HOW THE OTHER
THIRD LIVES . . .

ORBIS BOOKS

Maryknoll, New York 10545

HOW THE OTHER
THIRD LIVES . . .

Third World stories, poems,
songs, prayers, and essays
from Asia, Africa, and Latin America

Compiled and Edited by
Margaret B. White and **Robert N. Quigley**

The Catholic Foreign Mission Society of America (Maryknoll) re-
cruits and trains people for overseas missionary service. Through
Orbis Books Maryknoll aims to foster the international dialogue which
is essential to mission. The books published, however, reflect the opinions of their authors, and are not meant to represent the official
position of the Society.

Library of Congress Cataloging in Publication Data
Main entry under title:

How the other third lives ...

    Bibliography: p.
    SUMMARY: An anthology of prose and poetry from the various
countries of Africa, Asia, and Latin America reflecting their indi-
vidual social and cultural history.
    1.   Literature, Modern. [1.   Literature—Collections]
I. White, Margaret B.   II. Quigley, Robert N.
PN6014.H737   808.8'032   77-22499
ISBN 0-88344-190-X
ISBN 0-88344-191-8 pbk.

CONTENTS

v

GHANA

CAPE VERDE ISLANDS

NIGERIA

KENYA

ANGOLA

MOZAMBIQUE

SOUTH AFRICA

SHORT STORIES

ESSAYS

NOVELLA

JOURNALS

PREFACE

The initial motivation for this book arose out of my experiences as a teacher of literature in Korea and the Philippines. Teaching Shelley and Keats and Daniel Defoe, I came to feel that Western literature, as an exclusive literary diet, was as unhealthy and imbalanced as an exclusive diet of hamburgers and Coca-Cola. I began to seek out, and share with my students, poems and essays from countries which were our geographic neighbors in Asia, or whose literature reflected a national experience similar to the countries in which I was teaching.

The response of the students was immediate and electric. As we read and talked together, as I began to collect and compile the materials we were using, I, too, became increasingly excited with and intrigued by what we were studying. In most of the selections we found a freshness, a direct humor, and a sense of vibrant, immediate reality and urgency which is less available in most Western literature. I found that with few exceptions neither the poetry nor the prose required extensive explication, beyond a general discussion of the characteristics of the country from which a selection came. It is as though the directness of the authors' experiences grasped the imagination of the readers immediately, and student and teacher became sharers in the excitement of new discoveries. Before leaving the Philippines I put together all we had collected, materials we had enjoyed and shared, hoping that other teachers and students would continue to enjoy our discoveries.

Like many others who return to their homeland after some time abroad, part of my "culture shock" on returning to the United States was the realization of our isolation and insularity. Like other travellers I longed to share what I had learned, seen and experienced, and was frustrated in finding no viable mode for speaking. This volume, revised and expanded with the help of Robert N. Quigley, is my attempt to share.

Many people have contributed to the concept and compilation of this volume. First thanks must go to the students at Yonsei and Sogang Universities, in Seoul, Korea; Ateno de Manila University and Jose Abad Santos Memorial School in Quezon City, Philippines; and the Center for Open Education, Englewood, New Jersey.

Special thanks to Dr. Edward Wright, Director of the Fulbright Program in Korea; Mrs. Doreen Gamboa, Director of the Jose Abad Santos Memorial School; and to the staff of the International School in Manila, who prepared the text in its original mimeographed version.

I am grateful, too, to Herbert D. White, with whom I first went to Asia, and to my children, Eric and Susan, whose interests have sometimes been neglected on behalf of this volume.

MARGARET B. WHITE

INTRODUCTION

Literature is often likened to a mirror, within which we see our images more truly than in our daily lives or our history books; and to a lamp, shining out to guide us on our path. And so it is. The great literatures of the world have recalled us again and again from the pettiness of factionalism and the narrowness of provincial mores to the universal truths which bind all humankind together.

Until very recently the lamps and mirrors available to readers in the western world have been mainly limited to a body of work which, though marvelously rich, is limited in perspective. For most American students studies in literature have dealt almost exclusively with British and American authors. "Comparative Literature" or "World Literature" has often meant "European Literature." Lately young people have begun to discover, more or less on their own, the treasures of Asian literature, especially the religious and philosophic classics of India and the Far East.

This volume is presented in response to this developing interest in exploring literatures other than our own, particularly national literature from emerging nations.

This anthology is not presented as a scholarly text, or as an attempt to be learnedly representative of the best of the many literatures from which selections have been made. It is rather a personal offering, poems, stories, and essays from Africa, Asia, and Latin America, which we found exciting and memorable, and which have given us a new perspective on life in this world community. Most of the selections are modern, but not all. Most are by writers who are well-known in their own countries and abroad, but a few are by writers who produced only a few poems or stories in the course of careers primarily bent in other directions. Many very important figures in national and international literature do not appear here. This is due not to any desire on our part to slight or to overlook, or to value one writer more highly than another; it is due rather to our own limitations and to the limitations of the scope possible in one small volume trying to represent a vast world literature.

In presenting the material we have chosen a format as simple and unobtrusive as possible, hoping to allow for the widest possible variations in the manner of its use. The primary division is by genre—poetry, stories, essays, novella, journals. Within the poetry section the selections are arranged by continent and country of origin, moving from Asia to Latin America to Africa, thus allowing the reader who chooses to get some feeling for the similarities and dissimilarities from one country to another, one continent to another. The stories, on the other hand, are grouped so that those whose points of view are most dissimilar fall together, and by juxtaposition comment on one another.

All the essays, the journals, and the novella deal with one theme—the oppression of one group of human beings by another—and can usefully be read either as a body or in conjunction with poems and stories which deal in a different mode with the same set of circumstances. The three pieces from the Philippines, for example—the stories by Hamada and Dharam and the essay by Constantino—all deal with various racial, political, and religious groups, but from such disparate perspectives as to make it difficult for the reader to believe they are describing the same locale.

All the selections are valuable in themselves, as works of literature. They are equally valuable as documents of social and cultural history, providing those glimpses into the emotions, customs, and prejudices of a people which are absent in recordings of geographic, historic, or social "facts." The desperation and suicide of the servant girl in Sembene's "Black Girl," for example, speaks more directly and lastingly to the evils of colonialism than could many volumes of historical accounts of the subject. All the themes which appear daily in our papers—struggles for national independence, racist policies, the cruel inequities of rich and poor, the anguish of hunger—appear in these pages as specifically related to characters whose fears, hopes, and sufferings are readily identifiable with our own.

In spite of the continuous theme of oppression and injustice, brutality and viciousness, this is not a volume of despair. In the midst of pain there is humor, romantic love, love of country and of children, and even the petty deceits, selfishness, and bumbling which are equally the mark of humankind. A Korean poet of long ago speaks of his desire to lasso time, in order to prevent the growing old of his beloved parents. "The Truly Married Woman," in the story by Nicol, has never heard of woman's liberation, but discovers for herself the pride and self-fulfillment of claiming her proper status. The young revolutionary, Néstor Paz, dying of starvation, writes poignantly of his love for his young wife and his deep desire to be with her, raise a family and share with them and his compatriots a time of peace and honor.

In this mirror, then, it is hoped we will see more clearly those things in our own lives and the lives of our fellow citizens of the world which are merely idiosyncratic, and we will have more capacity to admit of, even to cherish and enjoy, the rich diversity of experiences of the peoples of the world. May it be a lamp to light the path to a world in which, as Luthuli says, the goal shall be "the recognition and preservation of the rights of man and the establishment of a truly free world."

POETRY FROM ASIA

INDIA

RABINDRANATH TAGORE

*Rabindranath Tagore (1861–1941) was the first poet in Asia to
win a Nobel Prize. He translated his poems from Bengali into
English himself.*

Songs from Gitanjali (Song Offerings)

I Have Ever Loved Thee

I have ever loved thee in a hundred forms and times,
Age after age, in birth following birth.
The chain of songs that my fond heart did weave
Thou graciously didst take around thy neck,
Age after age, in birth following birth.

When I listen to the tales of the primitive past,
The love-pangs of the far distant times,
The meetings and partings of the ancient ages,
I see thy form gathering light
Through the dark dimness of Eternity
And appearing as a star ever fixed in the memory of the All.

We two have come floating by the twin currents of love
That well up from the inmost heart of the Beginningless.
We two have played in the lives of myriad lovers
In tearful solitude of sorrow
In tremulous shyness of sweet union,
In old old love ever renewing its life.

The onrolling flood of the love eternal
Hath at last found its perfect final course.
All the joys and sorrows and longings of heart,
All the memories of the moments of ecstasy,
All the love-lyrics of poets of all climes and times
Have come from the everywhere
And gathered in one single love at thy feet.

My Heart, Like a Peacock

My heart, like a peacock on a rainy day,
spreads its plumes tinged with rapturous colors of thoughts,
and in its ecstasy seeks some vision in the sky,—
with a longing for one whom it does not know.
My heart dances.

The clouds rumble from sky to sky—
the shower sweeps horizons,
the doves shiver in silence in their nests,
the frogs croak in the flooded fields,—
and the clouds rumble.

O, who is she on the king's tower
that has loosened the braid on her dark hair,
has drawn over her breasts the blue veil?
She wildly starts and runs in the
sudden flashes of lightning
and lets the dark hair dance on her bosom.

Ah, my heart dances like a peacock,
the rain patters on the new leaves of summer,
the tremor of the crickets' chirp
    troubles the shade of the trees,
the river overflows its bank washing the village meadows.
My heart dances.

The Battle Is Over

The battle is over. After strife and struggle the treasure is
   gathered and stored.
Come now, woman, with your golden jar of beauty. Wash away
   all dust and dirt, fill up all cracks and flaws, make the heap
   shapely and sound.
Come, beautiful woman, with the golden jar on your head.

The play is over. I have come to the village and have set up my
   hearthstone.
Now come, woman, carrying your vessel of sacred water; with
   tranquil smile and devout love, make my home pure.
Come, noble woman, with your vessel of sacred water.
The morning is over. The sun is fiercely burning.
The wandering stranger is seeking shelter.
Come, woman, with your full pitcher of sweetness.

Open your door and with a garland of welcome ask him in.
Come, blissful woman, with your full pitcher of sweetness.

The day is over. The time has come to take leave.
Come, O woman, with your vessel full of tears.
Let your sad eyes shed tender glow on the farewell path and
   the touch of thy trembling hand make the parting hour full.
Come, sad woman, with your vessel of tears.

The night is dark; the house is desolate and the bed empty,
   only the lamp for the last rites is burning.
Come, woman, bring your brimming jar of remembrance.
Open the door of the secret chamber with your unbraided
   streaming hair and spotless white robe, replenish the lamp
   of worship.
Come, suffering woman, bring your brimming jar of remembrance.

Where the Mind Is Without Fear

Where the mind is without fear
  and the head is held high;
Where knowledge is free;
Where the world has not been broken up
  into fragments by narrow domestic walls;
Where words come out from the depth of truth;
Where tireless striving stretches
  its arms towards perfection;
Where the clear stream of reason has not lost
  its way into the dreary desert sand of dead habit;
Where the mind is led forward by thee
  into ever-widening thought and action—
Into that heaven of freedom, my Father,
  let my country awake.

MOHAN SINGH (1905–)

Evening

The sun horse panting and snorting
Reaches the shores of evening,
Kicking his hoofs and flicking red dust
His vermillion mane wet with perspiration
He throws red foam from his mouth.

The mellow-colored Evening comes
And places her hand between his pricked ears
Her long fingers
Feel the hot breath from his nostrils
And take off the bridle from his mouth.

The restive animal
Tamed and quietened
Walks behind the Evening slowly
And goes into the stable of darkness.

                            —Translated by Balwant Gargi

PAKISTAN

MUHAMMAD IQBAL

Pakistani poetry reflects the Islamic religion of Pakistan. Muhammad Iqbal (1873–1938) is sometimes considered the father of Pakistani poetry, as he is of the political state of Pakistan. His poem included here is called a "ghazal," which is something like a sonnet in English poetry; in the original language, Urdu, it has a strict rhyme scheme and traditional form. Ghazals were traditionally light love poems, but Iqbal's are rather serious.

Ghazal No. 9

Fabric of earth and wind and wave!
  Who is the secret, you or I,
Brought into light? or who the dark
  world of what hides yet, you or I?
Here in this night of grief and pain,
  trouble and toil, that men call life,
Who is the dawn, or who dawn's prayer
  cried from the minaret, you or I?
Who is the load that Time and Space
  bear on their shoulder? Who the prize
Run for with fiery feet by swift
  daybreak and sunset, you or I?
You are a pinch of dust and blind,
  I am a pinch of dust that feels;
Through the dry land, Existence, who
  flows like a streamlet, you or I?

             —*Translated by V.G. Kiernan*

TAUFIQ RAFAT

Taufiq Rafat (1927–) writes in English, in modern style.

Poem 4

The time to love
  is when the heart says so.

Who cares
  if it is muddy August
  or tepid April?—
for Love's infallible feet
  step daintily
  from vantage to vantage
  to the waiting salt-lick.

If Spring
has any significance,
it is for us,
  the rhymesters,
  who need
  a bough to perch on
  while we sing.

Love is a country
  with its own climate.

INDONESIA

J. E. TATENGKENG

Tatengkeng (1907–) wrote both of the following poems. Both indicate the close relationship between the islands of the Indonesian archipelago and the sea, but they are very different in tone and mood.

On the Shore: Twilight

The small waves break with a splash,
The great sun flickers.
It's a quiet, pleasant day,
With blue-red mountains all around.

The fishermen's boats sail along in clusters,
Out from the bay, into the shallows:
The sailors sing melancholy songs
Of old loves, lost loves.

The sun looks down the other side of the mountain,
The moon slips grinning into its place,

And this poet goes off into musing
And praise—and gathers in a poem.

The emptier, the lonelier the world
The more yearningly the Soul sings on . . .
   —Translated by Burton Raffel and Nurdin Salam

Traveler First Class

Before I was thirty
I was never more than a deck passenger.

Thanks to the efforts of my friends
And the transfer of sovereignty
I'm now a traveler first class.

I'm one of the army
Of inspection officials
Wandering from island to island
Building up the country.

Every evening I play bridge in the salon
And drink my beer
And rage at the waiter.

I've never written a report.

I disembark
And give half a rupiah
For the workers on the first of May.

—Translated by James S. Holmes

CHAIRIL ANWAR

Chairil Anwar (1922–1949) died when he was only twenty-seven. Though he wrote only about seventy poems, he became a major influence in Indonesian poetry.

At the Mosque

I shouted at Him
Until He came.

We met face to face.

Afterwards He burned in my breast.
All my strength struggles to extinguish Him.

My body, which won't be driven, is soaked with sweat.

This room
Is the arena where we fight,
Destroying each other,
One hurling insults, the other gone mad.
          —Translated by Burton Raffel and Nurdin Salam

My Love Far in the Islands

My love far in the islands,
    Loving girl,
Now passing the time alone.

The boat sails on, the moon is cool,
I carry a present round my neck,
The wind helps, the sea is clear,
Yet I know that I shall never reach her.

In the clear water, in the moaning wind,
In the feeling I have that all passes,
My death is speaking queenly words
"My lap must be your boat's harbor."

Why! how many years have I sailed
In my boat as fragile as me?
Why must my death begin to call me
Before I have kissed my love again?

My loving girl far in the islands,
    If I should die,
Will die passing the time alone.
          —Translated by Derwent May

W.S. RENDRA

Rendra (1935–) wrote the following poem to celebrate his marriage.

Little Sister Narti

I'm writing this letter
While the sky drips down
And two small wild ducks
Are making love in the pond
Like two naughty children,
Funny and nice,
Two flapping ducks
Making their feathers shake.
Hey, little sister Narti,
I want you for my wife!

Twelve angels
Have descended,
In this time of drizzling rain:
In front of the window-mirror
They stare and wash their hair
For the celebration.
Hey, little sister Narti,
In my fancy bridegroom clothes,
Covered with flowers and wearing a sacred sword,
I ache to lead you to the altar
And marry you.

I'm writing this letter
While rain drips
From the sky;
A sweet, spoiled child
Cries for her toys;
Two mischievous little boys
Are having fun in the ditch
And the jealous sky is watching.
Hey, little sister Narti,
I want you
To be the mother of my children!

—Translated by Burton Raffel

SITOR SITUMORANG

Sitor Situmorang (1924–) lived for some years in Paris. Some of his poetry is more western than other Indonesian poetry.

Swimming Pool

The child and I are stretched out
Carelessly on the edge of the pool,
Examining clouds in the blue sky
As if to find some special sign.

Reflected in the clear pool
I see the calm clarity of a face
Long since silenced and gone
But not yet pronounced dead.

Then the child asks of his own accord
If men go to heaven
When they die.

And because I know for sure
I nod quietly
And the child immediately understands.
            —Translated by Jean Kennedy and Burton Raffel

CHINA

WEN YI-TUO

Wen Yi-tuo (1899–1946) wrote poems which showed the influence of ancient Chinese tradition but also reflected modern thought and practice.

Dead Water

Here is a ditch of hopelessly dead water.
No breeze can raise a single ripple on it.
Might as well throw in rusty metal scraps
or even pour left over food and soup in it.

Perhaps the green on copper will become emeralds,
Perhaps on tin cans peach blossoms will bloom.
Then, let grease weave a layer of silky gauze,
and germs brew patches of colorful spume.

Let the dead water ferment into jade wine
covered with floating pearls of white scum.
Small pearls chuckle and become big pearls,
only to burst as gnats come to steal this rum.
And so this ditch of hopelessly dead water
may still claim a touch of something bright.
And if the frogs cannot bear the silence—
the dead water will croak its song of delight.

Here is a ditch of hopelessly dead water—
a region where beauty can never reside.
Might as well let the devil cultivate it—
and see what sort of world it can provide.

— *Translated by Kai Yu Hsu*

FENG CHIH

This is a poem about the liberation of the poor man through the miracles of modern industry. Feng Chih was born in 1906.

I Sing of Anshan Steel

I sing of Anshan steel.
Because of many wishes, I sing of Anshan steel.
When the train reaches the riverside, we wish for a bridge;
When the survey team arrives in wild mountains,
   it seeks deeper ore deposits;
For all these wishes, I sing of Anshan steel.

For much happiness, I sing of Anshan steel;
The farmers can have the proper tools they need;
And better looms weave more clothes;
For much happiness, I sing of Anshan steel.

For one famous saying, I sing of Anshan steel.
"What we don't understand we must learn."
The insight of this suggestion is proven here.
For one famous saying, I sing of Anshan steel.

For the many exemplars of man, I sing of Anshan steel.
Man tempers steel, and steel tempers man:
Heroes of a new order emerge without stop.
For the many exemplars of man, I sing of Anshan steel.

For the many marvelous sights, I sing of Anshan steel.
Molten iron flows from the furnaces,
   thick smoke surges towards the sky,
All day long ceaselessly, and every night the sky is red.
For the many marvelous sights, I sing of Anshan steel.

For a lasting peace, I sing of Anshan steel.
As the harvest of steel increases,
   so grows the strength of peace.
Let the brave white dove soar ever higher and farther.
For a lasting peace I sing of Anshan steel.

—Translated by Kai Yu Hsu

MAO TSE-TUNG

Mao Tse-tung (1893–1976) used many of the old forms of Chinese poetry. The two poems given here reflect two experiences in his life: the Long March of the Red Army in 1935 and his fondness for swimming the Yangtze River.

The Long March

None in the Red Army feared the distresses
of the Long March.
We looked lightly on the ten thousand peaks
and ten thousand rivers.
The Five Mountains rose and fell like rippling waves,
In the vast darkness we walked through the muddy hills.

Warm were the precipices
where Gold Sand River dashed into them.
Cold were the iron chains of the Tatu Bridge.
Delighting in the thousand snowy folds
of the Ming Mountains,
The last pass vanquished, the Three Armies smiled.

—Translated by Robert Payne

After Swimming Across the Yangtze River

Having just drunk the water of Changsha
Now I eat the fish of Wuchang.
Crossing the ten-thousand-li-long Yangtze River
I gaze at the unlimited sky of the southland.
Let the winds and waves batter me,
Still it is better than strolling in a quiet garden,
Now that I have found freedom in space.
Did not Confucius say when on a river:
"Such is that which passes and is gone!"

The sails stir
But the Snake and Tortoise hills remain still.
Here a grand scheme takes shape.
A bridge flying across
Turning into a broad road Heaven's Moat that used to
   separate the north from the south.
Building a stone wall to the west
Will cut off the rain fallen on the Wu Mountain,
To create a towering dam above a mirror-like lake,
The goddess of the Wu Mountain should be unchanged,
But only startled by the changed world.

—Translated by Kai Yu Hsu

NORTH VIETNAM

HO CHI MINH

Ho Chi Minh (1890–1969) was the first president of the independent republic of North Vietnam. These poems are taken from his Prison Diary.

On the Road

Although they have tightly bound my arms and legs,
All over the mountain I hear the song of birds,
And the forest is filled
with the perfume of spring-flowers.
Who can prevent me from freely enjoying these,
Which take from the long journey
a little of its loneliness?

Morning Sunshine

The morning sunshine penetrates into the prison,
Sweeping away the smoke and burning away the mist.
The breath of life fills the whole universe,
And smiles light up the faces of all the prisoners.

Cold Night

In the cold autumn night,
    without mattress, without blankets,
Lying with back curled round and legs folded up close,
I try in vain to sleep. The moonlight on the plantains
Increases the sense of cold,
    and through the window bars
The Great Bear draws up alongside and looks in.

KOREA

*These are not modern poems, but modern translations of
Korean poems from the sixteenth and seventeenth centuries.
They come from the Korean traditional form called "sijo."*

JONG CHOL

Out of Favor

There are moments when I am made aware
    I am not as fair as others.
But I will not pretty this face
    Or use rouge to seek your favor.
And I wish you to know this is not a ruse
    to draw your attention, my love.

KIM SANG-YONG

Perfumed Incense

The perfumed incense has turned to ashes
   in its golden vessel;
Drops falling from the water clock
   tell me the night is very deep.
Where did you go? With whom did you make love,
   That you come to me now when the moon is low?
Ah, you have come only to see
   How much you have scourged this heart.

Your Love Is a Lie

Love is a lie;
   your love for me is a lie.
You say you will visit me in my dreams—
   even that is a lie.
Since I cannot sleep,
   how can I see you in dreams?

BAK IN-RO

A Rope of Iron

I wish I could smelt and shape
   ten thousand pounds of iron;
I would twist it into a rope
   and lasso the traveling sun.
Perhaps then my father and mother
   would age a little more slowly.

The Three Brothers

From the union of two spirits
  three brothers came, living as one.
Two went I know not where;
  they have forgotten to return.
Every evening I go to the gate;
  I am overwhelmed with sighs.

JAPAN

Many readers are familiar with the haiku form in Japanese verse. We have included here a few haiku, a longer form known as the "tanka," and some other modern poems in various styles. The haiku in Japanese consists of three lines with a total of seventeen syllables. Its briefness allows it merely to suggest an idea or feeling and leaves it up to the reader to fill in the complete thought or translate the feeling into personal terms. The tanka expresses an emotion or impression in five lines of thirty-one syllables.

KOBAYASHI ISSA (1763–1826)

Repairs

A morning-glory vine,
all blossoming, has thatched
this hut of mine.

Heaven's River

A lovely thing to see:
through the paper window's hole
the Galaxy.

Winter

Now that I'm old
I am envied by people—
Oh, but it's cold!

KATO SHUSON (1905–)

Cold Winter Storm

Cold winter storm—
A safe-door in a burnt-out site
Creaking in the wind.

The Winter Sea Gulls

The winter sea gulls—
In life without a house,
In death without a grave.

—Translated by Donald Keene

TACHIBANA AKEMI (1812–1868)

It Is a Pleasure

It is a pleasure
When, spreading out some paper,
I take brush in hand
And write far more skillfully
Than I could have expected.

It is a pleasure
When, after a hundred days
Of twisting my words
Without success, suddenly
A poem turns out nicely.

It is a pleasure
When, in a book which by chance
I am perusing,
I come on a character
Who is exactly like me.

It is a pleasure
When, without receiving help
I can understand
The meaning of a volume
Reputed most difficult.

—Translated by Donald Keene

YOSANO AKIKO (1874–1941)

A Mouse

In my attic dwells a mouse.
The creaking noise he makes
Reminds me of a sculptor who carves
An image all night long.

Again when he dances with his wife,
He whirls like a race horse, round.
Though the attic dirt and dust flutter down
On this paper as I write,
How would he know?
But I stop to think:
   I am living with mice.
   Let them have good food
   And a warm nest.
   Let them drill a hole in the ceiling and,
   From time to time, peep down on me.
                 —Translated by Shio Sakanishi

KAORU MARUYAMA (1899–)

A Rhinoceros and a Lion

A rhinoceros was running;
A lion was clinging to his back,
Biting.
Blood spouted up and, twisting his neck in agony,
The rhinoceros was looking at the sky.
The sky was blue and quiet.
The daytime moon floated in it.

It was a picture,
An accidental moment in a far country of jungles,
So the landscape was silent,
The two animals remained as they were.
Only in the stillness
The lion was, moment by moment, trying to kill;
The rhinoceros was, eternally, about to die.
        —Translated by Satoru Sato and Constance Urdang

BAKU YAMANOGUCHI (1903–)

Marriage

Whenever poetry saw me
It cried out, "Marriage, marriage."
Thinking back, I see that I was
Most eager to marry.
In other words,
There are various states in this world:
The state of getting soaked in the rain,
The state of being blown by the wind,
Or the state of wishing to die; however,
In my state
I could not put marriage out of my mind.
Poetry, full of vigor,
Stuck to me wherever I went,
Crying, "Marriage, marriage."
Finally I married. Poetry
Stopped crying words altogether.
Now something other than poetry
Scratches at my heart from time to time
Or crouches behind the bureau,
Starting to cry, "Money, money."
            —*Translated by Satoru Sato and Constance Urdang*

POETRY FROM LATIN AMERICA

"Latin America" sometimes means the same as "Spanish America," plus Brazil; and sometimes it means all the territory south of the United States. Our selections come from Latin America in the second meaning: We include poems from Chile, Peru, Brazil, and from Mexico, Cuba, Jamaica, Haiti, and Martinique.

CHILE

PABLO NERUDA

Neruda (1904–1973) was born in Parral, Chile. He won the
Stalin Peace Prize in 1950 and the Nobel Prize in 1971. Neruda
is one of the world's best known and honored Latin American
poets and has been extremely prolific. There are English trans-
lations of many of his works, for example: Splendor and Death
of Joaquin Murieta, Song of Despair, We Are Many, Early
Poems *and* Neruda and Vallejo: Selected Poems. *He served as a*
diplomat for his country for many years.

Ode to Laziness

Yesterday I felt this ode
Would not get off the floor.
It was time, I ought
at least
show a green leaf,
I scratch the earth: "Arise,
sister ode
—said to her—
I have promised you,
do not be afraid of me,
I am not going to crush you,
four-leaf ode,
four-hand ode,
you shall have tea with me.
Arise,
I am going to crown you among the odes.

We shall go out together along the shores
of the sea, on a "bicycle."
It was no use.
Then,
on the pine peaks,
laziness
appeared in the nude,
she led me dazzled
and sleepy,
she showed me upon the sand
small broken bits
of ocean substance,
wood, algae, pebbles,
feathers of sea birds.
I looked for but did not find
yellow agates.
The sea
filled all spaces
crumbling towers,
invading
the shores of my country,
advancing
successive catastrophes of the foam.
Alone on the sand
spread wide
its corolla.
I saw the silvery petrels crossing
and like black creases
the cormorants
nailed to the rocks.
I released a bee
that was agonizing in a spider's net.
I put a little pebble
in my pocket,
it was smooth, very smooth
as the breast of a bird,
meanwhile on the shore,
all afternoon
sun struggled with mist.
At times
the mist was steeped

in thought,
topaz-like,
at others fell
a ray from the moist sun
distilling yellow drops.
At night,
thinking of the duties of my fugitive ode,
I pull off my shoes
near the fire;
sand slid out of them
and soon I began to fall
asleep.

–Translated by William Carlos Williams

The United Fruit Company

When the trumpets had sounded and all
was in readiness on the face of the earth,
Jehovah divided his universe:
Anaconda, Ford Motors,
Coca-Cola Inc., and similar entities:
the most succulent item of all,
The United Fruit Company Incorporated
reserved for itself: the heartland
and coasts of my country,
the delectable waist of America.
They rechristened their properties:
the "Banana Republics"—
and over the languishing dead,
the uneasy repose of the heroes
who harried that greatness,
their flags and their freedoms,
they established an *opera bouffe:*
they ravished all enterprise,
awarded the laurels like Caesars,
unleashed all the covetous, and contrived
the tyrannical Reign of the Flies—
Trujillo the fly, and Tacho the fly,
the flies called Carias, Martinez,

Ubico—all of them flies, flies
dank with the blood of their marmalade
vassalage, flies buzzing drunkenly
on the populous middens:
the fly-circus fly and the scholarly
kind, case-hardened in tyranny.

Then in the bloody domain of the flies
The United Fruit Company Incorporated
unloaded with a booty of coffee and fruits
brimming its cargo boats, gliding
like trays with the spoils
of our drowning dominions.

And all the while, somewhere, in the sugary
hells of our seaports,
smothered by gases, an Indian
fell in the morning:
a body spun off, an anonymous
chattel, some numeral tumbling,
a branch with its death running out of it
in the vat of the carrion, fruit laden and foul.

—Translated by Ben Belitt

NICANOR PARRA

Parra, a poet and physicist, was born in Chile in 1914. He became particularly known for his Poemas y antipoemas *(Poems and Antipoems). He is ten years younger than Neruda and some think his poetry may represent the beginning of a new way of writing in Chile.*

Epitaph

Of medium height,
With a voice neither shrill nor low,
The oldest son of an elementary school teacher
And a piecework seamstress,

Naturally thin
Though fond of good eating,
With drawn cheeks
And oversize ears,
A square face,
And slits for eyes,
And the nose of a mulatto boxer
Over an Aztec idol's mouth
—All this bathed
In a light halfway between irony and perfidy—
Neither too bright nor totally stupid,
I was what I was: a mixture
Of vinegar and olive oil,
A sausage of angel and beast!

–Translated by Jorge Elliott

PERU

CESAR VALLEJO

*Like Pablo Neruda, Peru's Vallejo (1895–1938) was a Marxist.
His translator says of him that even more than Neruda Vallejo
"attacks at root the Catholic-racist-colonial culture that many
of the best in South America are still in the nets of." The poem we
have selected is about being a son.*

Common Sense

"There is, mother, a place in the world, called Paris. A very
big place and far off and once again big."

My mother turns up my overcoat collar, not because it is
beginning to snow, but so it may.

My father's wife is in love with me, coming and advancing

backward toward my birth and breastward toward my death. For I'm hers twice: by the goodbye and by the return. I close her on returning. That's why her eyes gave so much to me, just with me, in flagrants with me, happening by terminated works, by consummated pacts.

My mother is confessed by me, pointed at because of me? How comes she doesn't give an equal part to my other brothers? To Victor, for example, the eldest, who is so old now people say: He looks like his father's younger brother! It must be because I've traveled much! Because I've lived more!

My mother grants a map of coloring principle to my stories of return. Facing my life of returning, remembering that I traveled two hearts along her womb, she blushes and stays mortally livid when I say in the treatise of the soul: That night I was happy. But more she becomes sad; more would she become sad.

"You look so old, my son!"

And steps along the yellow color to weep, for she finds me aged in the sword blade in the mouth of my face. Weeps for me, becomes sad for me. How can she miss my youth if I'm always to be her son? Why does a mother ache finding her sons aged, if their ages never reach hers? And why, when the sons the nearer the end they come, the nearer their parents? My mother weeps because I am old in my time and because never will I age in hers!

My goodbye started from a point in her being, more external than the point in her being to which I return. I am, because of the excessive deadline, of my shift, more man in my mother's eyes than son. There resides the pure whiteness that today sheds light upon us with three flames. I say to her, then, until I hush:

"There is, mother, in the world a place called Paris. A very big place and far off and once again big."

My father's wife, hearing me, eats her lunch and her mortal eyes lower softly by my arms.

–Translated by Clayton Eshleman

BRAZIL

MANUEL BANDEIRA

Bandeira (1886–1968) taught Spanish American Literature at the National Faculty of Philosophy in Rio de Janeiro.

Boardinghouse

Garden of the little bourgeois boardinghouse.
Cats lying boneless in the sun.
Shrubs besiege the flat flower beds.
The fuchsias, ti-singed, have withered.
The sunflowers
                    yellow!
                    endure.
And the dahlias, plump, plebeian in their Sunday best.
A kitten makes water.
With the gestures of a French waiter
It carefully covers the little piss-puddle.
It walks away, elegantly shaking its right paw
—The only creature of delicate refinement in the little
    bourgeois boardinghouse.
                    –Translated by William L. Grossman

DOM HELDER CAMARA

Dom Helder Camara was born in 1900 and is now archbishop of Olinda and Recife in North-East Brazil, the poorest region of the country. In a larger sense, he is the bishop of all those

everywhere who share his conviction that inhuman structures
can be changed by the violence of truth and justice.

Prayer Poems

If It Depended on Me

If it depended on me
   I would suppress
   all iron bars,
   all hedges,
   all walls.
If it depended on me
   doors and windows—
   except for the rare moments
   when they must shield
   the King's secrets—
   would remain open,
   generously letting in
   the air and light and life!

Ended Thy Miracles

Ended thy miracles,
   finished thy triumphs!
   Get out,
   disappear
   without meeting the multitudes
   as quick to hiss as to applaud!
I pity the masses
   that require portents
   but shun the every-day
   and exult at the unexpected, the unusual,
   who are childlike, infantile,
   and whom the demagogues
   nourish with sweets,
   encourage with gestures,
   amuse with chimeras.

If There Are Hare-Brained Streets

If there are hare-brained streets
   unable to preserve a secret
   arrogant streets
   that preen themselves
   on the glories of their past,
   there are also old dead-ends
   that silently preserve
   the simple joys they've witnessed,
   and the anonymous virtues
   that have sanctified their humble stones.

No One Has Comprehended

No one has comprehended
   how earnestly I've wanted
   with my own hands
   to relieve the weary horse
   of its harness and its saddle
   and its blinkers, most especially.
But I know that I have done so,
   praying for more than half—
   much more, much more than half
   of loved and destitute humanity.

There Are Horses

There are horses
   so concerned with independence
   that they would rather go unshod
   than to agree to go in irons.

The Aviator Asked Me

The aviator asked me
  if I would like
  to kiss the clouds
  (the plane would wait for me
  a few minutes).
I did not say anything,
  not wanting to offend the clouds
  but I have never wanted
  to kiss the void,
  the nothingness.

When I Was A Youngster

When I was a youngster
  I wanted to go out running
  among the mountain peaks
And when, between two summits
  a gap appeared,
  why not leap
  across the chasm?
Led by the angel's hand,
  all my life long
  this is what happened,
  this, exactly.

–Translated by Herma Briffault

MEXICO

JOSE JUAN TABLADA

Tablada (1871–1945) is the author of the following haiku. The haiku form is Japanese, the original language was Spanish, we read it in English.

The Monkey

from "Haiku of the Flowerpot"

The little monkey looks at me...
He wants to tell me something—
that he has forgotten!

–Translated by Robert Bly

OCTAVIO PAZ

Paz was born in Mexico in 1914 and like Chile's Pablo Neruda is a diplomat, most recently as Mexican Ambassador to India. In his work he is concerned with defining the separate Spanish and native American elements in his cultural heritage. In competition with poets throughout the world, he was given the Gran Premio Internacional de Poesía award in 1963. Among his writings are plays and over twelve books of poetry.

In Her Splendor Islanded

In her splendor islanded
This woman burning like a charm of jewels
An army terrifying and asleep

This woman lying within the night
Like clear water lying on closed eyes
In a tree's shadow
A waterfall halted halfway in its flight
A rapid narrow river suddenly frozen
At the foot of a great and seamless rock
At the foot of a mountain
She is lake-water in April as she lies
In her depths binding poplar and eucalyptus
Fishes of stars burning between her thighs
Shadow of birds scarcely hiding her sex
Her breasts two still villages under a peaceful sky
This woman lying here like a white stone
Like water in the moon in a dead crater
Not a sound in the night not moss nor sand
Only the slow budding of my words
At the ear of water at the ear of flesh
Unhurried running
And clear memorial
Here is the moment burning and returned
Drowning itself in itself and never consumed

–Translated by Muriel Rukeyser

CUBA

Like all of life in Cuba, literature became very different after the 1959 revolution. Two of the poems included here were written during the Castro regime.

"PLACIDO"

The author, whose real name was Gabriel de la Concepción Valdes (1809–1844), was the illegitimate son of a black father and a white Spanish dancer. At the age of thirty-five he was executed by the Spanish rulers of Cuba; thus, like the

Philippine's Rizal, he became a martyr and a hero in his country's struggle for liberty. The following poem was written in the chapel of the Hospital de Santa Cristina on the night before his execution.

Mother, Farewell!

If the unfortunate fate engulfing me,
The ending of my history of grief,
The closing of my span of years so brief,
Mother, should wake a single pang in thee,
Weep not. No saddening thought to me devote;
I calmly go to a death that is glory-filled;
My lyre before it is forever stilled
Breathes out to thee its last and dying note.

A note scarce more than a burden-easing sigh
Tender and sacred, innocent, sincere—
Spontaneous and instinctive as the cry
I gave at birth—And now the hour is here—
O God, thy mantle of mercy o'er my sins!
Mother, farewell! The pilgrimage begins.
—Translated by James Weldon Johnson

ROBERTO FERNANDEZ RETAMAR

Fernández Retamar was born in Havana in 1930 and was educated in Europe and America. His early work showed much French influence.

Of Reality

Those who marry in hired clothes

Oblivious,
forgetful

that within two days
all this princely finery,
accompaniment of the evening's chatter
and of the final tribute of tears,
must be returned with as few stains as possible
(The advertisement filled a square of an enormous wall
with its absurd poster—but all the same!):
and remembering on the other hand, no doubt,
that in five or six hours they will lie in glory,
they move forward, immaculate, pale
as their gloves.
    She
awkward and self-conscious;
      and he
happy, though they couldn't get a good fit,
for his back and his shoulder pinches a little
       —Translated by J.M. Cohen

DOMINGO ALFONSO

Alfonso (1925–) is an architect, and has also published one volume of poetry, Poemas del hombre común (Poems of the Common Man).

Arte poética

On the thirty-first of August nineteen sixty-four
Señor Ezequiel Sotomayor
read on page two of REVOLUTION the following text:
"This river, like all those we crossed before and after it,
 was in flood.
We were also hampered by the lack of boots
 in our company."

When he had finished he turned over the page
and mentally compared this
with the verses of a certain fifteenth-rate poet;
fearfully he consulted his sensibility
and to confirm his judgment sent for
his young niece who was reading literature.
They minutely examined both writings
and decided for the newspaper text.

—Translated by J.M. Cohen

JAMAICA

AGNES MAXWELL-HALL

Maxwell-Hall was born in Jamaica in 1894 but was educated in London, Boston, and New York City. She writes in English.

Jamaica Market

Honey, pepper, leaf-green limes
Pagan fruit whose names are rhymes,
Mangoes, breadfruit, ginger-roots,
Granadillas, bamboo-shoots,
Cho-cho, ackees, tangerines,
Lemons, purple Congo-beans,
Sugar, okras, kola-nuts,
Citrons, hairy coconuts,
Fish, tobacco, native hats,
Gold bananas, woven mats,
Plantains, wild-thyme, pallid leeks,
Pigeons with their scarlet beaks,
Oranges and saffron yams,

Baskets, ruby guava jams,
Turtles, goat-skins, cinnamon,
All-spice, conch-shells, golden rum.
Black skins, babel—and the sun
That burns all colours into one.

Lizard

O, what would people say if you
Ate bitter-tasting ants, drank dew,
Caught gnats as blue as summer skies,
And swallowed painted butterflies?

And what would people think, if then
You laid eggs—just like any hen—
Forgot them in a windy nest,
And left the sun to do the rest?

Leave everyone—come sit with me
In trees; the things you'll hear and see!
And lead a lizard-life—I'm one!
A pocket-dragon in the sun!

UNA H. MARSON

Marson (1905–) has held many important international posts.
She has written four books and several plays, one of which was
produced in London and the others in Jamaica.

Nightfall

How tender the heart grows
At the twilight hour,
More sweet seems the perfume
Of the sunless flower.

Come quickly, wings of night,
The twilight hurts too deep;
Let darkness wrap the world around,
My pain will go to sleep.

HAITI

EMILE ROUMER

Roumer (1903–) studied in France and England and writes in French. He is a lawyer but has also published books of poetry.

The Peasant Declares His Love

High-yellow of my heart, with breasts like tangerines,
you taste better to me than eggplant stuffed with crab,
you are the tripe in my pepper-pot,
the dumpling in my peas, my tea of aromatic herbs.
You are the corned beef whose customhouse is my heart,
my mush with syrup that trickles down the throat.
You are a steaming dish, mushroom cooked with rice,
crisp potato fries, and little fish fried brown . . .
My hankering for love follows you wherever you go.
Your bum is a gorgeous basket
   brimming with fruits and meat.
             —Translated by John Peale Bishop

MARTINIQUE

AIMÉ CÉSAIRE

Césaire was born in 1913 on the island of Martinique, which is one of the Windward Islands of the Caribbean. With Léopold Sédar Senghor and Léon Damas, he helped to found the influential Negritude movement in literature. In his concerns for the meaning and identity of the Negro race, for the stifling effects of the colonial mentality, and for the degrading effects of the whites' sense of superiority to his people, he shares many of the concerns of the African poets in the next section. The selection here is taken from his long poem Return to My Native Land.

Excerpts from Return to My Native Land

He was a very good nigger

And it did not occur to him that he might ever hoe
and dig and cut anything except the insipid
cane

he was a very good nigger.

And they threw stones at him, bits of scrap iron,
broken bottle ends, but neither these stones
nor this iron nor those bottles . . .

O quiet years of God on this clod of an earth

and the whip argued with the swarming flies over the
   sweet dew of our wounds.

I say Hurrah! more and more the old negritude
is turning into a corpse
the undone horizon is pushed back and stretched
Between the torn clouds a sign by lightning:
the slave-ship is splitting open. . . . Its belly in spasm
   ringing with noises.

The cargo of this bastard suckling of the seas is
   gnawing at its bowels like an atrocious tapeworm
Nothing can drown the threat of its growling intestines
in vain the joy of the sails filled out
   like a purse full of doubloons
in vain the tricks allowed by the fatal stupidity
   of the police frigates
in vain does the captain have the most troublesome
nigger hanged from the yard-arm, or thrown
overboard, or fed to his mastiffs.
In their spilt blood
the niggers smelling of fried onion
find the bitter taste of freedom
and they are on their feet the niggers

the sitting-down niggers

unexpectedly on their feet
on their feet in the hold
on their feet in the cabins
on their feet on deck
on their feet in the wind
on their feet beneath the sun
on their feet in blood
on their feet
         and
            free
on their feet and in no way distraught
free at sea and owning nothing
veering and utterly adrift
surprisingly
on their feet
on their feet in the rigging
on their feet at the helm
on their feet at the compass
on their feet before the map
on their feet beneath the stars
on their feet
         and
            free
and the cleansed ship advances fearless upon the
   caving waters
          —Translated by John Berger and Anna Bostock

POETRY FROM AFRICA

African poetry has many languages. The originals of some of the poems which follow were in French, some in one of the national languages, and some were written in English.

AFRICA

JOHN S. MBITI

Mbiti is Africa's best-known Christian theologian. Born in 1931, he has taught in several African universities and at Union Theological Seminary in New York City. Professor Mbiti is currently Director of the Ecumenical Institute of the World Council of Churches in Geneva. This sampling of African prayers, gathered by Mbiti in his Prayers of African Religion, *has been taken from different tribes and countries and reflects the riches of indigenous spirituality.*

National Deliverance

One body and possessor of strength,
Give me thy help,
That I may lead this people of thine
Free from all their sufferings.

Deliverance from Foreign Domination

Stars and moon which are in the heavens,
Blood of deng which you have taken [of the Dinka],
You have not summoned the ants [*Nuer*]
   of deng capriciously [in vain],
Blood of deng which you have taken,
The wing of battle on the river bank is encircled
   by [ostrich] plumes.
Dayim, son of God, strike the British to the ground,
Break the steamer on the Nile and let the British drown,
Kill the people on the mountains,

Kill them twice [i.e., two years in succession],
Do not slay them jestingly.
Mani goes with a rush,
He goes on for ever,
The sons of Jagei [Nuer people] are proud in the bryes,
Proud that they always raid the Dinka.

Strike the Chords of Praise

I shall sing a song of praise to God:
Strike the chords upon the drum.
God who gives us all good things—
Strike the chords upon the drum—
Wives, and wealth, and wisdom.
Strike the chords upon the drum.

A Litany for Rain

RECITATIVE:	RESPONSE:
We overcome this wind.	We overcome.
We desire the rain to fall,	
that it be poured in showers quickly.	Be poured.
Ah, thou rain, I adjure thee fall.	
If thou rainest, it is well.	It is well.
A drizzling confusion.	Confusion.
If it rains and our food ripens, it is well.	It is well.
If the young men sing, it is well.	It is well.
A drizzling confusion.	Confusion.
If our grain ripens, it is well.	It is well.
If our women rejoice,	It is well.
If the children rejoice,	It is well.
If the young men sing,	It is well.
If the aged rejoice,	It is well.
An overflowing in the granary,	Overflowing.
A torrent in flow,	A torrent.
If the wind veers to the south, it is well.	It is well.
If the rain veers to the south, it is well.	It is well!

Prayer of a Dying Man

And though I behold a man hate me,
I will love him.
O God, Father, help me, Father!
O God, Creator, help me, Father!
And even though I behold a man hate me,
I will love him.

Funeral Recitation

LEADER:

The creature is born,
  it fades away, it dies,
    and comes then the great cold.

The bird comes, it flies, it dies,
  and comes then the great cold.

The fish swims away,
  it goes, it dies,
    and comes then the great cold.

Man is born, he eats and sleeps,
  he fades away,
    and comes then the great cold.

And the sky lights up,
  the eyes are closed,
    the star shines.

Man is gone,
  the prisoner is freed,
    the shadow has disappeared.

Khmvoum [God], Khmvoum,
  hear our call.

GROUP RESPONSE:

It is the great cold of the
night, it is the dark.

It is the great cold of the
night, it is the dark.

It is the great cold of the
night, it is the dark.

It is the great cold of the
night, it is the dark.

The cold down here, the
light up there.

The shadow has disap-
peared.

Khmvoum, Khmvoum,
hear our call.

SENEGAL

LÉOPOLD SÉDAR SENGHOR

*Senghor was born in Senegal in 1906 and is probably the most
famous of all the African poets. He met the West Indian poet,
Aimé Césaire, in Paris, and they and others pondered together
what it means to be black in today's world. The philosophy they
evolved is what is now known as "Negritude." Senghor became a
teacher and a statesman and in 1960 was installed as the first
president of the Independent Republic of Senegal. He has published many books of poetry.*

Prayer to Masks

Black mask, red mask, you black and white masks,
Rectangular masks through whom the spirit breathes,
I greet you in silence!
And you too, my pantherheaded ancestor.
You guard this place, that is closed
    to any feminine laughter, to any mortal smile.
You purify the air of eternity,
    here where I breathe the air of my fathers.
Masks of maskless faces, free from dimples and wrinkles,
You have composed this image, this my face
    that bends over the altar of white paper.
In the name of your image, listen to me!
Now while the Africa of despotism is dying—
    it is the agony of a pitiable princess
Just like Europe to whom she is connected
    through the navel,
Now turn your immobile eyes towards your children
    who have been called
And who sacrifice their lives
    like the poor man his last garment
So that hereafter we may cry 'here' at the rebirth of the world

being the leaven that the white flour needs.
For who else would teach rhythm to the world
   that has died of machines and cannons?
For who else should ejaculate the cry of joy
   that arouses the dead and the wise in a new dawn?
Say, who else could return the memory of life
   to men with a torn hope?
They call us cotton heads, and coffee men, and oily men,
They call us men of death.
But we are the men of the dance whose feet
   only gain power when they beat the hard soil.

—Translated by Gerald Moore and Ulli Beier

DAVID DIOP

*Diop (1927–1973) was born in Bordeaux, France, but spent
many years of his life in Dakar, Senegal. He moved frequently
between Africa and France during his short life. His father was
Senegalese and his mother from the Cameroons. At the time of
his death, in an air crash near Dakar, his influence among
African poets was spreading. His volume of collected poetry and
essays, entitled* Hammerblows, *was published in the United
States in 1973.*

Africa

Africa my Africa
Africa of proud warriors in ancestral savannas
Africa of my grandmother's singing
Along the banks of her far-off river
I have never known you
But my gaze is charged with your blood
Your beautiful black blood spread abroad over the fields
The blood of your sweat
The sweat of your labor

The labor of your slavery
Slavery of your children.
Africa tell me Africa
Is it you, then, this back that bends
And sinks under the weight of humility
This trembling red-striped back
That says yes to the whip on the noonday roads?

Then gravely a voice answered me:
Impetuous son, that young and robust tree
That tree over there
Splendidly alone midst white faded flowers
It is Africa your Africa that springs up again
Springs up patiently obstinately
And whose fruits ripen with
The bitter flavor of freedom.

—Translated by Anne Atik

GAMBIA

LENRIE PETERS

*Peters (1932–) has studied surgery, been an amateur singer and
broadcaster, and has written a novel. In this poem he depicts
bitterly the adjustments people try to make to a modern, me-
chanized world they neither love nor understand.*

After They Put Down Their Overalls

After they put down their overalls
And turn off the lathes
They do not return to the women

After they have bathed
Instead, with hyena's thirst
They turn to the open-air bar
To swallow the hook of imported liquor
As they sit reckless across the log
Hypnotized by the bees.
They belch the arrogance of doubt
As they lie in refined stupor
Waiting for the sharp sun
To show them the way out.
Less sure than when they took the potion
They lumber back to the clever tools
They do not love and do not understand
Hoping the sun's anger would cool
So they can carry their dark glasses in their hand.

SIERRA LEONE

ABIOSEH NICOL

Abioseh Nicol (1924–) was born in Sierra Leone and educated there, in Nigeria, and in England. He has written short stories and articles as well as poetry and was awarded the Margaret Wrong Prize and Medal for Literature in Africa in 1952. This poem reflects an experience of many who have gone abroad for education and returned to their native place, with both hope and fear.

The Meaning of Africa

Africa, you were once just a name to me
But now you lie before me with sombre green challenge

To that loud faith for freedom (life more abundant)
Which we once professed shouting
Into the silent listening microphone
Or on an alien platform to a sea
Of white perplexed faces troubled
With secret imperial guilt; shouting
Of you with a vision euphemistic
As you always appear
To your lone sons in distant shores. . . .

Then the cold sky and continent would disappear
In a grey mental mist.
And in its stead the hibiscus blooms in shameless scarlet
    and the bougainvillea in mauve passion
    entwines itself around strong branches;
    the palm trees stand like tall proud moral women
    shaking their plaited locks against the
    cool suggestive evening breeze;
    the short twilight passes;
    the white full moon turns its round gladness
    towards the swept open space
    between the trees; there will be
    dancing tonight; and in my brimming heart
    plenty of love and laughter.

Oh, I got tired of the cold Northern sun
Of white anxious ghost-like faces
Of crouching over heatless fires
In my lonely bedroom.
The only thing I never tired of
Was the persistent kindness
Of you too few unafraid
Of my grave dusky strangeness.
So I came back
Sailing down the Guinea Coast,
Loving the sophistication
Of your brave new cities:
Dakar, Accra, Cotonou,
Lagos, Bathurst, and Bissau;
Liberia, Freetown, Libreville,
Freedom is really in the mind.

Go up country, so they said,
To see the real Africa.
For whosoever you may be,
That is where you come from.
Go for bush; inside the bush,
You will find your hidden heart,
Your mute ancestral spirit.
And so I went, dancing on my way—

Now you lie before me passive
With your unanswering green challenge.
Is this all you are?
This long uneven red road, this occasional succession
Of huddled heaps of four mud walls
And thatched, falling grass roofs
Sometimes ennobled by a thin layer
Of white plaster, and covered with thin
Slanting corrugated zinc.
These patient faces on weather-beaten bodies
Bowing under heavy market loads.
The pedalling cyclist wavers by
On the wrong side of the road,
As if uncertain of this new emancipation.
The squawking chickens, the pregnant she-goats
Lumber awkwardly with fear across the road.
Across the windscreen view of my four-cylinder kit car
An overladen lorry speeds madly towards me
Full of produce, passengers, with driver leaning
Out into the swirling dust to pilot his
Swinging obsessed vehicle along.
Beside him on the raised seat his first-class
Passenger, clutching and timid; but he drives on
At so, so many miles per hour, peering out with
Bloodshot eyes, unshaved face and dedicated look;
His motto painted across "Sunshine Transport, we get you
There, quick, quick. The Lord is my Shepherd ... "

The red dust settles down on the green leaves.
I know you will not make me want, Lord,
Though I have reddened your green pastures.
It is only because I have wanted so much

That I have always been found wanting.
From South and East, and from my West
The sandy desert holds the North:
We look across a vast continent
And blindly call it ours.
You are not a country, Africa,
You are a concept,
Fashioned in our minds, each to each,
To hide our separate fears,
To dream our separate dreams.
Only those within you who know
Their circumscribed plot,
And till it well with steady plough
Can from that harvest then look up
To the vast blue inside
Of the enamelled bowl of sky
Which covers you and say
"This is my Africa" meaning
"I am content and happy.
I am fulfilled, within,
Without and roundabout.
I have gained the little longings
Of my hands, my loins, my heart,
And the soul following in my shadow."
I know now that is what you are, Africa.
Happiness, contentment and fulfilment.
And a small bird singing on a mango tree.

GHANA

AQUAH LALUAH

Aquah Laluah (1904–1950) was born in that part of the former African Gold Coast now known as Ghana. She attended college in Wales and then returned to Africa to teach in a Girls' Vocational School in Sierra Leone. Her poems have been published in U.S. anthologies.

The Souls of Black and White

The souls of black and white were made
By the selfsame God of the selfsame shade.
God made both pure, and He left one white;
God laughed o'er the other, and wrapped it in night.

Said He, "I've a flower, and none can unfold it;
I've a breath of great mystery, nothing can hold it.
Spirit so illusive the wind cannot sway it,
A force of such might even death cannot slay it."

But so that He might conceal its glow
He wrapped it in darkness, that men might not know.
Oh, the wonderful souls of both black and white
Were made by one God, of one sod, on one night.

JAWA APRONTI

*Jawa Apronti (1940–) is one of the youngest poets represented
in this collection. He studied both in Ghana and in England. His
poem compares coldly civilized English funerals with those he
remembers in Africa.*

Funeral

At home Death claims
Two streams from women's eyes
And many day-long dirges;
Gnashes, red eyes and sighs from men,
The wailing of drums and muskets
And a procession of the townsfolk
Impeded
Only if the coffin decides
To take one last look at the home.

But here I see
Three cars in procession.
The first holds three—
A driver chatting gaily with a mate,
And behind them, flowers on a bier.
The second holds five, and the third too.

A procession
Efficiently arranged by the undertaker,
From the brass fittings on the bier
To the looks of sorrow on the mourners' faces.
And Death is escorted
Tearlessly but efficiently
By
Three cars in procession.

CAPE VERDE ISLANDS

AGUINALDO FONSECA

Fonseca was born in 1922 in the Cape Verde Islands, off the coast of West Africa. He has worked on literary reviews and has had his poems published in anthologies.

Tavern by the Sea

A distant glimmer
And a beacon spitting light
In the black face of night.

Everything is brine and yearning.

Winds with waves on their back
Make tremble the tavern
Which is an anchored ship.

Love passionate and brutal
Amidst the open knives
And the abandon
Of a prostitute's embrace.

Upon the air despairings rise
In heavy swells of smoke.

Bottles, glasses, bottles ...
—Oh! the thirst of a sailor ...

Tattooing pricked on skin
Proclaim the pain and the bravado
Of escapades in ports.

Men of every race,
Men without homeland or name
—Just men of the sea
With voice of salt and wind
And ships in unclouded eyes.

Boredom and longing appear
Chewing on aged pipes . . .
Appear and then depart
Staggering off with a drunk.

Cards, tables, and chairs,
Bottles, glasses, bottles
And the tavern-keeper's face
Stirring up ancient quarrels.

And everything is full of sin
And everything is full of sleep
And everything is full of sea!
                    —*Translated by Gerald Moore and Ulli Beier*

NIGERIA

JOHN PEPPER CLARK

*Clark was born in 1935 at Kiagbodo in midwestern Nigeria.
Clark is the editor of* Black Orpheus *and is on the faculty of the
University of Lagos, Nigeria. Ibadan, the subject of this poem,
is the largest city in Nigeria and its university is one of the most
influential institutions in Africa.*

Ibadan

Ibadan,
   running splash of rust
and gold—flung and scattered
among seven hills like broken
china in the sun.

WOLE SOYINKA

*Wole Soyinka, born in 1934, is an actor, musician, and producer
as well as poet. He studied at Ibadan and then in England and
taught for awhile and worked in the theater in London. His
return to Nigeria was an important event in the theatrical life of
the country. His poem reflects in very personal terms the bitterness of racial discrimination.*

Telephone Conversation

The price seemed reasonable, location
Indifferent. The landlady swore she lived
Off premises. Nothing remained
But self-confession. "Madam," I warned,
"I hate a wasted journey—I am African."
Silence. Silenced transmission of
Pressurized good-breeding. Voice, when it came,
Lipstick coated, long gold-rolled
Cigarette-holder pipped. Caught I was, foully.
"HOW DARK?" . . . I had not misheard. . . .
   "ARE YOU LIGHT
OR VERY DARK?" Button B. Button A. Stench
Of rancid breath of public hide-and-speak.

Red booth. Red pillar-box. Red double-tiered
Omnibus squelching tar. It *was* real! Shamed
By ill mannered silence, surrender
Pushed dumbfoundment to beg simplification.
Considerate she was, varying the emphasis—
"ARE YOU DARK? OR VERY LIGHT?" Revelation came.
"You mean—like plain or milk chocolate?"
Her assent was clinical, crushing in its light
Impersonality. Rapidly, wave-length adjusted,
I chose. "West African sepia"—and as afterthought,
"Down in my passport." Silence for spectroscopic
Flight of fancy, till truthfulness clanged her accent
Hard on the mouthpiece. "WHAT'S THAT?" conceding
"DON'T KNOW WHAT THAT IS." "Like brunette."
"THAT'S DARK, ISN'T IT?" "Not altogether.
Facially, I am brunette, but madam, you should see
The rest of me. Palm of my hand, soles of my feet
Are peroxide blond. Friction, caused—
Foolishly madam—by sitting down, has turned
My bottom raven black—One moment madam!" sensing
Her receiver rearing on the thunderclap
About my ears—"Madam," I pleaded, "wouldn't you rather
See for yourself?"

KENYA

JOSEPH E. KARIUKI

*Kariuki (1931–) was educated in Kenya and at Cambridge in
England. During his stay in Britain he wrote verse, some of
which was broadcast from the Overseas Service of the British
Broadcasting Corporation. He is now Director-General of the*

African Training and Research Center in Administration for Development, Tangier, Morocco.

New Life

It will rain tonight,
I smell it in the air,
And how we have waited.

My love said she would come with the rain.

A gentle knock at the door—
Palpable thudding in my breast.

A gust of wind blows out the tiny candle,
A momentary torrential outburst,
Then a flash that lights up
Scorching eyes.
A crack to end the world:
An unbearable brief eternity of silence
And then the rain.

It comes heaving, tearing, bearing down,
Surging in impatient billows to drain its source,
Till unable to bear its own forces
It settles to a timeless steady flow
Endless.

There is calm in the air,
And greater calm by my side.

Tomorrow the village women go planting
Their seed in the hungry ground:
And life is born anew.

ANGOLA

ANTONIO JACINTO

Jacinto was born in Luanda, Angola, in 1924; his poems have appeared in anthologies.

Monangamba

On that big estate there is no rain
it's the sweat of my brow that waters the crops;

On that big estate there is coffee ripe
and that cherry-redness
is drops of my blood turned sap.

   The coffee will be roasted,
   ground, and crushed,
   will turn black, black with the colour of the *contratado*.

Black with the color of the *contratado!*

Ask the birds that sing,
the streams in carefree wandering
and the high wind from inland:

   Who gets up early? Who goes to toil?
   Who is it carries on the long road
   the hammock or bunch of kernels?
   Who reaps and for pay gets scorn
   rotten maize, rotten fish,
   ragged clothes, fifty *angolares*
   beating for biting back?

Who?

Who makes the millet grow
and the orange groves to flower?
—Who?

Who gives the money for the boss to buy
cars, machinery, women
    and Negro heads for the motors?

Who makes the white man prosper,
grow big-bellied—get much money?
—Who?

And the birds that sing,
the streams in carefree wandering
and the high wind from inland
will answer:

   —Monangambeeee....

Ah! Let me at least climb the palm trees
Let me drink wine, palm wine
and fuddled by my drunkness forget

   —Monangambee....

—Translated by Alan Ryder

MOZAMBIQUE

JOSÉ CRAVEIRINHA

Craveirinha, born in 1922, is a poet and a journalist.

Poem of the Future Citizen

I came from somewhere
from a Nation which does not yet exist.
I came and I am here!

Not I alone was born
nor you nor any other . . .
but brothers.

I have love to give in handfuls.
Love of what I am
and nothing more.

I have a heart
and cries which are not mine alone
I come from a country which does not yet exist.

Ah! I have love in plenty to give
of what I am.

I!
A man among many
citizen of a Nation which has yet to exist.

Song of the Negro on the Ferry

If you could see me die
The millions of times I have been born . . .

If you could see me weep
The millions of times you have laughed . . .

If you could see me cry out
The millions of times I have kept silent . . .

If you could see me sing
The millions of times I have died
And bled. . .

I tell you, European brother

You would be born
You would weep
You would sing
You would cry out
And you would die
Bleeding . . .
Millions of times like me!!!

—*Translated by Philippa Rumsey*

SOUTH AFRICA

BLOKE MODISANE

Modisane was born in 1923 in Johannesburg, where he was educated and worked for some years on Drum *magazine. He fled from South Africa to London, where he worked as a writer, actor, and broadcaster. He is now living in Rome.*

Lonely

it gets awfully lonely,
lonely;
like screaming,
screaming lonely;
screaming down dream alley,
screaming of blues, like none can hear;
but you hear me clear and loud:
echoing loud;
like it's for you I scream.

I talk to myself when I write,
shout and scream to myself,
then to myself
scream and shout:
shouting a prayer,
screaming noises,
knowing this way I tell
the world about still lives;
even maybe
just to scream and shout.

is it I lack the musician's contact
direct?
or, is it true, the writer
creates
(except the trinity with God, the machine and he)
incestuous silhouettes
to each other scream and shout,
to me shout and scream
pry and mate;
inbred deformities of loneliness.

SHORT STORIES

The only common factor in these stories is that they come from cultures seldom represented in anthologies of the short story. They vary widely in literary merit as well as in subject and style. While we have been able to include stories from only a few countries—China, Cuba, India, Burma, Philippines, Korea, Senegal, Sierra Leone, and Israel—each gives a special glimpse of some of the humor, sadness, and strengths of the people of their lands.

In the first story, by the Senegalese writer and filmmaker Sembène Ousmane, a black servant girl experiences the bitterness of seeing her dreams of making her fortune in a foreign land turn to despair. The story contrasts sharply with the second, The Truly Married Woman, *in which Abioseh Nicol, a doctor, writer, and diplomat from Sierra Leone, captures the strength and humor of a strong indigenous culture.*

In many of the stories, war, civil disorder, or political turmoil provide either subject matter or setting. The Indian writer Khushwant Singh satirizes the basic meaninglessness of the constant turmoil between Hindus and Moslems in his country by showing in Riot *how a civil disorder may be started by a love affair between two dogs. Another kind of love affair is the subject of the Burmese* His Spouse, *by "Zawgyi" (pen name of U Thein Han). The story demonstrates how Zawgyi utilizes the common life of his country as his subject matter, a movement in which he was a pioneer in Burmese literature. In* Tehilah, *S.Y. Agnon writes of the poverty-stricken old Jewish community of Jerusalem and the spirituality of bygone days.*

The two stories from China and the one from Korea form a unit, with many interesting points of comparison and contrast. In neither China nor Korea has fiction been accorded a place of honor in the ranks of literature, a fact reflected in the rather

75

*stilted quality of these stories. The Chinese stories are heavy
with ideology, in marked contrast with the Cuban stories. Although written under the communist regime of Fidel Castro, the
Cuban stories reflect more influence of Sartre or Camus than
Mao or Castro. The Korean story and one of the Chinese stories,*
Maple Leaves *by He Guyan, are both set in Korea during the
Korean war. The Chinese story is written from the point of view
of the patriotic Chinese soldier; it stands in poignant contrast
to* The Nonrevolutionaries, *by Korea's Yu-Wol Chong-Nyon,
who sees in the war a senseless and meaningless carnage ravaging all the peoples of her homeland. The Moon on a Frosty
Morning by Fang Shumin is primarily ideological; through the
dogma, however, rings true the feelings of the young woman
cadre as she waits, with both dread and a degree of anticipation,
the return of her disgraced husband. In spite of Spanish,
Japanese, and American influences on the Philippines, which
are apparent in* Tanabata's Wife, *this story is a tale of basic
human needs. The next story,* Dada, *also takes place in the
Philippines, in and around the old central business area of
Manila and revolves around some members of the city's small
Hindu community.*

*Western influence is evident in both the story by Onelio Jorge
Cardoso (Cuba), which reminds us of Hemingway, and that of
Virgilio Piñera, which has some of the dark fantasy of the
French existentialists. The rhythm of the life of the fisherman
in the Cardoso story contrasts with the urban setting of the
story by Piñera.*

SEMBÈNE OUSMANE

Sembène Ousmane grew up in the former French colony of the Western Sudan, now the independent African state of Sudan. During the Second World War he served in the French army in Italy and Germany, returning after the war to work in Marseilles as a dock hand. Like his first novel, Le Docker Noir *(The Black Docker), his short story* Black Girl *captures the bitterness and despair of being black in a society based on the assumption of white supremacy.* Black Girl *was inspired by a letter printed in a French newspaper describing the desperate plight of a young black servant girl.*

Ousmane is both a writer and a filmmaker, whose film The Money Order *was shown at the 1969 Film Festival in New York. Perhaps his best novel is* God's Bits of Wood, *a fictionalized account of the 1947–48 railway strike on the Dakar-Bambako line. The deprivations of the workers and their families, the brutality of the French managers, the corruption of the blacks who are favored by the ruling class are vividly presented and stand as memorable testimony to the evils of colonialism.*

In Black Girl *the setting ranges from Dakar, Senegal's capital and most important port, to Antibes, on the French Riviera. Diouana, the servant, originally came from Casamance, the southernmost region of Senegal, rural and backward compared to the more affluent, modern, and sophisticated city of Dakar or the still more sophisticated European playground of the Riviera. Diouana's grand dreams of securing for herself a portion of the fabulous riches of the Europeans are soon shattered as she comes to realize that her race—even more than her status— renders her a non-person, a "useful object." Her desperation is complete when she begins to understand that "She wasn't the 'African' girl in her own right, but theirs." In her final act she reclaims, though briefly, the one possession she has left—her own life. (See O.R. Dathorne,* The Black Mind, A History of African Literature, *Minneapolis, University of Minnesota Press, 1974.)*

Black Girl

It was the morning of the 23rd of June in the year of our Lord nineteen hundred fifty-eight. At Antibes, along the Riviera, neither the fate of the French Republic, nor the future of Algeria nor the state of the colonial territories preoccupied those who swarmed across the beaches below La Croisette.

Above, on the road leading to the Hermitage, two old-style Citroens, one behind the other, were moving up the mountain. They stopped and several men quickly got out, rushing down the gravel walk towards a house on which a worn sign spelled out 'Villa of Green Happiness.' The men were the police chief of the town of Grasse, a medical officer, and two police inspectors from Antibes, flanked by officers in uniform.

There was nothing green about the Villa of Green Happiness except its name. The garden was kept in the French manner, the walks covered with gravel, set off by a couple of palm trees with drooping fronds. The Chief looked closely at the house, his eyes stopping at the third window, the broken glass, the ladder.

Inside were other inspectors and a photographer. Three people who seemed to be reporters were looking with rather absent-minded interest at the African statues, masks, animal skins, and ostrich eggs set here and there on the walls. Entering the living-room was like violating the privacy of a hunter's lair.

Two women were hunched together, sobbing. They looked very much alike, the same straight forehead, the same curved nose, the same dark circles about eyes reddened from crying. The one in the pale dress was speaking: 'After my nap, I felt like taking a bath. The door was locked from the inside —blowing her nose—'and I thought to myself, it's the maid taking her bath. I say "the maid," ' she corrected, 'but we never called her anything else but her name, Diouana. I waited for more than an hour, but didn't see her come out. I went back and called, knocking on the door. There was no answer. Then I phoned our neighbor, the Commodore. . . .'

She stopped, wiped her nose, and began to cry again. Her sister, the younger of the two, hair cut in a boyish style, sat hanging her head.

'You're the one who discovered the body?'

'Yes . . . that is, when Madame Pouchet called and told me that the black girl had locked herself in the bathroom, I thought it was a joke. I spent thirty-five years at sea, you know. I've roamed the seven seas. I'm retired from the Navy.'

'Yes, yes, we know.'

'Yes, well, when Madame Pouchet called I brought my ladder.'

'You brought the ladder?'

'No. It was Mademoiselle Dubois, Madame's sister, who suggested the idea. And when I got to the window, I saw the black girl swimming in blood.'

'Where is the key to the door?'

'Here it is, your Honour,' said the inspector.

'Just wanted to see it.'

'I've checked the window,' said the other inspector.

'I'm the one who opened it, after breaking the pane,' said the retired navy man.

'Which pane did you break?'

'Which pane?' he repeated. He was wearing white linen trousers and a blue jacket.

'Yes, I saw it, but I'd like to ask precisely.'

'The second from the top,' answered the sister.

At this, two stretcher-bearers came down, carrying a body wrapped in a blanket. Blood dripped on the steps. The magistrate lifted a corner of the blanket and frowned. A black girl lay dead on the stretcher, her throat cut from one ear to the other.

'It was with this knife. A kitchen knife,' said another man, from the top of the stairs.

'Did you bring her from Africa or did you hire her here?'

'We brought her back from Africa, in April. She came by boat. My husband is with aerial navigation in Dakar, but the company only pays air passage for the family. She worked for us in Dakar. For two and a half or three years.'

'How old is she?'

'I don't know exactly.'

'According to her passport, she was born in 1927.'

'Oh! The natives don't know when they are born,' offered the naval officer, plunging his hands in his pockets.

'I don't know why she killed herself. She was well treated here, she ate the same food, shared the same rooms as my children.'

'And your husband, where is he?'

'He left for Paris the day before yesterday.'

'Ah!' said the inspector, still looking at the knick-knacks. 'Why do you think it was suicide?'

'Why?' said the retired officer. . . . 'Oh! Who do you think would make an attempt on the life of a Negro girl? She never went out. She didn't know anyone, except for Madame's children.'

The reporters were getting impatient. The suicide of a maid—even if she were black—didn't amount to a hill of beans. There was nothing newsworthy in it.

'It must have been homesickness. Because lately, she'd been behaving very strangely. She wasn't the same.'

The police magistrate went upstairs, accompanied by one of the inspectors. They examined the bathroom, the window.

'Some boomerang, this story,' said the inspector.

The others waited in the living-room.

'We'll let you know when the coroner is finished,' said the inspector, on his way out with the police magistrate an hour after their arrival.

The cars and the reporters left. In the Villa of Green Happiness the two women and the retired naval officer remained silent.

Bit by bit, Madame Pouchet searched her memory. She thought back to Africa and her elegant villa on the road to Hahn. She remembered Diouana pushing open the iron gate and signalling to the German shepherd to stop barking.

It was there, in Africa, that everything had started. Diouana had made the six-kilometre round trip on foot three times a week. For the last month she had made it gaily, enraptured, her heart beating as if she were in love for the first time. Beginning at the outskirts of Dakar, brand new houses were scattered like jewels in a landscape of cactus, bougainvillea and jasmine. The asphalt of the Avenue Gambetta stretched out like a long black ribbon. Joyous and happy as usual, the little maid had no complaints about the road or her employers. Though it was a long way, it had no longer seemed so far the past month, ever since Madame had announced she would take her to France. France! Diouana shouted the word in her head. Everything around her had become ugly, the magnificent villas she had so often admired seemed shabby.

In order to be able to travel, in order to go to France, since she was originally from the Casamance, she had needed an identity card. All her paltry savings went to get one. 'So what?' she thought. 'I'm on my way to France!"

'Is that you, Diouana?'

'Viye, Madame,' came her answer in the Senegalese accent. She spoke from the vestibule, nicely dressed in her light coloured cotton, her hair neatly combed.

'Good! Monsieur is in town. Will you look after the children?"

'Viye, Madame,' she agreed in her childish voice.

Though her identity card read 'born in 1927,' Diouana was not yet thirty. But she must have been over twenty-one. She went to find the children. Every room was in the same condition. Parcels packed and tied with strings, boxes piled here and there. After ten whole days of washing and ironing, there wasn't much left for Diouana to do. In the proper sense of her duties, she was a laundress. There was a cook, a houseboy and herself. Three people. The servants.

'Diouana . . . Diouana,' Madame called.

'Madame?' she answered, emerging from the children's room.

Madame was standing with a notebook in her hands making an inventory of the baggage. The movers would be coming at any moment.

'Have you been to see your parents? Do you think they will be happy?'

'Viye, Madame. The whole family is agreed. I tell Mama for myself. Also tell Papa Boutoupa,' she said,

Her face, which had been radiant with happiness, fixed on the empty walls, and began to fade. Her heartbeat slowed. She would be ill if Madame changed her mind. Ready to plead her case, Diouana's ebony-black face grew gloomy, she lowered her eyes.

'You're not going to tell me at the last moment, on this very day, that you're leaving us in the lurch?'

'No, Madame, me go.'

They were not speaking the same language. Diouana wanted to see France, this country whose beauty, richness, and joy of living everyone praised. She wanted to see it and make a triumphal return. This was where people got rich. Already, without having left African soil, she could see herself on the dock, returning from France, wealthy to the millions, with gifts of clothes for everyone. She dreamed of the freedom to go where she wished, without having to work like a beast of burden. If Madame should change her mind, refuse to take her, it would truly make her ill.

As for Madame, she was remembering the last few holidays she had spent in France. Three of them. And then she had only two children. In Africa, Madame had acquired bad habits when it came to servants. In France when she hired a maid not only was the salary higher, but the maid demanded a day off to boot. Madame had had to let her go and hired another. The next one was no different from the first, if not worse. She answered Madame tit for tat. 'Anyone who is capable of having children should take a turn with them herself. I can't live in. I have my own children to take care of and a husband too,' she declared.

Used to being waited on hand and foot, Madame had yielded to her wifely duties, and clumsily fulfilled the role of mother. As for a real vacation, she had hardly had any. She soon persuaded her husband to return to Africa.

On her return, grown thin and thoroughly exasperated, she had conceived a plan for her next vacation. She put want ads in all the newpapaers. A hundred young girls answered. Her choice fell on Diouana, newly arrived from her native bush. Producing two more children during the three years that Diouana worked for her, between her last holiday and the one to come, Madame sang the praises of France. For three thousand francs a month, any young African girl would have followed her to the end of the earth. And to top it off, from time to time, especially lately, Madame would give Diouana little gifts of this and that, old clothes, shoes that could be mended.

This was the insurmountable moat that separated the maid and her employer.

'Did you give Monsieur your identity card?'

'Viye, Madame.'

'You may go back to your work. Tell the cook to give the three of you a good meal.'

'Merci, Madame,' she answered, and went off to the kitchen. Madame continued her inventory.

Monsieur returned on the stroke of noon, his arrival announced by the barking of the dog. Getting out of his Peugeot 403, he found his wife, indefatigable, pencil in hand.

'Haven't the baggage men come yet?' she said nervously.

'They'll be here at a quarter to two. Our bags will be on top. That way they'll be out first when we land in Marseilles. And what about Diouana? Diouana!'

The eldest of the children ran to fetch her. She was under the trees with the littlest one.

'Viye, Madame.'

'It's Monsieur who was calling you.'

'That's fine. Here are your ticket and your identity card.'

Diouana held out a hand to take them.

'You keep the identity card, I'll take care of the ticket. The Duponts are returning on the same ship, they'll look after you. Are you glad to be going to France?'

'Viye, Monsieur.'

'Good. Where are your bags?'

'At Rue Escarfait, Monsieur.'

'After I've had lunch we'll go fetch them in the car.'

'Bring the children in, Diouana, it's time for their nap.'

'Viye, Madame.'

Diouana wasn't hungry. The cook's helper, two years younger than she, brought the plates and took the empty ones away, noiselessly. The cook was sweating heavily. He wasn't happy. He was going to be out of work. This was how the departure affected him. And for this reason he was a bit resentful of the maid. Leaning out the wide window overlooking the sea, transported, Diouana watched the birds flying high above in the immense expanse of blue. In the distance she could barely make out the Island of Goree. She was holding her identity card, turning it over and over, examining it and smiling quietly to herself. The picture was a gloomy one. She wasn't pleased with the pose or with the exposure. 'What does it matter? I'm leaving!' she thought.

'Samba,' said Monsieur, who had come to the kitchen, 'the meal was excellent today. You outdid yourself. Madame is very pleased with you.'

The cook's helper stood at attention. Samba, the cook, adjusted his tall white hat and made an effort to smile.

'Thank you very much, Monsieur,' he said. 'I too am happy,

very happy, because Monsieur and Madame are happy. Monsieur very nice. My family big, unhappy, Monsieur leave, me no more work.'

'We'll be back, my good man. And then, with your talent you'll soon find another job!'

Samba, the cook, wasn't so sure. The whites were stingy. And in a Dakar filled with country people each claiming to be a master cook, it wouldn't be easy to find a job.

'We'll be back, Samba. Maybe sooner than you think. The last time we stayed only two and a half months.'

To these consoling words from Madame, who had joined her husband in the kitchen, Samba could only answer: 'Merci, Madame. Madame very nice lady.'

Madame was glad. She knew from experience what it meant to have a good reputation with the servants.

'You can go home this afternoon at four with Monsieur. I'll pack up the rest. When we come back I promise to hire you again. Are you pleased?'

'Merci, Madame.'

Madame and Monsieur were gone. Samba gave Diouana a slap. She hit him back angrily.

'Hey! Careful. Careful. You're going away today. So we shouldn't fight.'

'That hurt!' she said.

'And Monsieur, does he hurt you too?'

Samba suspected a secret liaison between the maid and her employer.

'They're calling for you, Diouana. I hear the car starting.'

She left without even saying goodbye.

The car moved along the highway. Diouana didn't often have the privilege of being driven by Monsieur. Her very look invited the pedestrians' admiration, though she dared not wave a hand or shout while going past, 'I'm on my way to France!' Yes, France! She was sure her happiness was plain to see. The subterranean sources of this tumultuous joy made her a bit shaky. When the car stopped in front of the house at Rue Escarfait, she was surprised. 'Already?' she thought. Next door to her humble house, at the Gay Navigator Café a few customers were seated at the tables and several were talking quietly on the sidewalk.

'Is it today you're leaving, little one?' asked Tive Correa.

Already tipsy, he steadied himself, legs apart, holding his bottle by the neck. His clothes were rumpled.

Diouana would have nothing to do with the drunkard. She didn't listen to Tive Correa's advice. An old sailor, Tive Correa had come home from Europe after twenty years absence. He had left, rich with youth, full of ambition, and come home a wreck. From having wanted everything he had returned with nothing but an excessive love for the bottle. For Diouana he predicted nothing but misfortune. Once, when she had asked his advice, his opinion had been that she shouldn't go. In spite of his serious state of inebriety, he made a few steps towards Monsieur, bottle still in hand.

'Is it true that Diouana's leaving with you, Monsieur?'

Monsieur did not answer. He took out a cigarette and lit it, blew the smoke through the car door, and looked Tive Correa over from head to toe. What a bum he was, greasy clothes, stinking of palm wine. Correa leaned over, putting a hand on the car door.

'I was there. I lived in France for twenty years,' he began with a note of pride in his voice. 'I, whom you see this way, ruin though I am today, I know France better than you do. During the war I lived in Toulon, and the Germans sent us with the other Africans to Aix-en-Provence, to the mines at Gardanne. I've been against her going.'

'We haven't forced her to go! She wants to,' Monsieur answered dryly.

'Certainly. What young African doesn't dream of going to France? Unfortunately, they confuse living in France with being a servant in France. I come from the village next to Diouana's, in Casamance. There, we don't say the way you do that it is the light that attracts the butterfly, but the other way round. In my country, Casamance, we say that the darkness pursues the butterfly.'

In the meantime, Diouana returned, escorted by several women. They were chatting along, each begging for a little souvenir. Diouana promised happily; she was smiling, her white teeth gleaming.

'The others are at the dock,' said one. 'Don't forget my dress.'

'For me, some shoes for the children. You've got the size in your suitcase. And remember the sewing machine.'

'The petticoats, too.'

'Write and tell me how much the hair straightening irons cost and also the price of a red jacket with big buttons, size 44.'

'Don't forget to send a little money to your mother in Boutoupa . . . '

Each one had something to tell her, some request to make of her; Diouana promised. Her face was radiant. Tive Correa took the suitcase, pushing it drunkenly but not roughly into the car.

'Let her go, girls. Do you think money grows on trees in France? She'll have something to say about that when she gets back.'

Loud protests from the women.

'Goodbye, little cousin. Take care of yourself. You have the address of the cousin in Toulon. Write to him as soon as you get there, he will help you. Come give me a kiss.'

They all kissed each other goodbye. Monsieur was getting impatient. He started up the motor to indicate politely that he wished they'd be done with it.

The Peugeot was moving. Everyone waved.

At the dock it was the same; relatives, friends, little commissions. Everyone pressed around her. Always under the watchful eye of Monsieur. She embarked.

A week at sea. 'No news,' she would have written if she'd been keeping a diary, in which case she'd also have had to know how to read and write. Water in front, behind, to port, to starboard. Nothing but a sheet of liquid, and above it, the sky.

When the boat landed, Monsieur was there. After the formalities, they quickly made their way to the Cote d'Azur. She devoured everything with her eyes, marvelling, astonished. She packed every detail into her head. It was beautiful. Africa seemed a sordid slum by comparison. Towns, buses, trains, trucks went by along the coastal highway. The heaviness of the traffic surprised her.

'Did you have a good crossing?'

'Viye, Monsieur,' she would have answered, if Monsieur had asked the question.

After a two-hour drive, they were in Antibes.

Days, weeks and the first month went by. The third month began. Diouana was no longer the joyous young girl with the ready laugh, full of life. Her eyes were beginning to look hollow, her glance was less alert, she no longer noticed details. She had a lot more work to do here than in Africa. At first her fretting was hardly noticeable. Of France, 'La Belle France,' she had only a vague idea, a fleeting vision. French gardens, the hedges of the other villas, the crests of roofs appearing above the green trees, the palms. Everyone lived his own life, isolated, shut up in his own house. Monsieur and Madame went out a good deal, leaving her with the four children. The children quickly organized a mafia and persecuted her. 'You've got to keep them happy,' Madame would say. The oldest, a real scamp, recruited others of like inclination and they played explorer. Diouana was the 'savage.' The children pestered her. Once in a while the eldest got a good spanking. Having picked up phrases from the conversations of mama, papa or the neighbors back in Africa—phrases in which notions of racial prejudice played a part—he made exaggerated remarks to his pals. Without the knowledge of his parents, they would turn up, chanting, 'Black Girl, Black Girl. She's as black as midnight.'

Perpetually harassed, Diouana began to waste away. In Dakar she had never had to think about the colour of her skin. With the youngsters teasing she began to question it. She understood that here she was alone. There was nothing that connected her with the others. And it aggravated her, poisoned her life, the very air she breathed.

Everything grew blunt; her old dreams, her contentment eroded. She did a lot of hard work. It was she who did all the cooking, laundry, babysitting, ironing. Madame's sister came to stay at the villa. making seven people to look after. At night, as soon as she went up to bed, Diouana slept like a log.

The venom was poisoning her heart. She had never hated anything. Everything became monotonous. Where was France? The beautiful cities she had seen at the movies in Dakar, the rare foods, the interesting crowds? The population of France reduced itself to these spiteful monsters, Monsieur, Madame and Mademoiselle, who had become strangers to her. The country seemed limited to the immediate surroundings of the villa. Little by little she was drowning. The wide horizons of a short while ago stopped now at the colour of her skin, which suddenly filled her with an invincible terror. Her skin. Her blackness. Timidly, she retreated into herself.

With no one from her universe to exchange ideas with, she held long moments of palaver with herself. A week ago, Monsieur and Madame had cleverly taken her along to visit their relatives in Cannes.

'Tomorrow we'll go to Cannes. My parents have never tasted African food. You'll do us African honour with your cooking.' Madame had said. She was nearly bare, and getting bronzed from the sun.

'Viye, Madame.'

'I've ordered some rice and two chickens. . . . You'll be careful not to spice it too much?'

'Viye, Madame.'

Answering this way, her heart hardened. It seemed the hundredth time that she'd been trailed from villa to villa. To this one's house and then to that one's. It was at the Commodore's—everyone called him the Commodore—that she had rebelled the first time. Some silly people, who followed her about, hanging on her heels in the kitchen, had been there for dinner. Their presence was an oppressive shadow on her slightest movement. She had the feeling of not knowing how to do anything. These strange, self-centered, sophisticated beings never stopped asking her idiotic questions about how African women do their cooking. She kept herself under control.

The three women were still chirping when she waited on them at the table, testing the first spoonful on the tip of their tongue, then gluttonously devouring the rest.

'This time, at my parents, you must outdo yourself.'

'Viye, Madame.'

Restored to her kitchen, her thoughts went to Madame's former kindness. She detested it. Madame had been good to her, but in a self-seeking way. The only reason for her attentiveness had been to wind the strings round Diouana, the better to make her sweat. She loathed everything. Back in Dakar, Diouana used to gather Monsieur and Madame's leftovers to take home to Rue Escarfait. She had taken pride then in working for 'important white people.' Now she was so alone their meals made her sick to her stomach. The resentment spoiled her relations with her employers. She stood her ground, they stood theirs. They no longer exchanged any remarks but those of a business nature.

'Diouana, will you do the washing today?'

'Viye, Madame.'

'Last time you didn't do a good job on my slips. The iron was too hot. And the collars of Monsieur's shirts were scorched. Do pay attention to what you're doing, will you?'

'Viye, Madame.'

'Oh, I forgot. There are some buttons missing on Monsieur's shirts and his shorts.'

Every little job was Diouana's. And then Madame started speaking to her in pidgin French, even in front of guests. And this was the only thing she did with honesty. In the end, no one in the house ever spoke to the maid any more except in terms of 'Missie,' Senegalese pidgin talk. Bewildered by her inadequacies in French, Diouana closed herself into a sort of solitary confinement. After long, lonely moments of meditation she came to the conclusion first of all that she was nothing but a useful object, and furthermore that she was being put on exhibit like a trophy. At parties, when Monsieur or Madame made remarks about 'native' psychology, Diouana was taken as an illustration. The neighbors would say: 'It's the Pouchets' black girl. . . . ' She wasn't the 'African girl' in her own right, but theirs. And that hurt.

The fourth month began. Things got worse. Her thoughts grew more lucid every day. She had work and work to spare. All week long. Sunday was Mademoiselle's favorite day for asking friends over. There were lots of them. The weeks began and ended with them.

Everything became clear. Why had Madame wanted her to come? Her generosities had been premeditated. Madame no longer took care of her children. She kissed them every morning, that was all. And where was 'La Belle France?' These questions kept repeating themselves. 'I am cook, nurse-maid, chambermaid; I do all the washing and ironing and for a mere three thousand francs a month. I do housework for six people. What am I doing here?'

Diouana gave way to her memories. She compared her 'native bush' to these dead shrubs. How different from the forest of her home in Casamance. The memory of her village, of the community life, cut her off from the others even more. She bit her lips, sorry to have come. And on this film of the past, a thousand other details were projected.

Returning to these surroundings, where she was doubly an outsider, her feelings hardened. She thought often of Tive

Correa. His predictions had come cruelly true. She would have liked to write to him, but couldn't. Since arriving in France, she had had only two letters from her mother. She didn't have the time to answer, even though Madame had promised to write for her. Was it possible to tell Madame what she was thinking? She was angry with herself. Her ignorance made her mute. It was infuriating. And besides, Mademoiselle had made off with her stamps.

A pleasant idea crossed her mind though, and raised a smile. This evening only Monsieur was at home, watching television. She decided to take advantage of the opportunity. Then, unexpectedly finding Madame there too, Diouana stopped abruptly and left the room.

'Sold, sold. Bought, bought,' she repeated to herself. 'They've bought me. For three thousand francs I do all this work. They lured me, tied me to them, and I'm stuck here like a slave.' She was determined now. That night she opened her suitcase, looked at the objects in it and wept. No one cared.

Yet she went through the same motions and remained as sealed off from the others as an oyster at low tide on the beach of her native Casamance.

'Douna'—it was Mademoiselle calling her. Why was it impossible for her to say Di-ou-a-na?

Her anger redoubled. Mademoiselle was even lazier than Madame: 'Come take this away'—'There is such-and-such to be done, Douna'—'Why don't you do this, Douna?'—'Douna, now and then please rake the garden.' For an answer Mademoiselle would receive an incendiary glance. Madame complained about her to Monsieur.

'What is the matter with you, Diouana? Are you ill or something?' he asked.

She no longer opened her mouth.

'You can tell me what's the matter. Perhaps you'd like to go to Toulon. I haven't had the time to go, but tomorrow I'll take you with me.'

'Anyone would think we disgust her,' said Madame.

Three days later Diouana took her bath. Returning home after a morning of shopping, Madame Pouchet went in the bathroom and quickly emerged.

'Diouana! Diouana!' she called. 'You are dirty, in spite of everything. You might have left the bathroom clean.'

'No me, Madame. It was the children, viye.'

'The children! The children are tidy. It may be that you're fed up with them. But to find you telling lies, like a native, that I don't like. I don't like liars and you are a liar!'

Diouana kept silent, though her lips were trembling. She went upstairs to the bathroom, and took her clothes off. It was there they found her, dead.

'Suicide,' the investigators concluded. The case was closed.

The next day, in the newspaper on page four, column six, hardly noticeable, was a small headline:

'Homesick African Girl Cuts Throat in Antibes.'

                    —*Translated by Ellen Conroy Kennedy*

ABIOSEH NICOL

This story comes from Sierra Leone, a former British colony in West Africa. The capital and chief port of Sierra Leone, Freetown, served a unique function as an anti-slave-trade base. Freed African slaves from England established a settlement there in 1787 and were subsequently joined by groups of former slaves from Nova Scotia and Jamaica. Between 1807 and 1864 more than 50,000 "recaptured" slaves, taken by the British navy from the by then illegal slave trade ships, were settled in Freetown. The British governor of the colony undertook a deliberate campaign to develop this settlement of "recaptives," originally from all over West Africa, into a homogeneous Christian community. With the aid of the Anglican Church Missionary Society, the Methodist Missionary Society, and the pastors of the churches of the first groups of freed settlers, this policy became a living reality. The colony became an independent state within the British Commonwealth in 1961.

Abioseh Nicol (born Davidson Nicol) is a diplomat, physician, and medical researcher as well as a well-known writer of fiction. He has been principal of Fourah Bay College, Freetown; vice-chancellor of the University of Sierra Leone; and ambassador to the United Nations. Like The Truly Married

Woman *(1965) many of his stories center upon life in government service, and upon the often humorous, sometimes tragic,
tangle of domestic and public relations existing in an emerging
nation.*

The Truly Married Woman

Ajayi stirred for a while and then sat up. He looked at the
cheap alarm clock on the chair by his bedside. It was six-
fifteen, and light outside already; the African town was slowly
waking to life. The night watchmen roused from sleep by the
angry crowing of cockerels were officiously banging the locks
of stores and houses to assure themselves and their em-
ployees, if near, of their efficiency. Village women were tramp-
ing through the streets to the market place with their wares,
arguing and gossiping.

Ajayi sipped his cup of morning tea. It was as he liked it,
weak and sugary, without milk. With an effort of will, he got up
and walked to the window, and standing there he took six deep
breaths. This done daily, he firmly believed, would prevent
tuberculosis. He walked through his ramshackle compound to
an outhouse and took a quick bath, pouring the water over his
head from a tin cup with which he scooped water from a bucket.

By then Ayo had laid out his breakfast. Ayo was his wife. Not
really one, he would explain to close friends, but a mistress. A
good one. She had borne him three children and was now three
months gone with another. They had been together for twelve
years. She was a patient, handsome woman. Very dark with
very white teeth and open sincere eyes. Her hair was always
carefully plaited. When she first came to him—to the exasperation of her parents—he had fully intended marrying her as
soon as she had shown satisfactory evidence of fertility, but he
had never quite got round to it. In the first year or so she would
report to him in great detail the splendour of the marriage
celebrations of her friends, looking at him with hopeful eyes.
He would close the matter with a tirade on the sinfulness of
ostentation. She gave up after some time. Her father never

spoke to her again after she had left home. Her mother visited her secretly and attended the baptismal ceremonies of all her children. The Church charged extra for illegitimate children as a deterrent; two dollars instead of fifty cents. Apart from this, there was no other great objection. Occasionally, two or three times a year, the pastor would preach violently against adultery, polygamy, and unmarried couples living together. Ajayi and Ayo were good churchpeople and attended regularly, but sat in different pews. After such occasions, their friends would sympathize with them and other couples in similar positions. There would be a little grumbling and the male members of the congregation would say that the trouble with the Church was that it did not stick to its business of preaching the Gospel, but meddled in people's private lives. Ajayi would indignantly absent himself from Church for a few weeks but would go back eventually because he liked singing hymns and because he knew secretly that the pastor was right.

Ayo was a good mistress. Her father was convinced she could have married a high-school teacher at least, or a pharmacist, but instead she had attached herself to a junior Government clerk. But Ayo loved Ajayi, and was happy in her own slow, private way. She cooked his meals and bore him children. In what spare time she had she either did a little petty trading, visited friends, or gossiped with Omo, the woman next door.

With his towel round his waist, Ajayi strode back to the bedroom, dried himself and dressed quickly but carefully in his pink tussore suit. He got down the new bottle of patent medicine which one of his friends who worked in a drug store had recommended to him. Ajayi believed that to keep healthy, a man must regularly take a dose of some medicine. He read the label of this one. It listed about twenty diseased conditions of widely differing pathology which the contents of the bottle were reputed to cure if the patient persevered in its daily intake. Ajayi underlined in his own mind at least six from which he believed he either suffered or was on the threshold of suffering: dizziness, muscle pain, impotence, fever, jaundice, and paralytic tremors. Intelligence and courage caused him to skip the obviously female maladies and others such as nervous debility or bladder pains. It said on the label too that a teaspoonful should be taken three times a day. But since he only remembered to take it in the morning and in any case believed in shock treatment, he took a swig and two big gulps. The medicine was bitter and astringent. He grimaced but was satisfied. It was obviously a good and strong medicine or else it would not have been so bitter.

He went in to breakfast. He soon finished his maize porridge, fried beans, and cocoa. He then severely flogged his eldest son, a ten-year-old boy, for wetting his sleepingmat last night. Ayo came in after the boy had fled screaming to the back yard.

'Ajayi, you flog that boy too much,' she said. 'He should stop wetting the floor, he is a big boy,' he replied. 'In any case, no one is going to instruct me on how to bring up my son.' 'He is mine too,' Ayo said. She seldom opposed him unless she felt strongly about something. 'He has not stopped wetting although you beat him every time he does. In fact, he is doing it more and more now. Perhaps if you stopped whipping him he might get better.' 'Did I whip him to begin doing it?' Ajayi asked. 'No.' 'Well, how will stopping whipping him stop him doing it?' Ajayi asked triumphantly. 'Nevertheless,' Ayo said, 'our own country-woman Bimbola, who has just come back from England and America studying nursing, told us in a women's group meeting that it was wrong to punish children for such things.' 'All right, I'll see,' he said, reaching for his sun helmet.

All that day at the office he thought about this and other matters. So Ayo had been attending women's meetings. Well, what do you know. She would be running for the Town Council next. The sly woman. Always looking so quiet and meek and then quoting modern theories from overseas doctors at him. He smiled with pride. Indeed Ayo was an asset. Perhaps it was wrong to beat the boy. He decided he would not do so again.

Towards closing time the chief clerk sent for him. Wondering what mistake he had made that day, or on what mission he was to be sent, he hurried along to the forward office. There were three white men sitting on chairs by the chief clerk, who was an aging African dressed with severe respectability. On seeing them, Ajayi's heart started thudding. The police, he thought; heavens, what have I done?

'Mr. Ajayi, these gentlemen have enquired for you,' the chief clerk said formally. 'Pleased to meet you, Mr. Ajayi,' the tallest said, with a smile. 'We represent the World Gospel Crusading Alliance from Minnesota. My name is Jonathan Olsen.' Ajayi shook hands and the other two were introduced.

'You expressed an interest in our work a year ago and we have not forgotten. We are on our way to India and we thought we would look you up personally.'

It transpired that the three Crusaders were en route and that their ship had stopped for refueling off the Africa port for a few hours. The chief clerk looked at Ajayi with new respect. Ajayi tried desperately to remember any connection with W.G.C.A. (as Olsen by then had proceeded to call it) whilst he made conversation with them a little haltingly. Then suddenly he remembered. Some time ago he had got hold of a magazine from his subtenant who worked at the United States Information Service. He had cut a coupon from it and posted it to W.G.C.A. asking for information, but really hoping that they would send illustrated Bibles free which he might give away or sell. He hoped for at least large reproductions of religious paintings which, suitably framed, would decorate his parlour or which he might paste up on his bedroom wall. But nothing had come of it and he had forgotten. Now here was W.G.C.A. as large as life. Three lives. Instantly and recklessly he invited all three and the chief clerk to come to his house for a cold drink. They all agreed.

'Mine is a humble abode,' he warned them. 'No abode is humble that is illumined by Christian love,' Olsen replied. 'His is illumined all right, I can assure you,' the chief clerk remarked drily.

Olsen suggested a taxi, but Ajayi neatly blocked that by saying the roads were bad. He had hurriedly whispered to a fellow clerk to rush home on a bicycle and tell Ayo he was coming in half an hour with white men and that she should clean up and get fruit drinks. Ayo was puzzled by the message as she firmly imagined all white men drank only whisky and iced beer. But the messenger had said that there was a mixture of friendliness and piety in the visitors' mien, which made him suspect they might be missionaries. Another confirmatory point was that they were walking instead of being in a car. That cleared up the anomaly in Ayo's mind and she set to work at once. Oju, now recovered from his morning disgrace, was dispatched with a basket on his head to buy soft drinks. Ayo whisked off the wall all their commercial calendars with suggestive pictures. She propped up family photographs which had fallen face downwards on the table. She removed the Wild

West novels and romance magazines from the parlour and put instead an old copy of Bunyan's *Pilgrim's Progress* and a prayer book which she believed would add culture and religious force to the decorations. She remembered the wine glasses and the beer-advertising table-mats in time and put those under the sofa. She just had time to change to her Sunday frock and borrow a wedding ring from her neighbor when Ajayi and the guests arrived. The chief clerk was rather surprised at the change in the room—which he had visited before—and in Ayo's dress and ring. But he concealed his feelings. Ayo was introduced and made a little conversation in English. This pleased Ajayi a great deal. The children had been changed too into Sunday suits, faces washed and hair brushed. Olsen was delighted and insisted on taking photographs for the Crusade journal. Ayo served drinks and then modestly retired, leaving the men to discuss serious matters. Olsen by then was talking earnestly on the imminence of Christ's Second Coming and offering Ajayi ordination into deaconship.

The visit passed off well and soon the missionaries left to catch their boat. Ajayi had been saved from holy orders by the chief clerk's timely explanation that it was strictly against Government regulations for civil servants to indulge in non-official organizations. To help Ajayi out of his quandary, he had even gone further and said that contravention might result in a fine or imprisonment. 'Talk about colonial oppression,' the youngest of the missionaries had said, gloomily.

The next day Ajayi called at the chief clerk's office with a carefully wrapped bottle of beer as a present for his help generally on the occasion. They discussed happily the friendliness and interest the white men had shown.

This incident and Ayo's protest against flagellation as a specific against enuresis made Ajayi very thoughtful for a week. He decided to marry Ayo. Another consideration which added weight to the thought was the snapshot Olsen took for his magazine. In some peculiar way Ajayi felt he and Ayo should marry, as millions of Americans would see their picture—Olsen had assured him of this—as 'one saved and happy African family.' He announced his intention of marrying her to Ayo one evening, after a particularly good meal and a satisfactory bout of belching. Ayo at once became extremely solicitous and got up looking at him with some anxiety. Was he ill? she asked. Was there anything wrong at the office? Had anyone insulted him? No, he answered, there was nothing wrong with his wanting to get married, was there? Or had she anyone else in mind? Ayo laughed, 'As you will,' she said; 'let us get married, but do not say I forced you into it.'

They discussed the wedding that night. Ajayi wanted to have a white wedding with veil and orange blossom. But Ayo with regret decided it would not be quite right. They agreed on grey. Ayo particularly wanted a corset to strap down her obvious bulge; Ajayi gave way gallantly to this feminine whim, chucking her under the chin and saying. 'You women with your vanity!' But he was firm about no honeymoon. He said he could not afford the expense and that one bed was as good as another. Ayo gave way on that. They agreed, however, on a church wedding and that their children could act as bridal pages to keep the cost of clothes within the family.

That evening Ajayi, inflamed by the idea and arrangements for the wedding, pulled Ayo excitedly to him as they lay in bed. 'No,' said Ayo, shyly, pushing him back gently, 'you mustn't. Wait until after the marriage.' 'Why?' said Ajayi, rather surprised, but obedient. 'Because it will not somehow be right,' Ayo replied seriously and determinedly.

Ayo's father unbent somewhat when he heard of the proposed marriage. He insisted, however, that Ayo move herself and all her possessions back home to his house. The children were sent to Ayo's married sister. Most of Ajayi's family were in favour of the union, except his sister, who, moved by the threat implicit in Ayo's improved social position, advised Ajayi to see a soothsayer first. As Ayo had got wind of this through friends at market on Saturday, she saw the soothsayer first and fixed things. When Ajayi and his sister called at night to see him, he consulted the oracles and pronounced future happiness, avoiding the sister's eye. The latter restrained herself from scratching the old man's face and accepted defeat.

The only other flaw in a felicitous situation had been Ayo's neighbour Omo, who had always on urgent occasions at short notice lent Ayo her wedding ring. She had suddenly turned cold. Especially after Ayo had shown her the wedding presents Ajayi intended to give her. The neighbour had handled the flimsy nylon articles with a mixture of envy and rage.

'Do you mean you are going to wear these?' she had asked.

'Yes.' Ayo had replied simply. 'But, my sister,' she had protested, 'you will catch cold with these. Suppose you had an accident
and all those doctors lifted your clothes in the hospital. They
will see everything through these.' 'I never have accident,'
Ayo answered, and added, 'Ajayi says all the 'Ollywood cinema
women wear these. It says so there. Look—' "Trademark
Hollywood." ' 'These are disgraceful; they hide nothing, it is
extremely fast of you to wear them,' the jealous girl said,
pushing them back furiously over the fence to Ayo.

'Why should I want to hide anything from my husband when
we are married?' Ayo said triumphantly, moving back to her
own kitchen and feeling safe in the future from the patroniz-
ing way the wedding ring had always been lent her.

The arrangements had to be made swiftly, since time and the
corset ribs were both against them; Ajayi's domestic routine
was also sorely tried, especially his morning cup of tea which
he badly missed. He borrowed heavily from a moneylender to
pay the dowry and for the music, dancing, and feasting, and for
dresses of the same pattern which Ayo and her female relations would wear after the ceremony on the wedding day.

The engagement took place quietly, Ajayi's uncle and other
relations taking a Bible and a ring to Ayo's father and asking
for her hand in marriage, the day before the wedding. They
took with them two small girls carrying on their heads large
hollow gourds. These contained articles like pins, farthings,
fruit, kola nuts, and cloth. The articles were symbolic gifts to
the bride from the bridegroom; so that she might be precluded
in future marital disputes from saying, 'Not a pin or a farthing
has the blackguard given me since we got married.'

On arrival at Ayo's father's house, the small procession
passed it first as if uncertain, then returned to it. This gave
warning to the occupants. Ajayi's uncle then knocked several
times. Voices from within shouted back and ordered him to
name himself, his ancestry, and his mission. He did this. Argument and some abuse followed on either side. After his
family credentials had been seriously examined, questioned,
doubted, and disparaged, Ajayi's uncle started wheedling and
cajoling. This went on for about half an hour to the enjoyment
and mock trepidation of Ajayi's relations. He himself had remained at home, waiting. Finally, Ayo's father opened the
door. Honour was satisfied and it was now supposed to be

clearly evident to Ajayi's relations, in case it had not been before, that they were entering a family and household which was distinguished, difficult, and jealous of their distinction.

'What is your mission here?' Ayo's father then asked sternly. Ajayi's uncle answered humbly:

'We have come to pluck a red, red rose
That in your beautiful garden grows.
Which never has been plucked before,
So lovelier than any other.'

'Will you be able to nurture our lovely rose well?' another of Ayo's male relations asked.

Ajayi's family party replied:

'So well shall we nurture your rose
'Twill bring forth many others.'

They were finally admitted; drinks were served and prayers offered. The gifts were accepted and others given in exchange. Conversation went on for about thirty minutes on every conceivable subject but the one at hand. All through this, Ayo and her sisters and some young female relations were kept hidden in an adjoining bedroom. Finally with some delicacy, Ajayi's uncle broached the subject after Ayo's father had given him an opening by asking what, apart from the honour of being entertained by himself and his family, did Ajayi's relations seek. They had heard, the latter replied, that in this very household there was a maiden chaste, beautiful, and obedient, known to all by the name of Ayo. This maiden they sought as wife for their kinsman Ajayi. Ayo's father opened the bedroom and brought forth Ayo's sister. Was this the one? he asked, testing them. They examined her. No it was not this one they replied, this one was too short to be Ayo. Then a cousin was brought out. Was this she? No, this one is too fat, the applicants said. About ten women in all were brought out. But none was the correct one. Each was too short or too fat or too fair, as the case was, to suit the description of the maiden they sought. At this point, Ajayi's uncle slapped his thigh, as if to show that his doubts were confirmed; turning to his party, he stated that it was a good thing they had insisted on seeing for themselves the bride demanded, or else the wrong woman would have been foisted on them. They agreed, nodding. All right, all right, Ayo's father had replied, there was no cause for impatience. He wanted to be sure they knew whom they wanted. Standing on guard at the bedroom door, he turned his back to the assembly, and with tears in his eyes beckoned to Ayo sitting on the bed inside. He kissed her lightly on the forehead to forgive the past years. Then he led her forth and turned fiercely to the audience. Was this then the girl they wanted, he asked them sternly?

'This is the very one,' Ajayi's uncle replied with joy. 'Hip, hip, hip, hooray,' everybody shouted, encircling Ayo and waving white handkerchiefs over her head. The musicians smote their guitars instantly; someone beat an empty wine bottle rhythmically with a corkscrew; after a few preliminary trills the flutes rose high in melody; all danced round Ayo. And as she stood in the centre, a woman in her mid-thirties, her hair slightly streaked gray, undergoing a ceremony of honour she had often witnessed and long put outside her fate, remembering the classic description of chastity, obedience, and beauty, she wept with joy and the unborn child stirred within her for the first time.

The next morning she was bathed by an old and respected female member of her family and her mother helped her to dress. Her father gave her away at the marriage service at church. It was a quiet wedding with only sixty guests or so. Ajayi looked stiff in dinner jacket with buttonhole, an ensemble which he wore only on special occasions. Afterwards they went to Ayo's family home for the wedding luncheon. At the door they were met by another of Ayo's numerous elderly aunts, who held a glass of water to their lips for them to sip in turn, Ajayi being first. The guests were all gathered outside behind the couple. The aunt made a conveniently long speech until all the guests had foregathered. She warned Ayo not to be too friendly with other women as they would inevitably steal her husband; that they should live peaceable and not let the sun go down on a quarrel between them. Turning to Ajayi, she told him with a twinkle in her eye that a wife could be quite as exciting as a mistress, and also not to use physical violence against their daughter, his wife.

After this they entered and the Western part of the ceremony took place. The wedding cake (which Ayo had made) was cut and speeches made. Then Ajayi departed to his own family home where other celebrations went on. Later he changed into a lounge suit and called for Ayo. There was weeping in Ayo's household as if she were setting off on a long journey. Her mother in saying goodbye remarked between tears that although she would not have the honour next morning of showing the world evidence of Ayo's virginity, yet in the true feminine powers of procreation none except the blind and the deaf could say Ayo had lacked zeal.

They called on various relations on both sides of the family and at last they were home. Ayo seemed different in Ajayi's eyes. He had never really looked at her carefully before. Now he observed her head held erectly and gracefully through years of balancing loads on it in childhood; her statuesque neck with its three natural horizontal ridges—to him, signs of beauty; her handsome shoulders. He clasped her with a new tenderness.

The next morning, as his alarm clock went off, he stirred and reached for his morning cup of tea. It was not there. He sprang up and looked. Nothing. He listened for Ayo's footsteps outside in the kitchen. Nothing. He turned to look beside him. Ayo was there and her bare ebony back was heaving gently. She must be ill, he thought; all that excitement yesterday.

'Ayo, Ayo,' he cried, 'are you ill?' She turned round slowly still lying down and faced him. She tweaked her toes luxuriously under the cotton coverlet and patted her breast slowly. There was a terrible calm about her. 'No, Ajayi,' she replied, 'are you?' she asked him. 'Are your legs paralyzed?' she continued. 'No,' he said. He was puzzled and alarmed, thinking that her mind had become unhinged under the strain.

'Ajayi, my husband,' she said, 'for twelve years I have got up every morning at five to make tea for you and breakfast. Now I am a truly married woman you must treat me with a little more respect. You are now a husband and not a lover. Get up and make yourself a cup of tea.'

KHUSHWANT SINGH

*Khushwant Singh, born in India in 1917, is a Sikh, a member of
a religion founded about 1500 which draws from both Hinduism
and Islam, but is distinct from both. Thus, in this story as well
as in his novel,* Train to Pakistan, *Singh is able to write with a
certain degree of detachment and sardonic humor. He is presently editor of* The Illustrated Weekly of India.

   *Factional rivalries, whether religious or political in origin
are the subject matter of many of the stories in this volume. In*
Riot *the conflict is the long-standing contest between India's
Muslims and Hindus, satirically presented in the context of a
dog-fight.*

Riot

The town lay etherized under the fresh spring twilight. The
shops were closed and house doors barred from the inside.
Streetlamps dimly lit the deserted roads. Only a few policemen
walked about with steel helmets on their heads and rifles
slung behind their backs. The sound of their hobnailed boots
was all that broke the stillness of the town.

   The twilight sank into darkness. A crescent moon lit the
quiet streets. A soft breeze blew bits of newspaper from the
pavements onto the road and back again. It was cooled and
smelled of the freshness of spring. Some dogs emerged from a
dark lane and gathered round a lamppost. A couple of policemen strolled past them smiling. One of them mumbled something vulgar. The other pretended to pick up a stone and hurl it
at the dogs. The dogs ran down the street in the opposite
direction and resumed their courtship at a safer distance.

   Rani was a pariah bitch whose litter populated the lanes and
by-lanes of the town. She was a thin, scraggy specimen, typical
of the pariahs of the town. Her white coat was mangy, showing
patches of raw flesh. Her dried-up udders hung loosely from
her ribs. Her tail was always tucked between her hind legs and
she slunk about in fear and abject servility.

   Rani would have died of starvation with her first litter of

eight had it not been for the generosity of the Hindu shop-keeper, Ram Jawaya, in the corner of whose courtyard she had unloaded her womb. The shopkeeper's family fed her and played with her pups till they were old enough to run about the streets and steal food for themselves. The shopkeeper's generosity had put Rani in the habit of sponging. Every year when spring came, she would find excuse to loiter around the stall of Ramzan, the Moslem greengrocer. Beneath the wooden platform on which groceries were displayed lived the big, burly Moti. Early autumn, Rani presented the shopkeeper's household with half a dozen or more of Moti's offspring.

Moti was a cross between a Newfoundland and a spaniel. His shaggy coat and sullen look were Ramzan's pride. Ramzan had lopped off Moti's tail and ears. He fed him till Moti grew big and strong and became the master of the town's canine population. Rani had many rivals. But year after year, with the advent of spring, Rani's fancy lightly turned to thoughts of Moti and she sauntered across to Ramzan's stall.

This time spring had come but the town was paralyzed with fear of communal riots and curfews. In the daytime people hung about the street corners in groups of tens and twenties, talking in whispers. No shops opened and long before curfew hour the streets were deserted, with only pariah dogs and policemen about.

Tonight even Moti was missing. In fact, ever since the curfew Ramzan had kept him indoors tied to a cot. He was far more useful guarding Ramzan's house than loitering about the streets. Rani came to Ramzan's stall and sniffed around. Moti could not have been there for some days. She was disappointed. But spring came only once a year—and hardly ever did it come at a time when one could have the city to oneself with no curious children looking on—and no scandalized parents hurling stones at her. So Rani gave up Moti and ambled down the road toward Ram Jawaya's house. A train of suitors followed her.

Rani faced her many suitors in front of Ram Jawaya's doorstep. They snarled and snapped and fought with each other. Rani stood impassively, waiting for the decision. In a few minutes a lanky black dog, one of Rani's own progeny, won the honors. The others slunk away.

In Ramzan's house, Moti sat pensively eyeing his master

from underneath his charpoy. For some days the spring air had made him restive. He heard the snarling in the street and smelled Rani in the air. But Ramzan would not let him go. He tugged at the rope—then gave it up and began to whine. Ramzan's heavy hand struck him. A little later he began to whine again. Ramzan had had several sleepless nights watching and was heavy with sleep. He began to snore. Moti whined louder and then sent up a pitiful howl to his unfaithful mistress. He tugged and strained at the leash and began to bark. Ramzan got up angrily toward the door dragging the lightened string cot behind him. He nosed open the door and rushed out. The charpoy stuck in the doorway and the rope tightened around his neck. He made a savage wrench, the rope gave way, and he leapt across the road. Ramzan ran back to his room, slipped a knife under his shirt, and went after Moti.

Outside Ram Jawaya's house, the illicit liaison of Rani and the black pariah was consummated. Suddenly the burly form of Moti came into view. With an angry growl Moti leapt at Rani's lover. Other dogs joined the melee, tearing and snapping wildly.

Ram Jawaya had also spent several sleepless nights keeping watch and yelling back war cries to the Moslems. At last fatigue and sleep overcame his newly acquired martial spirit. He slept soundly with a heap of stones under his charpoy and an imposing array of soda-water bottles filled with acid close at hand. The noise outside woke him. The shopkeeper picked up a big stone and opened the door. With a loud oath he sent the missile flying at the dogs. Suddenly, a human being emerged from the corner and the stone caught him squarely in the solar plexis.

The stone did not cause much damage to Ramzan, but the suddenness of the assault took him aback. He yelled "Murder!" and produced his knife from under his shirt. The shopkeeper and the grocer eyed each other for a brief moment and then ran back to their houses shouting. The petrified town came to life. There was more shouting. The drum at the Sikh temple beat a loud tattoo—the air was rent with war cries.

Men emerged from their houses making hasty inquiries. A Moslem or a Hindu, it was said, has been attacked. Someone had been kidnapped and was being butchered. A party of goondas were going to attack, but the dogs had started barking. They had actually assaulted a woman and killed her children. There must be resistance. There was. Groups of fives joined others of tens. Tens joined twenties till a few hundred, armed with knives, spears, hatchets, and kerosene-oil cans proceeded to Ram Jawaya's house. They were met with a fusillade of stones, soda-water bottles, and acid. They hit back blindly. Tins of kerosene oil were emptied indiscriminately and lighted. Flames shot up in the sky enveloping Ram Jawaya's home and entire neighborhood, Hindu, Moslem, and Sikh alike.

The police rushed to the scene and opened fire. Fire engines clanged their way in and sent jets of water flying into the sky. But fires had been started in other parts of the town and there were not enough fire engines to go round.

All night and all the next day the fire burnt—and houses fell and people were killed. Ram Jawaya's home was burnt and he barely escaped with his life. For several days smoke rose from the ruins. What had once been a busy town was a heap of charred masonry.

Some months later when peace was restored, Ram Jawaya came to inspect the site of his old home. It was all in shambles with the bricks lying in a mountainous pile. In the corner of what had once been his courtyard there was a little clearing. There lay Rani with her litter nuzzling into her dried udders. Beside her stood Moti guarding his bastard brood.

"ZAWGYI" (U THEIN HAN)

"Zawgyi" is the pen name of U Thein Han, a well-known Burmese writer who draws both his themes and his style from everyday life. Burma, in southeast Asia, is bounded on the west by India and Pakistan, on the north by China, and on the east by Thailand and Laos. It has been called the "Happy Land" because it has been able to produce more rice than needed to feed its people. Buddhism is the state religion and influences much of Burmese life—education, architecture, the arts, social customs. Women in Burma tend to have more freedom outside the home

*than in most of Asia, but within the family they are expected to
take second place to the men.*

In His Spouse *"Zawgyi" gives us a delightfully intimate view
of Burmese family life. Though Ko Hsin in the story is definitely not a typical husband and father, through this account of
his relations with his family we get a sense of the rhythms of
their daily life. The trip to market each morning, the watering of
the greens to make them weigh more, the quickness of the children to take advantage of their father's inattention—all of these
are at once representatively Burmese and very universal.*

*U Thein Han, formerly a librarian, is now an Education
Officer in Rangoon.*

His Spouse

1

Ma Paw, the wife of Ko Hsin, worked in the market. Each
morning she walked a mile to town with greens on a tray. If
business was brisk, she returned early; otherwise, only when
the sun had declined. Whenever she reached the bamboo
bridge that crossed the stream beside the village on her return, thoughts of her husband and children arose in her mind.

She was tall with reddish hair and slightly protruding teeth,
but it could not be said that she was ugly. Her husband, Ko
Hsin, was a man of leisure who sat and ate at home. It was not
wholly true that he did nothing. He had to cook the rice and
look after the children.

Ko Hsin had been a novice in the Buddhist Monastic Order
for nine years and had some learning. He was good-natured,
fond of laughter, and was the prime mover at charities and
weddings. He was not as tall as his wife, was small-chested,
had a fine crop of hair and a thin strip of moustache. He was
tattooed to his knees.

When they were married and after they had a son, Ma Paw
kept shop and ministered to Ko Hsin's needs. When the second
son was born, she could only keep shop. After the birth of their
daughter, Ma Paw often became very tired. Once when she was
hard hit by a business loss, her state was pitiable. But she did
not complain.

She was heartened when one of her friends told her: "You should listen to your husband read the eulogy and blessing at a wedding in the village. Magnificent! He is a learned man." She was heartened when her fourteen-year-old son sometimes met her at the bamboo bridge and relieved her of her tray and basket. At these times her thoughts turned in gratitude to her husband.

Once when she and her children were talking on the raised platform of their house, a tipsy drinker of today appeared on the road and made insulting eyes at them. The children ran into the house in fear. Ko Hsin hurriedly appeared from within the house and stood with arms akimbo on the platform. The drunkard's eyes turned and whirled, leading away his tottering feet. Ma Paw was thankful. Were it not for my man, we would have suffered great indignities, she thought.

Ma Paw was now in her thirty-seventh year. Ko Hsin was six years older.

Ko Hsin, for all his years, had never really worked. When people said of him that he supported himself by clutching the hem of a skirt, he would reply jokingly, "I am able to live in leisure as I live now because of my past meritorious deeds. Don't be jealous." Though he said this, in his heart he was hurt. But the pain was almost forgotten in pride of his brilliant repartee. Because of his replies the others frowned on him or thrust their chins at him in derision. In time these acts of his neighbors spurred him to action. He borrowed money from a cousin and entered the bamboo business. He lost heavily. The next rains, he went down to the fields to plow. He returned home with blood dripping from his foot where he had run in the plowshare. It took fifteen days for the wound to heal.

2

He was forty-three on the day he got well. The wound of the flesh had healed but the wound of the heart had swollen.

Ma Paw had set off to market as usual, the elder son had gone on to the monastery school. The other two children were playing beneath the tamarind tree in front of the house. As Ko Hsin sat drinking a pot of green tea, he saw the carpenter father of six set out with his box of tools from a neighboring house. The man from next door crossed the stream to cut dani leaves on the other bank. Even the old man from the opposite house whittled a piece of wood to make a puddling stick.

At first Ko Hsin was filled with a sense of ease and pleasure as he drank cup after cup of tea and watched his children at play. But when his neighbors began to stir to work, his pleasure faded, and he remembered that he had yet to get the pot of rice on the fire. He suddenly recalled the taunts of his neighbors and the procession of his life passed before his eyes. His foppishness since leaving the monastery, his marriage to Ma Paw, his business failure, his hurt foot. He became sad and ashamed. He desired to break out of this way of life. He thought it would be good to become a monk. Then he would not have to boil rice. He would be able to turn his eyes toward the Supreme Good. His wife and children would gain merit by him. He felt certain that the time for his release from the sorrows of rebirth was at hand. He would endeavor to become a small god. Thus did he think. But he remembered again that he must prepare the rice or he would have nothing to eat and the children would cry. He arose and entered the kitchen.

Meanwhile, in the market, Ma Paw was adding water to her greens to make them heavier, whereby she might earn more. With what more she earned, she intended to buy some nice cheroots for her husband.

Ko Hsin was skilled at preparing boiled rice. He called the children and gave them the rice with the remains of yesterday's curry. When the children had gone back to their play, he sat with his feet dangling from the raised platform and returned to his thoughts. When he became a monk, he would come with his begging bowl to Ma Paw's house every morning and get a chance to meet Ma Paw and the children. But Ma Paw was illiterate and ignorant of the religious Law. When she died, she would pass to the lower worlds. For this he pitied her. He wanted to open her eyes to the Law.

The quarrel of his children returned him to realities. The sister had scratched the brother's face; in retaliation he had pulled her hair. Now both were crying.

Ko Hsin called the children into the house and made them sit in different corners. He then tried to return to his reverie but could not pick up the chain of thought. He glanced at his children and saw their little heads nodding into sleep. He felt a yawn rise in him.

"Don't move," he commanded the children, and laid himself down for a nap.

The moment his eyes were closed the children opened theirs. They threw speaking glances at each other and at their father. They agreed to run down to play as soon as he fell asleep.

Ko Hsin awoke to Ma Paw's voice calling to her son in the tamarind tree.

"Get down from there at once; you'll fall. Where is your sister?"

"At the streamside," the boy replied.

"Ko Hsin," Ma Paw cried, "do you leave your children unattended like that? A good father you are!"

The daughter appeared with muddy hands and the boy climbed down from the tree.

Ko Hsin looked daggers at his children. They hid behind the mother.

"Here're cheroots for you," said Ma Paw, and thrusting them on him, she headed the children into the kitchen. Ko Hsin's eyes followed them. Ma Paw washed her daughter's hands and gave the children pea cakes to eat. Then, sitting down, Ma Paw spread her legs on the floor, untied her hair, bent forward, and let the hair hang above her legs.

"Massage my back with your elbows," she told her son. He did so while keeping his cake between his teeth. The shaking of the back under the pressure of the elbows and the swing of the spreading hair as her head swayed made Ma Paw appear as though possessed by the devil.

Ko Hsin looked and heaved a deep sigh of disgust. I must don the yellow robes, he thought.

However, he did not dare to tell his wife till the year had turned.

3

It was now three months, though Ko Hsin had said that he would wear the yellow robes for only a month. Ma Paw's aunt, who had come over to help look after the children, began to yearn for her own in her village.

"When will the Celibate return to lay life?" she had asked the monk one day.

The monk had not replied. Instead, he had quoted sacred verses extolling the life of a monk. The sacred verses did not enter the aunt's ears. Only anger rose in her because she felt that she was being kept here unfairly. When the monk had departed, she called Ma Paw to her.

"Ma Paw, I want to go back. Tell your monk to cast off the robes. I cannot stay on longer as a servant in your house," she threatened.

Ma Paw, too, wanted her husband to return home. She had alluded to the matter once or twice, only to have been turned back with sermons. Now the time was near when the monks would go into retreat for three months. Not knowing what to do, she conferred with a friend. After some talk they burst into laughter.

4

The morning was gold with sunlight. Doves cooed in the tamarind tree. Ma Paw did not go to market. Instead, she fried and cooked at home. Then she bathed and made herself fragrant with powder down to her toes. She smeared it lightly on her face. She gathered her straying strands and tied them in a knot to suit her features. The meager hair on her forehead was collected into a "dove's wing." She penciled her eyebrows in a wide sweep and made her lips red by chewing betel. She put on a jacket of fine white cloth and a new skirt of printed red flowers. The children, too, were dressed in clean clothes and the household things were packed. A bullock cart waited in readiness in the yard.

At ten o'clock the monk appeared, accompanied by his eldest son, who was in his monastery school. As he approached, he thought with apprehension, they will ask me again to forsake the life of a monk. He drew near the house and saw the cart. He entered the house and saw the packed household things. He sat on the mat the aunt had rolled out for him in the place of reverence in the house and searched in vain for Ma Paw.

After some time Ma Paw appeared with a tray of food. With sad eyes and movements, she offered the food. The monk took a quick glance at her. He noticed how dressed up she was. He took another glance. He was puzzled by her behavior, but his thoughts were occupied in steeling himself to refuse the request to return to lay life which he knew Ma Paw would surely make.

After the meal Ma Paw took away the tray and sat reverently at a distance. As the monk made to preach the sermon, Ma Paw spoke to her aunt.

"Aunt, hasn't the cartman arrived yet?"

The monk, unable to begin his sermon, looked toward the waiting cart.

"Ma Paw, what's going on here?" he asked.

"I will reveal all to the Celibate." Ma Paw addressed the monk without raising her head. "Aunt wants to return to her village. If she returns, I will be unable to keep shop and look after the children at the same time. That is why I beg permission of the Celibate to allow me and the two children to go live with Aunt in her village. The eldest son will be left in the Celibate's care."

She turned to her eldest son. "Son, stay behind with the Celibate," she said, and wiped away a tear from her downcast face.

The monk remained silently thoughtful.

"The Celibate may continue to be a monk throughout his life if that is his wish. His humble lay woman will try to make a living somehow. The Celibate's world and hers are different worlds; there is a vast gap between them. Henceforth, there can only be the relationship of monk and lay devotee between them. Since she still has two children, if she can find someone to depend upon somewhere else, she desires to accept him. That is why she wishes to make things clear now so that complications may not arise later."

The monk uttered a cry of amazement. Ma Paw raised her eyes slightly. The monk's hands fluttered about his robes. He looked at Ma Paw.

Ma Paw continued: "This is said for the benefit of both. The Celibate will be able to follow the Law in freedom, and his humble devotee will be able, should she find someone—"

"There are too many toddy drunkards in your aunt's village," the monk said. "I will return to the lay life."

Ma Paw became Ko Hsin's wife again.

—Translated by U Win Pe

S.Y. AGNON

Shmuel Yosef Agnon (1888–1970), whose works became classics of Hebrew literature in his lifetime, was born in Galicia, Poland. In 1925 he moved permanently to Israel. The city of Jerusalem figures largely in his writings, particularly in the religious and mystical associations of the city. Tehilah, which in addition to being a proper name is the Hebrew word meaning "praise" or "psalm," represents a time now vanished when, at least in Agnon's imagination, life in the old city of Jerusalem could be lived in an aura of holiness and reverence.

Though he writes of a former era—the old walled city, for example, no longer exists, having been destroyed in the Arab-Israeli war of 1948—Agnon gives us an important insight into the emotional anguish of the Middle East. Tehilah speaks with great love of Jerusalem: ". . . When I say 'Jerusalem,' I add nothing more, since the holiness is contained in the name; yes, in the very name itself." Yet she sees that the houses of the community have fallen into disrepair, the faithful leave them, or refuse to maintain them, "and the sons of Ishmael [Arabs] enter and take possession."

Tehilah's world, though it had a full share of personal grief, was a world in which both the justice and the mercy of God were sure, and surely to be known. Leaving it, at a great age, it is as though, for the narrator of the story, she has taken its certainties with her. The story is a eulogy, both for the saintly Tehilah, and for the nation of Israel.

Tehilah

Now there used to be in Jerusalem a certain old woman, as comely an old woman as you have seen in your days. Righteous she was, and wise she was, and gracious and humble: for kindness and pity were the light of her eyes, and every wrinkle in her face told of blessing and peace. I know that women should not be likened to angels: yet her would I liken to an angel of

God. She had in her, besides, the vigor of youth; so that she wore old age like a mantle, while in herself there was seen no trace of her years.

Until I had left Jerusalem she was quite unknown to me; only upon my return did I come to know her. If you ask why I never heard of her before, I shall answer: Why have you not heard of her until now? It is appointed for every man to meet whom he shall meet, and the time for this, and the fitting occasion. It happened that I had gone to visit one of Jerusalem's noted men of learning, who lived near the Wailing Wall. Having failed to find his house, I came upon a woman who was going by with a pail of water, and I asked her the way.

She said, "Come with me, I will show you."

I replied, "Do not trouble yourself. Tell me the way, and I shall go on alone."

She answered, smiling, "What is it to you if an old woman should earn herself a *mitzvah?*"*

"If it be a *mitzvah* ," said I, "then do so; but give me this pail that you carry."

She smiled again and said, "If I do as you ask, it will make the *mitzvah* but a small one."

"It is only the trouble I wish to be small, and not the merit of your deed," I said.

She answered, "This is no trouble at all, but a privilege; since the Holy One has furnished his creatures with hands that they may supply all their needs."

We made our way amongst the stones and through the alleys, avoiding the camels and the asses, the drawers of water and the idlers and the gossip-mongers, until she halted and said, "Here is the house of him you seek."

I found the man of learning at home at his desk. Whether he recognized me at all is doubtful; for he had just made an important discovery, which he at once began to relate. As I took my leave I thought to ask him who that woman might be, whose face shone with such peace and whose voice was so

---

Mitzvah: Literally, a commandment; a moral duty that confers spiritual reward.

gentle and calm. But there is no interrupting a scholar when he speaks of his latest discovery.

Some days later I went again to the Old City, this time to visit the aged widow of a rabbi; for I had promised her grandson before my return that I would attend to her welfare.

That day marked the beginning of the rainy season. Already the rain was falling, and the sun was obscured by clouds. In other lands this would have seemed like a normal day of spring; but here in Jerusalem, which is pampered with constant sunshine through seven or eight months of the year, we think it is winter should the sun once fail to shine with all its strength, and we hide ourselves in houses and courtyards, or in any place that affords a sheltering roof.

I walked alone and free, smelling the good smell of the rain as it fell exultantly, wrapping itself in mist, and heightening the tints of the stones, and beating at the walls of houses, and dancing on roofs, and making great pools beneath that were sometimes turbid and sometimes gleamed in the sunbeams that intermittently broke through the clouds to view the work of the waters—for in Jerusalem even on a rainy day the sun yet seeks to perform its task.

Turning in between the shops with their arched doorways at the street of the smiths, I went on past the shoemakers, and the blanket-weavers, and the little stalls that sell hot broths, till I came to the Street of the Jews. Huddled in their tattered rags sat the beggars, not caring even to reach a hand from their cloaks, and glowering sullenly at each man who passes without giving them money. I had with me a purse of small coins, and went from beggar to beggar distributing them. Finally I asked for the house of the *rabbanit*,* and they told me the way.

I entered a courtyard, one of those which to a casual passerby seems entirely deserted, and after mounting six or seven broken flights of stairs, came to a warped door. Outside I stumbled against a cat, and within a heap of rubbish stood in my way. Because of the mist I could not see anyone, but I heard a faint, apprehensive voice calling, "Who is there?" Looking

---

*Rabbanit: A form of address meaning "rabbi's wife."

up, I now made out a kind of iron bed submerged in a wave of pillows and bolsters, and in the depths of the wave an alarmed and agitated old woman.

I introduced myself, saying that I was recently come from abroad with greetings from her grandson. She put out a hand from under the bedding to draw the coverlet up to her chin, saying, "Tell me now, does he own many houses, and does he keep a maidservant, and has he fine carpets in every room?" Then she sighed, "This cold will be the death of me."

Seeing that she was so irked with the cold, it occurred to me that a kerosene stove might give her some ease; so I thought of a little stratagem.

"Your grandson," I said, "has entrusted me with a small sum of money to buy you a stove: a portable stove that one fills with kerosene, with a wick that burns and gives off much heat." I took out my wallet and said, "See, here is the money."

In a vexed tone she answered, "And shall I go now to buy a stove, with these feet that are on me? Feet did I say? Blocks of ice I mean. This cold will drive me out of my wits if it won't drive me first to my grave, to the Mount of Olives.* And look, you, abroad they say that the Land of Israel is a hot land. Hot it is, yes, for the souls in Gehenna."

"Tomorrow," I said, "the sun will shine out and make the cold pass away."

" 'Ere comfort comes, the soul succumbs.' "

"In an hour or two," I said, "I shall have sent you the stove."

She crouched down among her coverlets and bolsters, as if to show that she did not trust me as her benefactor.

I left her and walked out to the Jaffa Road. There I went to a shop that sold household goods, bought a portable stove of the best make in stock, and sent it on to the old *rabbanit*. An hour later I returned to her, thinking that, if she was unfamiliar with stoves of this kind, it would be as well to show her the method of lighting it. On the way, I said to myself: Not a word of thanks, to be sure, will I get for my pains. How different is one old woman from another! For she who showed me the way to the scholar's house is evidently kind to all comers; and this

---

*Before 1948, the Mount of Olives was the traditional burying ground for Jerusalem's Jews.

other woman will not even show kindness to those who are prompt to seek her comfort.

But here I must insert a brief apology. My aim is not to praise one woman to the detriment of others; nor, indeed, do I aspire to tell the story of Jerusalem and all its inhabitants. The range of man's vision is narrow: shall it comprehend the City of the Holy One, blessed be He? If I speak of the *rabbanit*, it is for this reason only, that at the entrance to her house it was again appointed for me to encounter the other old woman.

I bowed and made way for her; but she stood still and greeted me as warmly as one might greet one's nearest kinsman. Momentarily I was puzzled as to who she might be. Could this be one of the old women I had known in Jerusalem before leaving the country. Yet most of these, if not all, had perished of hunger in the time of the war. Even if one or two survived, I myself was much changed; for I was only a lad when I left Jerusalem, and the years spent abroad had left their mark.

She saw that I was surprised, and smiled, saying, "It seems you do not recognize me. Are you not the man who wished to carry my pail on the way to your friend's house?"

"And you are the woman," said I, "who showed me the way. Yet now I stand here bewildered, and seem not to know you."

Again she smiled. "Are you obliged, then, to remember every old woman who lives in the Old City?"

"Yet," I said, "you recognized me."

She answered, "Because the eyes of Jerusalem look out upon all Israel, each man who comes to us is engraved on our heart; thus we never forget him."

"It is a cold day," I said, "a day of wind and rain, and here I stand, keeping you out of doors."

She answered, with love in her voice, "I have seen worse cold than any we have in Jerusalem. As for wind and rain, are we not thankful? For daily we bless God, saying, 'Who causes the wind to blow and the rain to fall.' You have done a great *mitzvah*: you have put new life into old bones. The stove which you sent to the *rabbanit* is warming her, body and soul."

I hung my head, as a man does who is abashed at hearing his own praise. Perceiving this, she said:

"The doing of a *mitzvah* need not make a man bashful. Our fathers, it is true, performed so many that it was needless to publish their deeds. But we, who do less, perform a *mitzvah* even by letting the *mitzvah* be known: then others will hear, and learn from our deeds what they too must do. Now, my son, go to the *rabbanit*, and see how much warmth your *mitzvah* has brought."

I went inside and found the stove lit, and the *rabbanit* seated beside it. Light flickered from the perforated holes, and the room was full of warmth. A lean cat lay in her lap, and she was gazing at the stove and talking to the cat, saying to it, "It seems that you like this heat more than I do."

I said, "I see that the stove burns well and gives off a fine heat. Are you satisfied?"

"And if I am satisfied," said the *rabbanit*, "will that make it smell the less or warm me the more? A stove there was in my old home, that would burn from the last day of the Feast of Tabernacles to the first night of the Passover, and give off heat like the sun in the dog-days of the month of Tammuz; a lasting joy it was, not like these bits of stove which burn for a short while. But nowadays one cannot expect good workmanship. Enough it is if folk make a show of working. Yes, that is what I said to the people of our town when my dear husband, the Rabbi, passed away: may he speak for me in the world to come! When they got themselves a new rabbi, I said to them, What can you expect? Do you expect that he will be like your old rabbi? Enough it is if he starts no troubles. And so I said to the neighbors just now, when they came to see the stove that my grandson sent me through you, I said to them, 'This stove is like the times, and these times are like the stove.' What did he write to you, this grandson? Didn't write at all? Nor does he write to me. No doubt he thinks that by sending me this bit of a stove he has done his duty."

After leaving the *rabbanit*, I said to myself: I too think that by sending her this bit of a stove I have done my duty: surely there is no need to go again. Yet in the end I returned, and all because of that same gracious old woman; for this was not the last occasion that was appointed for me to see her.

Again I must say that I have no intention of recounting all that happened to me in those days. A man does many things, and if he were to describe them all he would never make an end to his story. Yet all that relates to that old woman deserves to be told.

On the eve of new moon I walked to the Wailing Wall, as we in

Jerusalem are accustomed to do, to pray at the Wailing Wall at the rising of each moon.

Already most of the winter had passed, and spring blossoms had begun to appear. Up above, the heavens were pure, and the earth had put off her grief. The sun smiled in the sky; the Old City shone in its light. And we too rejoiced, despite the troubles that beset us; for these troubles were many and evil, and before we had reckoned with one, yet another came in its wake.

From Jaffa Gate as far as the Wailing Wall, men and women from all the communities of Jerusalem moved in a steady stream, together with those newcomers whom the Place* had restored to their space, albeit their space had not yet been found. But in the open space before the Wall, at the booth of the Mandatory Police, sat the police of the Mandate, whose function it was to see that none guarded the worshippers save only they. Our adversaries, wishing to provoke us, perceived this and set about their provocations. Those who had come to pray were herded together and driven to seek shelter close up against the stones of the Wall, some weeping and some as if dazed. And still we say, How long, O Lord? How long? For we have trodden the lowest stair of degradation, yet You tarry to redeem us.

I found a place for myself at the Wall, standing at times amongst the worshippers, at times amongst the bewildered bystanders. I was amazed at the peoples of the world: as if it were not enough that they oppressed us in all lands, yet they must also oppress us in our home.

As I stood there I was driven from my place by one of the police who carried a baton. This man was in a great rage, on account of some ailing old woman who had brought a stool with her to the Wall. The policeman sprang forward and kicked the stool, throwing the woman to the ground and confiscating the stool; for she had infringed the law enacted by the legislators of the Mandate, which forbade worshippers to bring seats to the Wall. And those who had come to pray saw this, yet held their peace; for how can right dispute against might? Then came forward the same old woman whom I knew, and looked

*The Place: the Cabalistic name for God.

the policeman straight in the eyes. And the policeman averted her gaze, and returned the stool to its owner.

I went up to her and said, "Your eyes have more effect than all the pledges of England. For England, which gave us the Balfour Declaration, sends her officers to annul it; while you only looked upon that wicked one, and frustrated his evil intent."

She replied, "Do not speak of him so, for he is a good gentile, who saw that I was grieved and gave back her stool to that poor woman. . . . But have you said your afternoon prayer? I ask because, if you are free, I can put in your way the *mitzvah* of visiting the sick. The *rabbanit* is now really and truly ill. If you wish, come with me and I shall take you by a short route." I joined her and we went together.

From alley to alley, from courtyard to courtyard, we made our way down, and at each step she took she would pause to give a piece of candy to a child, or a coin to a beggar, or to ask the health of a man's wife or, if it were a woman, the health of her husband. I said, "Since you are concerned with everyone's welfare, let me ask after yours."

She answered, "Blessed be the Name, for I lack nothing at his hand. The Holy One has given to each of his creatures according to its need; and I too am one of these. But today I have special cause for thanking him, for he has doubled my portion."

"How is this?" I asked.

She replied, "Each day I read the psalms appointed for the day, but today I read the psalms for two days together." Even as she spoke, her face clouded over with grief.

"Your joy has passed away," I said.

She was silent for a moment. Then she said, "Yes, my son, I was joyful, and now it is not so." Yet even as she spoke, the light shone out again from her face. She raised her eyes and said, "Blessed be He, who has turned away my sorrow."

"Why," I asked, "were you joyful, yet afterwards sad, and now, joyful again?"

She said, very gently, "Since your words are not chosen with care, I must tell you, this was not the way to ask. Rather should you have said, 'How have you deserved it, that God should turn away your sorrow?' For in his blessed eyes, all is one, whether sorrow or joy."

"Perhaps in the future," said I, "my words will be chosen with care, since you teach me how one must speak. 'Happy is the man who does not forget Thee.' It is a text of much meaning."

She said, "You are a good man, and it is a good text you have told me; so I too shall not withhold good words. You asked why I was joyful, and why I was sad, and why I now rejoice. Assuredly you know as I do, that all a man's deeds are appointed, from the hour of his birth to the hour of his death; and accordingly, the number of times he shall say his psalms. But the choice is free how many psalms he will say on any one day. This man may complete the whole book in a day, and that man may say one section a day, or the psalms for each day according to the day. I have made it my custom to say each day the psalms for that day; but this morning I went on and said the psalms for two days together. When I became aware of this I was sad, lest it meant that there were no more need for me in the world, and that I was disposed of and made to finish my portion in haste. For 'it is a good thing to give thanks to the Lord'; and when I am dead I shall not be able to say one psalm, or even one word. Then the Holy One saw my grief, and showed his marvellous kindness by allowing me to know that such is his own very will. If it pleases the Name to take my life, who am I that I should grieve? Thus He at once turned away my sorrow. Blessed be He and blessed be his name."

I glanced at her, wondering to myself by what path one might come to a like submission. I thought of the men of ancient times, and their virtuous ways; I spoke to her of past generations. Then I said, "You have seen with your own eyes more that I can describe in words."

She answered, "When a person's life is prolonged for many days and years, it is granted him to see many things; good things, and yet better things."

"Tell me," I said to her, "of these same good things."

She was silent for a while; then she said, "How shall I begin? Let me start with my childhood. When I was a little girl, I was a great chatterbox. Really, from the time I stood up in the morning till the time I lay down at night, words never ceased pouring from my lips. There was an old man in our neighborhood, who said to those delighting in my chatter: 'A pity it is for this little girl; if she wastes all her words in childhood, what will be left for her old age?' I became terribly frightened, thinking this meant that I might die the very next day. But in time I came to fathom the old man's meaning, which was that a person must not use up in a short while what is allotted him for a whole lifetime. I made a habit of testing each word to see if there was real need for it to be said, and practiced a strict economy of speech. Through this economy, I saved up a great store of words, and my life has been prolonged until they are all used up. Now that only a few words remain, you ask me to speak them. If I do so it will hasten my end."

"Upon such terms," said I, "I would certainly not ask you to speak. But how is it that we keep walking and walking, yet we have still not come to the house of the *rabbanit?*"

She said, "You still have in mind those courtyards we used to take for a short cut. But now that most of the Old City has been settled by the Arabs, we must go by a roundabout way."

We approached one of these courtyards. She said, "Do you see this courtyard? Forty families of Israel once lived here, and here were two synagogues, and here in the daytime and night-time there were study and prayer. But they left this place, and Arabs came and occupied it."

We approached a tumble-down house. She said, "Do you see this house? Here was a great academy where the scholars of the Torah lived and studied. But they left this house, and Arabs came and occupied it."

We came to the asses' stalls. She said, "Do you see these stalls? Here stood a soup-kitchen, and the virtous poor would enter in hungry and go forth satisfied. But they abandoned this place, and Arabs came and occupied it. Houses from which prayer and charity and study of the Torah never ceased, now belong to the Arabs and their asses. . . . My son, we have reached the courtyard of the *rabbanit's* house. Go in, and I shall follow you later. This unhappy woman, because of the seeming good she has known abroad, does not see the true good at home."

"What is the true good?" I asked.

She laughed, saying, "My son, you should not need to ask. Have you not read the verse, 'Happy the man thou choosest to dwell in thy courtyards?' For these same courtyards are the royal courts of the Holy One, the courts of our God, in the midst of Jerusalem. When men say 'Jerusalem,' their way is to add the words, 'Holy City.' But when *I* say 'Jerusalem,' I add nothing more, since the holiness is contained in the name; yes, in the very name itself. . . . Go up, my son, and do not trip on the stairs. Many a time have I said to the keeper of the community funds that these stairs are in need of repair; and what answer did he give me? That this building is old and due to be demolished, therefore it is not worthwhile spending a penny on its upkeep. So the houses of Israel fall into disuse until they are abandoned, and the sons of Ishmael enter and take possession. Houses that were built with the tears of their fathers—and now they abandon them. But again I have become a chatterer, and hasten my end."

I entered, and found the *rabbanit* lying in bed. Her head was bandaged and a poultice had been laid upon her throat. She coughed loudly, so that the medicine bottles placed by her bedside would shake at each cough. I said to her, "Rabbanit, are you ill?" She sighed and her eyes filled with tears. I sought for words of comfort, but the words would not come. All I could say, with my eyes downcast, was "So you are ill and deserted."

She sighed again and replied, "Yes, I am ill as ill can be. In the whole world there is no one so ill as I am. All the same, I am not deserted. Even here in Jerusalem, where nobody knows me, and nobody knows the honors done to me in my own town, even here there is one woman who waits on me, who comes to my room and fetches a drop of soup for my royal feast. What do you hear from my grandson? He is angry with me, to be sure, because I have not written to thank him for the stove. Now I ask you, how shall I go out to buy ink and pen and paper for the writing of letters? It is hard enough even to fetch a spoonful of soup to my lips. . . . I am surprised that Tilli has not come."

"If you are speaking," said I, "of that gracious old woman who brought me here, she told me that she would come very soon."

"I cannot tell whether she is gracious," said the *rabbanit;* "at least she makes herself useful. Look you, how many holy, holy women there are about Jerusalem, who go buzzing like bees with their incantations and supplications, yet not one of them has come to me and said, 'Rabbanit, do you need help?'. . . My head, my head. If the pains in my heart won't take me off soon, the pains in my head will take me off first."

I said to her, "I can see that speech is a burden to you."

She answered, "You say that speech is a burden to me; and I say that my whole existence is a burden to me. Even the cat knows this, and keeps away from his home. Yet people say that cats are home-loving creatures. He finds my neighbor's mice more tasty, to be sure, than all the dainties I feed him. What was I meaning to say? I forget all I mean to say. Now Tilli is different. There she goes, with the bundles of years heaped up on her shoulders, bundle on bundle; yet all her wits serve her, although she must be twice my age. If my father—God bless his pious memory—were alive this day, he would be thought of as a child beside her."

I urged the *rabbanit* to tell me about this Tilli.

"And did you not mention her yourself? No-vadays people don't know Tilli; but there was a time when everyone did, for then she was a great, rich woman with all kinds of business concerns. And when she gave up all these and came to Jerusalem, she brought along with her I can't say how many barrels of gold, or if not barrels, there is no doubt that she brought a chest full of gold. My neighbors remember their mothers telling them how, when Tilli came to Jerusalem, all the best men here came courting, either for themselves or for their sons. But she sent them packing and stayed a widow. At first she was a very rich widow, and then a quite well-to-do widow, until at last she became just an old woman."

"Judging from Tilli's appearance," said I, "one would think that she had never seen hard times in her life."

The *rabbanit* replied with scorn, "You say that she has never seen hard times in her life, and I say that she has never seen good times in her life. There is no enemy of mine whom I would bless with the afflictions that Tilli has borne. You suppose that, because she is not reduced to living off the public funds, she has enjoyed a happy life, but I believe that there is not a beggar knocking on the doors who would exchange his sorrows for hers. . . . Oh, my aches and my pains. I try to forget them, but they will not forget me."

I perceived that the *rabbanit* knew more than she cared to disclose. Since I felt that no good would come of further questioning, I showed myself ready to leave by rising from my chair.

" 'The sweep hadn't stepped into the chimney, but his face was already black,' " said she. "You have scarcely sat down in your chair, and already you are up and away. Why all this haste?"

I said, "If you wish me to stay, I will stay."

She made no answer; so I began speaking of Tilli again, and asked if I might be told her story.

"And if I tell you," said the *rabbanit*, "will it benefit you, or benefit her? I have no liking for tale-bearers: they spin out their cobwebs, and call it fine tapestry. I will only say this, that the Lord did a mercy to that good man when He put the evil spirit into that apostate, may her name be blotted out. Why are you gaping at me? Don't you understand Yiddish?"

"I understand Yiddish quite well," said I, "but I cannot understand what you are saying, *rabbanit*. Who is the good man, and who is the apostate you have cursed?"

"Perhaps I should bless her then, perhaps I should say, 'Well done, Mistress Apostate, you who have changed the gold coin for the brass farthing.' See, again you are staring at me as if I were speaking Turkish. You have heard that my husband of blessed memory was a rabbi, wherefore they call me *rabbanit*; and have you not heard that my father too was a rabbi? Such a rabbi, that in comparison with him, all other rabbis might rank as pupils in a school for infants: and I speak of real rabbis, look you, not of those who wear the mantle and give themselves airs. . . . What a world, what a world it is! A deceitful world, and all it contains is deceit and vanity. But my father, of blessed and pious memory, was a rabbi from his childhood, and all the matchmakers in the province bustled about to find him a wife. Now there was a certain rich widow, and when I say rich, you know that I mean it. This widow had only one daughter —would she had never been born. She took a barrel full of gold dinars, and said to the matchmakers, 'If you wed that man to my daughter, this barrel full of gold will be his; and if it is not sufficient, I shall add to it! But her daughter was not a fit match for that holy man; for she was already tainted with the spirit of perverseness, as is shown by her end, and she fled away from her home, and entered the house of the nuns, and deserted her faith. Yes, at the very hour when she was to be led to her bridal, she ran away. That poor stricken mother wasted half her fortune in trying to reclaim her. Her appeal went up to the Emperor himself; and even the Emperor was powerless to help. For they who have once entered the house of the nuns may never go out alive. You know now who that apostate was; the daughter of . . . hush, for here she comes."

Tilli entered the room. She was carrying a bowl of soup, and seeing me she said:

"Ah, you are still here! But stay, my friend, stay. It is a great *mitzvah* to visit the sick. *Rabbanit,* how much better you look! Truly, salvation comes in the wink of an eye; for the Name is healing you every minute. I have brought a little soup to moisten your lips, now, my dear, raise your head and I shall prop up your pillow. There, my dear, that's better. My son, I am sorry that you do not live in the City, for then you would see for yourself how the *rabbanit's* health is improving day by day."

"And do I not live in Jerusalem?" I said. "Surely Nachlat Shivah is Jerusalem?"

"It is indeed," answered Tilli. "God forbid that it should be otherwise. Rather may the day come when Jerusalem extends as far as Damascus, and in every direction. But the eye that has seen all Jerusalem enclosed within her walls cannot accustom itself to viewing what is built beyond the walls as the City itself. It is true that all the Land of Israel is holy and, I need hardly say, the surroundings of Jerusalem: yet the holiness that is within the walls of the City surpasses all else. My son, there is nothing I have said which you do not know better than I. Why then have I said it? Only that I might speak the praise of Jerusalem."

I could read in the eyes of the *rabbanit* a certain resentment, because Tilli was speaking to me rather than to her. So I took my leave and went away.

Various preoccupations kept me for a while from going to the Old City; and after that came the nuisance of the tourists. How well we know these tourists, who descend upon us and upon the land, all because the Place has made a little space for us here! They come now to see what has happened; and having come, they regard us as if we were created solely to serve them. Yet one good thing may be said for the tourists: in showing them "the sights," we see them ourselves. Once or twice, having brought them to the City to show them the Wailing Wall, I met Tilli there. It seemed to me that a change had come over her. Although she had always walked without support, I noticed that she now leaned on a stick. Because of the visitors, I was unable to linger. For they had come to spy out the whole land, not to spend time upon an old woman not even mentioned in their itineraries.

When the tourists had left Jerusalem, I felt restless in myself. After trying without success to resume work, I bestirred myself and walked to the City, where I visited of my own accord all the places I had shown to the visitors. How can I describe what I saw? He who in his goodness daily renews the works of creation, perpetually renews his own City. New houses may not have been built, nor new trees planted, yet Jerusalem herself is ever new. I cannot explain the secret of her eternal variety. We must wait, all of us, for those great sages who will one day enlighten us.

I came upon that same man of learning whom I had visited earlier, and he drew me to his house, where he set before me all his recent findings. We sat together in deep contentment, while I asked my questions, and he replied; or spoke of problems, which he resolved; or mentioned obscure matters which he made clear. How good it is, how satisfying, to sit at the feet of one of the scholars of Jerusalem, and to learn the Law from his lips! His home is simple, his furnishings austere, yet his wisdom ranges far, like the great hill ranges of Jerusalem which are seen from the windows. Bare are the hills of Jerusalem; no temples or palaces crown them. Since the time of our exile, nation after nation has come and laid them waste. But the hills spread their glory like banners to the sky; they are resplendent in ever-changing hues; and not least in glory is the Mount of Olives, which bears no forest of trees, but a forest of tombs of the righteous, who in life and in death gave their thoughts to the Land.

As I stood up to go, the mistress of the house entered and said to her husband, "You have forgotten your promise." He was much perturbed at this, and said, "Wonder of wonders: all the time I have known Tehilah she has never asked a favor. And now she wants me to say that she wishes to see you."

"Are you speaking," said I, "of Tilli, the old woman who showed me the way to your house? For it seems to me that you call her by another name."

"Tehilah," he answered, "is Tilli's true name, that was given to her in the synagogue. From this you may learn that even four or five generations ago our forebears would give their daughters names that sound as though they had been recently coined. For this reason my wife's name is Tehiyah, or Reborn, which one might suppose to have been devised in our own age of rebirth. Yet in fact it belongs to the time of the great Gaon,* who required my wife's great-grandfather to call his daughter Tehiyah; and my wife bears her name."

I said, "You speak now of the custom four or five generations ago. Can it be that this Tehilah is so old?"

He smiled, saying, "Her years are not written upon her face, and she is not in the habit of telling her age. We only know it because of what she once let slip. It happened that Tehilah came to congratulate us at the wedding of our son; and the blessing she gave to our son and his bride was that it might be granted for them to live to her age. My son asked, 'What is this blessing with which you have blessed us?' And she answered him, 'It is ninety years since I was eleven years old.' This happened three years ago; so that now her age is, as she might express it, ninety years and fourteen: that is to say, a hundred and four."

I asked him, since he was already speaking of her, to tell me what manner of woman she was. He answered:

"What is there to say? She is a saint; yes, in the true meaning of the word. And if you have this opportunity of seeing her, you must take it. But I doubt if you will find her at home; for she is either visiting the sick, or bringing comforts to the poor, or doing some other unsolicited *mitzvah*. Yet you may perhaps find her, for between *mitzvah* and *mitzvah* she goes home to knit garments or stockings for poor orphans. In the days when she was rich, she spent her wealth upon deeds of charity, and now that nothing is left her but a meagre pittance to pay for her own few needs, she does her charities in person."

The scholar accompanied me as far as Tehilah's door. As we walked together he discoursed on his theories; but realizing that I was not attending to his words, he smiled and said, "From the moment I spoke of Tehilah, no other thought has entered your mind."

"I would beg to know more of her," I replied. He said:

"I have already spoken of her as she is today. How she was before she came to our land I do not know, beyond what

---

*Literally, "genius," a title given to pre-eminent rabbinical scholars.

everyone knows; that is to say, that she was a very wealthy woman, the owner of vast concerns, who gave up all when her sons and her husband died, and came here to Jerusalem. My late mother used to say, 'When I see Tehilah, I know that there is retribution worse than widowhood and the loss of sons.' What form of retribution this was, my mother never said; and neither I, nor anyone else alive, knows; for all that generation which knew Tehilah abroad is now dead, and she herself says but little. Even now, when she is beginning to change, and speaks more than she did, it is not of herself. . . . We have come to her house; but it is unlikely that you will find her at home; for towards sunset she make the rounds of the schoolrooms, distributing sweets to the younger children."

A few moments later, however, I stood in the home of Tehilah. She was seated at the table, expecting me, so it seemed, with all her being. Her room was small, with the thick stone walls and arched ceiling that were universal in the Jerusalem of bygone days. Had it not been for the little bed in a corner, and a clay jar upon the table, I would have likened her room to a place of worship. Even its few ornaments—the hand-lamp of burnished copper, a copper pitcher and a lamp of the same metal that hung from the ceiling—even these, together with the look of the table, on which were laid a prayer-book, a Bible, and some third book of study, gave to the room the grace and simplicity of a house of prayer.

I bowed my head saying, "Blessed be my hostess."

She answered, "And blessed be my guest."

"You live here," said I, "like a princess."

"Every daughter of Israel," she said, "is a princess; and, praised be the living God, I too am a daughter of Israel. It is good that you have come. I asked to see you; and not only to see you, but to speak with you also. Would you consent to do me a favor?"

"Even to the half of my kingdom," I replied. She said:

"It is right that you should speak of your kingdom; for every man of Israel is the son of kings, and his deeds are royal deeds. When a man of Israel does good to his neighbor, this is a royal deed. Sit down, my son: it makes conversation more easy. Am I not intruding upon your time? You are a busy man, I am sure, and need the whole day for gaining your livelihood. Those times have gone when we had leisure enough and were glad to spend an hour in talk. Now everyone is in constant bustle and haste. People think that if they run fast enough it will speed the coming of the Messiah. You see, my son, how I have become a chatterer. I have forgotten the advice of that old man who warned me not to waste words."

I was still waiting to learn the reason for her summons. But now, as if she had indeed taken to heart the old man's warning, she said nothing. After a while she glanced at me, and then looked away; then glanced at me again, as one might who is scrutinizing a messenger to decide if he is worthy of trust. At last she began to tell me of the death of the *rabbanit*, who had passed away during the night, while her stove was burning, and her cat lay warming itself at the flame—till the hearse-bearers came and carried her away, and someone unknown had taken the stove.

"You see, my son," said Tehilah, "a man performs a *mitzvah*, and one *mitzvah* begets another. Your deed was done for the sake of that poor woman, and now a second person is the gainer, who seeks to warm his bones against the cold." Again she looked me up and down; then she said, "I am sure you are surprised that I have troubled you to come."

"On the contrary," I said, "I am pleased."

"If you are pleased, so am I. But my pleasure is at finding a man who will do me a kindness; as for you, I do not know why you should be pleased."

For a moment she was silent. Then she said, "I have heard that you are skilful at handling a pen—since you are, as they nowadays call it, an author. So perhaps you will place your pen at my service for a short letter."

I took out my fountain pen. She looked at it with interest, and said, "You carry your pen about with you, like those who carry a spoon wherever they go, so that if they chance upon a meal, the spoon is ready to hand."

I replied, "For my part, I carry the meal inside the spoon." And I explained to her the working of my fountain pen.

She picked it up in her hand and objected, "You say there is ink inside, but I cannot see one drop."

I explained the principle more fully, and she said:

"If it is so, they slander your generation in saying that its inventions are only for evil. See, they have invented a portable stove, and invented this new kind of pen: it may happen that they will yet invent more things for the good of mankind. True it is that the longer one lives, the more one sees. All the same, take this quill that I have myself made ready, and dip it in this ink. It is not that I question the usefulness of your pen; but I would have my letter written in my own way. And here is a sheet of paper; it is crown-paper, which I have kept from days gone by, when they knew how good paper was made. Upwards of seventy years I have kept it by me, and still it is as good as new. . . . One thing more I would ask of you: I want you to write, not in the ordinary cursive hand, but in the capital letters of the prayer book and the Torah. I assume that as a writer you must at some time have transcribed, if not the Torah itself, at least the Scroll of Esther that we read on Purim.

"As a boy," I answered, "I copied such a scroll exactly in the manner prescribed; and, believe this or not, everyone who saw that scroll praised it."

"Although I have not seen it," said Tehilah, "I am sure you know how to write the characters as is required, without a single flaw. Now I shall make ready for you a glass of herb tea, while you proceed with your writing."

"Please do not trouble," I said, "for I have already taken something to drink."

"If so, how shall I show hospitality? I know: I shall cut you a piece of sugar-loaf; then you can say a blessing, and I can add, Amen."

She gave me some of the sugar. Then, after a short silence, she said:

"Take up the quill and write. I shall speak in the vernacular, but you will write in the holy tongue. I have heard that now they teach the girls both to write and to speak the holy language: you see, my son, how the good Lord is constantly improving his world from age to age. When I was a child, this was not their way. But at least I understand my Hebrew prayer book, and can read from the Torah, and the Psalms, and the Ethics of the Fathers. . . . Oh dear, oh dear, today I have not finished my day."

I knew that she meant the day's portion of the Psalms, and said to her, "Instead of grieving you should rather be glad."

"Glad?"

"Yes," I said, "for the delay is from heaven, that one day

more might be added to your sum of days." She sighed, and said:

"If I knew that tomorrow our Redeemer would come, gladly would I drag out another day in this world. But as day follows day, and still our true Redeemer tarries and comes not, what is my life? And what is my joy? God forbid that I should complain of my years: if it pleases Him to keep me in life, it pleases me also. Yet I cannot help but ask how much longer these bones must carry their burden. So many younger women have been privileged to set up their rest on the Mount of Olives, while I remain to walk on my feet, till I think I shall wear them away. And is it not better to present oneself in the Higher World while one's limbs are all whole, and return the loan of the body intact? I do not speak of putting on flesh, which is only an extra burden for the hearse-bearers. But at least it is good to die with whole limbs. . . . Again I am speaking too much: but now what does it matter a word less, or a word more. I am fully prepared to return the deposit of my body, earth back to earth. . . . Take up your quill, my son, and write."

I dipped the quill-pen in the ink, made ready the paper and waited for Tehilah to speak. But she was lost in her thoughts and seemed unaware of my presence. I sat there and gazed at her, my eyes taking in every wrinkle and furrow of her face. How many experiences she had known! She was in the habit of saying that she had seen good things, and yet better things. From what I had been told, these things seemed far from good. The adage was true of her, that the righteous wear mourning in their hearts, and joy upon their faces.

Tehilah became aware of me and, turning her head, said, "Have you begun?"

"You have not told me what I am to write."

She said, "The beginning does not need to be told. We commence by giving praise to God. Write: *With the help of the Holy Name, blessed be He.*"

I smoothed the paper, shook the quill, and wrote, *With the help of the Holy Name, blessed be He.*

She sat up, looked at what I had written, and said: "Good, very good. And now what next? Write as follows: *From the Holy City, Jerusalem, may she be built and established, speedily and in our days, Amen.* In speech I only say 'Jerusalem,' without additions. But in writing, it is proper that we should bring to mind the holiness of Jerusalem, and add a plea for her to be rebuilt: that the reader may take Jerusalem to his heart, and know that she is in need of mercy, and say a prayer for her. Now, my son, write the day of the week, and the portion of the Torah for the week, and the number of years since the creation."

When I had set down the full date, she continued:

"Now write, in a bold hand, and as carefully as you can, the letter *Lamed*. . . . Have you done this? Show me how it looks. . . . There is no denying that it is a good *Lamed*, though perhaps it could have been a trifle larger. Now, my son, continue with *Khaf*, and after the *Khaf* write *Bet*, and after it *Vav*. . . . *Vav*, I was saying, and now comes *Dalet*. Show me now the whole word, *Likhvod*, 'In honor of.' Very fine indeed. It is only right that the respectful address should be suitably written. Now add to that, 'the esteemed *Rabbi*' . . . ah, you have already done so! You write faster than I think: while I am collecting my thoughts, you have already set them down. Truly your father—may the light of God shine on him—did not waste the cost of your education. . . . My son, forgive me, for I am so tired. Let us leave the writing of the letter till another day. When is it convenient for you to come?"

"Shall I come tomorrow?" I said.

"Tomorrow? Do you wish it? What day is tomorrow?"

"It is the day before new moon."

"That is a good day for this thing. Then let it be tomorrow."

I saw that she was inwardly grieved, and thought to myself: The day before new moon is a time for prayer and supplication, a time for visits to the tomb of Rachel our Mother; surely she will not be able to attend to her letter. Aloud I said to her, "If you are not free tomorrow I shall come on some other day."

"And why not tomorrow?"

"Just because it *is* the day before the new moon."

She said, "My son, you bring my sorrow before me, that on such a day I should be unable to go to Rachel our Mother."

I asked why she could not go.

"Because my feet cannot carry me there."

"There are carriages," I said, "and buses as well."

"When I first came to Jerusalem," said Tehilah, "there were none of these buses, as they call them now, and a foolish word it is, too. There were not even carriages; so we used to walk. And since I have gone on foot for so long, it is now hardly worth changing my ways. Did you not say you are able to come tomorrow? If it pleases the Name to grant my wish, my life will be prolonged for yet a day more."

I left her and went on my way; and the following day I returned. I do not know if there was any real need to return so soon. Possibly if I had waited longer, it would have extended her life.

As soon as I saw her, I perceived a change. Tehilah's face, that always had about it a certain radiance, was doubly radiant. Her room shone out too. The stone floor was newly polished, and so were all the articles in the room. A white coverlet was spread over the little bed in the corner, and the skirtings of the walls were freshly color-washed blue. On the table stood the jar, with its parchment cover, and a lamp and sealing wax were placed at its side. When had she found time to color-wash the walls, and to clean the floor, and to polish all her utensils? Unless angels did her work, she must have toiled the night long.

She rose to welcome me, and said in a whisper, "I am glad that you have come. I was afraid you might forget, and I have a little business matter to attend to."

"If you have somewhere to go," I said, "I shall come back later."

"I have to go and confirm my lease. But since you are here, sit down, and let us proceed with the letter. Then afterwards I shall go about my lease."

She set the paper before me and fetched the ink and the quill pen. I took up the pen and dipped it in the ink and waited for her to dictate her message.

"Are you ready?" she said. "Then I am ready too!"

As she spoke the word "ready," her face seemed to light up and a faint smile came to her lips. Again I prepared to write, and waited for her next words.

"Where did we leave off?" she said. "Was it not with the phrase, *In honor of the esteemed rabbi?* Now you shall write his name."

Still I sat waiting.

She said in a whisper, "His name is Shraga. . . . Have you written it?"

"I have written."

She half-closed her eyes as if dozing. After some time she raised herself from her chair to look at the letter, and whispered again, "His name is Shraga. His name is Shraga." And again she sat silent. Then she seemed to bestir herself, saying, "I shall tell you in a general way what you are to write." But again she lapsed back into silence, letting her eyelids droop.

"I see," she said at last, "that I shall have to tell you all that happened, so that you will understand these things and know how to write. It is an old story, of something which happened many years ago; yes, three and ninety years ago."

She reached for her walking stick and let her head sink down upon it. Then again she looked up, with an expression of surprise, as a man might who thinks he is sitting alone and discovers a stranger in his room. Her face was no longer calm, but showed grief and disquiet as she felt for her stick, then put it by, and again took it up to lean upon, passing her hand over her brow to smooth out her wrinkles.

Finally she said, "If I tell you the whole story, it will make it easier for you to write. . . . His name is Shraga. . . . Now I shall start from the very beginning."

She raised her eyes and peered about her; then, reassured that no one else could be listening, she began:

"I was eleven years old at the time. I know this, because Father, of blessed memory, used to write in his Bible the names of his children and the dates of their births, his daughters as well as his sons. You will find the names in that Bible you see before you; for when I came to Jerusalem, my late brothers renounced their right to my father's holy books and gave them to me. As I said before, it is an old story, three and ninety years old; yet I remember it well. I shall relate it to you, and little by little you will understand. Now, are you listening?"

I inclined my head and said, "Speak."

"So you see, I was eleven years old. One night, Father came home from the synagogue, bringing with him some relative of ours, and with them Petachya Mordechai, the father of Shraga. When she saw them enter, my dear mother—peace be upon her soul—called me and told me to wash my face well and put on my Sabbath dress. She too put on her Sabbath clothes and bound her silk kerchief round her head and, taking my hand, led me into the best room to meet Father and his guests.

Shraga's father looked at me and said, 'Heaven shield you, you are a pretty child.' Father stroked my cheek and said, 'Tehilah, do you know who spoke to you? The father of your bridegroom-to-be spoke to you. May the influences be happy, my child: tonight you are betrothed.' At once all the visitors blessed me with happy influences, and called me 'the bride.' Mother quickly bundled me back to her room to shield me from any evil eye, and kissed me, and said, 'Now and henceforth, you are Shraga's betrothed; and God willing, next year, when your bridegroom comes of age at thirteen for wearing the phylacteries, we shall make your wedding.'

"I knew Shraga already, for we used to play with nuts and at hide-and-seek, until he grew too old and began to study the Gemara. After our betrothal I saw him every Sabbath, when he would come to Father's house and repeat to him all he had learned through the week. Mother would give me a dish of sweets which I would take and offer to Shraga, and Father would stroke my cheek and beam upon my bridegroom.

"And now they began to prepare for the wedding. Shraga's father wrote out the phylacteries, and my father bought him a prayer shawl, while I sewed a bag for the phylacteries and another bag for the prayer shawl that is worn on a Sabbath. Who made the large outer bag for both prayer shawl and phylacteries I cannot remember.

"One Sabbath, four full weeks before the day fixed for the wedding, Shraga failed to come to our house. During the afternoon service, Father enquired at the house of study, and was told that he had gone on a journey. Now this journey was made to one of the leaders of the Hasidim, and Shraga had been taken by his father in order that he might receive a direct blessing on the occasion of his first wearing of the prayer shawl and phylacteries. When my father learned this, his soul nearly parted from his body; for he had not known until then that Shraga's father was of the Sect. He had kept his beliefs a secret, for in those days the Hasidim were despised and persecuted, and Father was at the head of the persecutors; so that he looked upon members of the Sect as if (God forbid) they had ceased to belong to our people. After the Havdalah ceremony at the close of the Sabbath, Father tore up my marriage contract and sent the pieces to the house of my intended father-in-law. On the Monday, Shraga returned with his father, and they came to our house. My father drove them out with abuse; whereupon Shraga himself swore an oath that he would never forgive us the insult. Now Father knew well that he who cancels a betrothal must seek pardon from the injured party; yet he took no steps to obtain this. And when my mother implored him to appease Shraga, he made light of her entreaties, saying, 'You have nothing to fear: he is only of the Sect.' So contemptible were the Hasidim in my father's eyes that he took no heed in this thing wherein all men take heed.

"Preparations for the wedding had been made. The poultry was ordered, and the house was cluttered with sacks of flour and casks of honey for the making of loaves and cakes. In short, all was ready, and there lacked nothing but a bridegroom. My father summoned a matchmaker; another bridegroom was found for me; and with him I went to my bridal.

"What became of Shraga, I do not know, for Father forbade any of our household to mention his name. Later I heard that he and all his people had moved to another town. Indeed they were in fear for their very lives, since, from the day when Father ended my betrothal, they were not called to the Law in synagogue—not even at the Rejoicing of the Law, when every man is called. They could not even come together for worship, for my father as head of the community would not let them assemble outside the fixed houses of prayer; and had they not moved to another town where they might be called to the Torah, they could not have gone through the year.

"Three years after the wedding, I was granted the birth of a son. And two years later, another son was born to me. And two years after that, I gave birth to a daughter.

"Time passed uneventfully, and we lived at our ease. The children grew and prospered, while I and my husband watched them grow and were glad. I forgot about Shraga, and forgot that I had never received a note of pardon at his hand.

"Mother and Father departed this life. Before his death, my father of blessed memory committed his affairs to his sons and his sons-in-law, enjoining them all to work together as one. Our business flourished, and we lived in high repute. We engaged good tutors for our sons, and a foreign governess for our daughter; for in those days pious folk would have nothing to do with the local teachers, who were suspected of being freethinkers.

"My husband would bring these tutors from other towns;

and whereas the local teachers were obliged to admit any student who came, even if he was not suitably qualified, tutors who had been brought from elsewhere were dependent upon those who engaged them and under no such obligation. Coming, as they did, alone, they would dine at our table on Sabbath days. Now my husband, who because of the pressure of his affairs could not make set times for study of the Torah, was especially glad of one such guest and his learned discourses. And I and the children delighted in the tuneful table chant he would sing us. We did not know that this tutor was a Hasid, and his discourses the doctrines of Hasidism, and the airs that he sang us, Hasidic airs; for in all other respects he conducted himself like any other true believer of Israel. One Sabbath eve, having discoursed of the Torah, he closed his eyes and sang a hymn of such heavenly bliss that our very souls went forth at its sweetness. At the end, my husband asked him, 'How may a man come to this experience of the divine?' The tutor whispered to him, 'Let your honor make a journey to my *rebbe*,* and he will know this and much more.'

"Some days later, my husband found himself in the city of the tutor's *rebbe*. On his return, he brought with him new customs, the like of which I had not seen in my father's house; and I perceived that these were the customs of the Hasidim. And I thought to myself, who can now wipe the dust from your eyes, Father, that you may see what you have done, you who banished Shraga for being a Hasid, and now the husband you gave me in his stead does exactly as he did? If this thing does not come about as atonement for sin, I know not why it has come about.

"My brothers and brothers-in-law saw what was happening, but they said not a word. For already the times had changed, and people were no longer ashamed to have Hasidim in the family. Men of wealth and position had come from other towns and married amongst us; they followed the customs of Hasidim, and even set up a house of prayer for their sect, and would travel openly to visit their *rebbes*. My husband did not attend their services, but in other respects he observed Hasidic customs and educated his sons in their ways, and from time to time would make journeys to his *rebbe*.

---

*Yiddish for rabbi; usually applied to Hasidic leaders in Eastern Europe.

"A year before our first-born son came of age, there was plague in the world, and many fell sick. There was not a house without its victims, and when the plague reached us, it struck our son. In the end the Lord spared him—but not for long. When he rose from his sickbed, he began to study the practice of the phylacteries from the great code of the Shulhan Aruch. And I saw this and was glad, that for all his Hasidic training, his devotion to the Law was not lessened.

"One morning our son rose up very early to go to the house of study. As he was about to enter, he saw there a man dressed in grave clothes, resembling a corpse. It was not a dead man he had seen, but some demented creature who did many strange things. The child was overcome with terror and his senses left him. With difficulty was he restored to life. Restored to life he was indeed, but not to a long life. From that day on, his soul flickered and wavered like a candle flame, like the soul of a man at the closing prayer of the Day of Atonement, when his fate is about to be sealed. He had not come of age for wearing phylacteries when he gave up his ghost and died.

"Through the seven days of mourning I sat and meditated. My son had died after the Havdalah at the ending of Sabbath, thirty days before he came of age for phylacteries. And at the end of a Sabbath, after the Havdalah, thirty days before I was to go to my bridal with Shraga, Father had torn up the marriage contract. Counting the days I found to my horror that the two evils had come about on the same day, at the same hour. Even if this were no more than chance, yet it was a matter for serious reflection.

"Two years later, the boy's brother came of age—came, and did not come. He happened to go with his playfellows to the woods outside our town to fetch branches for the Pentecost. He left his comrades in the woods, intending to call on the scribe who was preparing his phylacteries; but he never returned. We thought at first that he had been stolen by gypsies, for a troop of them had been seen passing the town. After some days his body was found in the great marsh beside the woods; then we knew he must have missed his way and fallen in.

"When we stood up from our mourning, I said to my husband, 'Nothing remains to us now but our one daughter. If we do not seek forgiveness from Shraga, her fate will be as the fate of her brothers.'

"Throughout all those years we had heard nothing of

Shraga. When he and his people left our town, they were forgotten, and their whereabouts remained unknown. My husband said, 'Shraga is the Hasid of such and such a *rebbe:* I shall
make a journey to this man, and find out where he lives.'

"Now my husband was not the Hasid of this same *rebbe:* on
the contrary, he was opposed to him, because of the great
dispute that had broken out between the *rebbes*, on account of
a cattle slaughterer, whom one had appointed and the other
had dismissed. In the course of that quarrel a man of Israel
was killed, and several families were uprooted, and several
owners of property lost their possessions, and several persons
ended their days in prison.

"Nevertheless, my husband made the journey to the town
where this *rebbe* lived. Before he arrived there, the *rebbe* died,
after dividing his ministry amongst his sons, who went away
each to a different town. My husband journeyed from town to
town, from son to son, inquiring of each son where Shraga
might be. Finally he was told, 'If you are asking after Shraga,
Shraga has become a renegade and joined our opponents.' But
no one knew where Shraga now lived.

"When a man is a Hasid, you may trace him without difficulty. If he is not the disciple of one *rebbe*, he is the disciple of
another. But with any ordinary unattached Jew, unless you
know where he lives, how may he be found? My husband, peace
be upon his soul, was accustomed to making journeys, for his
business took him to many places. He made journey after
journey inquiring for Shraga. On account of these travels his
strength in time began to fail and his blood grew thin. At last,
having traveled to a certain place, he fell sick there and died.

"After I had set up his tombstone, I went back to my town
and entered into business. While my husband was still alive, I
had helped him in his affairs: now that he was dead, I speeded
them with all my might. And the Lord doubled my powers until
it was said of me, 'She has the strength of a man.' It would have
been well, perhaps, had wisdom been granted me in place of
strength, but the Lord knows what he intends and does not
require his own creatures to tell him what is good. I thought in
my heart: all this toil is for my daughter's sake. If I add to my
wealth, I shall add to her welfare. As my responsibilities became ever greater, I found I had no leisure to spend at home,
except on Sabbaths and holy days, and even these days were
apportioned, half to the service in synagogue, and the other

half to the reception of guests. My daughter, so it seemed, was in no need of my company, for I had engaged governesses, and she was devoted to her studies. I received much praise on account of my daughter, and even the gentiles, who deride our accent, would say that she spoke their language as well as the best of their people. Furthermore, these governesses would ingratiate themselves with my daughter, and invite her to their homes. In due course, I called the matchmakers, who found her a husband distinguished for his learning, and already qualified for the rabbinate. But I was not to enjoy a parent's privilege of leading my daughter to her bridal, for the evil spirit took possession of her, so that her right reason was perverted.

"And now, my son, this is what I ask of you: Write to Shraga for me, and say that I have forgiven him for all the sorrows that befell me at his hand. And say that I think he should forgive me, too, for I have been stricken enough."

For a long, long time I sat in silence, unable to speak a word. At last, secretly wiping a tear from my eye, I said to Tehilah:

"Allow me to ask a question. Since the day when your father tore up the marriage contract, ninety years and more have passed. Do you really believe that Shraga is still alive? And if so, has anyone informed you where he may be found?"

Tehilah answered, "Shraga is not alive. Shraga has now been dead for thirty years. I know the year of his death, for in that year, on the seventh day of Adar, I went to a synagogue for the afternoon service. Following the week's reading from the Prophets, they said the memorial prayer for the dead, and I heard them pray for the soul of Shraga. After the service, I spoke to the beadle of the synagogue, and asked him who this Shraga might be. He mentioned the name of a certain kinsman of the dead man, who had given instructions for his soul to be remembered. I went to this kinsman, and heard what I heard."

"If Shraga is dead, then, how do you propose to send him a letter?"

Tehilah answered, "I suppose you are thinking that this old woman's wits are beginning to fail her, after so many years; and that she is relying upon the post office to deliver a letter to a dead man."

I said, "Then tell me, what will you do?"

She rose, and picking up the clay jar that stood on the table, raised it high above her head, intoning in a kind of ritual chant:

"I shall take this letter—and set it in this jar; I shall take this wax—and seal up this jar; and I shall take them with me—this letter and this jar."

I thought to myself, and even if you take the jar and the letter with you, I still do not see how your message will come to Shraga. Aloud I said to her, "Where will you take your jar with its letter?"

Tehilah smiled and said softly, "Where will I take it? I will take it to the grave, my son. Yes, I shall take this jar, and the letter inside it, straight to my grave. For up in the High World they know Shraga well and will know where to find him. And the postmen of the Holy One are dependable, you may be sure; they will see that the letter is delivered."

Tehilah smiled again. It was a little smile of triumph, as of a precocious child who has got the better of an argument with her elders. After a while she let her head sink upon her walking stick and seemed again to be half asleep. But soon she glanced up and said, "Now that you understand the whole matter, you can write of your own accord." And again her head dropped over her stick.

I took up the pen and wrote the letter. When I had finished, Tehilah raised her head and inquired, "Is it done now?" I began to read the letter aloud, while she sat with her eyes closed, as if she had lost interest in the whole matter and no longer desired very greatly to hear. When the reading was over, she opened her eyes and said:

"Good, my son, good and to the point. Perhaps it might have been phrased rather differently, but even so, the meaning is clear. Now, my son, hand me the pen and I shall sign my name. Then I can put the letter in the jar; and after that I shall go about my lease."

I dipped the pen in the ink and handed it to her, and she took it and signed her name. She passed the pen over certain of the characters to make them more clear. Then she folded the letter and placed it inside the jar, and bound the piece of parchment over the top. Then she kindled the lamp, and took wax for sealing, and held it against the flame until the wax became soft; then she sealed the jar with the wax. Having done these things, she rose from her place and went towards her bed. She lifted up the coverlet and placed the jar under the pillow of the bed. Then she looked at me fairly, and said in a quiet voice:

"I must make haste to confirm my lease. Bless you, my son,

for the pains you have taken. Now and henceforth I shall not trouble you more."

So saying, she made smooth the coverlet of her bed, and took up her stick, and went to the door, and reached up that she might lay her lips to the mezuzah, and waited for me to follow. She locked the door behind us and walked ahead with brisk steps; and I overtook her and continued at her side.

As she walked, she looked kindly upon every place that she passed and every person she met. Suddenly she stopped and said, "My son, how can they abandon these holy places and these faithful Jews?"

At that time, I still did not comprehend all she meant by these words. When we reached the parting of the ways, she stopped again and said, "Peace with you." But when she saw that I was resolved not to leave her, she said no more. She went up the wide steps that lead to the courtyard of the Communal Center, and entered, and I followed.

We went into the Communal Center, which administers the affairs of the living and the dead. Two of the clerks sat there at a desk, their ledgers before them and their pens in their hands, writing and taking sips of their Turkish coffee as they wrote. When they saw Tehilah, they set down their pens and stood up in respect. They spoke their welcome, and hastened to bring her a chair.

"What brings you here?" asked the elder of the clerks.

She answered, "I have come to confirm my lease."

He said, "You have come to confirm your lease: and we are of the opinion that the time has come to annul it."

Tehilah was amazed. "What is all this?" she cried.

He said, "Surely you have already joined the immortals?"

Laughing at his own joke, the clerk turned to me, saying, "Tehilah, bless her, and may she live for many, many years, is in the habit of coming every year to confirm the bill of sale on the plot for her grave on the Mount of Olives. So it was last year, and the year before that, and three years ago, and ten and twenty and thirty years ago, and so will she go on till the coming of the Redeemer."

Said Tehilah, "May he come, the Redeemer: may he come, the Redeemer. Would to God he would hasten and come. But as for me, I shall trouble you no more."

The clerk asked, assuming a tone of surprise, "Are you going to a kibbutz, then, like these young girls they call 'pioneers'?"

Tehilah said, "I am not going to a kibbutz, I am going to my own place."

"What," said the clerk, "are you returning to your home country?"

Tehilah said, "I am not returning to my home country, but I am returning to the place whence I came: as it is written, '*And to the dust thou shalt return.*'"

"Tut-tut," said the clerk, "do you think that the Burial Society has nothing to do? Take my advice, and wait for twenty or thirty years more. Why all this haste?"

She said quietly, "I have already ordered the corpse-washers and the layers-out, and it would be ill-mannered to make sport of these good women."

The clerk's expression changed, and it was evident that he regretted his light words. He then said:

"It is good for us to see you here, for so long as we see you, we have before us the example of a long life; and should you desert us—God forbid—it is as if you take away from us this precedent."

Tehilah said, "Had I more years to live, I would give them gladly to you, and to all who delight in life. Here is the lease for you to sign."

When the clerk had endorsed the bill of sale, Tehilah took it and placed it in the fold of her dress.

"Now and henceforth I shall trouble you no more," she said. "May the Name be with you, dear countrymen; for I go to my place."

She rose from her chair, and walked to the door and reached up to lay her lips to the mezuzah, and kissed the mezuzah, and so went away.

When she saw that I still went with her, she said, "Return to your own life, my son."

"I thought," said I, "that when you spoke of confirming the lease, you meant the lease of your house; but instead . . . "

She took me up in the midst of my words. "But instead," said she, "I confirmed the lease of my long home. Yet may the Holy One grant that I have no need to dwell there for long, before I rise again, with all the dead of Israel. Peace be upon you, my son. I must make haste and return to my house, for I am sure that the corpse-washers and the layers-out already await me."

I stood there in silence and watched her go, until she passed out of sight among the courts and the alleys.

Next morning I went to the Old City to enquire how she fared. On my way, I was stopped by the man of learning to whose house Tehilah had led me. For some while he kept me in conversation, and when I wished to take my leave, he offered to accompany me.

"I am not going home yet," I said. "I am going to see Tehilah."

He said, "Go only after a hundred and twenty years."

Seeing my surprise, he added, "You will live. But that saint has now left us."

I parted from him and went on alone. As I walked I thought again and again: Tehilah has left us, she has gone on alone; she has left us, and gone on alone. I found that my feet had carried me to the house of Tehilah, and I opened her door and entered.

Still and calm was the room, like a house of prayer after the prayer has been said. There, on the stone floor, flowed the last tiny rivulets of the waters in which Tehilah had been cleansed.

—Translated by Walter Lever

HE GUYAN

The setting for Maple Leaves *is the same as that for* The Nonrevolutionaries. *But the perspective is exactly opposite. Where the narrator of* The Nonrevolutionaries *is Korean, apolitical, and trained in western thought, the soldiers in* Maple Leaves *are Chinese, highly ideological, and Asian in orientation.*

When the Japanese were defeated in 1945, an old civil conflict burst into full flame in China, the struggle between the Kuomintang of Chiang Kai-shek and the communist forces led by Mao Tse-tung. The conflict ended in victory for the Communists in 1949. With Chiang's forces pushed off the mainland to Taiwan, Mao's army could turn its attention to the support of the communist regime of North Korea in the hope of uniting the whole peninsula under the Red flag. In this conflict, however, the North Korean and Chinese troops had to cope with the powerful and technologically advanced U.S. military machine, which pitted a superlatively well-equipped air force against much more vulnerable ground forces.

Maple Leaves embodies the passionate intensity and dedication to communist ideals which characterize much of modern Chinese literature. The story reflects a kind of unquestioning loyalty to the cause and total willingness to sacrifice the individual self to the greater good.

We do not know anything about the writer, He Guyan, but it seems likely he is one of the peasant-worker-soldier class who predominate in modern Chinese literature.

Maple Leaves

One autumn evening, as the sun was reddening the western sky, Hu Wenfa walked briskly out of the gully in which he was billeted. He was a driver in the Second Transport Company. He stuffed his last steamed bread roll into his mouth and brushed the dirt and crumbs off his uniform with his greasy hands as he walked to the shelters where the trucks were kept.

The shelters were in a wood to his right. Of the dozen or so that had been dug along the foot of a hill all were now empty except the one in which Hu Wenfa's new GAZ truck squatted like a great dark green beast with its shoulders hunched. Outside the shelter Hu Wenfa's assistant Wang Zhixiu was stretched out snoring happily on his greatcoat, which was by now dirt-brown right through to the fleece lining.

Hu Wenfa smiled at the sight, kicked him gently on the leg, and said, 'Wake up, we're going.'

Wang Zhixiu scrambled to his feet, looking blearily at Hu Wenfa. Then without a word he took the bucket that was beside him and went down to the river to fetch some water. Hu Wenfa opened the bonnet, inspected the engine closely, and oiled it. It was only when they were both sitting in the cab that Wang Zhixiu asked, as if he had only just been woken up, 'What's it this time?'

'Taking ammo from divisional stores to the strongpoint on Height Four One Two.'

'But haven't three trucks gone already?'

'Yes. Three went, but planes got two of them on the way. I don't know how the hell it happened. How could two grown men let their trucks be hit by a ruddy plane? They're still waiting for the ammunition on Height Four One Two. We've got a tough one today, young Wang. We've got to cross some air-strafed interdiction zones and another that's under artillery fire. If a plane gets us tonight our record of thirty-five thousand kilometres of safe driving will be snatched from under our noses.'

'We won't let it happen.'

'I hope not. Let's get one thing clear from the word go—no sleep for you this evening.'

Young Wang yawned as if to suggest that Hu Wenfa was wasting his breath saying anything so obvious and replied, 'Start her up.'

The motor roared into life. Long after the truck had bumped its way up to the military road Hu Wenfa kept looking round to see if Wang Zhixiu had gone to sleep.

Wang Zhixiu was an odd sort of bloke. Although he was only just twenty there were already two deep furrows in his brown forehead. He was quiet, unflappable, and always seemed to have the hint of a smile on his face. His eyesight was good and he worked with a will. The only thing wrong with him was that he was such a glutton for sleep. It made no difference where he was: whenever he had a moment to spare he would spread his greatcoat out on the ground and lie down on it. Within two minutes he would be right out, and neither wind nor rain could wake him.

There were two things that could shake him out of this habit. One was when something had gone wrong with the truck. This would fill him with so much energy that even the company commander or the political instructor would be wasting their breath telling him to go to sleep. His soft warm greatcoat might have turned into a bed of nails as he climbed over the truck or lay underneath to repair it. If it was a minor fault he might take a nap when he had put it right; but if there was something seriously wrong he would work at it all day through till the truck had to be moving again at night. He could not be bothered to eat properly on the job. He would ask someone to fetch him a couple of steamed rolls, and if there were none of those to be had, he would wash a biscuit down with a mug of hot water. He never let Hu Wenfa have anything to do with day-time repairs because he felt that the driver needed sleep more than his mate did. He only asked Hu Wenfa's advice when the problem was one he could not cope with himself.

The other thing that could stop him from sleeping was an urgent assignment like today's. Hu Wenfa need not have worried on that score. When they came across enemy aircraft at night they drove without lights under a blanket of darkness. Wang Zhixiu would rock to and fro breathing lightly as he sat beside Hu Wenfa as if he were asleep, but at any moment he might suddenly shout, 'Stop! Bomb crater!' then jump down from the truck to see how deep it was and whether it was possible to go round it. If it was not possible he would take his shovel from the truck without a word. Within ten minutes the hole would have been skillfully filled.

Hu Wenfa's character was the opposite of Wang Zhixiu's. He was an alert and active man of inexhaustible energy who wanted to get on with any job he was doing as quickly as possible, and was never happy when driving at less than sixty kilometres an hour. This often made Wang argue with him. Once when they had been crossing a zone under artillery fire Hu had wanted to go flat out, but Wang had been dead set against it. Instead of going into all the details he just said slowly, 'However fast you drive you aren't going to be able to race the shells.'

'What do you suggest then?' Hu had asked him.

'I'm all in favour of going fast along decent roads, but the ground in front of us here is honeycombed with craters. If you drive like a madman a crash will be enough to write off the lorry even if we dodge the shells.'

On Wang's advice Hu had taken it quietly. All that happened to them was that shrapnel tore some holes in the truck's canopy.

Another time they had to cross a river in winter when the water, covered in a thin sheet of ice, was higher than the surface of the bridge. The wooden bridge itself, about a kilometre long, was invisible; all that could be seen of it were a few wooden posts. Hu Wenfa's idea was to go straight along the line of the posts, reckoning that as the rivers were never flooded in winter the bridge was bound to be there under the ice. Wang Zhixiu would have nothing of it. After an argument he jumped down from the truck. 'A truck costs a fortune,' he said, 'and we can't fool about with it. I'm going to make sure.' He took off his cotton-padded trousers, socks, and boots, then leapt into the river. Although lumps of ice kept bumping noisily into him he said nothing as he felt his way across along the posts and confirmed that the bridge really could be crossed. His teeth were still chattering audibly when he came back and climbed into the cab. When Hu Wenfa advised him to put his greatcoat back on at once he replied in a matter-of-fact way, 'It's nothing to what our mates have to put up with at the front.'

Wang Zhixiu was a meticulous but slow worker. Hu Wenfa was always pulling his leg about the way he took his time, to which Wang would coolly reply that by taking their time the Chinese People's Volunteers would wear the Americans out.

The difference between the driver and his mate was like that between a straight and hard Cunninghamia tree and a tough, flexible mountain creeper. Hu Wenfa had not liked working with Wang Zhixiu at all to begin with; but by now he felt he would never find a better Number Two.

Wang's life was very simple, and seemed to consist of nothing other than driving, going to classes, eating, and sleeping. He was not interested in singing, dancing, or playing cards, and as far as Hu Wenfa could see there were only two things of which he was really fond. One was a coloured picture of Chairman Mao he had bought at a stationer's when he went back to Andong (on the Chinese side of the Korean frontier) three months earlier. As Hu liked it too he let him paste it up in the right-hand corner of the cab. The other thing Wang liked was the maple leaf of the Korean autumn. Before every journey he would break off a spray of the red leaves to put in the cab by the picture of Chairman Mao, and when they withered he would replace them with fresh ones. Hu Wenfa, with the veteran truck-driver's passion for tidiness, liked to keep his cab as neat as a bridal chamber. Once he removed the leaves and threw them out when Wang was not around, but a new spray was there when they set out the next day. 'What do you want those mucky leaves in the truck for?' he asked. 'They get in the way.' 'No they don't,' replied Wang. 'I didn't put them in your steering wheel.'

'You're going sissy with all your leaves and flowers.'

'Don't you like them then?' asked Wang with a grin.

'No.'

'You will soon enough.'

'Never. They smell bad and they look worse.'

Putting the leaves to his nose Wang replied, 'I suppose you've never been to my province, Jehol?'

'No.'

'Our maple forests cover mountains and plains. You should see them in autumn. Whole mountains turn red—from light red to purple and crimson. The most beautiful flowers in the world aren't a patch on them. When I joined the army the head of our engineering team took me to the top of a hill and showed me where the construction site had been measured out below. "When you come back from Korea after victory," he said to me, "a big factory will have been built there. By then you won't be able to recognize your own front door." I heard that they'd started work on it soon after I joined up. It's a great thing to have a factory built, but I wish I'd remembered to tell him not to cut the maples down.'

'We're industrializing now,' interrupted Hu Wenfa, 'so of course trees must be cut down when necessary.'

'The fewer the better. If they're really in the way they can be moved and replanted. It would be very good to have a line of maples round the outside of the factory.'

When the first star began to shimmer in the sky a lorry loaded with ammunition was roaring south. It was too dark for its number-plate to be readable, but a spray of red maple leaves danced like a flame behind the ammunition lorry's windscreen when another truck coming towards it flashed its headlights.

Wang was feeling sleepy again. 'We haven't had a single plane so far,' he said with a gigantic yawn. 'I hope it's all going to be as peaceful as the last few miles.'

'Not a chance. The Yanks won't be that obliging. Where are we coming to now?'

'We're almost at Jiuhuali.'

'We'll have to be careful. This is where it begins.'

'Stop and let me climb on top. I can see a lot farther from up there.'

At just the moment when the truck stopped one, two, and then a dozen flares lit up in an S-shaped pattern in front of them, turning the sky a lurid white. The truck's shadow was picked out clearly in the road. 'Damn,' said Hu furiously. 'Talk of the devil. You're too bloody clever.'

'Let's go then.'

'O.K.'

Hu slammed the cab door shut and shouted. 'Hold tight, Wang.' The truck shot forward like a hurricane. Knowing that the enemy aircraft was circling above him Hu could not leave his lights on all the time. But there was the danger of driving into a bomb crater. He used all his skill as he shot forward, flashing his lights on obstacles for about as long as it takes to blink. They were out again before the pilot had time to mark his position. Hu Wenfa had played blind-man's-buff with enemy aircraft more often than he could remember, and he had always won.

Young Wang was clinging to the top of the truck and probing into the night with his eyes as if they were searchlights. One or two kilometres later, when they were almost through the area lit by flares, he suddenly heard a grating roar. He turned and saw the black form of an aircraft diving towards them under the flares. Instinctively he banged the top of the cab three times and shouted, 'Stop!' As the brakes slammed on, a stream of blue tracer shells exploded and sent sparks dancing on the road two or three yards in front of the truck. The aircraft could not come back straight away, so after this strafing run the lorry raced forward even faster than before. Wang felt his stomach being all but shaken right out of him as he clung to the sides of the truck, his eyes fixed on the sky. The aircraft was soon diving on them again, coming in lower and faster this time. Wang thumped the cab three times again to tell Hu to stop. Instead Hu turned his lights on and drove flat out for several dozen yards. Then the lights went out again as the truck made a fast right-hand turn off the road and into a wood. Wang heard three explosions behind him and saw that thick smoke was blotting out the stars. Blue streaks were bouncing off the road.

Hu Wenfa stopped the truck under a tall tree, jumped down from the cab, blew his nose hard, and said, 'Blast! It's like a toad jumping on your foot—it gives you a scare even though it doesn't bite you.'

'Is the truck O.K.?' asked Wang, scrambling down from the top.

'Yes.'

'When you did that crash turn I thought it was because you couldn't stop.'

'If you try the same trick twice you give the game away. The sod would have got me if I'd done it again.'

Wang was full of admiration for Hu Wenfa as he remembered where the three rockets had just exploded. 'That's another tip I've picked up from you,' he said. 'You know your stuff all right.'

As the aircraft had now lost its target it dropped more flares. The tree just covered the truck. Wang looked at the sky that was a pale yellow in their glare and said, 'The bloody plane's still hanging about.' Hu pulled his greatcoat over his head, lit a cigarette, took a deep drag, exhaled and replied, 'He's welcome to fly round in circles up there. The more of their fuel they burn the better.'

Ten minutes or so later the sound of its engine faded away in the sky. The last flare slowly burned itself out and dropped as a glowing red spark. They climbed back into the cab and drove back to the road. Some half a dozen kilometres later a large mountain loomed up in front of them, and on the other side of it were flashes like sheet lightning. Hu stopped the engine and leaned out of the truck to listen. There was an unbroken roar of exploding shells. 'We'll have to be careful on the way up that: it's the King of Hell's Nose. The road's narrow, the mountain's high, and it's under permanent shelling. You can't use your headlights or drive fast. Being hit by a shell isn't worth worrying about, but if we go into a ravine that'll be our lot.'

'Start the engine. They won't be able to get us.' Wang opened the side window of the cab and put his head and arms outside to watch the narrow, winding road the truck was climbing. Wang's clipped shouts could be heard clearly over the shells and the engine: 'Left . . . further left . . . that's it . . . straight ahead . . . slower . . . slower, shell hole . . . right. . . . '

The truck kept stopping for Wang to jump out, grab his shovel, and walk ahead to find which way they could go. After countless stops and bends they were almost at the top. Just when they were going to follow the hairpin bends down the southern side there was a great flash and what sounded like a roll of thunder as a huge volley of shells exploded on the slope. Stones and branches showered on the truck. They were choked by the shell smoke that swept into the cab. Hu Wenfa cursed furiously and stopped the engine. Wang hesitated for a moment, quietly jumped out, and strode southwards through the smoke. It was two or three minutes before he came back. 'What's it like?' Hu Wenfa asked.

'The road surface has been blown to bits. I think we can get across if we take it a bit faster. Whatever you do, don't stop. Let's go.'

Wang leant out and shouted as he had before: 'Left ... left ... that's it ... careful ... right ... straight ahead.'

The lorry rocked from side to side in the shellfire like a small boat in a stormy sea. At times the cab was tilted at such an angle that they fell out of their seats, and Hu only righted the truck with a tremendous effort. As Hu clung to the steering-wheel his hands ran with sweat, and he clenched his teeth till they hurt. On either side were cliffs and deep ravines, and at any moment a whole cluster of shells might explode beside him. Not that he was worrying about this; the one thought in his mind was to follow Wang's instructions and press on without stopping.

'Left ... left ... ,' Wang was shouting hoarsely. 'Mind the crater ... slower ... slower ... right. ...'

As soon as the last word was out of his mouth flames leapt up all around the truck with powerful shock-waves that almost lifted it clear off the road. Wang was thrown back into his seat. Hu grabbed his arm with one hand and asked, 'Are you all right, Wang?'

'Don't stop. Never mind about me. Keep going.' Wang dragged himself up and seized hold of the window. 'Faster,' he shouted, louder than ever. 'Left ... left ... that's it ... carry on ... right, shell hole. ... '

The lorry went down the southern slope of the mountain round the hairpin bends. There was a continual explosion of shells on the road and the mountainside that showered the truck with a hail of stones and shrapnel. All Hu could hear was Wang's voice shouting, 'Left ... turn right ... carry on ... ' until they drove into a deep gully. Hu breathed a sigh of relief. 'We're through,' he said. Then he turned to Wang and added, 'But for your sharp eyes we'd have ended up in a ravine tonight.'

They drove along the gully for nearly a mile until somebody appeared from behind a boulder, stopped the lorry and asked, 'Are you the ammunition truck?'

Hu Wenfa jumped down from the cab and said, 'Yes. Are you the Second Detachment of the Zhenjiang unit?'

Before the other man had time to reply a group of men came out of another gully saying softly to each other, 'Hurry, the ammo's here.' They were all round the lorry in a moment.

'Have you come to help unload the truck?' Hu asked one of them who was wearing a greatcoat.

'No. We've come to collect the ammunition.'

'Blimey,' interrupted another soldier, 'you really had us worried. If you'd been any longer we'd have run right out. Got any grenades?'

'Plenty.'

'Do we need them! We've been hard at it ever since sunset. Let's get the stuff unloaded.'

Hu Wenfa could hear a continuous rumble of hand-grenades going off almost as fast as machine-guns on the other side of a nearby mountain. 'Wang,' he shouted in his excitment, 'come and help unload.'

The others were bustling on and around the lorry. With so many men on the job the load was soon off. Because he had been sweating heavily Hu was very thirsty, so he went into a dug-out with the ammunition for a drink of water. Thinking that Wang must be thirsty too after shouting so many instructions on the journey he filled a water-bottle for him. When he was almost back at the truck he called Wang a couple of times but nothing moved. He looked into the cab and saw Wang still slumped against the window with one arm dangling and the other cradling his head. Hu shook him by the shoulder. 'Hey, wake up. Time to turn round and go back.'

Wang still did not move.

Hu Wenfa put his hand out to feel his head and was horrified. He jumped into the cab, groped for the torch, and saw in its light that Wang's face was the colour of earth. There was no light in his half-closed eyes. One of Wang's hands was clutching the clothes on his chest. Blood was dripping from his wrist down to his trousers and the seat.

Hu Wenfa lifted him up and poured a little warm water into his mouth. He shouted loudly at him a couple of times. It was a very long time before he heard the familiar voice murmuring, 'Hu. . . .We got through . . . I won't be going back with you ... be very careful.... Whatever you do ... don't stop in the interdiction zones....'

Wang was growing heavier and heavier. Hu lifted up his head and looked through the windscreen at the lightning-like flashes from the other side of the black mountain in the distance and the red fireballs climbing into the sky. 'Open your eyes again and look, Wang,' he was thinking. 'Our boys are going to wipe them out.' As he brushed against Wang's icy cold hand his heart contracted and something warm welled up in his throat. He buried his head in Wang's chest and wept.

After Wang's death Hu Wenfa became rather quiet. He rarely rocked his head and whistled as he had before, and he was often seen lost in thought in front of the lorry. The political instructor and his comrades all felt sympathy and concern for him. They too were all saddened by Wang's sacrifice. Some of them even said anxiously when Hu Wenfa was not in earshot that they doubted whether he would finish his 35,000 kilometres of safe driving now that he had lost so good a mate.

In the tense days of that autumn Hu Wenfa's truck drove as usual along roads knee-deep in mud. He beat 42,000 kilometres before 7 November. The whole company held a meeting to celebrate and they expected that this would certainly cheer him up. He was as gloomy as ever. Even he could not have explained what was on his mind. As the truck drove through the Korean mountains pock-marked with craters, maple woods would flash past the windows. Every time he saw the rows of maples on some mountain pass he would think of his dead friend. Wang had been like a single maple tree on the plains of China. Compared to the vast forests it was next to nothing, but it was just such trees that made up the forests. Although maples did not have the scent of flowers they were more beautiful than any flower on earth, particularly when the cold winds of autumn bit through to the bone after the heavy frosts had begun.

His new mate had not been in the company long before he discovered that his teacher, Hu Wenfa, had the strange habit of putting a spray of maple leaves beside the picture of Chairman Mao in the corner of the cab. Once the truck started, the pink, crimson, and purple leaves would rustle and dance. In the light of an oncoming headlight they were like flames.

—Translated by W.J.F. Jenner

YU-WOL CHONG-NYON

Korea, the setting of The Nonrevolutionaries, *lies between China on the west, Japan on the east, and the Soviet Union on the north. Over the centuries of its history, the Korean nation has been buffeted by economic, political, and military struggles between its geographic neighbors, and further harassed by frequent interventions by other foreign powers (United States, Great Britain, France, Germany).*

In 1894 a war broke out between Japan and China, from which Japan emerged victorious and was ceded power over Korea. From 1894 to 1945 Korea was almost continuously under Japanese rule.

With the defeat of Japan, which ended World War II, Korea was partitioned at the 38th parallel. The country north of the parallel came under the influence of the U.S.S.R. South of the parallel, Korea was under a U.S. military government. This unnatural and unpopular decision created continual and growing tension on the peninsula which erupted in June 1950, when troops from North Korea launched a full-scale invasion of South Korea. The North Koreans, under the leadership of Kim Il-Sung, a former major in the Chinese Red Army, were determined to unify all of Korea under his communist government. During the war, which lasted from 1950 to 1953, North Koreans, augmented by Soviet aid and Chinese troops, and the South Koreans, augmented by United Nations (primarily U.S.) military assistance, fought a bloody contest. At one point the Communists pushed the southern forces almost off the southern end of the peninsula, so that only the port city of Pusan remained in South Korean control. Then, as the U.S. stepped up its assistance, the South Korean forces advanced to the Manchurian border at the Yalu river. Once again the North Koreans and Chinese pushed back, retaking Seoul. Finally the forces came to a general stalemate near the old 38th parallel division, which subsequently was re-established as the dividing line, in an armistice agreement signed on July 27, 1953.

In the story The Nonrevolutionaries *the confusion and anguish of the war is seen through the eyes of a young woman returning from a year's study in the West, "coming back to bring*

*the wisdom of the West to my 'underdeveloped' homeland." Her
horror at the senseless and brutal killings is heightened by an
acute awareness of the absurdity of the way "the fate of the world
was decided"—by presidents, chiefs of staff, and "other experts
on human welfare," arbitrarily drawing lines on a map. Reality
in this story is not political ideology but the rice and wine, the
flute and the harp, of the beloved homeland.*

*Yu-Wol Chong-Nyon is the pseudonym of a young Korean
woman. It means, literally, "Month-of-June-Youth," referring to
the generation coming to adulthood during and since the civil
war.*

The Nonrevolutionaries

Revolution, counterrevolution, nonrevolution.

The revolutionaries are executed by the counterrevolutionaries and the counterrevolutionaries by the revolutionaries.

The nonrevolutionaries are sometimes taken for revolutionaries and executed by the counterrevolutionaries, sometimes taken for counterrevolutionaries and executed by either
the revolutionaries or the counterrevolutionaries for no apparent reason at all.

—*Lu Hsun (1881–1936)*
—*Translated from Chinese by Chi-chen Wang*

Cursed be the men of the East. Cursed be the men of the West.
Cursed be those who have left my beloved homeland bleeding
and torn.

They banged on the doors. They hammered at the walls. Out!
Out! Everybody out! Everybody to the playfield.

With fear and with trembling we all got up, we got up out of
our blankets into the chilly dawn. My father and my mother,

my sisters and my brother. Out. *Out.* The shouting and the hammering continued. Out to the playfield.

"What about Ok-Sun?" my mother said to my father, pointing to me. "They don't know she's here. Maybe she should hide?"

"No, no," said my father. "They'll surely find her."

"But why? If we keep her hidden in the back, no one will see her."

"They will, they will. They're breaking in without warning. Only the night before they broke into twelve houses in our district. In the middle of the night, at two and three in the morning. They banged at the doors and pushed their way in, stamped into the houses with their muddy boots on and dragged the men away.

"With their boots on!" My mother was silent for a moment, shocked at this revelation of incredible boorishness. The poorest rag-picker, the most unlearned peasant, would never dream of entering another's home without removing his footwear.

But she returned to the argument. "I'm sure we can hide her safely—"

"No! No!" my father again protested. "Too dangerous. Better she go with all of us."

"But—"

But there was no time to argue. Out! *Out!* The shouting and the banging went on. They were still there, rounding up every man, woman, and child. Out I went, too, with my sisters and brother, my father and mother, out to the playfield.

I had returned home only a month ago. My year's scholarship had ended, and I was coming back to bring the wisdom of the West to my "underdeveloped" homeland. The boat had arrived at Seoul a day earlier than expected, but late at night. When I had reached home after midnight, none of the neighbors had seen me come. My father, glad as he and all the family were to see me, had said, "Enough. We'll go to bed and talk in the morning. She must be tired."

Tired I was, tired of the long, long voyage, still ill-adjusted to the many-houred change in time, so tired that I developed a fever of exhaustion that night. It was as though I had been holding it in until I could get back to my own bed before letting it go. For weeks I lay there sick.

It was at the beginning of my illness that the armies suddenly and without warning swarmed down from the north, blasting their way through my homeland, leaving us overnight under a strange regime, ruled by men of our own nation, but men warped and twisted by their training in a foreign land, by the rule of an oppressive hand, of cruel and unfeeling heart and mind.

In a faraway country on the other side of the globe, the President of the United States, the Prime Minister of His Majesty's Government, and the chairman of the Supreme Soviet, accompanied by their Chiefs of Staff and other experts on human welfare, had met. The map had glistened brightly before them with its greens and reds and yellows and blues. The fate of the world was decided. Here a cut, there a snip, and here a line. "For purposes of military convenience," the history books say, my beloved homeland was cut in two. Our minds and hearts, our families and lives were cut into shreds.

My beloved homeland! Will your rice and your wine ever taste the same again? Will your flutes and your harps ever sound the same again?

We were at the playfield once more. The playfield of so many mixed memories, now to be the site of the most sharply etched memory of them all. The playfield where with the girls of my class I had spent so many happy hours of childhood and adolescence. The playfield which had been built during the days of our Japanese lords, the days where here as everywhere in Korea we were taught to speak, write, and think only in a foreign tongue, when a phrase spoken in our mother tongue in a public place brought a slap on the face from the lords or their Korean vassals. The playfield where my father with all the other fathers had had to go so often to prostrate himself before the Shinto shrines. The playfield where our masters revealed a change of heart to us, where they suddenly called us brothers, members of the same race, fruit of the same cultural heritage, and "invited" our young men to join their armies to fight for the glory of our "common primordial ancestors." Then we knew that the war was truly going badly for them, that their men were dying.

The playfield! We waited in the chilly dawn for our new lords to guide us. We were there by the thousand, fathers and mothers, children and elders. I saw many neighbors I hadn't seen for well over a year, but they were too preoccupied to be surprised at my sudden reappearance. We waited in the chilly dawn for our new lords to guide us.

They came. They came with their heavy boots and their heavy rifles. They came dragging twelve men behind them. Twelve men we all knew. Twelve men we had grown up with.

The men with the boots and the rifles distributed themselves among the crowd. A hundred men or more. A man here, a man there. Everyone felt the alien presence close to his skin, everyone felt the gnawing cancer digging into his soul.

Their leader climbed up on the platform and slowly turned his eyes over us, at the sea of faces all around him. A signal, and one of the twelve men was set up next to him, one of the twelve men we knew. He was a clerk in our municipal office, a man as inoffensive as he was inefficient, a man who did his insignificant work as well as his limited abilities permitted him, a man whose main interest in his job consisted in receiving his pay regularly and going home to his family at the end of each day.

I had noticed his wife and children in the crowd.

"Comrades!" bellowed the leader. "Behold a traitor to the people. As you all know, the man you see before you has for years held in his hands the lives and well-being of all the people of this community. It is he who handles the rationing records, he who can decide how much rice you are to receive and when you are to get it. Comrades, an investigation of his records has revealed gross mismanagement of the rationing system of our community. When this treacherous criminal was directed to mend his ways, he offered nothing but resistance and reactionary proposals. For ten days now he has deliberately and malevolently sabotaged every effort on our part to establish the system of food distribution in this community on a rational and an honest basis. Comrades," he cried out again to the crowd, "what shall we do with this traitor?"

"Kill him!" The hundred men who had distributed them-

selves among the crowd had raised their fists and roared out this response with a single voice: *"Kill him!"*

The leader on the platform nodded in approval. "Thank you, comrades. That is indeed the only proper treatment for traitors."

He took his heavy pistol out of its holster, held it against the man's temple, and pulled the trigger. The clerk slumped to the boards of the platform. The crowd gasped.

"Death to traitors!" roared the hundred men. The man's blood trickled through the cracks between the boards and stained the soil of the playfield.

Another man was hoisted up onto the platform to take his place.

"Comrades," again cried the leader, "behold a traitor to the people. . . ."

An excited murmur went through the crowd as we recognized the man. I heard my brother whisper to my father, "Daddy! Isn't he the leader of the Communists?"

"Yes!"

"Then why?"

"Three kinds—Communists who've been in South Korea all the time; those trained in Russia and China; those trained in North Korea since the partition. They're fighting among themselves already."

The leader had finished his charges. Again he cried to the crowd: "Comrades, what shall we do with this traitor?"

"Kill him!" the hundred shouted as before.

But this time the leader looked displeased. "Comrades, I ask you what to do with a traitor and there is hardly any response! Comrades, think it over well. Take your time and reflect on the matter. I will ask once again a minute from now."

The hundred men glared at us, swung around in their places, and looked us each in the eye in turn. "I wonder if there could be any traitors here among us," they said for all to hear.

Then again the leader turned to the crowd. "Comrades," he bellowed once more, "What shall we do with this traitor to the people?"

"Kill him!" roared the hundred.

"Kill him!" we cried with our lips.

The leader looked pleased. He again unholstered his pistol,

pressed it to the man's head, and his blood joined that of the other, dripping down to the soil of the playfield.

Ten more times did the leader harangue us. Ten more times did we shudder as we cried aloud with our lips, *"Kill him!"* Ten more times did the blood of a Korean stain the soil of Korea.

We watched and we trembled as the chilly dawn unfolded into the chilly day.

> My beloved homeland!
> Will your rice and your wine
>   ever taste the same again?
> Will your flutes and your harps
>   ever sound the same again?
>
> Cursed be the men of the East.
> Cursed be the men of the West.
> Cursed be those
>   who have left my beloved homeland
>   bleeding and torn.

—Translated from the Korean by the author
and Daniel L. Milton

FANG SHUMIN

This story from the People's Republic of China reflects the same ideological commitments as are evident in Maple Leaves. *As in most modern Chinese literature, politics comes first, artistry second.*

While Maple Leaves *was set in the war-time era of the early 1950s,* The Moon on a Frosty Morning *reflects the peaceful but difficult times of the early 1960s in China. Owing to a succession of bad harvest years, the collective agriculture system had come under great strain. Some workers, like Cassia's husband in the story, grew weary in the struggle and opted for an easier*

way of life. Such recalcitrance only pointed up in sharper con-
trast the heroism of the faithful.

Characteristic of the commitments of modern Chinese litera-
ture is the representation of a young woman as the dominant
figure in the story. While Cassia is kind to her mother-in-law
and loving to her children, her primary concern is for the com-
munal life and integrity of the village. It is one of the striking
social changes of the Chinese revolution that women, who for
centuries were kept in extraordinarily subordinate roles in
China, have been pushed to the forefront in the social, political,
and literary life of the country.

One reason for the selection of this story, which is very simi-
lar in style and theme to much of modern Chinese short fiction,
is that there is a subtle element of human ambiguity coexisting
with the ideological message. As Cassia waits for the return of
her despised and cowardly husband, we are made aware that, in
spite of her heroic facade, she is a real person with real human
emotions—anger, pity, desire, regret, revenge. The lack of a
definite, final resolution adds to the general air of credibility.

The Moon on a Frosty Morning

Cassia had just fed her one-year-old baby and was covering her
head with a towel to go to the fields, when her four-year-old son
Shigour said to his granny, 'Why are you making shoes for my
father? He's away.'

'I'm not making them for that spineless father of yours.' She
rubbed the awl against her hair and thrust it hard and angrily
through the sole of the shoe. 'I'm making them for your
mother.'

'But her feet are too small for those shoes,' Shigour protested solemnly.

'Out of the way, brat.' With Shigour driven away the old lady
handed her daughter-in-law the black canvas shoes for which
she had just finished making the sole.

'Oh well,' she said, smiling till her eyes creased right up, 'you
can't blame the boy. You've been so busy these last few months
rushing all over the place through mud and water. No wonder
these great boots aren't proper women's shoes. Try them on.'

Cassia tried on the new shoes and found that they fitted

perfectly. Even she could not help laughing. Then she tucked a sickle in her belt and hurried off to the threshing-ground.

The threshing-ground lay to the north of Bean Hamlet, as the village was called. It was bigger than last year, and heaped within new fencing in the middle of it were two huge mounds of bright red sorghum that had yet to be milled; the corn-cobs stacked in frames built of sorghum stalks gleamed in the autumn sun like a golden palace, and the piles of late millet were pushing at the fence round the threshing-floor, making it lean like an overhanging cliff.

The rich fragrance of grain drifted across the threshing-floor. Although it was now late autumn and the light northwest wind blowing across the field was reminding everyone that the cold season had begun, Cassia felt only warmth at the sight of the fine harvest on the floor as she cut off the sorghum tops with her sickle.

Eyes sparkled as people returning to other counties from market passed the threshing-floor. They sighed with admiration and said, 'What a good harvest they've had in this team.'

'Indeed,' somebody agreed awkwardly. 'Looks even better than the Cherry Orchard Team we passed earlier.'

'A fat lot you know. They left the famous Cherry Orchard Team behind months ago.'

'Which team is this then?' asked the ill-informed man with another sigh.

'Bean Hamlet.'

'At last. So this is the famous "poor Bean Hamlet",' a voice said with a hoarse chuckle. 'The paupers have managed a decent harvest this year—like a blind man catching an eel.'

This last remark stung Cassia as she worked. There was an explosion in her head as she flung a bundle of sorghum tops to the ground, flicked her short, untidy hair back and shot a furious glare at the hoarse, middle-aged man. He blushed in fear and embarrassment. She softened her expression, suddenly realizing that she had no reason to lose her temper like an eighteen-year-old. A woman of thirty-two should be more tolerant; besides, she was deputy work-team leader. She waved to the men in the road and smiled at them. 'Are you thirsty, friends? Take a rest on the threshing-floor.'

'No thanks,' one of them replied. 'Looks like a good harvest you've had this year.'

'It certainly is,' she shouted happily, stepping back with her strong legs. An old man in a little felt hat jumped off his grey donkey and croaked, 'Hey, comrade, come here, comrade.'

A cheeky youth beside him who was grinning all over his face grabbed him and whispered: 'You're asking for trouble, you shameless old devil. You're not on comrade terms with her.'

When Cassia heard this she ran to the fence and said to the old man, 'Never mind that nonsense, uncle. You go ahead and call me "comrade" as bold as you please. What do you want to say?'

The old man shifted the pouch-sack on his shoulder before relaxing and letting himself reply. 'I came through here on the way to market during the floods in July, and the oceans of water covering the fields made me think that you'd been washed out again. After two bad years running I was sure you'd be going hungry again this year. I'd never have dreamed you could get this good a harvest.'

Cassia waved her sickle and laughed, her eyebrows raised. 'You can't have been to market since then. You may have seen the floods, but you didn't see how we fought against them.'

The old man now apparently understood everything. He took off his hat, nodded, jumped back on his donkey, and rode away. Cassia smiled as she watched them go off towards the Grand Canal ferry. The full evening sun cast a golden light over her tanned face. The boundless plain beyond the village and the fields of green wheat shoots that covered it gave her a feeling of expanse and excitement. At the same time she was a little depressed. She had wanted badly to tell those strangers who did not know the story how their village had fought against the flood. But she must put all such ideas out of her head. Anyone would think that Bean Hamlet was not tough enough. As she gazed into the distance deep in thought she saw a trail of yellow dust rising from the road behind the brick-kiln. She knew it came from a rider and trembled as she realized that it must be Big Wu galloping at that speed. Just then she heard some women on the threshing-floor crying out, 'It's Big Wu, it's him, it's Big Wu.' Unable to think of anything else she dropped her sickle and ran after the other women and the children towards the road. Shielding her eyes with her right hand she made out a chestnut horse pounding through the dust, and the bare-chested man astride it was indeed Big Wu, the team leader.

'Big Wu.' She was waving and shouting.

The chestnut horse carried its rider to the fence. The tall rider, a man in his forties, dismounted with a leap into a cloud of dust and put his hand on the horse's back.

'Have you been impatient waiting for me to come back? Come and take a look at our horse.'

Cassia was the first to reach it. 'It's a fine sturdy beast,' she said.

'It's kicking,' shouted Big Wu, deliberately frightening the women and children so that they scattered like chickens. Cassia alone stepped forward and grabbed it by the mane. When it shook its head violently, she pinched its nostrils shut and forced its mouth open.

'Be quiet, you devil.' It whinnied, pawed the ground, and then calmed down. 'What did you want to make it do that for?' she said to Big Wu, adding, 'Tell me quickly, how old is it?'

'Six. It's a strong one all right.'

As she kneaded the horse's back she could not hold back her praises. 'And such a glossy coat. What breed is it?' 'It's Mongolian—from beyond the Great Wall.' 'Good.' Then she anxiously asked, 'Have we bought her yet?' 'I paid on the nail and I've got the papers to prove it.' 'Good.' Cassia tugged at the reins as she said, 'Yesterday Tiedan and I built the stable, and last night Grandpa Baishun was chosen as stock-keeper. He's so pleased he's spent the morning cooking and rolling feed. I'll take him along to be watered and fed. I've got the cart with iron-rimmed wheels ready at the granary door to take the state grain, so you'd better go there and check the grain. Now that we've got our horse we must load the cart tomorrow morning, and I'm going to drive it. After two years on relief grain from the government our team must be first to deliver.'

'Fine, fine,' Big Wu cut in. 'You take him over to Grandpa Baishun for a feed, and I'll be with you when I've checked the grain.' Just as they were about to move Big Wu suddenly remembered something. 'Cassia,' he shouted. 'Wait a moment. I've got good news for you.'

'I didn't hear a magpie this morning,' she said, turning her head, 'so I don't see how there can be any good news for me.'

'Shigour's dad, your husband Waizi, is coming back from Cherry Orchard tonight.'

Cassia was shattered. This sudden news was like being hit on the head with a brick. Try as she did to control the anger that surged up inside her she could not help her face turning pale and her voice shaking as she replied, 'Don't you dare mention his name. Our family is getting along very well without him.'

'Keep your temper, Cassia,' said Big Wu. 'If he's seen he was in the wrong and is willing to come back you should be ready to help him. The return of the prodigal is something to be pleased about.'

'So am I expected to send a bridal chair with eight porters to fetch him?' Cassia asked indignantly. 'If he had the nerve to leave he can have the nerve to sleep out in the village's reed beds.'

'Hmm,' said Big Wu. 'Waizi wasn't in that sort of mood at all. When we met at the market he grabbed hold of me and wouldn't let me go. And when he asked me about his mother, yourself, and the two kids, his eyes were red although he is a grown man.'

'It's none of his business,' Cassia cut in, sounding as if she were gnashing her teeth. 'We haven't starved to death.'

'Listen,' said Big Wu. ' "Waizi," I said to him, "your wife has changed. These last months she's really been doing things. She's a candidate Party member and has been elected deputy team leader." '

'You seem to have enjoyed gossiping with him, you old gas-bag,' she interrupted again.

'The best part of the story is still to come,' grinned Big Wu. 'He hung on to my hand until I said, "Let me go, I've got to buy a horse for the team." Tears were pouring down his cheeks, so I asked him if he wasn't all right staying with his in-laws. "Don't ask me about that," he said. "I've heard all the news from Bean Hamlet. If they'll have me back again I'll. . . . " "What'll you do?" I asked him, and he started howling. "Never mind, Waizi," I said. "If you know you've gone wrong you should come back and admit it; from now on you must forge ahead with all the rest of us. I'll back you up this time. When will you be coming home?" His answer came back like a shot: "Tonight".'

Cassia was so angry that she stamped her foot and flung out her arm. 'I never signed any undertaking to have him. Even if he does come I won't have him back.'

'Oh, well,' said Big Wu, still trying to win her round, 'you should at least let him stay tonight. He's coming back this evening, whether you let him stay on can be decided later.

After all, we can't ignore him now that he's turning over a new leaf. Look! The horse is eating Old Deng's fence. Take him away this moment!'

It was night by now. The north-west wind that had been blowing across the plain had dropped, and the frozen stars shivered in the late autumn cold. Cassia let the horse relieve itself, then watered it beside the well. Grandpa Baishun tethered it in its newly-built stable and fed it as carefully as if he were fingering a jewel. A moment later Big Wu was there, standing under the swinging hurricane lamp and saying happily, 'Mmm. That feed smells good.' With a nod to Grandpa Baishun he said to Cassia, 'I've checked the state grain. The stuff in the sacks is all up to standard—first-rate stuff—so it can be taken in first thing tomorrow. When I've had a drink of water I must be off to the river bend to hear how the labourers from our village are getting on with the canal. Which of the men should take the cart?'

She stretched out her arm. 'I told you I was going to drive, didn't I?' He shot a sidelong glance at her and, seeing the determined way her eyebrows were raised, could only smile. It would have been a waste of time to say anything more.

She was a long time settling in the new horse with Grandpa Baishun before going home. As it was the end of the lunar month there was not even a sliver of moon above the trees. She felt her way into the courtyard and grimly remembered to wedge the gates shut by sticking a pole hard against them. In the house she heard her mother-in-law ask sleepily from the darkness, 'Is that you back? Shall I light the lamp?'

'No,' Cassia replied quickly. 'Are the children asleep? Why are you still awake?'

'I rocked them to sleep. Why did you have to make such a noise shutting the gates? We haven't used the date-wood pole for months, so why shut the gates with it tonight?'

'I thought the wind would blow them open.'

'Fool,' the old woman went on, 'idiot. Didn't you notice that the wind had dropped ages ago?'

Cassia did not want to tell her mother-in-law that Waizi was coming back that night in case the news gave her a seizure and killed her. She climbed on to the kang, but no matter which way she lay she could not get to sleep. She gritted her teeth and hardened her heart, longing to hear him trying to force the gates while she lay there on the kang and would not get up to open them. He could freeze—he had asked for it. As she lay there her heart would start to pound at the slightest sound from the yard, but as she waited she heard no loud noise to follow.

An evening in July flashed before her eyes. That night when, with one cloudburst following another, she had waded home from a team meeting through the floods, her feet heavy with mud, supporting herself with difficulty on the vegetable-garden fence. Just as she and her mother-in-law had been looking for a big spade in the shed they had heard squelching footsteps in the yard. She had opened the door and said, 'Oh, you're back.'

The stocky Waizi had come in and was wiping the mud off his feet while she lit the lamp and asked him, 'Where've you been? We shouted ourselves hoarse trying to get you to the team meeting.'

'I went to Cherry Orchard,' he had said.

'What a thing to do,' she had replied, flaring up. 'You just don't care about the team's crops. Big Wu's been elected team leader and he'll be a good one. He's taken men and women from our village down to the river bend as fast as they can go to drain the water out. But you had time to go and visit the children's granny. What do you mean by it at a time like this?'

'You want to know what I was doing?' said Waizi with a laugh. 'I was negotiating. It's all settled. Tomorrow the whole family moves to Cherry Orchard.'

Cassia had been stunned. 'What? What did you say?'

'What's the point of thinking about nothing but work all the time? Can't you see that this poverty-ridden hollow has been a frog pond for two years running? Even the team's donkey has starved to death. Now this year's rains have drowned us again. There's nothing to stay for. The sooner we find some dry land the better.'

Cassia had realized at once what he was thinking. 'Frightened of starving?' she had said. 'Want to sneak off, don't you?'

Waizi had tilted his head to one side and replied, 'Say what you like as long as you understand that tomorrow we're shutting the place up and going, bedding and all.'

'Who's going?' she had asked.

'All of us,' he had said.

At this she had flared up and shouted furiously, 'You can clear off by yourself. You may have it all nicely worked out, but nobody's going with you.'

The stocky Waizi had rushed forward and grabbed her. 'Stay where you are. Where are you going with that spade?'

'Get away from me,' Cassia had said, breaking away from him. 'I'm going to drain off the water and guard the dike with Big Wu. This is a crisis. I've got no time to waste talking to you.' Waizi had raised his hand, but Cassia had moved her spade instantly to parry it, screaming 'Don't touch me. If you lay a finger on me you'll get a dose of this.' With their quarrel the room had felt as hot as a kiln; gongs were being beaten outside to tell everyone to go to the dike at once, the boy was crying, and the adults were shouting at each other. It had been too much for the old woman, who released a torrent of abuse on him: 'Worthless wretch, evil son, get the hell out of here and eat and drink as well as you can.'

When Cassia had come back the next day from her work at the river she had tried to win him round, but he was so set in his twisted ideas that when she had finished he just replied, 'The flood waters are here to stay. This dump won't ever get rich. Are you coming with me or aren't you?'

'No,' Cassia had said, steeling herself, 'I won't go.'

'If you're not coming that's your lookout. Mother and Shigour are coming with me.'

The old lady had jabbed her finger at his nose and said, 'You're not going to take even a hair of any of us, not one hair.'

Red-faced and hoarse, Waizi had issued his last warning: 'Very well then; don't come if you don't want to. But don't expect me to be nice to you when you come begging from me in the autumn.'

This had made the old lady angrier than ever: 'If that's how you're going to talk to us you'd better clear out at once. Go off and hatch your plans, my fine lad. There may not be much flesh on us but our bones are hard, really hard.'

Waizi had wrapped up his bedding and gone, his pipe between his teeth.

His last superior glance at them was deeply etched on Cassia's mind. The thought of it still made her almost burst with indignation; she gave an involuntary and contemptuous

snort. This woke her mother-in-law, who rolled over and asked:
'Are you cold?'

'No, mother, I'm boiling hot.'

She tried as hard as she could to calm herself down as she lay there in the dark, her eyes wide open, struggling to drive away the image that flickered in front of them. But it hovered there more clearly than ever. She imagined him coming back and apologizing to her. She would tell him straight out that what he'd done had been completely wrong, and it had all been because he had not had confidence in the group and the people's commune.... She fell into a doze. When she woke again a little later there was still no sound from the courtyard. 'He hasn't come back,' she thought. The crescent moon setting in the south-west was filtering its light through the window, and she could hear the first cock-crow of the morning. She could stay in bed no longer. The old lady leant over to her and said:

'Why are you tossing and turning so?'

'Keep your voice down, mother.' Cassia sat up smartly and felt for her clothes. 'I've got to get up early to take the tax grain in.'

'You'll be frozen right through this early in the morning,' the old lady said, 'so mind you wear a jacket over your green tunic. I finished the soles of your new shoes last night and put them by your pillow. Have you found them?'

'I've put them on,' Cassia replied.

'It'll be a long, cold journey, so wait till I've boiled you some noodles and egg.'

'No thanks.' Cassia got down from the kang. 'I must be on my way before the third cock-crow. I can get something to eat on my way through Zimu township.'

She groped lightly for her child's head, kissed his lips, and went out. She felt the cold in the courtyard at once, pulling her warm hands straight away from the frozen window-sill and sucking in her breath. There had been a frost that night, the first since last winter, and the young crows perched in the locust tree in the yard were cheeping miserably. Some dead leaves, covered in white, were drifting to the ground. She looked up again at the golden crescent of the moon in the southwestern sky and at the stars shimmering in the cold air, overcome with a warm feeling of pity. It had been the height of summer when Waizi left wearing only a thin shirt and trousers. He would choose the cold season to come back, the pig-headed fool. Well, if he wanted to come back he'd have to change his way of thinking.

She regretted her anger of the previous night. He hadn't come back, so she need not have blocked the gates too securely. She went over and worked the heavy date-wood pole loose. As she stepped through the gates all her courage could not stop her from gasping with fright: there was somebody squatting in the shadows outside.

'Who's that?' she called.

The man did not look up. He stayed there with his arms clasping his shoulders and his head buried in them.

There was no need to ask any question. The faint moonlight was bright enough for her to see that it was Waizi.

—Translated by W.J.F. Jenner

SINAI C. HAMADA

Tanabata's Wife *is set in Baguio, sometimes called the summer capital of the Philippines. Located in the mountains some 150 miles north of Manila, the cool, clear air of Baguio provides a welcome relief from the summer heat of the central plains. The United States maintains a large recreation area, Camp John Hay, in the city of Baguio; primarily used as a vacation spot for U.S. military personnel, Camp John Hay is a major source of employment for the local Filipino population.*

The Philippines endured, throughout its history, long periods of colonial occupation, first by the Spanish and then by the Americans. During the Second World War the Americans were driven out by the Japanese, who controlled the islands until 1944. The Philippines became an independent republic in 1946, though continuing to maintain close ties with the United States.

Evidence of all these influences appears in the story. Fas-ang is an Igorot, a mountain tribe centered in Bontoc, toward the northern end of the island of Luzon. Her language is a mixture of her native tongue ("kaingins"), with elements of Spanish ("gracias"). Her husband, Tanabata, may well be one of the many Japanese soldiers who chose to remain in the Philippines after the war or returned to settle there when hostilities were over. Camp John Hay, at which Fas-ang's lover was employed, and the cine (movies) in Baguio to which Fas-ang becomes so attracted, are evidences of continuing American influence.

The story presents these elements without political overtones. It is a tale of basic human needs and desires, which transcend cultural bounds.

Sinai Hamada is a practicing lawyer and the editor of the Baguio Midland Courier.

Tanabata's Wife

Fas-ang first came to Baguio by way of the Mountain Trail. When at last she emerged from her weary travel over the mountains, she found herself just above the Trinidad Valley. From there, she overlooked the city of Baguio itself.

Baguio was her destination. Along with three other women, she had planned to come to work on the numerous roads that were being built around the city. Native women were given spades to shovel the earth from the hillsides, and so make way for the roads that were being cut.

They had almost arrived. Yet Fas-ang knew of no place where she could live in the city while waiting to be taken in as a laborer. Perhaps she would stay in the workers' camp and be packed with the other laborers in their smelly quarters. She had heard a lot about tiered beds, the congestion in the long, low-roofed house for the road workers.

It was mid-afternoon. The four women and three men, new immigrants from Bontoc, walked on the long straight road of the Trinidad Valley. They had never before in their lives seen a road so long and straight. After the regular up and down journey over the hills, the level road was tedious and slow to travel on.

Plodding along, they at last left the valley behind, passed through the narrow gap of the Trinidad River, and entered

Lukban Valley. All along the road, the sight was a succession of cabbage plots, more and more.

And when they passed Lukban Valley and came to Kisad Valley still there were rows and rows of cabbage.

But now the sun was sinking low behind the brown hills in the west. And the company thought of their shelter for the night. For they had one more steep hill to climb before the city laborers' camp. So they had been told. And their feet ached painfully. Was there no door open for them among the thatched homes in the valley?

It was then that they came to the house of Tanabata-san. The Japanese gardener was looking out through his tiny window as they were about to pass on. He halted them.

"Are you looking for work?" the gardener called out in his broken dialect.

"Indeed we are, my lord," one of the strangers replied.

"If you like, I have work for two women, in my garden," Tanabata offered.

The men looked questioningly at the women. "Which of you would like to stay?" one man asked.

Only Fas-ang was willing to consider the gardener's offer. She stepped forward. "How much would you give me?" she demanded.

"Ten pesos."

"Ten pesos?" Fas-ang asked for twelve, but Tanabata would not agree to that. Fas-ang reflected for a moment, and then confided to her companions. "Guess I'll stay. There is but a difference of two pesos between what I'll get here and my wage if I become a road worker. Who knows? My lot here may even be better."

One of the remaining three women was also persuaded to stay after Fas-ang had made her decision. Tanabata was smiling as he watched the two make up their minds.

The rest of the company were going on their way. "So, you two will stay," the eldest of the group said, affecting a superior air. "Well if you think it is best for both of you, then it is all right. You need not worry over us, for we shall go on and reach the camp early tonight."

In this way, Fas-ang first lent herself to Tanabata. She was then at the height of womanhood. Her cheeks were ruddy, though not as rosy as in her girlhood. She had a buxom breast, the main charm of her sturdy self. As she walked, her footsteps were heavy. And anyone would admit that she was indeed pretty.

Tanabata had had no wife. For a long time now, he had been looking for one among the native women, hoping he would find one who might consent to marry him. But none did he ever find, until Fas-ang, guided by fate, came. He had almost sent for a Japanese wife from his homeland. He had her picture. But it would have cost him much.

Would Fas-ang, by chance, learn to like him and later agree to their marriage? This was only a tiny thought in the mind of Tanabata as he sat one evening looking wistfully at Fas-ang. She was washing her feet by the water ditch in front of the house. Every now and then, she lifted her skirt above her knees, and Tanabata saw her clear, bright skin, tempting him.

After a time, Fas-ang herself would watch Tanabata. As they sat before their supper, she would cast furtive glances at him across the low, circular table. He was bearded. Sometimes, he let his beard grow for three days, and his unshaven, hairy face was ugly to look at. Only with a clean countenance and in his blue suit did Fas-ang like him at all.

Well-dressed, Tanabata-san would walk on Sundays to the market fair. Close behind him followed one of his laborers, carrying two heavy baskets over his shoulder. The baskets overflowed with the minor produce of the garden: strawberries, celery, tomatoes, spinach, radishes, and "everlasting" flowers. Fas-ang, in her gayest Sunday dress would trail in the rear. She was to sell garden products at the market.

In the afternoon, the fair would be over. Fas-ang would go home with a heavy handbag. She would arrive to find Tanabata, usually tipsy, with a half-emptied bottle still before him on the table.

Fas-ang would lay the bag of money on his crossed legs. "That is the amount the vegetables have brought us," she would report.

"Good." And Tanabata would break into a happy smile. He always said *gracias* after that, showing full trust in Fas-ang. He would pick out two half-peso pieces and give them to her. "Here, take this. They are for you. Buy yourself whatever you like with them." For he was a prosperous, generous gardner.

On weekdays, there was hard and honest work in the garden. The other native woman had gone away when she saw that she was not favored as Fas-ang was. So, Fas-ang, when she was not cooking, stayed among the cabbage rows picking worms. All that Tanabata did was to take care of the seedlings in the shed house. Also, he did most of the transplanting, since he alone had the sensitive fingers that could feel the animate sense of the soil. He had but little area to superintend, and only three farmhands to look after.

Fas-ang liked the daily turns that were her lot. Little by little she learned to do the domestic chores. Early in the morning she rose to cook. Before noon she cooked again. And in the evening likewise. She washed clothes occasionally, and more when the laundress came irregularly. She swept the house. And, of course, she never forgot to leave a tea kettle steaming over live embers. Anytime, Tanabata might come in and sip a cup of tea.

Immediately after noon on weekdays, when the sun was hot and the leaves were almost wilting, Tanabata liked to stroll and visit his neighbor, Okamoto-san. They were of the same province in Japan, Hiroshimaken. Okamoto had a Benguet woman for a wife. Kawane was an industrious and amiable companion. The only fault Okamoto found in Kawane was her ignorance. She had no idea of the world beyond her small valley.

One afternoon, Tanabata as usual paid his friend a visit. This was of great consequence, for he had a mind to ask Okamoto if he thought Fas-ang could be a fit wife for him. Tanabata was slow in broaching the subject to his friend, but he was direct:

"I think I shall marry that woman," Tanabata said.

"Which woman—Fas-ang?" Okamoto asked.

"Yes."

"She is a good woman, I think. She seems to behave well."

"I have known her only for a short time. Do you think she will behave as well always?" Tanabata asked earnestly.

Okamoto was hesitant and would not be explicit. "I cannot tell. But look at my wife. She's a peaceful woman," he answered simply.

"There, my good friend," Tanabata reminded his neighbor, "you forget that your wife is of the Benguet tribe, while Fas-ang is of the Bontoc tribe."

"Yet they are good friends—as much as we are," was Okamoto's bright rejoinder. And they both laughed.

Two days later Tanabata proposed to Fas-ang. He had frequently teased her before. But now he was gravely concerned about what he had to tell. He had great respect for this sturdy native woman.

He called Fas-ang into the big room where she heretofore seldom entered except to clean. It was dimly lighted. Fas-ang went in, unafraid. It seemed she had anticipated this. She sat close beside him on a trunk. Tanabata talked carefully, convincingly, and long. He explained to her as best as he could his intentions. At last, she yielded. Without ceremony and without the law, they were wedded by a tacitly sworn agreement between themselves.

As before Fas-ang did not find it difficult to tend the truck garden. To be sure, it was sometimes dull. Now and then she would get exasperated with the routine work. But only for a short time. Ordinarily, she was patient, bending over the plants as she rid them of their worms, or gathering them for the sale in the market. Her hands had been trained now to handle with care the tender seedlings, which had to be prodded to grow luxuriantly.

When the sunbeams filled the valley, and the dewy leaves were glistening, it was a joy to watch the fluttering white butterflies that flitted all over the garden. They were pests, for their coming in the bright morning would stir the laborers to be up and doing before they, themselves, were outdone by the insects.

In time, Fas-ang was introduced to Japanese customs. Thus she learned to use chopsticks after being prevailed upon by Tanabata; they had a zinc tub outside their hut in which they heated water and took a bath in the evening; Fas-ang pickled radishes after the Japanese fashion, salting them in a barrel; she began to use wooden shoes, though of the Filipino variety, and left them outside their bedroom before she retired; she became used to drinking tea and pouring much *toyo* sauce on their food; mattresses too, and no longer a plain mat, formed her bedding.

A year after they were married they had a child, a boy. The baby was a darling. Tanabata decided to celebrate. He gave a baptismal party to which were invited his Japanese friends. They drank *saki*, ate Japanese seaweeds, pickles, canned fish, and many other dainties.

But Fas-ang, in all this revelry, could not understand the chattering of her guests. She was very quiet, holding the baby in her arms.

The men (there were no women visitors) had brought gifts for the baby and the mother. Fas-ang was very much delighted. She repeatedly muttered her *gracias* to all as the gifts were piled before her.

Then the men consulted the Japanese calendar. The child was given the name Kato. And the guests shouted *banzai* many times, tossing glassfuls of *saki* to the ceiling. They wished the mother and child good luck.

Tanabata was most solicitous toward Fas-ang as she began to recover from the emaciation caused by her strenuous childbirth. He would not allow her to go out. She must stay indoors for a month. It was another Japanese custom.

At length, when August had passed, Fas-ang once more stepped out into the sunshine, warm and free. The pallor of her cheeks had gone. She was alive and young again. Her usual springy steps came back and she walked briskly, full of strength and passion.

But what news of home? Fas-ang yearned to hear from her people back in Bisao, Bontoc. Had the *kaingins* been planted with *camote* and corn? Her kinsmen had heard of her delivering a child, and they sent a boy-cousin to inquire about her. He was told to see if Fas-ang lived happily, and if her Japanese husband really treated her well. If not, they would do him harm. The Bontocs, or *busok* are very fierce.

The cousin came. Tanabata entertained the cousin well. He bought short pants for the Igorot boy and told him to do away with his G-string. The boy was much pleased. After a week, the boy said he would go back. And Tanabata bought some more clothes for him.

Fas-ang saw her cousin off. Tanabata was then in the shed house, cultivating the seedlings. Fas-ang instructed her cousin well; "Tell Ama and Ina I am happy here. They must not worry about me. My husband is kind, and I'm never in want. Give them this little money that I have saved for them. You see, I have a child, so I shall live here long yet. But I do wish to go home sometime and see Ama and Ina. Often I feel homesick."

She wept. And when her cousin saw her tears, he wept too. Then they parted.

It was no hidden truth that Tanabata loved his wife dearly. In every way, he tried to show his affection. Once, he had not allowed her to go to the city to see the movies. But he repented afterwards and sent her there without her asking.

Fas-ang soon became a *cine* addict. She went to shows with one of the garden boys. Sometimes, she took her baby along. She carried the baby on her back. They had to take a kerosene lamp with them to light their way coming home. They would return near midnight.

Tanabata, alone, would stay at home. He sat up late reading his books of Japanese novels. When Fas-ang arrived, she would be garrulous with what she had seen. Tanabata would tuck her under the thick blankets to warm her cold feet. She would then easily fall asleep, and after she had dozed off, he would himself retire.

More, and more, Fas-ang liked to attend the shows. The city was two miles away. But that did not matter. The theater was fascinating. Moreover, Fas-ang admitted, she often met several of her relatives and townmates in the theater. They, too, had learned to frequent the *cine*. Together they had a good time.

Tanabata asked Okamoto what he thought of Fas-ang's frequenting the shows. Okamoto, being less prosperous and more conservative, did not favor it. He advised Tanabata to stop her. But Tanabata was too indulgent with Fas-ang even to intimate such a thing to her. Though inclined to be cautious, he loved her too much to deny her any pleasure she desired.

Thus Fas-ang, after the day's duties, would run off to the show. Tanabata had grown even more lenient. He could never muster courage to restrain her, much less scold her. She never missed a single change of program in the theater. Tanabata did not know what to do with her. He could not understand what drew her to the *cine*. For his part, he was wholly uninterested in the screen shows; he had attended but once and that a long time ago, and he had been disgusted. Still Fas-ang continued to attend them as devotedly as ever.

One night she did not come home. She returned in the morning. Tanabata asked where she had slept, and she said, "With my cousin at the Campo Filipino." She had felt too lazy to walk all the way down to the valley, she said.

That whole day she remained at home. Tanabata went out to the garden. Fas-ang rummaged among her things. She tied them into a bundle which she hid in the corner and she dressed her child.

Then, at midnight, when Tanabata was sound asleep, she escaped. She carried her child and ran down the road where her lover was waiting. They would return to Bontoc, their native place. The man had been dismissed from the military post at Camp John Hay.

Fas-ang left a note on the table before she left. It had been written by the man who had seduced her. It read: *Do not follow us. We are returning home to Bontoc. If you follow us, you will be killed on the way!*

When Tanabata had the letter read to him, he dared not pursue the truant lovers. The note was too positive to mean anything but death if disobeyed. He was grieved. And for three days, he could hardly eat. He felt bitter, being betrayed and deserted. Helpless, he was full of hatred for the man who had lured his wife away.

Okamoto, faithful indeed, came to comfort his friend. He offered to come with his wife and live with Tanabata. But Tanabata would not consider the proposition. Nor could he be comforted. He politely begged his friends to leave him alone. He had suddenly become gloomy. He sat in his hut all day and drank much liquor. He shut himself in. The truck garden was neglected.

Months passed. The rows of cabbage were rotting; Tanabata was thought to be crazy. He did not care what happened to the plants. He had dismissed the new helpers that were left him. Weeds outgrew the seedlings. The rainy season set in, and the field was devastated by a storm. Tanabata lived on his savings.

The rainy season passed. Sunny, cold November came to the hills. In a month more, Tanabata would perhaps go home to die in Japan. His despondency had not been lessened. When he thought of his lost boy, he wept all the more.

Then, one evening, Fas-ang came back. She stood behind the

house, surveying the wreck left of what was formerly a blooming garden. She had heard back home, from wayfarers who had returned, of Tanabata. The man who had stolen the affections of Fas-ang had left her.

"Your Japanese husband is said to be ruining himself," some reported.

"He pines for you and his boy," others brought back.

"It is said he is thinking of going home across the sea, but he must see his little son first," still others told her.

Fas-ang at once decided. "Then I must return to him before it is too late." And so she came.

In the twilight, she stood, uncertain, hesitant. She heard the low mournful tune arising from the bamboo flute that Tanabata was playing. What loneliness! Fas-ang wondered if that now seemingly forbidding house was still open to her. Could she disperse the gloom that had settled upon it? There was a woman's yearning in her. But she wavered in her resolve, feeling ashamed.

The music had ceased. She almost turned away when the child, holding her hand, cried aloud. Tanabata looked out of the window, startled. He saw the mother and child. He rushed outside, exultant. Gently, he took them by the hands and led them into the house. Then he lighted the big lamp that had long hung from the ceiling, unused.

MORLI DHARAM

The characters in Dada *are members of Manila's small Hindu community. "Dada," the fat, rich merchant who is the object of his terrified nephew's entreaties in the story, owns the "Taj Mahal Silk Emporium" on the Escolta. The Escolta is the old, central business area of Manila, seldom visited by tourists, but a crowded, bustling, thriving area of tiny shops and small department stores. The merchants are Filipino, Chinese, and Indian, and, having no other common language, use English as the language of trade and general discourse. Thus it is in keeping that Dada's wife speak to the nephew, who was born and educat-*

ed in the Philippines, in broken English, while the men at table,
all Indians, speak in their native tongue.

Morli Dharam attended the University of the Philippines,
and also studied in the United States. He writes both fiction and
drama, has been a reviewer for the Manila Times, and also
teaches creative writing and Philippine Literature at Arellano
University.

Dada

As he went up the stairs he felt the old fear return. There was a
dryness in his throat and his hand sliding along the banister
left wet imprints on the polished wood.

He had not wanted to come. There was that leaden weight
within him when his mother had said he was well enough now
to meet his uncle. He had thought up evasions, had put up
various subterfuges, and when these did not avail him, had
pitted a stolid stubborn front against his mother's nagging
insistence. But she had been equally stubborn. Through the
years, he did not remember a time when she had not had her
way with him. However headstrong he might have been, she
always won her point, always routed his resistance, so that in
the end, his will broken, and the fortress of his desire battered
down, a cold shuddering sensation would force him to say the
one conciliatory word that stopped his torment. Such scenes
with his mother left him shaken. That cold shuddering sensation would be the precursor to a strangling fit that turned him
in one staggering moment into a mute. And when under such a
fit the need to speak arose because his mother, unaware of his
anguish, had spoken to him and he must needs answer her, the
words would come limping out of his mouth in the gaspy stut-
tering whine of an imbecile. At such times his mother's eyes
narrowed to a steely glare and with her strong thin arms
akimbo, she would taunt him with her strident: "Idiot! Can't
you talk straight?" And she would bring about his utter annihilation with her grotesque mimicry of his splintered
speech: "Ah-ah-ah-ah . . . !" until hatred for her would so well
up in him that the explosive desire to wreak violence would stir
his hands to trembling.

"Don't be a baby," his mother whispered to him as she followed him up the stairs. "Speak up to him and tell him outright the things I told you to say. Make him listen to you. You're old enough now to demand his attention. Talk straight and don't be a baby."

At the top of the stairs he wiped his sweating hands, moistened his lips. Behind him he felt his mother's hand straighten his shirt collar, heard her emphatic whisper in his ear: "Do as I told you."

From where she was playing with her paper dolls on the Persian rug, his cousin Silawahnti looked up at them in calm wonder, her round eyes black buttons on the thin fabric of her face.

"Mummee-e-e, Mummee-e-e-e," the little girl rose and ran into the kitchen. "Luisa is here with Rama."

His aunt Jhamna came out of the kitchen wiping her floury hands on a towel. Among the Hindu women he had known, she was the most nearly Caucasian in color and features. She was tall, slender, upright as a reed, had auburn hair which she wore in fat twin plaits behind her head; and she had hazel eyes and a spray of freckles on her face and arms which deepened her complexion to a most becoming beige. Draped around her shoulders and trailing to the floor was a large white cambric stole (which when the moment called for it became the characteristic veil, the symbol of reverence all Hindu women wore in the presence of their menfolk). One side of her beak-like nose was pierced. The tiny eyelet was at the moment bared of its diamond stud which, were she dressed up, would lie embedded there, small and glittering. On her wrists she wore a loose cluster of thin gold bangles.

She bade them be seated on the low capacious chairs grouped around the glass-topped table on the center of the huge red Persian carpet that covered the living room floor. When his aunt Jhamna sat down, she drew up a trousered leg, rested the ball of her foot on the edge of the chair, leaned an elbow on the apex of her drawn-up knee, and in the course of their conversation, gently swung her sandal that hung by a thong on her big right toe.

He noticed that his aunt Jhamna drew up her veil over her head as she sat opposite him, and the full import of her action as it swiftly dawned on him caused a sharp flicker of shyness, inferiority, self-consciousness, to clutch at his already suffering ego so that he felt constrained to lower his eyes and fix his gaze vacantly on the folded newspaper at the glass-topped table. She had never before covered her head solely in his presence, had never before looked at him with this new intentness, this utterly confusing attention, this new respect as from one adult to another and she had never before addressed him by his full name, Ramchand, as she did now. So that there was that one second of stupefied awareness when his aunt Jhamna in her high hoarsey voice said, "*Aré*, Ramchand, how are you?"

He shifted his gaze from the table to his aunt's smiling face now framed like a madonna's in the thin white veil, swallowed, and gave her a shy, lank smile. "Fine," he said.

His aunt Jhamna turned to his mother. There was a gently teasing humor in her cold-husky voice when she spoke, "*Aré*, Luisa, now you have big boy. Soon he marry, then what you do? You like him marry Indian girl? Or you like him marry Filipino girl? What you like?"

His mother suggested that his aunt Jhamna ask him the question herself and determine his preference.

His aunt Jhamna turned to him again, and in the scant English she had learned from her husband, his uncle Vassanmal, she said, her gold bangles jingling thinly as she swept her arm out in a large gesture of admonition: "Filipino girl no good. Talk too much. Go out alone. Maybe fight with mother-in-law. Maybe fight with husband. But Indian girl good. She no talk too much. No fight mother-in-law. No fight husband. Can sew. Can cook. She bring you big dowry. Then you have money to open store. What you say?"

Both his aunt Jhamna and his mother turned on him the combined barrage of their appraisal, awaiting his answer; his aunt's, with that new attention and respect he found so disturbing; his mother's, with her possessive proprietary air that always made him squirm and which always loosed within him a hot swift tide of resentment against her.

"I don't know," he finally said, flushing under their probing stares.

His aunt Jhamna's freckles stood out clearly in the tiny mounds of her cheeks now raised in a smile of amusement suddenly widening and breaking into a gale of wheezy mirth. The little girl, Silawahnti, barefoot and in red silk trousers and yellow tunic, leaned inside the parenthesis of his aunt

Jhamna's thighs, looking at him with dark wondering eyes as her lips convolved about a dirty thumb. Amused tolerance softened his mother's eyes but there lingered about her firmly set mouth the taint of smug triumph.

Then his mother snapped her fan open and while she employed it she launched, in broken English so his aunt would readily understand, into a spirited account of his recent, almost fatal bout with pneumonia. His mother was a large spare-boned woman with small restless eyes and a firmly set mouth sharp like an old knife grown thin with use. Her face had gone slack with the encroachment of age, and her neck was long and flabby like the pitiable obscene throat of an unfledged bird. She wore her hair bobbed, allowed herself the illusion of make-up which somehow was not incongruous with her thighs and legs which were well-preserved and had remained through the years firm and rounded and virginal.

His aunt Jhamna listened, asked questions, from time to time glanced at him. Meanwhile, he had opened the folded newspaper on the glass-topped table and had desperately tried to engross himself in its contents.

"You no more sick?" his aunt asked him, her hazel eyes soft like a doe's.

He was startled when his mother jarred with her fan the paper he was reading and in dialect snapped at him. "Pay attention when you're spoken to!"

He lowered his paper and hastily smoothed out the consternation from his face.

His aunt Jhamna's hazel eyes slanted, crinkled in their corners as she laughingly repeated her question.

"I'm all right now," he said, the words coming out low, depleted of their vocal force from squeezing past a parched, constricted throat. Catching the grim look in his mother's eyes, he lowered his gaze to the paper on his lap.

His mother snapped her fan in a weary, impatient gesture of disgust and said, her voice shrill with held-back anger: "He's very stubborn. Very hard-headed. Only likes reading. Always, always reading." Her face worked with exasperation and folding her fan with a snap, exclaimed: "I don't know what more to do with him."

His aunt Jhamna lowered her foot from the edge of her chair and discovering that Silawahnti was sucking her thumb, slapped the child's hand away and hoarsely chided her daughter: "How many times I told you no put finger in mouth? You also hardheaded like Ramchand? *Hala*, go! Go take bath now! Tell Felisa give you bath!"

Silawahnti wriggled her toes on the Persian rug and made no move to go.

"If you no take bath," his aunt continued, "Dada get angry and Dada no take you in auto to Luneta this afternoon."

Silawahnti considered this, then quickly turning on her heels, she scampered to the kitchen shouting as she ran: "Felisa, you give me bath now. I go Luneta this afternoon."

"Foolish child!" His aunt Jhamna told his mother. "Also very hard-headed. Even I beat her sometimes she still hard-headed."

"Beating is good for children." His mother's tone was firmly authoritative. "They never behave unless you beat them. Look at Rama. When he makes me very angry I still beat him."

"Yes?" A husky chuckle gurgled in his aunt Jhamna's throat. "Suppose he have wife, you still beat him?"

"Why not?" His mother's tone bristled with righteousness. "Even if he has wife, he's still my son."

"Oh, yes." Then leaning toward him, her bangles again jingling thinly in her series of admonitory gestures, his aunt Jhamna said. "*Aré*, Ramchand! You always obey mother. You be good boy. Mother makes sacrifice for you. Many sacrifice she make. When your father die she no marry again because she afraid maybe new husband no love you same like true son. She afraid maybe new husband beat you. Always happen. Even in India. So your mother make sacrifice ... no more marry ... always take good care of you ... make many sacrifice when you sick ... "

"That's true." His mother's voice went crumbly with tears. "He never will know all the suffering I've gone through bringing him up after his father died ... when he was barely six months old. I always tell him: Even if his body were cut into a thousand pieces he never will be able to repay what it cost me to bear him and raise him into a decent boy."

"So you must love mother. You always be good boy," his aunt Jhamna said. Then as an afterthought, she asked, "You love mother?"

He was acutely ill at ease. His stomach was hot, tight with

embarrassment. It was all he could do to manage a soft "Of course" from a throat and mouth arid with shame.

As his mother further related the details of his illness, her voice became by turns whining with self-pity, petulant with grief, somber with martyrdom.

Try as he would he could not avoid hearing all that was said, and what he heard brought a faint roaring in his ears, hot flushes raising through his body. He was sick with shame at his mother's volubly remembered instances of his obstinacy and her consequent distress on their account. He raised the newspaper he was reading so that it hid him from the two women in the room.

"Now, he's well." His mother's voice contained a contrary note of hopeless resignation as if his being well were not at all what she had wished. "Doctor said give him special kind of food. To make him strong. He is thin, you see. And still he takes injections. And that cost money. We have not as yet paid the doctor. And the hospital." Over the rim of his paper, he saw his mother; the turned-down corners of her sharp mouth gave her care-worn face a tragic cast.

His aunt Jhamna became bothered with her sniffles and searching for a corner of her cambric stole, blew her nose on it.

"What time will Dada come?"

"Maybe twelve. Maybe one o'clock. Today Sunday. They fixing store, putting new *estante*. Maybe new goods come this afternoon."

His aunt Jhamna rose from her chair, adjusted the cambric stole about her shoulders, hunted for one sandal that had somehow wedged itself under her chair. She pulled it out with her foot, slipped it on, and turning to his mother said, "Better I finish making *pan* now. By and by Dada come. If *pan* not yet make, he angry." Her hazel eyes took on a glint of mischief. "Maybe he beat me also, no Ramchand?" She arched her neck back, snuffling out her rustling laughter at him. "Come Luisa. I have buttermilk in ice box. I give you for Ramchand." She approached him at the same time pulling the veil over her head so that when, feeling her close presence, he looked up at her, he saw her head entirely covered with that symbol of reverence as if he were a man fully grown and in accordance with strict dictates of her caste she must needs defer to his superior position. "You like buttermilk, Ramchand?"

Slightly flushing, he met her gaze and softly said, "Yes, Jhamna."

She turned and while she walked to the kitchen she said, "You wait and Luisa bring you buttermilk. You be big boy now. You be good. No make mother angry. She make many sacrifice for you," she added, her voice coming to him, remote, from the kitchen.

He had drunk his buttermilk, eaten *pakhorra* and drunk ice water copiously to relieve his mouth of its peppery sting, read and yawned many times through the one newspaper on the glass-topped table when at precisely a quarter of two o'clock he heard the car arrive, heard the metallic slam of its door, the noisy babel in Sindhi floating up the stairwell, the leathery scrape of shoes on the stair treads.

He had a moment of quick terror until he remembered to hold the newspaper before his panic-stricken face and spare himself the cold impact of greeting any of the arrivals. He felt them enter the room, felt their actual bodily nearness slap at his senses, felt the room saturated with their oily pungent foreign talk.

Over the top of his newspaper he discerned his uncle Vassanmal's swarthy round head pass by, and, remembering his mother's stern injunctions, he manfully surmounted his panic and threw in his uncle's direction, what he intended to be a casually affectionate "Hello, Dada," but what instead came out as an inaudible, abortive, croak-like mumble. Almost at once he saw himself impaled on the spear of his terror, felt his stomach contract in a series of shuddery tremors.

"*Aré*, Mr. Ramchand, how are you?"

The voice was deep, throaty, bland with the spurious geniality of the subtly obsequious Indian salesman who comes to a customer with a silky smile and a "What can I do for you, Miss? Is there anything I can show you in the way of rayon, silk, satin?" The boy looked up into the droll beaming face of Mr. Krishinchand Lalchand seated beside Mr. Sehwani Bhagwani on the sofa opposite him, the two of them accompanied by their wives, having come with his uncle Vassanmal obviously for Sunday dinner. They were large portly men with paunchy middles; dark-visaged, thick-necked, and their wives, big handsome women swathed in yards and yards of silk *sari*, were likewise sleek and fat. The two men visitors owned the two Indian bazars adjoining his Uncle's "Taj Mahal Silk Emporium" on the Escolta. The arrivals, aside from the two couples who were guests, included the three Indian salesmen apprenticed to his uncle's store, his cousin Shewakram who was a young man of twenty, and Arjhani, his uncle Vassanmal's only son, age five.

He knew them all and they in turn remembered him from the small chubby boy they had seen through the years lagging behind the heels of a large spareboned dour-faced woman who jerked him out front whenever he had the tendency in the presence of strangers to disappear behind her skirt. They had twitted the small boy with the round dark eyes that looked at you as if he might at any moment burst into tears, had tweaked his nose, waggled his cheeks, balanced bits of a broken toothpick on his long upcurving lashes, swung him up in the air by his armpits until he fairly shrieked with terror, stuffed him with candies, a bit of money, and mechanical toys during Christmas, inveigled him to stay with them *(Arè, Rami! Better you stay with us. No more go home to Luisa. You stay and we take you to India. You like go India?)*, teased his mother by hiding him behind showcases, behind bales of goods, inside empty crates, until he gave himself away by bawling out loud, "Mama! Mama!"

He could feel them all looking at him, seeing a pale thin slat of a boy, his dark eyes rounder than ever but no longer seeming at any moment to burst into tears, now inscrutable rather and deep with only a trace of his boyhood chubbiness remaining on his lean hard cheeks now blotched with the eruptions of adolescent acne.

"What you do? You big boy now. You open store or you study more? Maybe you have sweetheart now, ha? When you marry?" Mr. Krishinchand Lalchand enjoyed his joke hugely, and the fat smirk across his shiny face gave him the aspect of a coarse billiken. The others in the room snickered deliciously like a pack of dark horses whinnying.

At dinner the two men visitors continued to discuss him with his uncle Vassanmal. As was customary, the men sat down to dinner first, his uncle at the head of the table, the two men visitors next, then the three Indian salesmen, his uncle's nephew Shewakram, himself, and at the foot of the table, the little boy Arjhani (perched on his high chair) whom his mother was trying to feed. His aunt Jhamna with the maid Felisa in her wake shuttled back and forth between the kitchen and the table, ladling out platters of the spice-fragrant thick-gravied foods, passing around bottles of ice water, replenishing the rapidly emptied bread platter with stacks of piping-hot *pan* wet with lard.

He watched the diners tear small chunks of *pan*, shape these into tiny cornucopias, dip these into the gravy saucers before them, scoop up gravy and pieces of goat meat and chuck the succulent morsels into their mouths; and the moist tongue-lapping sounds of their eating—*ptak-ptchak, ptak-ptchak, ptak-ptchak*—were, he thought, kin to the splashy gustatory sounds in a sty.

He did not understand Sindhi very well but occasionally he was able to grasp the gist of a sentence, the essence of their talk about him, and what he heard turned the food in his mouth into wads of thick fuzzy wool. It was a pity, the two men visitors said, clucking their tongues, that his uncle Vassanmal had sadly neglected the boy's upbringing. With the proper coaching in Sindhi reading and writing and a bit of fattening up, he would undoubtedly turn out into as fine a specimen of young Hindu manhood as any young buck born and raised in India, and would command no less a handsome dowry in the Indian marriage mart.

He became aware of the three Indian salesmen teasing him with their eyes like black velvet swatches in the thin pasteboard of their faces. Across the table from him, his cousin Shewakram sniggered salaciously and ground a shoe on his foot under the table. He swung his leg in a vicious kick, stubbing his toe on the hard edge of the other's chair, and as he chafed at his futile retaliation, he saw Shewakram lifting the corners of his grease-coated lips in a grin of triumph.

The diners gorged themselves, and he saw a beatific expression like a brooding Buddha's spread over his uncle's face as he hoisted his mammoth pot-belly, shifted his weight on one buttock, and slowly, casually, matter-of-factly, broke wind. The others exhaled fat zestful belches and rose from the table.

At the lavatory he waited until everybody had finished washing their hands, rinsed their mouths, before he moved toward it. As he did so, he saw Shewa deliberately taking his

own sweet time about soaping his hands. He stood to one side of
Shewa, prepared to wait patiently for his turn and was indeed
startled when Shewa, by inserting a finger in the tap nozzle,
directed a taut squirt of water at him, catching him pointblank
on the belly. Facing him, Shewa smiled wickedly, and hurrying
past him, flicked the drops of water from his still wet hands
into the boy's astonished face. As Rama washed his hands
clean of their goaty smell, his thwarted anger stirred them to
trembling, twitched his jaws in a quivery spasm.

"*Now!*" his mother said over his shoulder as he dried his
hands on a towel hung on a nail above the washbowl. "There he
goes into his room. Follow him, plant yourself squarely before
him, so he'll have no reason to ignore you. Tell him outright the
things I told you to say. Catch his attention for he'll soon be
sitting down at the card table and you know that once he's
there, not even cannon shot can dislodge him. Make him understand, talk straight, and don't be a baby. Get results or
you'd better take care when we return home. Better take
care!" She left him then, for his aunt Jhamna was calling her
to come to dinner.

He walked into the living room and saw that Krishinchand
Lalchand and Sehwani Bhagwani were setting up the card
table. Lhadu, the eldest of the three Indian salesmen, was
mixing brandy and soda at the cellarette beside the cabinet
radio, while the others were sprawled on chairs, leisurely picking their teeth. Shewakram, with one leg flung over the arm of
his chair, was intent on the movie page of the newspaper, now
and then rooting into the inner corner of his thigh where
apparently the soft plump worm of his sex was snagged upon
the crotch of his tight trousers. The boy waited until he was
sure no one was paying him the least attention and then,
swiftly crossing the living room, entered his uncle
Vassanmal's room.

As he paused on the threshold, he felt his stomach tighten.
His uncle Vassanmal, like a gross idol, was sitting on his bed,
one leg bent and raised upon a knee. Slowly, his uncle leaned
forward and unlaced a shoe which he dropped on the floor. He
raised his other foot and in the same laborious manner unlaced
and shucked the shoe off, thumping it on the floor. He then
emitted a faint belch after which he rested his hands on his

hammy thighs as he worked his toes up and down inside their brown silk socks. It was then his uncle noticed him leaning there by the doorjamb and his uncle spoke across the room to him in a natural perfunctory tone: "*Aré*, Rama, how're you?"

With marked diffidence, the boy walked into the room, stopped by a chair beside the round table with the crocheted lace tablecloth, watched his uncle wheeze as his enormous potbelly pressed on the edge of the bed while he leaned over to peel off his socks, then tenderly rub his bunions. He was of middle height but enormously fat so that his bloated torso and mammoth potbelly were in grotesque contrast to his rather small-calved spindly legs. Still discernible on his swarthy face were the ravages of smallpox he once had many years ago, the pockmarks no longer distinct but shallow and blurred by time. His black slick hair, austerely brushed down, hugged his head in the round clasp of a skullcap and fringed the edge of his narrow brow with a tiny fluted curl. His face was broad, his mouth wide, and the high ridge of his nose dominated the landscape of his face like a mountain peak.

As he watched his uncle wipe his toes with his socks, he felt the desire to speak erupt within him like a shooting geyser. He must have spluttered an involuntary mumble, for his uncle looked up at him and said, still quite perfunctorily: "You go school?"

The boy's tenseness, like boiling liquid when the heat is lessened, ebbed a little and he was glad for this release of tension, for this brief respite from the fear that his uncle, as he had habitually done in the past, would leave to him the sole burden of their conversation while maintaining, as he struggled and suffered the damnation of the chronic stutterer, a cold stoic silence. His fear of meeting his uncle had stemmed from those excruciating moments in the past when he had stood before him mute and tongue-tied, a welter of words stillborn on the threshold of his lips, while the other regarded him with an impassive stare and did not by so much as a gesture, a look, a word, ease the torment that clotted in his belly like tangled twine. *Now* his uncle had spoken to him *first*, wanted to know if he went to school, was kind, was generous, was altogether not the hard, mean, avaricious bogeyman of his childhood fancy; oh, he'd been wrong, now all *that* would be past, his uncle would speak to him, would be kind, would have sympathy, would above all understand how it was, how it is with a chronic stutterer who every waking moment of his day must strain and struggle and try to break away from the crippling tenacious strands of shyness, inferiority, self-consciousness that hamstrung him and made of him a suffering prisoner.

He managed a clumsy smile and when he replied, his voice, at first unsteady and quavering, became more natural, normal, even warm towards the end of his little speech. "No, Dada, we have no school. We are on vacation since March. School will open in June, next month. Then I'll . . . I'll be fourth year. I got 92 average. That is second highest. The first is 94. She's a girl. Teacher said maybe if I study more I can be first in class."

He watched his uncle wheeze again as he leaned over and tried to hunt for his slippers under the bed. "You find slippers, Rama, I think they go there . . . in corner, there!"

The boy was glad for this preoccupation. He had long wanted to move; standing there by the chair was making him feel absurd, only he didn't quite know how to manage any movement without attracting attention, without appearing awkward. He always felt glad whenever he could be of use to anybody even if it were only in doing the least little thing. If only people kept asking him to do something for them instead of, as often happened, staring at him and what was most intolerable, trying to make fun of him and speaking to him as if he were a dimwit or a child! He walked over to the bed, crouched on his hands and knees, and thrusting an arm under the bed, reached for the slippers that lay there against the wall. He dropped the sandals before his uncle's feet and shyly sat himself on the edge of the bed. Now that he was closer to his uncle, his fear was no longer as potent as before; in fact it had almost completely disappeared, and he was only hoping that their relation could stay forever thus, without terror, closer, more congenial.

His uncle rose from the bed and the sudden release of his enormous weight shot the bedsprings upward into position bouncing the boy on his back. He laughed, scrambling to his feet, and quickly looked at his uncle to see if he had noticed his momentary discomfiture. Apparently he hadn't for he was at the moment standing before his clothes bureau rummaging in its drawers. His uncle pulled out pyjama trousers and a house shirt, slung these over one shoulder, started unbuckling his belt. He dropped his trousers to the floor, shook loose the silk pyjamas and stooped over to step into these. His uncle wore no underwear and the sight of his swollen half-nudity made the boy turn away and study the linear pattern on the chenille bedspread. When he looked up again his uncle was clad in wide loose silk pyjamas over which his pin stripe silk house shirt hung to his knees. He watched his uncle grunt and stoop over to pick up his trousers and empty the pockets of balled dirty handkerchiefs, keys, loose bills, coins, receipts, swatches of men's suiting, a button, string, a checkbook which he tossed on the lace-covered round table.

The boy remained seated on the bed with his knees crossed, swinging one foot in an attempt at nonchalance while deep down, tiny licking tongues of panic crept inward from the outer fringes of his well-being. Between his uncle and himself there had been silence perhaps for the better part of five minutes, and the thought, that if he didn't quickly think of something to say next this silence would rise like a flood and submerge him completely into a vortex of speechlessness, tormented him because he now knew as well as if the other had explicitly told him that his uncle had nothing more to say to him, would not attempt anything else to say to him, was in fact, as was his habit in the past, ignoring him, snubbing him, as a Brahmin, a pariah. The simmer of anger in him clove his tongue to the roof of his parched mouth. Words started seething inside him, clamoring for release, for utterance, for spitting out against an injustice he felt was being done him. He started taking deep breaths to still his violently agitated heart and retain a measure of calm with which to speak out his mind clearly, lay out his plea coherently, manfully. He was no longer a child. His aunt Jhamna had covered her head in his presence, the Messrs. Krishinchand Lalchand and Sehwani Bhagwani, including their wives, thought him mature enough to warrant marriage speculations, his mother was now ever more hysterically careful about his making acquaintances with girls; no, he was no longer a child. His uncle had better realize the fact here, now, at once.

He watched his uncle seated at the lace-covered round table appearing to balance the stubs in his checkbook. After several false starts in his mind, he managed to blurt out: "Dada, I . . . I . . . I've been sick. I've been sick with pneumonia. I stayed in hospital for three weeks. Doctor said my illness serious." He paused to lick his dry lips, and suddenly frightened at the lengthening silence, hurtled on, impelled with the notion to let the momentum of his excitement push out everything he had to say. "D-d-doctor said if I not careful I'll have p-p-pleurisy. I'm all right now but I take injections. We have n-n-n-not yet paid the doctor and the hospital. Mama already paid part but there's still a balance of ninety pesos. Mama said you please give me the money including the thirty pesos for tuition and books I need next month. So next month I no bother you again. That makes a total of one hundred twenty pesos in all. Mama said you please give me because doctor is waiting and she is ashamed."

Halfway in his speech his uncle looked up, turned to him, hitching his armpit over the back of his chair. "*Aré*, Rama," his uncle said in a voice only a little less loud than a shout. The tone made the boy wince for he did not wish the people in the living room to know the nature of his talk with his uncle. "I have idea for you . . . Nice idea I have for you. What grade you now, ha?"

"I just finished third year. Next month in June, I'll start the fourth year."

"No use going back school. I have better idea for you. You stop school. You work for me. I send you Zamboanga with Lhada. I open branch there. You have nice house, nice food, nice clothes. You no more sick. I tell Lhada give you small money for cinema, for ice cream. Luisa stay here. She can go here every month, get small money. What you say?"

All the food he had eaten turned into a grey blubbery lump that weighted him down, inclined him on the brink of nausea. He sat dumbfounded staring at his uncle who stared back at him, his mammoth potbelly resting between his thighs, looking now more than ever like a toad. When he was a child, he had regarded his uncle's belly with awe, remembering a remark heard from his mother that if you pierced his uncle's stomach and slashed a hole thereon, the money his uncle had seized from his father when the latter died would come tumbling out like pennies from a slot machine.

"B-b-but I can't stop now. This is my last year. I have to

finish high school to go to college."

"Study? Study? Why you always study? What you like? Become governor-general of Philippines?"

"I must go to college to study medicine. I-I-I want to be a doctor."

"Why you want to be doctor? That crazy idea. Like Filipino idea. Always doctor, always lawyer. No attend to business. What I do with doctor? Many doctors poor people, no make money. Why you want be like that?"

The boy squirmed on the bed, cast his eyes down, toyed with his fingers, cracking them one by one.

"*I* no study," his uncle continued. "*I* finish only third grade in India. *I* make good business. *I* work hard. Why you no do the same? In Zamboanga you learn little Sindhi. Then later you go India. Learn some more reading, writing. Then you marry. I arrange for you. Maybe you get ten thousand, fifteen thousand rupees dowry. *I* keep money for you. Maybe *I* make you partner in business. What more you like? You own half store, half mine. You have money, you live nice. What more you want?"

He was sick, miserable and it was a struggle to say this: "D-d-doctors also get to make a lot of money."

His uncle looked at him sharply. "Where you get money for study?" His uncle's tone was low, packed with muffled thunder.

Inside the boy's head, his thoughts ran like frightened mice. He had a desperate time of it trying to collect them, to align them in one convincing rebuttal. "I-I-I get money from you. Bef-bef-before, you promised you send me through school."

"*I* no have money." His uncle rose from the chair, lumbered toward the clothes bureau where he tossed his checkbook into a drawer. "What you think I am, millionaire?"

"But—but Dada, I need one hundred twenty pesos now for doctor and school—"

"*I* no have money. I give you twenty pesos, that enough. When you go home, you get from Jhamna. I tell her give you twenty pesos. *I* no millionaire."

From the living room the bland throaty voice of Mr. Krishinchand Lalchand rose in a shout for his uncle. "*Aré*, Vassu," — the boy caught the gist of the Sindhi words—"you hurry up if we are going to play. Also bring a new deck of cards, will you?"

Now panic gripped him. In a moment his uncle would waddle out of the room, leaving him and his plea for money washed dry like wreckage in the tide of their argument. He had to think fast, speak fast, try to hold his uncle's attention a little longer. Words hurled themselves against the gates of his mind, and he became frantic with worry, fear, panic, that he would never be able to use them, unleash them to assist him, avenge him. But his throat and mouth were again dry, and speech became an effort, strenuous and tiring.

"But—but—but Dada, I need the money b—b—badly. This is my last-last-last year in school. I have to finish that."

"You hard-headed," his uncle said, rummaging in his bureau drawers for a pack of cards. "Luisa spoil you. She teach you wrong things. *I* give you nice idea but you hard-headed. *I* no have money to give you. *I* have many expense. *I* pay house rent, store rent, I pay salary. Why *I* give you money? Why *I* always give you?"

"Be—beb—because—because—" His heart was thumping faster. He wondered whether he had the nerve to say what his mother had coached him to say if his uncle proved difficult. Be—beb—because it's much more mine than it is yours. It's my father's money!"

His uncle slowly turned and fixed him across the room with a black flashing glare.

His audacity surprised him, and curiously enough, it gave him a pervading sense of calm. As from afar he heard his voice say, slowly, distinctly with dreamy langor, "It's . . . my . . . father's . . . money . . . you . . . stole . . . it . . . when . . . he . . . died." An impulse cranked him to say, like a record needle caught in a groove, softly, dreamily—"s-s-stole it . . . s-s-stole it . . . s-s-stole it. . . . "

The slap jarred his head back. His cheeks burned and his head rang with the force of the blow.

His mind screamed: *You hog! You toad! You thief! It's true! You took over Papa's store when he died, took his money, that's why you promised the lawyer you'd support us . . . send me through school . . .* But his mouth said: "Mh . . . mh . . . mh . . . mh . . . ," the whimpery syllables borne on shuddery gusts of breath that escaped through locked teeth.

His uncle towered over him, hunched there on the bed, one hand raised to his cheek now radiating heat like a flat iron. For a minute his uncle looked at him with scorn, then turned and walked away. Halfway across the room his uncle whirled, spat an Indian obscenity at him, thrust a beefy hand toward him, its fingers stretched apart, the thumb pointed downward—the whole brown hand seemingly a fat obscene spider dangling in the air. His uncle regarded him once more, then picking up a deck of cards from the drawer, walked slowly out of the room.

Hunched there on the bed, he felt cold perspiration break out on his brow, felt his blood roar and recede and scamper inner- wards to a cold leaden core somewhere in his belly. The sensa- tion was like a foot going to sleep, only this time, magnified to the height and breadth of his whole body. The palms of his hands itched and he felt a bowel movement coming on.

When his mother entered the room and confronted him with her "Well, what did he say? What did he say?" he swung his stricken face to her and, as his bleary senses made out her sharp features thrust before him like a blade, there dropped out of his mouth, like the whir of an unraveled spring in a snapped mechanical toy, the dry gaspy splintered whine of idiot syllables.

ONELIO JORGE CARDOSO

Cardoso's story about a Cuban fisherman blends elements of Hemingwayesque romanticism with revolutionary doctrine. Like the old man in Hemingway's Old Man and the Sea, *the fisherman Robles singlehandedly captures an impressively large fish. In Hemingway's tale, however, the conflict is that of a strong individualist bravely and with great endurance strug- gling with the forces of nature, which he both fears and loves.*

In Cardoso's story, however, the primary values are those of the revolution: personal integrity, community spirit, dedica- tion to the common good. Robles's temptation is to follow the example of his old master, Crespo, "The Cat," who had lived by an "each man for himself" motto. Confronted with the patriotic and generous spirit of Damaso, however, Robles is won over to a behavior nobler than his own desires.

Onelio Cardoso was born in Cuba in 1914. He has not written a great deal, but his work is of high quality.

The Cat's Second Death

Robles sat watching the daylight come as he leant back in the stern of the boat, with his left elbow pressed against the boards and his right arm stretched out holding the fishing line which ran over the end of his finger. He saw the rim of the sun rising slowly over the tip of his bare foot. This was not at all new to him. He could turn round then and there and be sure as always of seeing the scattered lights of Cojimar still burning. It had been deeply familiar to him for the last thirty years, since the time he began hauling up the stone anchor at the age of twelve for the old man Crespo who used to sit in the stern and address him as he worked, formally, but with harsh interjections.

Robles would have thought of the old man that morning, the same as those other mornings when the light had revealed him sitting in his place, but the night's catch had been small and now he could not help thinking about his own affairs. And so, leaving the sun on the side, his thoughts returned to the bottom of the boat and dwelt on the few fish he had caught one by one: two sea-bream, three red-coloured river fish and four piddling guatiberos. With that lot nobody could say he had been fishing; unless of course it was one of those people with fancy hats and loud shirts who hired boats on Sundays, messed up all the hooks and went off ecstatic about a couple of roncos which anyone could have caught with no trouble at all.

With his line full out, then, he needed luck to hand him a couple of ten-or-twelve-pound jew-fish. But the jew-fish were not to be had and the sun was gradually turning the black water of the night into the intense deep blue water of the day. If that old villain Crespo had been there ... he would have been sure to shout to him that he didn't know how to place himself in order to get the fish. But the old man was dead; fifteen years of red earth lay on top of what he had been, and now Robles could feel more at ease. Though really, the old man had taught him all he knew, even the other business: stealing fish off a long line, under the owner's nose, as you might say.

He had not done this himself up to now, but he could; he knew how to. He was simply a fisherman who was capable of keeping himself on what he caught in three anchorings and no more, depending of course on how the current was: if it was flowing up or down, on or offshore. Nobody was better at the job. He owed that to the old man and was grateful . . . as well as that wealth of tricks; because the day he felt like it he could also become a cat like the old man, and he almost burst out laughing at the thought: a cat.

They called old Crespo a cat because of the way he could smell out and grab other people's fish. And you certainly had to have something of a sharp-eyed feline in you to go along the coast and see from the distance where a chap was setting his nets and to remember the place the next night and go up to it, rowing in your skiff without a sound, with no lights and under the cover of darkness, to take his catch. Yes, you certainly had to be cat-like, and like a fairly superior cat at that. And, honestly, it took old Crespo to do it!

The business has its merits; but they are not good ones because as it's tricky you feel you've overcome real risks and imagine you're a big man. It's a bad thing to start it in the first place.

He felt a pull on the line and waited with all his senses concentrated in the tip of his finger, but then he scowled:

"Bah! A jiniguano or a wrasse."

The off-shore wind was still blowing and the water was smooth and calm. In such a calm and with no current at all the old man would not have waited around a moment longer: "Bring up your anchor, you lout!" he would have said, and at once set about lighting the end of his broken cigar.

Your anchor, your knife, your bail, your sounding-line, your tiller, your cleaning sponge; for when it was a question of doing something aboard it was as if he owned everything, although in fact if he had taken no more than the bail away Crespo would have flayed him alive even if he had fled to the very bottom of the sea.

True; but the old man had taught him all he knew and that meant he should always be grateful to him. He had only to think of the first day to remind himself of the old man. It was when he was left an orphan. Passing close by Crespo's hut he caught the smell and saw the fish he was frying. His mouth watered and the cat's small eyes noticed him from the very first moment, but he went on frying away; then he turned his pointed nose towards the boy:

"Hungry, aren't you?"

"Yes."

"Fine, nobody's got everything he wants."

And it seemed as though he were going to drop the subject, when he said:

"If you can get me some bait, sure I'll save you this one." And grabbing a snapper by the tail he put it to fry in the sizzling fat.

The twelve-year-old Robles did not say anything to that; he just went away, walked all over Cojimar and then down to the beach and stole, for the first time, a handful of sardines. Then he came and showed them to the old man. He smelt them first, threw them one by one into salt water together with others he had already and eventually said to him:

"Come on, take it."

The twelve-year-old's hand went to take one of the fried snappers, but stopped still when the cat's voice said:

"That's not the one I said."

Then he looked carefully so as not to make a mistake and luckily picked just the one the old man had said.

"Ah! At times memories are like the dorado, you don't know where they come from and then there they are hovering in the sky, every one of them like a slender, black forked thing above the boat, the water and the soul."

Thinking of the dorados Robles looked up at the sky. Seeing one would have been a piece of good luck because there was always a good chance that there was a companion fish swimming along beneath it. But in the sky there was only the waxing sun and Robles felt it burning in his eyes. Then the off-shore wind over the bows gradually lulled him into a trance and that was how he was when he heard the water slapping and he sat up at once. Perhaps it was the companion fish approaching. He thought that sometimes you attract things like that, just by thinking about them. Then he got up bit by bit while over the stern, barely seven yards away, the ripples were spreading over the broken mirror of the sea. That's where the splash had been. Now it would probably happen again closer by, and without taking his eyes off the point he had calculated he crouched down, feeling for the spinning-tackle. But he had no time to, for his eyes were suddenly filled with amazement.

"Christ!" he said, and was speechless.

In the very centre of the ripples a dark back which Robles knew only too well had just appeared.

A sawfish so far inshore and with the sun already up is something quite incredible. Sawfish always pass by, swimming at night along the main stream of the gulf, where the long lines with their floats and lights are laid to stop their progress. But if they are not caught they are never seen. To see one was a miracle. But Robles confronted a still greater miracle, when to his even greater amazement he saw that the sawfish had its saw stuck tight as a nail in a piece of drift-wood.

"You've had it!" he said and with three long strides he was in the bows. He jerked the jib sheet free and let it run out so that the off-shore breeze should bring him round on the fish.

It could not put up much of a fight, first because of the piece of wood and second because of the time it must have been struggling already. But a sawfish is a sawfish after all, and so when you pick up the cudgel you've got to be sure of hitting it right between the eyes, otherwise things can be awkward.

Then he thought of what he had to hand: the boat hook, the knife and the cudgel. A pity about the harpoon, he had lost it one night out at sea. Anyway, it was a question of sticking the hook in him now; then he would be able to feel in his wrist how alive or dead the sawfish was.

And when he was six inches away he stuck the hook in; water splashed up over him and as it poured down over his eyes and blurred them, he had the sensation that a man in the sea was trying to wrench the hook from his hands. But he stood firm, with his left foot in the bottom of the boat and his right pressed against the gunwhale straining all out. It went on for a time and then resistance suddenly weakened. Robles quickly wiped the water from his eyes with his left hand and saw the hook firmly embedded and a trickle of blood spreading out in the water. That was not good, for blood always drew a shark. He then realized that he would have to be quick, and pulling gently, he freed his right hand and grasped the cudgel. Three times he struck, right between the eyes, knowing he had done the trick after the first blow. When Robles had completed his task the round, dark back had become blue. The base of the bill, cut in three places, ended a foot or so from the mouth. What had happened when the sun rose had been repeated: black became blue.

But Robles hardly thought of such things. He hardly even looked at the sawfish, for between his eyes and the twelve stone of fish the old man's face had appeared again. At first he thought he was smiling, but then he remembered that the cat had never smiled. He had laughed it is true, but it was a short, snorting little laugh which sounded broken and never got farther than a few inches beyond his nose. He was just recalling that laugh when the thought which brought it on came naturally to him:

"Ha, ha! You can't fool me, you lout, anyone can hook a fish that's been hooked already!"

All right, he had to accept it: half the battle had been won by the night and the wooden plank. Then Robles's expression changed. He hesitated for a moment and taking hold of the knife he thrust his hands in through the gills. He was almost clumsy about it. Amongst the bleeding flesh he felt desperately for the smooth steel of the fish-hook and when he had brought this piece of tackle out whole through the gills, he looked at the eye.

"Damaso spliced that!" he said to himself and his voice sounded disconsolate.

You could recognize a splice made by Damaso amongst splices made by a thousand skillful hands. It was the same with his laugh. Amongst a thousand laughs you heard his and picked it out straight-away; perhaps it was because of that secret power he had of infecting others with his directness. So that you were soon laughing too at what he was laughing about, without really knowing what the hell Damaso was laughing about.

All these thoughts rushed through his head in a moment; however, what impinged on him most was the information he had just gained: the tackle was Damaso's and so the sawfish was too.

"What shall I do?" he said to himself, but inevitably the cat's pointed nose was already before him, and his two eyes shining with delight:

"Steal it, you lout! What I'd do is go out to sea a bit and say I caught it with my spinning-tackle, that's what I do."

Robles roused himself. For the second time in his life he could take something that wasn't his. The first time did not count of course, because he had been hungry and a child. This one would though, because it was not hunger but the gesture of an independent mind like the cunning mind of the cat.

A short time later Robles was coming into Cojimar. The

breeze had already begun to blow from behind him and the water was beginning to rise in white spray against the rocks along the coast. Damaso could not possibly be in Cojimar. It was Sunday and he was sure to have done what he always did: go off with the others to do what they called voluntary work. So all would be well. He would clean the fish on the jetty. Somebody might come by and be curious, and he would say quite calmly what he had thought out: "It was luck . . . out at sea . . . got it at dawn with the spinning-tackle."

But when he was actually tying his boat to the jetty a loud laugh made him rise his head in the direction of the Cooperative building.

"Damaso!" he said frantically tightening the knot in the rope.

And there was no way out of it: Damaso's bare powerful feet were approaching along the jetty.

"Congratulations, Robles, sixteen stones at least!"

"Twelve," he answered without looking up and asked immediately:

"Didn't you feel like joining the working party today?"

"I couldn't make it," the other said simply. Then with two lithe steps he was in the boat, sitting on the gunwhale, so that his bare feet dangled above the sawfish.

"You're in my way there," Robles said, but Damaso did not seem to hear. He was delightedly admiring the fish.

"A fine hunk, Robles. . . . Bit of a tussle to get it then?"

"You're right."

"Sawfish is the thing. . . . You know how much it is a pound?"

"Yes, eighteen."

"Not likely, it's twenty-nine; that's from today and they can't get enough of it!"

Robles looked up at him. It was good news, but difficult to relish in the face of Damaso's light eyes.

"There's enough for everybody today," Damaso said.

This time it was Robles who did not seem to hear, and his movements were awkward as if he did not know where to begin. At this point he went to get hold of the sawfish's bill in order to lift up, but Damaso's left hand was there first and did it for him.

"Leave it to me," Robles said.

"Cut it," the other answered and held the bill up until Robles began cutting. For a time the two of them concentrated on the job, but Damaso had not abandoned his thoughts:

"In the old days people didn't play fair. They even played the cat sometimes."

Because he had been looking at the fish's tail Damaso could not see the furtive, suspicious glance which fell on him.

"A cat like old Crespo, you remember?"

He had sunk the knife home but did not start cutting. When he turned his expression was disturbed:

"Don't forget the old man taught me everything I know."

Damaso held his look without wanting to insinuate anything, but he seemed to measure the words he spoke:

"No, not everything, there was something you didn't learn; you go out to fish, not to steal what other people have caught."

At this point Robles got up, but Damaso remained calm and went on talking as if the other man had not moved.

"There's no reason why I should be praising you, but it's funny in a way; the cat adopted you but you never chased a mouse and it's a mystery to me why a man like you shouldn't be working in with everybody else the way we do these days."

"I owe everything to the old man," he shouted: "Get that straight, I owe him for what he taught me as well and for the bread he gave me."

"He owes more to you."

"What do you mean!"

"He owes you more, if you think it out properly, Robles. You were hungry once, and he got twenty years of work out of you because of it."

"You know nothing about it. The old man taught me how to get along on my own."

"Nobody is ever alone. We know that now, Robles. Look, even when you go out to sea you're not alone."

"I've got a pair of hands with me, what else?"

"What about the chaps on land who made your boat-hook for you, the harpoon, the line, everything you've got. . . ."

"Come on now, that's ridiculous. . . . " he screamed, but he got caught up in his words as if rage had stifled his voice.

"Take it easy," Damaso said; "if you're right there's no need to shout—truth finds its own way into people's ears."

He spoke so calmly that Robles felt ashamed. For in fact he

had never raised his voice like that to anybody before. He crouched again and cut away furiously so that the knife slipped out of his hand and fell at the other man's feet. He went to pick it up, but Damaso's hand was there first once again, only it was his right hand this time. When he saw it, Robles did not know what to think: it was almost purple and horribly swollen. The hand was withdrawn immediately and the left hand took its place holding the knife and giving it to him. Robles took it uneasily and began cutting without looking what he was doing. He kept quiet for a while until he suddenly stopped working and asked, without raising his head:

"How did your hand get like that?"

"Last night, out at the long line . . . Number six float. . . . I went to collect a fish. . . . It had lost the fight and was flipping about on the surface. I thought it would be easy as usual and hauled the float aboard; I untied the hundred and twenty from the stanchion and when I saw it wasn't threshing carelessly wrapped the line round my hand. . . . It got stuck to the gunwhale and went crazy and if it hadn't been for the stay severing the line it would have pulled my hand off, I tell you. . . . It took the stay and a piece of line with it."

Damaso was speaking in a flat voice thinking he would calm the other man that way, but he could not know why Robles had knelt motionless in front of the fish with the knife in his hand. He would have asked him if something was wrong but Robles did not give him time for that either; he quickly went back to the bow, put his hand down and fetched up in front of Damaso's eyes the complete piece of tackle:

"Look, do you recognize it?"

"I should think so, it's my splice!"

"Then it's your fish too, for Christ's sake!" he shouted furiously and threw himself back against the gunwhale waiting to hear how the hell he'd answer that.

—Translated by J.G. Brotherston

VIRGILIO PIÑERA

Virgilio Piñera was born in 1912 in Cuba, but spent many years in Argentina. He is a poet, dramatist, short-story writer and novelist.

The Dragée reflects strong associations with the main stream of western literature. It is complex and inconclusive, requiring more active participation by the reader to note and follow up on the subtle clues and suggestions scattered throughout the story than is the case in either the more folk-oriented or the message-oriented stories in this volume. Piñera seems to have been influenced by the writings of western existentialists, such as Kafka and Sartre.

Set in Havana, the story reflects something of the pattern of life in that city. It is possible to follow the movement of the story by looking at a map of Havana. The fact that the story is set on a bus is typical in a city in which the primary mode of transportation is the bus service. The "Ten Cents" restaurant may well be one of the chain of government-run cafés located throughout the city, which provide meals free to students and at very low cost to workers. The protagonist in the story, a "traveller calling on doctors," very likely began his journey near the Plaza de la Revolución, near the center city, where many of the government buildings are located. Intending originally to call on customers in Vedado, an ultra-modern section of the city north of the Plaza de la Revolución, he decides instead to go south, toward the suburb of Víbora, in order to avoid crossing the street in the heavy rain. The events detailed in the story mingle with his day dreams, his philosophizing about "bus life," his relations with his wife, Berta, and the torrential tropical rain, to give the story a surrealistic tone.

A dragée (drah-zhey) is a small candy, frequently chocolate or silver coated, and filled with a liquid center.

The Dragée

In the end I got to like having breakfast in the Ten Cents. One of the few things I'm now grateful to my wife Berta for is that

at ten minutes to eight on that wet October morning she gave
me a shove and called me a fool for failing to get seats near the
door. She says she prefers them because in case of fire they are
only two steps from the exit. She says this every morning and
that day as usual of course I didn't get the wretched seats.
That's why we sat down near the fat assistant, whom Berta
can't stand for the simple reason that, being indecently fat
herself, she feels uncomfortable in front of the woman. To calm
her, I said it's only a question of ten minutes and that to cut the
meal short I could do without the strawberry pie, but she
ordered me one and another for herself, and two coffees with
milk. 'Don't look at her,' she said in my ear, 'she thinks all the
men fall for her.' I went on looking where I pleased ignoring
Berta's warning. Every morning she tells me not to look at
that assistant, and she does so even when my eyes are fixed on
the street. That's one of her many tricks. . . . Because today I
was watching an enchanting schoolgirl spreading butter on
her bread, picking it up in the laziest way, dipping it in her
milky coffee and lifting it to her mouth. With a mental bound I
went up to her. 'Good morning, my love. Tired of waiting for
me? I thought the right bus would never come.' And I kissed
her on one of her divine little ears. The reply to all this was
Berta's scolding voice saying out of the blue. 'See what you can
do to raise some money. The television people say they won't
wait another day.' I almost shoved the whole pie into my
mouth. The assistant laughed; fortunately Berta didn't see
her. I finished my coffee somehow, swallowing the last gulps
mixed with words like 'idler,' 'skinflint' (how does that apply to
me?), 'bad husband.' I put a peso on the counter and left her
still talking. I went into the streets. Now it was almost a
deluge—but never mind. Berta called something after me,
which fortunately I didn't hear. As the stop was two blocks
away, I went under the Galiane arcade. Actually my calls that
morning were in Vedado, but as I'd gone in the direction of the
Zanja stop and didn't want to cross the street, I decided on the
spot to visit my customers in Vibora. I am a traveller calling on
doctors. I hoped those in Vibora might prove more profitable
than those in Vedado!

It's like the end of the world, I thought, but anyhow it's a day
entirely at my disposal. I shan't see Berta again until eight.
Although we live only two blocks from her work, she is an
incorrigible patron of the Ten Cents and loves their 'blue plate'

lunch. Last night she accused me of bigamy. What will she accuse me of tonight? She loves liqueur dragées, so I'll bring her a bag. Probably she'll ask me if they're poisoned. The day's like the end of the world, but so long as I'm alive I'll manage somehow. There comes the bus. It's raining even harder. Now I'm beginning to get wet, but there's always some charitable soul around.

A building worker offered to shelter me under his cape. He began to tell me something about poor deliveries of material. But the bus's arrival saved me from a practical course in building.

It was full. All the same, if one's lucky. . . . I pinched the seat of a priest who got off at the corner of Reina and Manrique, on one of those benches along the side that take three passengers. Beside me a woman in her sixties with a baby on her knee; on the other side a chick. Normal situation. So I made no inward protest. What sets my nerves on edge with apprehension is a vacant seat. Who will fill it? I will say that I have very bad luck. In ninety-nine per cent of cases someone unpleasant does. I could count the times on my hand in which I get one of those enchanting schoolgirls that bring a devilish little glow to my fifty-year-old frame. One thinks things, feels things. . . . Unfortunately the enchantment is short-lived. The sylph gets down at the corner, and the seat she left is now occupied by another passenger.

This is all part of a very special type of human relationship: bus life. It is as if we spent lives in movement, and their duration was one of minutes. At the same time it's a way of feeling anguish. The face that moved us, the soul which peeped throught it, and for which we are now building enchanting plans, perhaps of eternal union . . . probably we shall never see it again! In fact the bell is rung and the face disappears, followed by our despairing eyes. Bus life is a crossword puzzle, a parcel that others help us to carry. It's overhearing conversations that throw us into perplexity, because we lack the personal history of the passenger that would give us an adequate scenic background. And the flood of people continues to flow in and out, getting on and off without a pause. It's all glances and silent questionings, tragedies which one thinks one has divined and which are probably only absurd comedies. Everything is in motion, as if within the earth's gravitational field there were another gravity, different from the common one because perceptible. At the same time one has the agonized feeling that this 'special time' will be of no use to one.

But the mysterious world remains with us. It seems unique, not even challenged by the much lauded world of the theatre. I don't deny that the stage has its mystery. But alas it is soon dispelled. If we go to the theatre at all often we come to know who the actors are, what they eat and even what they think. Of course I know I'm exaggerating. This is only a manner of speaking. All the same, when we see them night after night they certainly come to lose their magic. In the bus, on the other hand, everything is mysterious owing to the very fluidity of the human mass that continuously fills it. Isn't it astounding to think that I shall never again see that man in a blue suit who is signalling to the driver that he wants to get down at the corner? And isn't it equally astounding that this very reasonable possibility doesn't make me think that what I have taken for a man in a blue suit isn't merely a phantom? But doesn't there really come a moment when by reason of this fluidity I feel that the material object which conveys me from here to there is itself a nightmare? Of course this bus question seems at first sight most superficial and devoid of real interest. But the moment we fix our attention on it, a world of questions opens up before us.

Questions moreover that defeat every hypothesis. Here 'Who is he?' 'What's he going to do?' 'Where does he live?' 'What's he thinking?'—and all the infinite conjectures of the human brain—remain unanswered. Let no one cite those cases of a meeting in the bus at which two beings become united forever. From the moment when one identifies the other, that is to say the second they cease to be strangers, they automatically cease to belong to the bus world. They can get off at the next corner because now they have nothing to do with it.

In the complex world of bureaucratic jargon these locomotary services are called 'wheeled transport.' I would dare to maintain that the bus is the king of all these 'creatures.' Car drivers view it with respect, even with terror. One driver said to me once: 'There's no more exquisite food for a bus than a private car.' As I was travelling in his car at that moment I felt literally crushed. Their foolhardiness, moreover, is spine-chilling. They haven't the least hesitation in measuring up against a specimen as fearful as the road tanker, or the eight-wheeled lorry. I would say that the bus's purpose is not so much to follow a route as to elude the countless dangers that rise in its path with elegant effrontery, and at the same time, to produce copious new ones. That twofold reef of danger which produces cries of horror, curses, and virulent interchanges, with much hooting and flashing of signals, reminds me of a shipwreck, with the sensible difference that here nothing sinks but everything smashes.

Meanwhile the bus continued on its way. I must explain that these reflections didn't belong to that particular journey. My mind was then a blank; I was merely observing the landscape. A landscape which I viewed from one side and which gave me the impression that the houses were disappearing into one another. This distorted vision amused me. I much preferred it to what I should see with my right eye were I to look at the woman with the child on her knee. An old woman—there are plenty of them—who exclaimed when the vehicle pulled up sharp, 'Oh, these bus drivers!' and then dropped her head again like a dog who gives up because the affair isn't worth more than one bark. Not her exclamation (we know well enough that phrases like this form part of the bus ritual) but the tone in which it was uttered made me stop my ears. I said to myself: 'There's something behind this voice. . . ' At the same time I saw with the tail of my eye that the old woman was trying to settle the child between her enormous thighs and enormous breasts, as if to protect him against other possible jolts. The child, on the other hand, whose stillness was disturbing (it seemed to be under anaesthetic) presented to me only one-half of its face which, like the known surface of the moon, appeared, despite its extreme youth, to be peppered with craters, full of blotches and, again like the moon, to shine with a yellow, waxen light that made it look like a corpse. This little monster (I find myself compelled to give it this unpleasant description) had been endowed by nature with an excessive hairiness for its tender years (it couldn't be more than five): its arms and legs had thick black hairs like boar's bristles; its head was covered from the brows to the nape of the neck with a curly mane that was briskly blowing in the breeze from the bus window and falling like a cascade on its marble forehead.

I found this spectacle highly displeasing. Consequently I

decided to turn my eyes away. Probably at a circus there would be some more pleasing attraction beside the habitual program. But here in the bus, to which I certainly wouldn't deny its circus-like character (though with the sensible difference that the attraction is never known in advance) this child-old woman or this old woman-child, this impossible union of infancy and old age had a shattering effect on me. I started looking at the street again, thinking at the same time and with no proof at all that they were going to get out at the next corner.

Just at this moment the child exclaimed with the un-modulated voice of a savage, I would almost say, with a grunt, 'Granny, give me a sweet.'

I couldn't possibly help looking again. Its face remained as stiff as before, and although I didn't see it at the moment of speaking I am sure it didn't stir a muscle. The chattering of a parrot would have sounded more human. This 'Granny, give me a sweet,' reminded me of the imperious tone of a morphin-omaniac demanding his dose.

The grandmother, as if worked by a spring, opened one of those handbags that were fashionable back in the twenties —handbags whose elegance consists of a line of black fringe at the top and a scattering of gleaming rhinestones over its printed cloth. Immediately it exhaled a wave of cheap perfume mixed with the peculiar smell of ancient silk.

Now the old woman, whose black brocade dress followed the lines of her swelling flesh, as if in memory that once upon a time it had maintained a proper proportion to the cloth, took out a lozenge-tin on whose lid was a hunting scene, and with the tips of her fingers extracted a sweet so small that it was more like a wafer. It was green, but at the same time appeared black; it had a solid look, but you would have thought it was on the point of dissolving in the old woman's fingers; what is more, it gave off a smell that I should call unusual in this sort of object.

The old woman, the very image of imperturbability, held the sweet between her fingers, and gave a distrustful look to left and right. Upon this the child, with even more complete stolid-ity, if that was possible, produced a bass voice in which to say as in a single word that expressed a whole world of animality, 'Gimmeit!'

And it opened a huge mouth. As she reached out her hand,

she glanced at the girl in the seat beside her. Fascinated by this repulsive scene, she had been unable to look away. Then the old woman, who already had the sweet almost beside the child's mouth, took another look at the girl and said: 'Now be a polite boy, Pepito, and ask this nice girl if she'd like a sweet too.' Thereupon, Pepito, without a protest, without any reluctant grimace, with the complete unconcern of a murderer choosing his victim, took the sweet with the tips of his fingers and offered it to her. There must have been something imperious in this gesture or perhaps a deeper significance that she could not understand. I say this because the girl mechanically took the sweet, looking at the same time first at the child, then at the old woman. I was just about to turn my attention away from all this and return to my 'landscape' when I heard the child's unearthly voice: 'Eat it up.' She hesitated for a moment, gave a half-smile, and was just going to caress the child when it turned to the old woman who had followed the scene as anxiously as if it were a matter of life and death. The old woman turned to the girl: 'Please do eat the sweet. If you don't my grandson won't want to eat his.' And all this to the accompaniment of much bobbing and bowing of the head and smiles of complicity, as if this were a matter to be discussed between adults. At the same time she took from the lozenge-tin two sweets, not green or greenish black but white. One of these she offered to Pepito and took the other herself. Now Pepito, with his mouth open, looked at the girl as if waiting for her to do as he wished, and the old woman opened her mouth too. Some passengers were laughing, the driver made a heavy joke, the girl began to get annoyed. But no doubt she had decided that the best thing would be to eat the sweet. I was on the point of telling her not to (I don't know why I should have done so for there's no possible danger in a sweet offered you by a child) because people who look like that augur no good. But my invincible timidity, my confounded habit of not mixing myself up in other people's business compelled me to remain silent.

And as was to be expected, she ate it. And of course they ate theirs. Now what sent me into a cold sweat was the scornful attitude or rather the attitude of 'severed communication' that the singular pair assumed once they had gained their objective, if you can apply such a term to the act of persuading someone to eat a sweet. In fact they didn't take the slightest notice when the girl said: 'It tastes rather like medicine.' They sank so deep into themselves indeed that they seemed to be made of clothes rather than flesh. I am speaking literally, you understand. The old woman enclosed the child even tighter, if that were possible, between her knees and her breasts, then covered him completely with a kind of black cloak that hung from her shoulders. At the same time she raised her knees as far as her excessive fatness would allow and, hunching her shoulders, let her head fall on her chest.

A rude old woman and an ill-brought-up child, I said to myself, and this explanation seemed to leave me satisfied. Yet I was quite certain that the explanation was too simple. It hadn't the power to stop my thoughts, which started to flow. For the fact is that nobody, absolutely nobody in this world offers a sweet—despite any motives they may have for doing so—and then immediately adopts a public and obvious air of distance. One lets one's thoughts run on, and does not notice the traps they set for one. This is what happened to me when I thought about the question of motives. What can I know about the possible motives of this pair, who present such a contrast in ages? What can I know, a simple passenger in a bus, I who don't turn over mountains of papers or spend sleepless nights spying on people's actions? And why shouldn't the old woman and the child have hidden motives? Or the old woman at least, not to bring the child into this sticky business (as it seemed to me). For although he looked like a monster, he was in all probability the very model of innocence. No, I said to myself again, it's no more than this; a rude old woman and an ill-brought-up child.

Defeated, I returned at a bound to the simple explanation. No, it can't, it can't be more than this. There are no hidden motives; there is merely a sweet. And even if the girl did remark that it tasted like medicine, there's no reason to attach exaggerated importance to that.

So, hanging in the abyss of doubt, I opted for the simple explanation, which is of course infinitely more comfortable. I repeated in my head: Rude old woman, ill-brought-up child. . . . And just at that moment of charming compromise I saw the girl fall forward with all the weight of her body.

I would not say that she fell dead (which is what happened)

then and there, but that she fell owing to death. I know that the sentence is forced, but so too was the situation. For she fell owing to death, as if first she had had to transform herself into an inert object in order afterwards to fall dead at our feet. When I saw her body strike the floor of the bus I had the impression of a Pharaoh's mummy falling by accident on the floor of the museum. And while I'm on the subject of mummies. . . . I had plunged down to save the poor girl. I took her in my arms and laid her on her back. I should never have done it! That smooth, rosy untarnished skin now looked wrinkled, black, and scaly. Her face seemed to reflect a deliberate desire to arouse terror, disgust, even irreverence. It was as if, in addition to being forced to die a violent death (and indubitably this had been the case) she also had to leave a foul impression behind.

These were my reflections as I knelt on the floor of the bus holding in my arms hatred transformed into a corpse. Seeing the hatred in this face I felt moved; they hadn't even left her the enjoyment of her role as victim. In this infernal plan (did such a plan really exist?) there was the implacable design of turning a simple corpse (a corpse is a simple thing and no more) into something offensive. And this was the situation. For when I saw the passengers' attitude I could feel that the hatred reflected in that face awoke hatred in the rest of the faces there assembled. A woman said emphatically: 'Throw her out of the window.' It was obvious that the window was too narrow for such an operation, but this woman, in her sudden and justified hatred, had lost the idea of measurement.

Here everyone had lost his head. The bus had stopped; in front and behind our vehicle could be heard the deafening hooting of many other vehicles. To crown everything, a torrential rain began which compelled us to close the windows and doors. This made the scene even more sordid. It made us think indeed that very soon we would all suddenly strike the floor like the girl, and, like her, fall ridiculously, owing to death.

A policeman, who was travelling with us, started to force his way from the back of the bus, flourishing a revolver. He looked so absurd that despite the tragedy I was holding in my arms, I couldn't help smiling inside, thinking how often (as was the case then) they arrive too late to prevent a death. But his police mechanism had already started up; he had to make a

way for himself, to approach the corpse and ask the inevitable
question: 'What's going on here?' And then: 'Did anyone see
the killer?' And after that: 'Are there any eyewitnesses?' followed by 'Everyone stay where he is!'

This was what he did, though despite his mechanism he
could not prevent the terror reflected in his face at the sight of
the dead girl, because this was not foreseen by a policeman
whose view of death, the most fascinating, is a knife in the
belly or a bullet in the head. The moment he was confronted
with that face, he was on the defensive, and it would have
taken very little to make him open fire on her.

Once more she produced the desired effect, the sinister invi-
tation to go on tirelessly killing her which the policeman felt in
his straightforward animal nature. For leaping to one side he
said in a chucking voice: 'This is a case for the captain' . . . and
opening the bus door he went out in a water-spout, disappearing into the rain.

Then I put the corpse on the floor. Mechanically I took out
my handkerchief and covered the face. All the time the rain
was getting heavier; absolute water-spouts were striking the
windows, and at the same time a veritable river was forming in
the street, which prevented the relief of the traffic jam caused
by our vehicle. As a result, the fluid life of the bus gathered us
inside once more and obliged us to look at one another as at
inhabitants of different planets. The rare case had occurred of
some dozens of persons watching a corpse to which not only
were they not attached by any ties of friendship, but to which
they could not even give a name. They did not know in what
suburb she lived, who—singular or plural—would really
mourn her, or finally and most important, what illness she had
died of.

Therefore gossip, misrepresentation, speculation, and
compassion—indispensable ingredients in the sauce of a
proper wake—were scandalously lacking in the present case.
We had the dead but lacked its personal history; this corpse
was of no use. True, she would never take the bus again (in this
sense she had ceased to be the living enigma that all passengers are), but now thrown on the floor, it obliged us to concen-
trate our thoughts on it. And what thoughts? Thoughts of
manifest impotence, of dumb rage, of the sadness of a hidden
mystery. Dying so suddenly in the bus, the girl had cancelled

216 *Virgilio Piñera (Cuba)*

all possibilities of reaching the source, her source, by converting us as she did so into pillars of salt for having looked
back, that is to say, at her past, which was for us only a blank
page.

A building worker, whose boots were almost touching the
dead girl's feet, expressed it exactly when he said slyly; 'Tell us
a little something, puss. . . . ' Then turning his head, he observed next moment to the company: 'She isn't one of my birds.
She got into this trouble of her own.'

Brutal but convincing. There was a collective guffaw; but it
was followed by a chill, because once the joke had had its effect
we fell back into depression. A depression which did not affect
the old woman and the child; they had not woken up. I hadn't
looked at them again since the tragedy, for the corpse had
stolen all attention. Indeed one monstrosity will always be
eclipsed by another. The dead girl's face reduced my disgust
and horror at those other two faces to nothing; if I noticed
them again and if I listened to their stertorous noise it was
because of the silence that followed our laughter, as if we had
been deflated by one explosion of hilarity. We remained in this
state, the very image of collapse like a balloon after it has
burst.

I returned to my seat. Good, I said to myself. Now there are
only the formalities. In a few minutes the policeman will be
back, bringing the captain with him and very likely the police
surgeon as well. They'll arrest the old woman, and if there's a
trial we'll be summoned as witnesses. If the autopsy proves
that the victim swallowed toxic substances some minutes before her death, then it will be fully proved that the old woman
is a murderess.

On the other hand this hypothesis would be abandoned if it
should be proved that the girl died a natural death. The mere
thought of this made me cross. It isn't that I set myself up as a
detective—far from it—but my inner judgement couldn't
agree that things had happened in such a simple way. My
principal suspicion was based on the colour of two sweets
—green or greenish black, the one they gave the girl; white,
the ones eaten by the grandmother and grandchild. I reasoned
in this manner: (1) the old woman carries a lozenge-tin with
poisoned sweets and with sweets (let's call them so) that are

harmless. Some are green or greenish black, the others white, which means that at a single glance there is no possibility of an irreparable mistake. (2) The grandchild, who no doubt is innocence personified, is at the same time a tool in the grandmother's hands. She has trained him as you train a dog or a monkey. (3) At a certain signal (in this case secret) the innocent child asks for a sweet. (4) Not the child but the old woman makes the offer. This feature struck me as a masterstroke in the art of deception. If Pepito were to proffer the sweet on his own, there would be the possibility of a polite refusal; there would be nothing rude in rejecting a child's offer. With an adult it would be a different story; the grandmother, by putting the child forward makes any refusal impossible. (5) Let us remember the girl's last words: 'It tastes rather like medicine': words which, as we have seen, aroused a whole series of sinister conjectures in me, which were unfortunately confirmed a few minutes later. Obviously that sweet must have contained a mortal poison. I would swear it publicly before the court of God and man.

Pleased and proud of my brilliant inductions and deductions, I stared barefacedly at the old woman, her lips moved continuously, reflecting the wandering course of her dreams. She seemed to ask me the question: Have you examined the intestines yet, sir?

I was on the point of shaking her awake and shouting at her: Don't worry about that. I'll take out the intestines in a minute and they'll speak for themselves, you devilish old hag! But as the intestines were still in the dead girl's belly, the argument was valid. Since there was still the possibility (which I obstinately considered remote) that it was not poisoning, I had no alternative but to examine the case from the point of view of pure coincidence. At the moment when the girl is ripe for death someone offers her a completely harmless sweet. Then all the scaffolding on the alleged wickedness of the old woman falls to the ground. In this case I should have to admit that my imagination had played me a dirty trick. But . . .

But it is just crazy human vanity to affirm positively that an examination of the intestines alone can disprove poisoning by the injection of a toxic substance. Consequently I conclude: overwhelming accusations, crushing evidence, sentence of death . . . and my 'sagacity' puts me in such a state of euphoria that I mutter in my teeth as I again look at the old woman: 'Tropical locust!'

At this moment a woman who had been mumbling prayers mixed with such profane phrases as 'Won't this rain ever stop?' 'They'll close the shop before I get there,' 'I shall catch a terrible cold,' rested her eyes on the sleeping pair. No doubt because the rain was now beating rather less hard and the snoring was really deafening, she leant forward, not having noticed them before, opened her eyes wide, and adopted the posture of one listening to an invalid's laboured breathing: 'They're lucky! They aren't even aware that there's been a death!'

Upon which the builder, who had already pronounced his verdict against the sleepers, took a sidelong glance which moved from the body to the woman's face. Then, as if looking for approval in her eyes, which he certainly expected, for in his opinion no one in the world could feel the slightest sympathy for people of that stamp, he said: 'Don't they look suspicious to you?'

The question had the virtue of giving me limitless possibilities of accusation. After my last reasonings I had found myself at the dead point where doubts are as imperious as certainties. But now someone was coming to my help, and in the plain language of the people, without mental contortions or elaborate surmises, was putting my theories on the plane of verisimilitude. I felt myself flushing as my hands began to move nervously, uncertain where to rest on my body. I looked once or twice at the builder, waiting for him to add something, for him to show greater eloquence in fact. For all I wanted were arguments, dozens of them, thousands of them if they could be found, as brilliant, subtle, and irrefutable as possible, so that the old woman's guilt should shine out like a star with its own light, outshining all those other stars of innocence whose rays hurt my eyes, forcing me to depart from my fixed idea.

Overcoming my inveterate timidity, I told myself that all I had to do was to 'agitate' the passengers. Now the builder had pronounced that sinister word which has the strange power of converting a human being into a cornered animal. Certainly I must not let the suspicion evaporate; I must give it body, 'circulate the rumour' as they say. The captain would soon arrive, and it suited my plans that he should find public opinion suitably prepared. So, making up my mind once and for all, I said, pointing at the snorers: 'No more than suspicious?'

The woman who had been praying gave me an unfriendly look since I had forestalled her reply. Completely ignoring my person, she said to the builder:

'That's just what I was thinking. There's something fishy about this.'

'Then you saw what I saw, did you?' I asked, looking her in the eyes.

'May I inquire what you saw?' she asked in an irritated voice. 'Nothing wrong would be likely to escape this person's notice,' (and she pointed to herself).

'Good,' said the builder, 'I saw the child give her a sweet.'

'A sweet? . . . And to whom?'

'To this . . . ' and the builder pointed to the dead girl.

'What about it? . . . ' said the woman. 'It's the most natural thing in the world. I like sweets too. I always carry some in my bag. Would you like one?'

The builder turned pale and made a gesture of refusal.

'But poisoned ones?' I asked her as if it were the most natural thing in the world.

'What? What does he say? . . . Poisoned?' and as she spoke she swayed her body backwards and forwards like someone trying to dodge an attack. I see what's coming . . . but it's no business of mine.

'Didn't you see, then?'

'See? . . . What . . . ?' and passing behind me she planted herself in front of the sleepers and looked carefully at them.

'If you didn't see before, there's nothing to see now,' I said as she came close to me.

'You must have been dreaming, dear,' shouted the woman who had suggested throwing the body out of the window. 'Didn't you see when the old woman told the kid to give that girl a sweet?' Then she turned straight to me. 'Look, sir, I was going to tell the policeman, but really I don't like getting mixed up in trouble!'

'The captain will be here in a minute,' I answered. 'I think it's our duty to tell him what we saw.'

'And you believe that the old woman poisoned her?' the

woman who had been praying asked me. 'More likely she died because her hour had come.'

'All the same,' and I gave her a look to show that I had caught her in a contradiction, 'you said there was something fishy about it.'

'Yes, I said that because . . . ' She glanced towards the bus door as if afraid the captain would appear, and added with a stammer: 'I'm not going to be mixed up in any arguments. I didn't see anything.'

'So, that was it . . . ' I said to her with a mocking smile. 'You saw nothing but thought it all up. Probably you went further and thought that the bird and the old woman were enemies, that when they caught the bus the old woman had already given her the poison, perhaps in the Ten Cents, mixed with her coffee and milk.'

'In the Ten Cents, what a horrible idea,' she shouted in a fury. 'Don't start making accusations against me. Did you ever see me in a Ten Cents?'

'I didn't say you were in the Ten Cents. I mentioned the Ten Cents as I might mention any other place. That's where you'd go for a meal, or a cool drink, or to have a coffee and milk, unless you considered it more appropriate to go to the undertaker's.'

'God forbid!' and the woman crossed herself. Her poor head was swimming with confusion. Lost in a welter of half thoughts, she said to me with an accusing air:

'Perhaps you walked through the Ten Cents and saw it all.'

Unintentionally she had succeeded in shaking me with this stupid sally. Obviously I wasn't going to tell her that I had breakfasted in the Ten Cents. By a paradox very frequent in people of her kind, her total lack of imagination had put it into her head that I was the assassin. So it would be prudent on my part to conceal from her my innocent visit to this place. All the same, I repeat, I felt shaken because the hypothetical example was strong enough to lead my fancy to the point where the trap awaits us that we have ourselves prepared. Unintentionally she made me see the unhappy girl taking her breakfast at the counter beside me, with those charming affectations that girls put on when they know that a man is persistently watching them. It was such a heavenly vision and agreed so well with my

eternal and unfulfilled aspiration to enjoy the love of one of
these little creatures hardly beyond the age of puberty that I
was on the point of proclaiming aloud: 'Yes, of course I'm the
murderer. I poisoned her because she refused me again.'

The woman's commanding voice roused me from my brief
musing.

'Answer. Haven't you got a tongue in your head?'

'Don't get so excited, mother,' said the builder, 'the gentleman wasn't in the Ten Cents.'

'And how do you know, mister?' she asked distrustfully.

'Are you deaf or pretending to be a fool? The gentleman
said. . . . '

'I don't care what he said,' she interrupted. 'I asked him if he
was in the Ten Cents and he's got to answer me.'

'With pleasure,' I said to her, allowing a mocking smile to
pass over my lips, 'I regret to tell you that I wasn't in the Ten
Cents.'

'Then,' she answered, slapping me in the face, 'stop talking
all this rubbish. . . . ' She paused as if about to say something
conclusive. Finally: 'Leave me out of this . . . !' And to clinch it;
'I haven't been in the Ten Cents for months.'

'Then you've missed their strawberry pies,' I said. 'They're
beautiful. If I do have breakfast in the Ten Cents it's for those
pies.'

'Then you didn't have strawberry pie today?' the woman at
the window asked. 'Quite right,' I answered, assuming an air of
great disappointment. 'I had to go to the Ministry to fetch my
identity card.'

'But you got on the bus near the Ten Cents,' said the builder.
'You got on with me. Don't you remember?'

'With you?' I asked disconcerted.

'Yes, with me. It was pouring with rain, and there was no bus
for ages. So I invited you to shelter under my cape. This . . . '
and he waved in my face a hood-shaped piece of white nylon.

'Now I remember,' I exclaimed, pretending to be surprised.
'If it wasn't for you I should have been soaked.' Then to dispel
his suspicions I added: 'I had to see my wife. She works two
blocks from the Ten Cents. So from the Ministry . . . '

'Right,' the builder interrupted me. 'Then do you intend to
accuse the old woman?'

'I shall say what I saw. I shall confine my answers to that.'

'And what did you see?' asked the woman who had been praying.

'Now we're back where we were! You're making no progress, friend . . . ' and the builder gave a laugh.

'I shall say that the old woman gave the girl a sweet.'

'It was the child who gave it to her,' said the woman who had made the suggestion about the window.

'Yes, but at the old woman's bidding,' I argued. 'You're not going to tell me that the child was the prime mover in this . . . crime.'

'Tell me something,' and the builder looked at me in a funny way. 'D'you know much about this business of poisoning?'

I must have turned very pale at this question. For the prayer woman who bore me a grudge over the matter of the Ten Cents, asked me:

'Are you feeling bad?'

'No,' I said pretending to be unmoved, 'I feel perfectly well.' (Actually my head was spinning, and I had to pause for some seconds before going on.) Finally I asked the builder:

'Why do you want to know?'

'I asked because I wanted to know whether poison can kill a person the moment it's administered.' And without giving me time to answer he added: 'I remember that when they gave my dog strychnine pills, it was quite a time before he fell over. It was more than an hour, and he foamed at the mouth.'

'I don't know anything about poisons,' I said, 'but I've read that some are instantaneous.'

'That looks bad for her,' he exclaimed, turning his gaze to the grandmother and child. 'Some people are capable of anything.' He brooded for a moment then pointed at the old woman and asked: 'Are you going to accuse her?'

I couldn't answer. Someone was thumping on the bus door; there was a confused shouting and whistling. The driver, coming out of his doze, pressed a button and the door opened. The captain, the policeman, and a sergeant came in.

'What's going on here?' asked the captain. The question was superfluous, but he had asked it out of pure automatism, as if he couldn't proceed to an ocular, forensic, or expert examination without first asking: 'What's going on here?'

'Captain,' I began, but he cut me short brusquely:

'Who asked you anything?'

He immediately bent down beside the corpse, removed the handkerchief that covered her face and looked at her attentively.

'My god, what's this?' he asked in consternation. Then, turning to the sergeant who was also looking at the corpse, he asked: 'What's this, lad? This is very strange.'

'Yes, Captain, it . . . it gives you the shivers,' he mumbled.

The captain was slowly getting up, making an evident effort to prevent his body from too quickly assuming an upright position; meanwhile his eyes reflected the perturbation produced in him by a situation that was so out-of-the-ordinary. But he had to do something; as he couldn't refrain from giving orders, and as authority can't stand with folded arms, he repeated his question, but this time in the past tense:

'What's been going on here?'

And thinking that no one would have the courage to answer him in view of the snub he had given me he added:

'Come on, tell us what happened. You tell me . . . ' and he pointed to me. 'You wanted to talk, didn't you? Well, talk.'

'Captain,' I began. But my voice was so quiet and hesitant that, already furious at this tiresome interruption when he was probably just getting ready to go to lunch, he shouted at me, putting the same urgency into his voice that he had hoped I would put into mine:

'Speak up. Tell me exactly what happened. Stop "sirring" me, and no theories, please.'

In less than five minutes I'd put him in the picture. A large part of my brief explanation had been devoted to presenting the old woman as the presumed guilty party. I based my accusation on the different colours of the sweets. The captain, who wasn't as foolish as he looked, interrupted me to object that this was no conclusive proof because sweet manufacturers usually offer them to the consumer in a variety of colours. Seeing that he would not swallow this, I tried to influence him by describing the old woman's suspicious manoeuvres, in the matter of her elaborate offer of the sweet in question. This argument had no more success than the last.

'We should have some trouble in the legal department,' he said, 'if we were to take everyone as a murderer who offers anyone a sweet.'

Caught in a predicament, I resorted to the dramatic method. I extended my arm towards the old woman:

'Look at her, Captain. She and her grandchild started snoring the moment the crime was committed'; then I added these words which, by my calculation, would put the old woman into grave difficulties:

'Why don't you wake her up and question her?'

Alas, on that ground I was to be beaten by the old woman herself. She had a masterstroke in store for me. I somewhat foresaw this, but my impatience was such that I dared to touch the captain's uniform and urge him once more to wake the old woman from her torpor.

Ignoring me entirely, he turned to the sergeant and said:

'Tell the ambulance team to come and fetch the corpse.' And to the policeman: 'Start taking the names and addresses of the passengers.' The prayer woman took up her position in front of the captain: 'Shall we have to go to court?' 'You'll be notified in due course,' was all that he said. One passenger asked: 'Shall we be able to go when we've given our particulars?' And a woman: 'When will the case be?' Everybody began asking questions. The captain shouted: 'Quiet!'

This command was so peremptory that the policeman himself stopped asking questions and looked at the captain, whose ill humour was increasing in this closed bus. He had undone two buttons of his shirt and quite obviously wanted to 'liquidate' the case as quickly as he possibly could. Again he cried: 'Quiet!'

Now when the quiet that reigned in the bus after this second threat could be characterized as 'deathly,' the old woman, from the distant country in which she was then travelling, was finally able to notify the captain of her real and effective presence on the field of action by snoring more loudly, if possible, than ever. And to increase the efficacy of her announcement, the full blast of her snores was counterpointed by nasal, grunting sounds from her grandson.

It was then that he decided to follow my suggestion. After listening to a few snores (he was no doubt trying to guess the nature of this deep sleep), he began to move in the direction of the snorers, but he did so by slow stages as if anxious to postpone an unpleasant encounter as long as possible. Finally he planted himself in front of the old woman and gave her a brisk shake. Showing no signs of the natural confusion you would expect in a waking person, she looked the captain up and down as if to say: I knew that you would come. Well, here I am. Start questioning me.

Meanwhile, feeling her grandson stirring under the cloak she began to rock him on her knees, supporting herself on the tips of her toes to do so. But the devilish child who was no doubt just waking up, struggled to put out his head, emitting sounds, moreover, which made the captain open his eyes wide. As for me, they froze the blood in my veins.

The old woman seemed to be afflicted with Saint Vitus' Dance. Her grandson's struggles were becoming increasingly wild and violent, obliging her to pull her cloak tight in one place and tug her dress down in another and, to press down with her elbows that bulk which she was having great difficulty in holding between her legs. As a result the imperturbable lady was quickly transformed into a being consisting of a series of unrelated muscular contractions.

At this point the captain, who had made no further comment despite all this struggle, took hold of the cloak, as if about to pull it off once and for all.

'Can't you see that the child's just going to suffocate?' he said.

'What child?' she asked with a tremendous show of astonishment which I took for cynicism.

'Why the child you've got underneath your cloak, of course, your grandson who gave the girl that sweet.'

'What are you talking about?' asked the old woman in annoyance.

'I haven't got any grandchildren and I don't care for sweets.'

'We'll find out about that at the station,' said the captain, who was towering with rage. 'But you can tell me for a start what it is you've got under that cloak.'

'A suckling pig,' answered the old woman with the broadest of smiles. 'A pretty little suckling pig, I bought it just now.'

'Granny,' said the captain with a very grim expression. 'Stop your stupid jokes. Everybody on this bus knows that you were carrying your grandson in your arms when you got on.'

'Me?' exclaimed the old woman. 'Got on with my grandson?

Where did you get that story from. I've already told you I'm not a grandmother and I haven't got any grandchildren. What are they getting at me for?'

On hearing this effrontery I leapt like a lion on the old woman.

'I confirm what the captain just said. I call all the passengers to witness. How can she deny that this is her grandson?' And I pointed an accusing finger at the shape. 'Will you deny that he put the sweet in the girl's mouth? An finally, will you deny that you poisoned her?'

'Jesus, Mary, and Joseph!' and the old woman crossed herself. 'Why, I wouldn't even kill a fly . . . '

'Perhaps you're not interested in flies, but you do poison human beings. And you rely on this innocent babe to help you do it.' I turned to the captain: 'And now she brings out this story about a suckling pig. . . .You're a liar!'

The old woman was hardly managing to control the shape which was struggling with increasing violence under her cloak. But she raised her eyes, looked at me with a shake of the head, looked at the captain and was opening her mouth, no doubt intending to protest her innocence once more, when a sharp and prolonged grunt was heard, followed by others in crescendo. The captain, absolutely beside himself, leant over the old woman and pulled at the cloak. Before everyone's eyes there appeared a little black pig with thick bristles. There was a frightened look in his eyes, which he closed when they found the captain's riveted upon them. The pig then turned right round trembling and tried to hide in the old woman's lap.

'She was telling the truth,' said the captain, looking first at the pig and then at the old woman. 'It's the truth, all right.'

'Of course it's the truth,' insisted the old woman, 'I said I was carrying a pig, and here it is.'

'What do you make of this, lad?' the captain asked the sergeant.

'Either the passengers have been seeing things, Captain,' answered the sergeant, 'or somebody's trying to fix something on the old woman.'

'This is the devil of a business,' muttered the captain. Then, raising his voice: 'Who was sitting next to the lady.'

'Your humble servant, Captain,' I answered. 'At the moment

of decease I was sitting between the lady and the murdered person.'

'And what did you see?'

'The lady took out a black sweet and gave it to the child.'

'To what child?'

'To the child who was sitting on her lap, of course.'

'You mean to the pig, because that was what she had under her cloak.'

'I saw a child,' I said, totally confounded. 'I'm prepared to swear to it.'

'You may have seen ten thousand children, but what we have here is a pig,' thundered the captain. He paused a moment and added. 'You'd better accept that.'

Finding myself at a loss, I resorted to extreme measures. Pointing to the old woman, I said to the captain:

'Tell her to show you the lozenge-tin that she took her sweets out of.'

'A lozenge-tin! What blasted lozenge-tin?' shouted the old woman. 'I'm fed up to the teeth with this man. Just look now, Mr. Captain, and see if I've got any lozenge-tin.' And keeping the pig down with her left hand, she held out her bag to the captain with her right.

He opened it in manifest haste. All that it contained was a purse, a handkerchief, some papers, and a small picture of the Infant Jesus.

'You and your suspicions,' she shouted at me in a fury, waving her bag under my nose. 'Here, take it. Look for the lozenge-tin! Look for it! Enjoy yourself, mister detective.'

'That's floored you,' said the builder. 'That's floored you. You're an artist, Granny,' he added, turning to the old woman.

'She's a witch,' I shouted. 'That's what she is, a witch.'

'Me a witch,' muttered the old woman, 'I'm a Christian, apostolic, catholic, and roman.' Then, raising her voice: 'Maybe it's you that's a wizard . . . '

'Very likely he is, Granny,' said the prayer-woman with a laugh. 'Because he's got the gift of gab . . . '

'That's enough,' shouted the captain. 'There are no witches here, but everyone's bewitched. But if the lozenge-tin isn't a fairy-tale it's bound to turn up.'

He was going to continue, but at that moment the policeman

came in followed by two stretcher-bearers, and said, springing to attention:

'As soon as you're ready, Captain.'

'So they've come for her already.' He paused, lit a cigarette and puffed a sharp mouthful of smoke. 'It's getting out of hand, I tell you . . . '

'What is, Captain? The corpse?'

'I shoudn't mind that. No, this whole business is getting out of hand.'

The bearers placed the corpse on the stretcher, covered it with a canvas and looked at the captain, as if waiting for orders.

'To the mortuary. I'll follow.'

They carried it out; as they went out of the bus door it was within an inch of slipping off the stretcher. But one of the men steadied it by putting a hand on its chest. It had stopped raining, and now we could hear the deafening noise of the car horns behind us. No doubt news of the tragedy had got about, for a large crowd was gathered beside the bus door. The captain, evidently disturbed by the aspect that the business was taking, and wishing to end it as soon as possible, ordered the driver to shut the door and told the sergeant, who was preparing to follow the stretcher-bearers, to stay where he was. In the meanwhile, the old woman and the pig had fallen back into a heavy sleep, and the bus was again thunderous with their snores. This finally drove the captain to exasperation. Taking off his cap, he scratched his head, pondered a little, and said:

'Stand up, everyone! Hands above your heads! Start searching them, Sergeant. And you,' he said to the policeman, 'search those at the back.'

As the sergeant was standing beside the captain when he gave the order, and I was next to him, my turn came first. He began his examination with professional skill. Although all this seemed to me the height of absurdity I couldn't help trembling when I felt the sergeant's expert fingers in my pocket.

'I'm afraid we shan't find anything,' said the captain dispiritedly.

'Oh no, Captain? cried the sergeant with a burst of detective pride. 'I've got something here . . . It looks like a little box.'

'Bring it out whatever it is and be done with it,' bawled the captain.

'Is this it?' asked the sergeant, displaying the famous lozenge-tin. 'What a pretty little object!'

The captain snatched it from his hands.

'You've made an awkward slip.' he said to me. 'Very awkward ... even the sharpest customers give themselves away ... '

'Captain,' I began to stammer, 'don't go and believe ... '

'Don't you worry! I don't believe anything,' he answered ironically, opening the lozenge-tin. 'I don't believe anything at all. Did you say green and white sweets? Were they like these?' And he showed me half a dozen dragées of those colours.

'Captain, I swear to you ... '

'Don't trouble. You made an awkward slip,' and he laughed. 'Good, now we're on firm ground. And the matter's concluded.' He moved to the door, and as he was about to get down, he turned on his heel, looked at me slyly, and said: 'Say, Sergeant, bring him along!'

—Translated by J.M. Cohen

ESSAYS

All the essays in this section deal with one subject: the promises and problems of freedom.

The first selection is the American Declaration of Independence. *In it the founders of the American republic declared their conviction that "all men are created equal," and that "whenever any form of Government becomes destructive . . . it is the Right of the people to alter or to abolish it, and to institute new Government. . . . " This conviction, and the success of the people of the United States, has served as inspiration to many leaders in today's emerging nations.*

Thus Ho Chi Minh, in preparing the Declaration of Independence *of the Democratic Republic of Vietnam, deliberately patterned his document after the style and spirit of the American statement. In Ho's document, the French and the Japanese are the colonialist counterparts to the British in the American declaration.*

Whereas Ho draws on the U.S. Declaration of Independence, Martin Luther King, Jr., in his famous speech, I Have A Dream, *points to another American work, Lincoln's* Gettysburg Address. *In moving language, Dr. King called on his people to rise in nonviolent struggle against the oppression of the whites. Ironically, he himself was to die from an assassin's bullet, the victim of the very violence he had dedicated his life to combat. The dream he describes in the speech remains only a dream, or, to many American blacks, a shattered hope, a bitter disillusionment.*

The two African writers, Peter Abrahams and Albert Luthuli, pick up the same theme of people's broken dreams. Abrahams is a South African who was a friend of the well-known African leaders Kwame Nkrumah and Jomo Kenyatta. The essay by

Albert Luthuli is taken from his acceptance speech of the Nobel Peace Prize in 1961. The prize was awarded him for his long struggles, both in political life and in writing, in the cause of nonviolent militancy in South Africa. His attack on "the most terrible dream in the world"—the South African doctrine of apartheid, is a striking counterpart to King's dream of freedom ringing from every hillside and mountaintop in America. Like King, Luthuli does not call for freedom only for his own people, for he knows that where any are in bondage, none is truly free.

The Filipinos in the Philippines, *by Renato Constantino, is an ironic counterpoint to the first selection, in which the fledgling American republic proudly asserted the equality and dignity of all people. Constantino's style is sardonic; by means of ridicule and inverted logic he attempts to demonstrate the absurdities of U.S.-Philippines relations.*

In the essay by Cuba's Fidel Castro, we look at problems of freedom from a post-revolutionary perspective. Art is almost necessarily in opposition to governments, for it asserts the necessity of individuals to make their own decisions and to make commitments to goals larger than those of the State. Castro discusses the problems of the artist in revolutionary society.

The Declaration of Independence

The unanimous Declaration of the thirteen United States of America.

When, in the Course of human events, it becomes necessary for one people to dissolve the political bands which have connected them with another, and to assume, among the Powers of the earth, the separate and equal station to which the Laws of Nature and of Nature's God entitle them, a decent respect to the opinions of mankind requires that they should declare the causes which impel them to the separation.

We hold these truths to be self-evident, that all men are created equal, that they are endowed by their Creator with certain unalienable Rights, that among these, are Life, Liberty, and the pursuit of Happiness. That, to secure these rights, Governments are instituted among Men, deriving their just Powers from the consent of the governed. That, whenever any form of Government becomes destructive of these ends, it is the Right of the People to alter or abolish it, and to institute new Government; laying its foundation on such Principles, and organizing its Powers in such form, as to them shall seem most likely to effect their Safety and Happiness. Prudence, indeed, will dictate that Governments long established should not be changed for light and transient causes; and, accordingly, all experience hath shown, that mankind are more disposed to suffer, while evils are sufferable, than to right themselves by abolishing the forms to which they are accustomed. But, when a long train of abuses and usurpations, pursuing invariably the same Object, evinces a design to reduce them under absolute Despotism, it is their right, it is their duty, to throw off such Government, and to provide new Guards for their future Security. Such has been the patient sufferance of these Colonies; and such is now the necessity which constrains them to alter their former Systems of Government. The history of the present King of Great Britain is a history of repeated injuries and usurpations, all having in direct object the establishment of an absolute Tyranny over these States. To prove this, let Facts be submitted to a candid world.

He has refused his Assent to Laws the most wholesome and necessary for the public good.

He has forbidden his Governors to pass Laws of immediate and pressing importance, unless suspended in their operation till his Assent should be obtained; and when so suspended, he has utterly neglected to attend to them.

He has refused to pass other Laws for the accommodation of large districts of People, unless those People would relinquish the right of Representation in the legislature; a right inestimable to them and formidable to tyrants only.

He has called together legislative bodies at places unusual, uncomfortable, and distant from the depository of their Public Records, for the sole Purpose of fatiguing them into compliance with his measures.

He has dissolved Representative Houses repeatedly, for opposing, with manly firmness, his invasions on the rights of the People.

He has refused for a long time, after such dissolutions, to cause others to be elected; whereby the Legislative Powers, incapable of Annihilation, have returned to the People at large for their exercise; the State remaining in the meantime exposed to all the dangers of invasion from without, and convulsions within.

He has endeavoured to prevent the Population of these States; for that purpose obstructing the Laws for Naturalization of Foreigners; refusing to pass others to encourage their migrations hither, and raising the conditions of new Appropriations of Lands.

He has obstructed the Administration of Justice, by refusing his Assent to Laws for establishing Judiciary Powers.

He has made Judges dependent on his Will alone, for the tenure of their offices, and the amount and payment of their salaries.

He has erected a multitude of New Offices, and sent hither swarms of Officers to harass our People, and eat out their substance.

He has kept among us, in times of Peace, Standing Armies, without the Consent of our legislatures.

He has affected to render the Military independent of and superior to the Civil Power.

He has combined with others to subject us to a jurisdiction

foreign to our constitution, and unacknowledged by our laws; giving his Assent to their Acts of pretended Legislation:

For quartering large bodies of armed troops among us:

For protecting them, by a mock Trial, from Punishment for any Murders which they should commit on the Inhabitants of these States:

For cutting off our Trade with all parts of the world:

For imposing Taxes on us without our Consent:

For depriving us, in many cases, of the benefits of Trial by Jury:

For transporting us beyond Seas to be tried for pretended offences:

For abolishing the free System of English Laws in a neighboring province, establishing therein an Arbitrary government, and enlarging its Boundaries, so as to render it at once an example and fit instrument for introducing the same absolute rule into these Colonies:

For taking away our Charters, abolishing our most valuable Laws, and altering fundamentally the Forms of our Governments:

For suspending our own Legislatures, and declaring themselves invested with Power to legislate for us in all cases whatsoever.

He has abdicated Government here, by declaring us out of his protection, and waging War against us.

He has plundered our seas, ravaged our Coasts, burnt our towns, and destroyed the Lives of our People.

He is at this time transporting large Armies of foreign Mercenaries to complete the works of death, desolation and tryanny, already begun with circumstances of Cruelty and perfidy scarcely paralleled in the most barbarous ages, and totally unworthy the Head of a civilized nation.

He has constrained our fellow Citizens, taken Captive on the high Seas, to bear Arms against their Country, to become the executioners of their friends and Brethren, or to fall themselves by their Hands.

He has excited domestic insurrections amongst us, and has endeavoured to bring on the inhabitants of our frontiers, the merciless Indian Savages, whose known rule of warfare, is an undistinguished destruction of all ages, sexes and conditions.

In every stage of these Oppressions, We have Petitioned for

Redress, in the most humble terms: Our repeated Petitions, have been answered only by repeated injury. A Prince, whose character is thus marked by every act which may define a Tyrant, is unfit to be the ruler of a free People.

Nor have We been wanting in attentions to our British brethren. We have warned them from time to time of attempts by their legislature to extend an unwarrantable jurisdiction over us. We have reminded them of the circumstances of our emigration and settlement here. We have appealed to their native justice and magnanimity, and we have conjured them by the ties of our common kindred, to disavow these usurpations, which, would inevitably interrupt our connexions and correspondence. They too have been deaf to the voice of justice and consanguinity. We must, therefore, acquiesce in the necessity, which denounces our Separation, and hold them, as we hold the rest of mankind, Enemies in war, in Peace Friends.

We, therefore, the Representatives of the United States of America, in General Congress assembled, appealing to the Supreme Judge of the World for the rectitude of our intentions, Do, in the Name, and by Authority of the good People of these Colonies, solemnly Publish and Declare, That these United Colonies are, and of Right, ought to be Free and Independent States; that they are Absolved from all Allegiance to the British Crown, and that all political connexion between them and the State of Great Britain, is and ought to be totally dissolved; and that, as Free and Independent States, they have full Power to levy War, conclude Peace, contract Alliances, establish Commerce, and to do all other Acts and Things which Independent States may of right do. And for the support of this Declaration, with a firm reliance on the protection of divine Providence, we mutually pledge to each other our Lives, our Fortunes, and our sacred Honour.

HO CHI MINH

For his "Declaration" Ho Chi Minh took as his model the
Declaration of Independence *of the United States, a document
which he had studied and greatly admired. Written in 1945,
after the defeat of the Japanese which ended World War II, the
declaration briefly sketches the history of French colonial rule
in Vietnam, as well as the French unwillingness to ally themselves with the Vietnamese freedom fighters, the Viet Minh, even
to struggle against the Japanese.*

*It is ironic that almost thirty years were to pass before the
independence which Ho is claiming in this document became a
reality and doubly ironic that in the end the force which prevented that independence was the same power which provided
the model for the declaration—the United States.*

*Ho Chi Minh was a scholar, a poet, a statesman, and a deter-
mined fighter for the freedom of his people.*

*Ho left his country at the age of twenty and remained away for
nearly thirty years. All that time he was working for the cause of
Vietnamese liberty, finding in international communism the
best hope of bringing independence and freedom to his country.
He was, during the years, frequently imprisoned, hungry, cold,
sick, near starvation. In his* Prison Diary *he wrote: "Fortunately, being stubborn and patient, never yielding an inch,
though physically I suffer, my spirit is unshaken."*

Declaration of Independence of the Democratic Republic of Vietnam

All men are created equal; they are endowed by their Creator
with certain inalienable Rights; among these are Life, Liberty, and the pursuit of Happiness.

This immortal statement was made in the Declaration of
Independence of the United States of America in 1776. In a
broader sense, this means: All the peoples on the earth are

equal from birth, all the peoples have a right to live, to be happy and free.

The Declaration of the French Revolution made in 1791 on the Rights of Man and the Citizen also states: "All men are born free and with equal rights, and must always remain free and have equal rights."

Those are undeniable truths.

Nevertheless, for more than eighty years, the French imperialists, abusing the standard of Liberty, Equality, and Fraternity, have violated our Fatherland and oppressed our fellow citizens. They have acted contrary to the ideals of humanity and justice.

In the field of politics, they have deprived our people of every democratic liberty.

They have enforced inhuman laws; they have set up three distinct political regimes in the North, the Center, and the South of Viet-Nam in order to wreck our national unity and prevent our people from being united.

They have built more prisons than schools. They have mercilessly slain our patriots; they have drowned our uprisings in rivers of blood.

They have fettered public opinion; they have practiced obscurantism against our people.

To weaken our race they have forced us to use opium and alchohol.

In the field of economics, they have fleeced us to the backbone, impoverished our people and devastated our land.

They have robbed us of our rice fields, our mines, our forests, and our raw materials. They have monopolized the issuing of bank notes and the export trade.

They have invented numerous unjustifiable taxes and reduced our people, especially our peasantry, to a state of extreme poverty.

They have hampered the prospering of our national bourgeoisie; they have mercilessly exploited our workers.

In the autumn of 1940, when the Japanese fascists violated Indochina's territory to establish new bases in their fight against the Allies, the French imperialists went down on their bended knees and handed over our country to them.

Thus, from that date, our people were subjected to the double yoke of the French and the Japanese. Their sufferings and miseries increased. The result was that, from the end of last year to the beginning of this year, from Quang Tri Province to the North of Viet-Nam, more than two million of our fellow citizens died from starvation. On March 9 (1945), the French troops were disarmed by the Japanese. The French colonialists either fled or surrendered, showing that not only were they incapable of "protecting" us, but that, in the span of five years, they had twice sold our country to the Japanese.

On several occasions before March 9, the Viet Minh League urged the French to ally themselves with it against the Japanese. Instead of agreeing to this proposal, the French colonialists so intensified their terrorist activities against the Viet Minh members that before fleeing they massacred a great number of our political prisoners detained at Yen Bay and Cao Bang.

Notwithstanding all this, our fellow citizens have always manifested toward the French a tolerant and humane attitude. Even after the Japanese Putsch of March, 1945, the Viet Minh League helped many Frenchmen to cross the frontier, rescued some of them from Japanese jails, and protected French lives and property.

From the autumn of 1940, our country had in fact ceased to be a French colony and had become a Japanese possession.

After the Japanese had surrendered to the Allies, our whole people rose to regain our national sovereignty and to found the Democratic Republic of Viet-Nam.

The truth is that we have wrested our independence from the Japanese and not from the French.

The French have fled, the Japanese have capitulated, Emperor Bao Dai has abdicated. Our people have broken the chains which for nearly a century have fettered them and have won independence for the Fatherland. Our people at the same time have overthrown the monarchic regime that has reigned supreme for dozens of centuries. In its place has been established the present Democratic Republic.

For these reasons, we, members of the Provisional Government, representing the whole Vietnamese people, declare that from now on we break off all relations of a colonial character with France; we repeal all the international obligation that

France has so far subscribed to on behalf of Viet-Nam, and we abolish all the special rights the French have unlawfully acquired in our Fatherland.

The whole Vietnamese people, animated by a common purpose, are determined to fight to the bitter end against any attempt by the French colonialists to reconquer their country.

We are convinced that the Allied nations, which at Teheran and San Francisco have acknowledged the principles of self-determination and equality of nations, will not refuse to acknowledge the independence of Viet-Nam.

A people who have courageously opposed French domination for more than eighty years, a people who have fought side by side with the Allies against the fascists during these last years, such a people must be free and independent.

For these reasons, we, members of the Provisional Government of the Democratic Republic of Viet-Nam, solemnly declare to the world that Viet-Nam has the right to be a free and independent country—and in fact it is so already. The entire Vietnamese people are determined to mobilize all their physical and mental strength, to sacrifice their lives and property in order to safeguard their independence and liberty.

MARTIN LUTHER KING, JR.

The son of the pastor of the Ebenezer Baptist Church in Atlanta, King was ordained in 1947 and became the minister of a Baptist church in Montgomery, Alabama. He attained national prominence by advocating a policy of passive resistance to segregation. His philosophy of nonviolent resistance led to his arrest on numerous occasions in the 1950s and 1960s. He organized, in 1963, the massive March on Washington, which brought more than 200,000 people together. In 1964 he was awarded the Nobel Peace Prize. His leadership was challenged in the 1960s by more militant groups. King's interest widened from civil rights to criticism of the Vietnam War and to a concern for poverty.

On April 4, 1968, he was shot and killed by an assassin's bullet on the balcony of the motel where he was staying in Memphis.

He is the author of Stride Toward Freedom *(1968),* Why We
Can't Wait *(1964), and* Where Do We Go From Here: Chaos or
Community? *(1967).*

I Have a Dream

Five score years ago, a great American, in whose symbolic
shadow we stand, signed the Emancipation Proclamation.
This momentous decree came as a great beacon light of hope to
millions of Negro slaves who had been seared in the flames of
withering injustice. It came as a joyous daybreak to end the
long night of captivity.

But one hundred years later, we must face the tragic fact
that the Negro is still not free. One hundred years later, the
life of the Negro is still sadly crippled by the manacles of
segregation and the chains of discrimination. One hundred
years later, the Negro lives on a lonely island of poverty in the
midst of a vast ocean of material prosperity. One hundred
years later, the Negro is still languished in the corners of
American society and finds himself an exile in his own land. So
we have come here today to dramatize an appalling condition.

In a sense we have come to our nation's Capital to cash a
check. When the architects of our republic wrote the magnificent words of the Constitution and the Declaration of Independence, they were signing a promissory note to which every
American was to fall heir. This note was a promise that all men
would be guaranteed the unalienable rights of life, liberty, and
the pursuit of happiness.

It is obvious today that America has defaulted on this promissory note insofar as her citizens of color are concerned. Instead of honoring this sacred obligation, America has given
the Negro people a bad check; a check which has come back
marked "insufficient funds." But we refuse to believe that the
bank of justice is bankrupt. We refuse to believe that there are
insufficient funds in the great vaults of opportunity of this
nation. So we have come to cash this check—a check that will
give us upon demand the riches of freedom and the security of
justice. We have also come to this hallowed spot to remind

America of the fierce urgency of now. This is no time to engage in luxury of cooling off or to take the tranquilizing drug of gradualism. Now is the time to make real the promises of Democracy. Now is the time to rise from the dark and desolate valley of segregation to the sunlit path of racial justice. Now is the time to open the doors of opportunity to all of God's children. Now is the time to lift our nation from the quicksands of racial injustice to the solid rock of brotherhood.

It would be fatal for the nation to overlook the urgency of the moment and to underestimate the determination of the Negro. This sweltering summer of the Negro's legitimate discontent will not pass until there is an invigorating autumn of freedom and equality. 1963 is not an end, but a beginning. Those who hope that the Negro needed to blow off steam and will now be content will have a rude awakening if the nation returns to business as usual. There will be neither rest nor tranquility in America until the Negro is granted his citizenship rights. The whirlwinds of revolt will continue to shake the foundations of our nation until the bright day of justice emerges.

But there is something that I must say to my people who stand on the warm threshold which leads into the palace of justice. In the process of gaining our rightful place we must not be guilty of wrongful deeds. Let us not seek to satisfy our thirst for freedom by drinking from the cup of bitterness and hatred. We must forever conduct our struggle on the high plane of dignity and discipline. We must not allow our creative protest to degenerate into physical violence. Again and again we must rise to the majestic heights of meeting physical force with soul force. The marvelous new militancy which has engulfed the Negro community must not lead us to a distrust of all white people, for many of our white brothers, as evidenced by their presence here today, have come to realize that their destiny is tied up with our destiny and their freedom is inextricably bound to our freedom. We cannot walk alone.

And as we walk, we must make the pledge that we shall march ahead. We cannot turn back. There are those who are asking the devotees of civil rights, "When will you be satisfied?" We can never be satisfied as long as the Negro is the victim of the unspeakable horrors of police brutality. We can never be satisfied as long as our bodies, heavy with the fatigue of travel, cannot gain lodging in the motels of the highways and the hotels of the cities. We cannot be satisfied as long as the Negro's basic mobility is from a smaller ghetto to a larger one. We can never be satisfied as long as a Negro in Mississippi cannot vote and a Negro in New York believes he has nothing for which to vote. No, no, we are not satisfied, and we will not be satisfied until justice rolls down like waters and righteousness like a mighty stream.

I am not unmindful that some of you have come here out of great trials and tribulations. Some of you have come fresh from narrow jail cells. Some of you have come from areas where your quest for freedom left you battered by the storms of persecution and staggered by the winds of police brutality. You have been the veterans of creative suffering. Continue to work with the faith that unearned suffering is redemptive.

Go back to Mississippi, go back to Alabama, go back to South Carolina, go back to Georgia, go back to Louisiana, go back to the slums and ghettos of our northern cities, knowing that somehow this situation can and will be changed. Let us not wallow in the valley of despair.

I say to you today, my friends, that in spite of the difficulties and frustrations of the moment I still have a dream. It is a dream deeply rooted in the American dream.

I have a dream that one day this nation will rise up and live out the true meaning of its creed: "We hold these truths to be self-evident; that all men are created equal."

I have a dream that one day on the red hills of Georgia the sons of former slaves and the sons of former slaveowners will be able to sit down together at the table of brotherhood.

I have a dream that one day even the state of Mississippi, a desert state sweltering with the heat of injustice and oppression, will be transformed into an oasis of freedom and justice.

I have a dream that my four little children will one day live in a nation where they will not be judged by the color of their skin but by the content of their character.

I have a dream today.

I have a dream that one day the state of Alabama, whose governor's lips are presently dripping with the words of interposition and nullification, will be transformed into a situation where little black boys and black girls will be able to join hands with the little white boys and white girls and walk together as sisters and brothers.

I have a dream today.

I have a dream that one day every valley shall be exalted,

every hill and mountain shall be made low, the rough places will be made plain, and the crooked places will be made straight, and the glory of the Lord shall be revealed, and all flesh shall see it together.

This is our hope. This is the faith with which I return to the South. With this faith we will be able to hew out of the mountain of despair a stone of hope. With this faith we will be able to transform the jangling discords of our nation into a beautiful symphony of brotherhood. With this faith we will be able to work together, to pray together, to struggle together, to go to jail together, to stand up for freedom together, knowing that we will be free one day.

This will be the day when all of God's children will be able to sing with new meaning

> My country, 'tis of thee
> Sweet land of liberty,
> Of thee I sing:
> Land where my fathers died,
> Land of the pilgrims' pride,
> From every mountain-side
> Let freedom ring.

And if America is to be a great nation this must become true. So let freedom ring from the prodigious hilltops of New Hampshire. Let freedom ring from the mighty mountains of New York. Let freedom ring from the heightening Alleghenies of Pennsylvania!

Let freedom ring from the snowcapped Rockies of Colorado!

Let freedom ring from the curvacious peaks of California!

But not only that; let freedom ring from Stone Mountain of Georgia!

Let freedom ring from Lookout Mountain of Tennessee!

Let freedom ring from every hill and molehill of Mississippi. From every mountainside, let freedom ring.

When we let freedom ring, when we let it ring from every village and every hamlet, from every state and every city, we will be able to speed up that day when all of God's children, black men and white men, Jews and Gentiles, Protestants and Catholics, will be able to join hands and sing in the words of the old Negro spiritual, "Free at last! thank God almighty, we are free at last!"

PETER ABRAHAMS

Peter Abrahams, born in 1919 in a Johannesburg slum of an Ethiopian father and a "Cape Coloured" mother, is the best known of the South African Negro writers. He has written Mine Boy *and other novels, as well as an autobiography,* Tell Freedom. *He was a friend of the well-known African leaders Kwame Nkrumah and Jomo Kenyatta. As young men, these three had been part of a group of Africans residing in London, who dreamed dreams of the glory that was to be Africa.*

Kenyatta returned to his country, Kenya, where he became president of the Kenya Africa Union party and was subsequently arrested and charged with being the leader of the terrorist Mau-Mau movement. After about ten years in prison he was released and was shortly elected prime minister and later the first president of Kenya, which had become a republic within the British commonwealth.

Nkrumah led his country's drive for independence and was elected president. Later the Ghanaian National Assembly voted to extend his term of office to life, lending credence to accusations that he had become a dictator. Riots against him broke out in the early 1960s, and attempts were made on his life. His great goal was the unity of all African nations, and in that interest he called the first conference of independent African states in 1958.

Abraham's essay was written in 1959, and may on some political points be dated. In it he relates what had happened to the two men he had known as friends and fellow students in London. While much has changed in Africa since 1959, the conflicts of old and new, modern and traditional, tribal ways and western ways, black and white, still remain.

Richard Wright, who is mentioned in the essay, is a well-known American writer, author of Native Son *and other works.*

Nkrumah, Kenyatta, and the Old Order

It was a hot, humid, oppressive August day in Accra, capital of the Gold Coast that was to become Ghana. The air had the stillness of death. I walked down toward the sea front. Perhaps there would be the hint of a breeze there. As I neared the sea front I was assailed by a potent stench of the sea with strong overtones of rotting fish.

The houses were drab, run-down wooden structures or made of corrugated iron, put together any way you please. The streets were wide and tarred, and each street had an open-drainage system into which young boys and old men piddled when they needed to relieve themselves. I have seen women empty chamber pots into these drains in the early morning. The fierce sun takes care of the germs, but God help you if smells make you sick.

In about eight minutes of walking, some fifteen "taxis" pulled up beside me: "Hi, massa! Taxi, massa! Me go anywhere you go cheap!" They are all private taxis with no meters and driven by strapping young men with flashing teeth. The place is full of taxi drivers willing to go anywhere and do anything cheap.

The street traders here are women. "Mammy traders," they are called. They trade in everything. They sell cigarettes, one at a time; round loaves of bread and hunks of cooked meat on which the big West African flies make sport. They love bargaining and haggling. They are a powerful economic factor in the life of the country. The more prosperous ones own their own trucks, some own fleets of trucks. These "mammy trucks" are the principal carriers of the country. They carry passengers as well as produce and go hurtling across the countryside with little regard for life or limb. Each truck has its own distinctive slogan, such as: Repent For Death is Round the Corner, or Enter Without Hope, or The Last Ride, or If It Must It Will. My own favorite, and I traveled in this particular truck, pleaded, Not Today O Lord Not Today.

I passed many mammy traders, many mammy trucks, before I reached the sea front. I crossed a street, jumped over an open drain, and there was the sea. But there was no breeze, and no shade from the terrible sun. In the end I gave in to the idea of "taxi, massa, taxi" and looked about for one. But now there was no taxi in sight. Instead, I saw, suddenly, a long procession of many women and a few men. The procession swung around a corner and came into full view, twenty or thirty yards long. The women wore white flowing robes and white kerchiefs on their heads. The faces were painted into grotesque masks made with thick streaks of black, red, white, and yellow paints. The heavy thud of bare feet rose above the hum of the sea.

Then, all at once, the drums burst forth and there was no other sound about me. The marching women began to jig, then dance. As the tail of the procession passed me the drums reached a frenzy. A thin, pure note from a reed rose above the drums. The whole procession became a shivering, shaking mass. The reed note held longer than seemed human. And then, dramatically, there was silence. The thudding feet faded away out of sight and sound. There was silence and a slight racing of my heartbeat and the hum of the sea, and, of course, the overpowering fishy stench.

I thought of Richard Wright, with whom I had had breakfast that morning. This was his first visit to any part of Africa and he seemed to find it bewildering. Countee Cullen, the late American Negro poet, had speculated:

> One three centuries removed
> From the scenes his fathers loved,
> Spicy grove, cinnamon tree,
> What is Africa to me?

Wright was finding the answers and finding them disconcerting. He had been astounded by the casual attitude to sex. There was, he had said, too much sex, too casually given and taken; so that it worked out as no sex, with none of the emotional involvement associated with sex in the western mind. He shook his head with a slight disgust. The open drains into which young boys and old men piddled had led him to conclude that Africans piddled rather more than other people. The sight of young men dancing together, holding hands, disturbed the puritan in him. He expressed to me that morning what he later summed up in his book on the Gold Coast: "I was black and they were black but it did not help me."

What Wright did not understand, what his whole background and training had made difficult for him to understand, was that being black did not of itself qualify one for acceptance in tribal Africa. But how could he, when there are thousands of urban-bred Africans up and down the vast continent who do not themselves understand this? The more perceptive of the urban Africans are only now beginning to comprehend, but slowly.

Being black is a small matter in tribal Africa because the attitude toward color is healthy and normal. Color does not matter. Color is an act of God that neither confers privileges nor imposes handicaps on a man. A man's skin is like the day: the day is either clear or dark. There is nothing more to it until external agencies come in and invest it with special meaning and importance.

What does matter to the tribal African, what is important, is the complex pattern of his position within his own group and his relations with the other members of the group. He is no Pan-African dreaming of a greater African glory when the white man is driven into the sea. The acute race consciousness of the American Negro, or of the black South African at the receiving end of Apartheid, is alien to him. The important things in his life are anything but race and color—until they are forced on him. And "Mother Africa" is much too vast to inspire big continental dreams in him. She is a land of huge mountains, dark jungles, and vast deserts. In her rivers and in her jungles and in her grasslands lurk creatures that are the enemies of man: the leopard and the lion, the snake and crocodile. All this makes travel, by the old African methods, extremely difficult and makes for isolation between one group of people and another. The African who is in Britain is likely to be a deal better informed on what is happening all over the continent than would be his fellow African in any of the main centers of both tribal and non-tribal Africa. In terms of communications the man in the tribe lives in the Dark Ages.

Richard Wright was surprised that even educated Africans, racially conscious literate people, had not heard of him and were skeptical of a grown man earning his living by writing. They could not understand what kind of writing brought a man enough money to support a family. Wright really wanted to understand the African, but—"I found the African an oblique, a hard-to-know man."

My sympathies were all with Wright.

The heat and salty rancid fish smell had made me desperately thirsty. Across the way a mammy trader squatted beside her pile of merchandise: cooked meat, sweet potatoes—a whole host of edibles—and some bottles of opaque white liquid that could be either coconut milk or palm juice, as well as the inevitable little pile of cigarettes priced at a penny apiece. I had been warned of the risks involved in eating anything sold by the street traders. But to hell with it, I was thirsty and not exactly a stranger to African germs. I crossed the street, felt the bottles, and chose the one that seemed coolest and looked the least opaque.

"How much?"

"One shilling." The carved ebony face looked at me with dead eyes.

I pulled the screwed-up newspaper stopper from the bottle, wiped its mouth, and took a swig. I could not decide whether it was coconut milk or palm juice. It had been heavily watered down and sweetened. But it was wet and thirst-quenching. I drank half the bottle, firmly ignoring the little foreign bodies that floated in the liquid. Then I paid her and drank the rest. I put down the empty and began to move away.

"You African?" she asked in her harsh, cold, masculine voice.

I stopped, turned and looked at her face. It was as deadly cold and impersonal as before: not a flicker of feeling in her eyes. Like an African mask, I thought. But unlike Wright, I did not try to penetrate it. I knew the futility of trying. She would show feeling if and when she decided. Not before.

"Yes," I said, and added, "from the south. Far, far south."

She paused for so long that I began to move again.

"You like here?" Nationalism had obviously touched her.

I turned back to her. "No," I said.

"Why you don't like?"

"I don't say I don't like."

"But you don't like?"

I showed her my teeth, African-wise, which is neither smile nor grimace but a blending of the two. "You like Africa?" I asked.

Now it was her turn to show me her teeth. There was a flicker of feeling in her eyes, then they went dead again. She nodded. I had established my claim. Only outsiders—white people or the Richard Wrights—liked or disliked Africa.

I left the mammy trader and carried on up the smelly and hot street. Much and little had passed between us. Out to sea some fishing boats appeared on the sky line. About me were the citizens of Accra. Some wore the cloth of the country—the men looking like pint-sized citizens of ancient Rome painted black and the women looking extraordinarily masculine—and others wore western dress.

My thoughts shifted to my forthcoming meeting with Kwame Nkrumah, Ghana's first Prime Minister. It was well over seven years since I had last seen him, in London. Then he was a poor struggling student; now he was the head of a state and the spokesman for the great Pan-African dream of freedom and independence.

This was the man who later made common cause with the people of French Guinea, when they voted for independence in 1958 and against membership in DeGaulle's Fifth Republic—a move by Nkrumah that can have great significance for the British Commonwealth. Prime Minister Macmillan has indicated that Whitehall is watching Nkrumah's "closer association" moves with Guinea with keen interest. Prediction would be idle, yet it is intriguing to speculate that an ex-colony of Britain might bring an ex-colony of France into the Commonwealth. This could be a dramatic underscoring of the changing nature of colonialism in Africa. And at the center of it is Kwame Nkrumah.

I remembered our past friendship and wondered what changes I would find in him. Anyway, it was now 9:00 A.M. and my date with him was for 9:30. I would soon know.

A few minutes later I flagged a taxi and simply said, "Kwame's office."

A pale-brown West Indian miss was the Prime Minister's secretary. She welcomed me as though I was a V.I.P. The Prime Minister had not come back from a conference yet. This tribal business was taking up a lot of his attention. She told me with indignation how members of the Ashanti tribe had to crawl on their bellies for some twenty yards into the presence of their king, the Asantehene, and how tribalism had to give way or there would be no progress. If she was any indication, then Nkrumah was very worried about the opposition the tribesmen were offering his western-style Convention People's Party.

A number of officials came in. The lady stopped assailing the tribes. Then there was some bustle and the Prime Minister arrived. In something just over five minutes he had seen and dealt with these officials and I was ushered into his office. It was a big pleasant, cool room.

Nkrumah came round his big official desk, took my hand and led me to a settee near the window. The now famous smile lit up his face. As we exchanged greetings, felt each other out with small talk in an attempt to bridge the gap of years, my mind went back to our London days. This poised, relaxed man, with the hint of guarded reserve about him, was a far cry from the friend I had last seen nearly eight years earlier.

For me, the most striking change of all was in his eyes. They reflected an inner tranquility which was the one thing the Nkrumah in Europe never had.

Even his name had been subtly different then. He had been our friend Francis Nkrumah, an African student recently arrived from the United States, and he had not seen Africa for a decade and more. He had quickly become a part of our African colony in London and had joined our little group, the Pan-African Federation in our protests against colonialism.

He was much less relaxed than most of us. His eyes mirrored a burning inner conflict and tension. He seemed consumed by a restlessness that led him to evolve some of the most fantastic schemes.

The president of our federation was an East African named Johnstone Kenyatta, the most relaxed, sophisticated, and "westernized" of the lot of us. Kenyatta enjoyed the personal friendship of some of the most distinguished people in English political and intellectual society. He was subtle, subtle enough to attack one's principles bitterly and retain one's friendship. He fought the British as imperialists but was affectionate toward them as friends.

It was to this balanced and extremely cultured man that Francis Nkrumah proposed that we form a secret society called The Circle, and that each of us spill a few drops of our blood in a bowl and so take a blood oath of secrecy and dedication to the emancipation of Africa.

Johnstone Kenyatta laughed at the idea; he scoffed at it as childish juju. He conceived our struggle in modern, twentieth century terms with no ritualistic blood nonsense. In the end Francis Nkrumah drifted away from us and started his own little West African group in London. We were too tame and slow for him. He was an angry young man in a hurry.

Then he went back to his part of Africa, and Francis Nkrumah became Kwame Nkrumah. He set himself at the head of the largely tribal populace and dabbled in blood ritual. There was some violence, a spell in prison, and finally Nkrumah emerged as the first African Prime Minister in a self-governing British African territory.

Tribal myths grew up around him. He could make himself invisible at will. He could go without food and sleep and drink longer than ordinary mortals. He was, in fact, the reincarnation of some of the most powerful ancestral spirits. He allowed his feet to be bathed in blood.

By the time I visited the Gold Coast the uneasy alliance between Nkrumah and the tribal chiefs had begun to crack. A week or so before my arrival he had threatened that, unless they cooperated with his government in turning the Gold Coast into an efficient twentieth century state, he would make them run so hard that they would leave their sandals behind them. This was a calculated insult to the tribal concept that a chief's bare feet must never touch the earth.

That was the beginning of the secret war. Nkrumah thought he would win it easily. He was wrong. The chiefs have not run, and today their opposition to him is even more clear cut. Some of his own followers, like Joe Appiah, who married the daughter of the late Sir Stafford Cripps, have defected to the tribalists. They are biding their time: waiting and watching.

And they have, negatively, scored their victories too. They have pushed him to a point where his regime is, today, intolerant of opposition. The tribal society brooks no opposition. Nkrumah's government banishes its most active opponents. As a modern socialist leading a western-style government he justifies this as a temporary expedient. But his less sophisticated ministers frankly talk the tribal language of strength, frankly express the tribal impulse to destroy those who are out of step.

There was an air of delicacy about our conversation and we were both aware of this. I asked him how he was getting on with those civil servants who, a little time earlier, had labeled him an "irresponsible agitator." He had nothing but praise for those who had remained. Some resigned, among them the officer in charge of the prison where Nkrumah had been detained, who refused openly to serve under one of his former inmates. One or two other die-hards of the old colonialism also pulled out, but in the main the expatriate civil servants stayed on and rendered loyal service. But he was preoccupied with Africanizing the service, something which has largely come about now.

We touched on local politics. He let off a full blast against the tribalist. I told him I had heard that the Accra Club was still exclusively European. His eyes lit up. "You wait and see," he said.

Then, in relation to nothing either of us had said, he leaned toward me and exclaimed, "This place is rich! God, man, there's so much riches here!"—as though revelation had just been made to him.

But always, throughout our talk, I sensed a new reserve, a new caution that had not been there in the young student I had known in Europe.

As we talked in Nkrumah's cool office that hot August day in Accra, my mind kept slipping back to our mutual friend Jomo or Johnstone Kenyatta, (later to be) imprisoned in his native Kenya for leading the Mau-Mau movement. Significantly, though we mentioned many friends, both Nkrumah and I avoided mentioning Kenyatta. I had decided not to mention him first. I had hoped Nkrumah would. He did not.

A year earlier, I had flown up to Kenya from South Africa and visited Kenyatta. I felt terribly depressed as I got off the plane. Things had grown so much uglier in the Union. The barricades were up in the ugly war of color. When I had left South Africa in the dim-and-distant past, there were isolated islands where black and white could meet in neutral territory. When I went back in 1952, the islands were submerged under the rising tide of color hatreds, and I was glad to quit that dark, unhappy land which yet compelled my love.

It was in this mood that I got off the plane. I had not seen my friend Jomo for years. Now there he was, just outside the airport terminal building, leaning on a heavy cane, bigger than I remembered him in Europe, paunchy, his face looking puffy. And behind him was a huge crowd of Africans.

I began to move toward him when a lean-faced, lean-hipped white colonial-administrator type suddenly appeared beside me and said: "Mr. Abrahams."

I stopped and thought, "Oh, Lord."

Kenyatta also came forward. The two men ignored each other. Lean-face introduced himself and said the Colonial Office had alerted them that I was coming to do some writing for the London Observer and they had drawn up a provisional schedule for me. Had I done anything about accommodation?

Before I could answer, Kenyatta said, "You are staying with me, of course." The old detachment was back in his eyes. They seemed to say, "You've got to choose, pal. Let's see how you choose."

Lean-face said, "We've got something set up for you tomorrow and—"

"I live in the bush," Kenyatta added.

It dawned on me that I had become, for the moment, the battlefield of that horrible animal, the racial struggle. I made up my mind, resenting both sides and yet conscious of the crowd of Africans in the background. A question of face was involved.

"I've promised to spend this weekend with Mr. Kenyatta," I said.

Lean-face was graceful about it. I promised to call at the Secretariat first thing on Monday morning. He gave me a copy of the schedule that had been prepared for me and wondered, *sotto voce*, whether I knew what I was letting myself in for. Kenyatta assured me that I would be perfectly safe, that nobody was going to cut my throat. I was aware that they were talking to each other through me. I was aware that they knew I was aware, and that made me bad-tempered.

"Then I'll say good night, Mr. Abrahams," Lean-face said pointedly.

As soon as he was out of hearing Kenyatta began to curse.

"It's good to see you again, Johnstone," I gripped his hand.

"Jomo," he replied. The hint of ironic speculation was back in his eyes. A slightly sardonic, slightly bitter smile played on his lips.

"Welcome to Kenya, Peter," he said. Then, abruptly: "Come meet the leaders of my people. They've been waiting long."

We moved forward and the crowd gathered about us. Jomo made a little speech in Kikuyu, then translated it for my benefit. A little old man, ancient as the hills, with huge holes in his ears, then welcomed me on behalf of the land and its people. Again Jomo translated.

After this we all bundled into the fleet of rattling old cars and set off for the Kikuyu reserve in the heart of the African bush. Kenyatta became silent and strangely remote during the journey.

We stopped at the old chief's compound, where other members of the tribe waited to welcome me. By this time the reception committee had grown to a few hundred. About me, pervading the air, was the smell of burning flesh; a young cow was being roasted in my honor. Before I entered the house a drink was handed to me. Another was handed to the old chief and a third to Kenyatta. The old man muttered a brief incantation and spilled half his drink on the earth as a libation. Jomo and I followed suit. Then the three of us downed our drinks and entered the house.

A general feasting and drinking then commenced, both inside and outside the house. I was getting a full ceremonial tribal welcome. The important dignitaries of the tribe slipped into the room in twos and threes, spoke to me through Kenyatta for a few moments, and then went away, making room for others.

"Africa doesn't seem to change," Kenyatta murmured between dignitaries. There was a terrible undercurrent of bitterness behind the softly murmured words. I was startled by it and looked at his face. For a fleeting moment he looked like a trapped, caged animal.

He saw me looking at him and quickly composed his face into a slightly sardonic humorous mask. "Don't look too closely," he said.

And still the dignitaries filed in, had a drink, spoke their welcome and went out.

The ceremonial welcome reached its high point about midnight. Huge chunks of the roasted cow were brought in to us, and we gnawed at the almost raw meat between swigs of liquor. Outside, there was muted drumming. Voices were growing louder and louder.

Suddenly, in the midst of a long-winded speech by an immensely dignified Masai chief from a neighboring and friendly tribe, Kenyatta jumped up, grabbed his heavy cane and half staggered to the door.

"Come, Peter," he called.

Everybody was startled. I hesitated. He raised his cane and

256   *Peter Abrahams (South Africa)*

beckoned to me with it. I knew that this would be a dreadful breach of tribal etiquette.

"Come, man!" he snapped.

I got up, aware of the sudden silence that had descended on the huge gathering. By some strange magic everybody seemed to know that something had gone wrong.

"Jomo," I said.

"I can't stand any more," he snapped. "Come!"

I followed him to the door. I knew the discourtesy we were inflicting on the tribe. I also knew that my friend was at the breaking point. We walked through the crowd of people, got into Kenyatta's car and drove off into the night. The African moon was big and yellow, bathing the land in a soft light that almost achieved the clarity of daylight.

He took me to his home. It was a big, sprawling, empty place on the brow of a hill. Inside, it had nothing to make for comfort. There were hard wooden chairs, a few tables, and only the bed in the bedroom. There were no books, none of the normal amenities of western civilization. When we arrived two women emerged from somewhere in the back and hovered about in the shadows. They brought in liquor, but I never got a clear glimpse of either of them. My friend's anguish of spirit was such that I did not want to ask questions. We sat on the veranda and drank steadily and in silence until we were both miserably, depressingly drunk.

And then Kenyatta began to speak in a low, bitter voice of his frustration and of the isolated position in which he found himself. He had no friends. There was no one in the tribe who could give him the intellectual companionship that had become so important to him—consequential conversation, the drink that represented a social activity rather than the intention to get drunk, the concept of individualism, the inviolability of privacy—all these were alien to the tribesmen in whose midst he lived. So Kenyatta, the western man, was driven in on himself and was forced to assert himself in tribal terms. Only thus would the tribesman follow him and so give him his position of power and importance as a leader.

To live without roots is to live in hell, and no man chooses voluntarily to live in hell. The people who could answer his needs as a western man had erected a barrier of color against him in spite of the fact that the taproots of their culture had become the taproots of his culture too. By denying him access to those things which complete the life of western man, they had forced him back into the tribalism from which he had so painfully freed himself over the years.

None of this was stated explicitly by either Kenyatta or myself. But it was there in his brooding bitter commentary on both the tribes and the white settlers of the land. For me Kenyatta became that night a man who in his own life personified the terrible tragedy of Africa and the terrible secret war that rages in it. He was the victim both of tribalism and of westernism gone sick. His heart and mind and body were the battlefield of the ugly violence known as the Mau-Mau revolt long before it broke out in that beautiful land. The tragedy is that he was so rarely gifted that he could have made such a magnificent contribution in other circumstances.

ALBERT LUTHULI

Albert Luthuli (1898–1967) is a native of South Africa. He grew up at a local mission where his father was serving as an interpreter and evangelist. At the age of thirty-six he gave up a comfortable academic career to become an elected tribal chief and eventually president of the African National Congress. The Congress, a multi-racial organization, was dedicated to the principles of passive resistance to the racist policies of the South African government. The government became so incensed by the existence of this organization and by its policies that thousands of Africans, including Luthuli, were jailed, placed under house arrest, or banished to their home districts. In 1959 Luthuli was sent to his home district and restricted to his farm for a period of five years.

It was during this period of banishment that he was awarded the Nobel Peace Prize for his long nonviolent struggle for his people's rights. The Dignity of Man *is Luthuli's Nobel Peace Prize Acceptance Speech.*

The Dignity of Man

The Nobel Peace Award that has brought me here has for me a threefold significance. On the one hand it is a tribute to my humble contribution to efforts by democrats on both sides of the color line to find a peaceful solution to the race problem. This contribution is not in any way unique.

To remain neutral in a situation where the laws of the land virtually criticized God for having created men of color was the sort of thing I could not, as a Christian, tolerate.

On the other hand the award is a democratic declaration of solidarity with those who fight to widen the area of liberty in my part of the world. As such, it is the sort of gesture which gives me and millions who think as I do tremendous encouragement.

There are still people in the world today who regard South Africa's race problem as a simple clash between black and white.

Our government has carefully projected this image of the problem before the eyes of the world. This has had two effects.

It has confused the real issues at stake in the race crisis. It has given some form of force to the Government's contention that the race problem is a domestic matter for South Africa.

This, in turn, has tended to narrow down the area over which our case could be better understood in the world.

From yet another angle, it is a welcome recognition of the role played by the African people during the last fifty years to establish, peacefully, a society in which merit and not race would fix the position of the individual in the life of the nation.

This award could not be for me alone, nor for just South Africa, but for Africa as a whole.

Africa presently is most deeply torn with strife and most bitterly stricken with racial conflict.

Ours is a continent in revolution against oppression. And peace and revolution make uneasy bed fellows.

There can be no peace until the forces of oppression are overthrown. Our continent has been carved up by the great powers. In these times there has been no peace. There could be no brotherhood between men.

But now, the revolutionary stirrings of our continent are

setting the past aside. Our people everywhere from north to south of the continent are reclaiming their land, their right to participate in government, their dignity as men, their nationhood.

Thus, in the turmoil of revolution, the basis for peace and brotherhood in Africa is being restored by the resurrection of national sovereignty and independence, of equality and the dignity of man.

It should not be difficult for you here in Europe to appreciate this. Your age of revolution, stretching across all the years from the eighteenth century to our own, encompassed some of the bloodiest civil wars in all history.

By comparison, the African revolution has swept across three-quarters of the continent in less than a decade, its final completion is within sight of our own generation.

Again, by comparison with Europe, our African revolution to our credit is proving to be orderly, quick and comparatively bloodless.

Our goal is a united Africa in which the standards of life and liberty are constantly expanding, in which the ancient legacy of illiteracy and disease is swept aside, in which the dignity of man is rescued from beneath the heels of colonialism which have trampled it.

This goal, pursued by millions of our people with revolutionary zeal, by means of books, representations, demonstrations and in some places armed force provoked by the adamancy of white rule, carries the only real promise of peace in Africa. Whatever means have been used the efforts have gone to end alien rule and race oppression.

There is a paradox in the fact that Africa qualifies for such an award in its age of turmoil and revolution. How great is the paradox and how much greater the honor that an award in support of peace and the brotherhood of man should come to one who is a citizen of a country where the brotherhood of man is an illegal doctrine.

Outlawed, banned, censured, proscribed, and prohibited; where to work, talk, or campaign for the realization in fact and deed of the brotherhood of man is hazardous, punished with banishment or confinement without trial or imprisonment; where effective democratic channels to peaceful settlement of the race problem have never existed these 300 years, and where white minority power rests on the most heavily armed and equipped military machine in Africa.

This is South Africa.

Even here, where white rule seems determined not to change its mind for the better, the spirit of Africa's militant struggle for liberty, equality, and independence asserts itself, I, together with thousands of my countrymen, have in the course of struggle for these ideals been harassed and imprisoned, but we are not deterred in our quest for a new age in which we shall live in peace and in brotherhood.

It is not necessary for me to speak at length about South Africa. It is a museum piece in our time, a hangover from the dark past of mankind, a relic of an age which everywhere else is dead or dying.

Here the cult of race superiority and of white supremacy is worshiped like a god. The ghost of slavery lingers on to this day in the form of forced labor that goes on in what are called farm prisons.

It is fair to say that even in present-day conditions, Christian missions have been in the vanguard in initiating social services provided for us. Our progress in this field has been in spite of, and not mainly because of, the Government. In this the church in South Africa—though belatedly—seems to be awakening to a broader mission of the church, in its ministry among us.

I, as a Christian, have always felt that there is one thing above all about "apartheid" or "separate development" that is unforgivable.

It seems utterly indifferent to the suffering of individual persons, who lose their land, their homes, their jobs, in the pursuit of what is surely the most terrible dream in the world.

This terrible dream is not held on to by a crack-pot group on the fringe of society. It is the deliberate policy of a Government, supported actively by a large part of the white population, and tolerated passively by an overwhelmingly white majority, but now fortunately rejected by an encouraging white minority who have thrown in their lot with nonwhites who are overwhelmingly opposed to so-called separate development.

Thus it is that the golden age of Africa's independence is also the dark age of South Africa's decline and retrogression.

Education is being reduced to an instrument of subtle

indoctrination. Slanted and biased reporting in the organs of public information, a creeping censorship, book-banning, and black-listing, all these spread their shadows over the land.

But beneath the surface there is a spirit of defiance.

The people of South Africa have never been a docile lot, least of all the African people. We have a long tradition of struggle for our national rights, reaching back to the very beginning of white settlement and conquest 300 years ago.

We, in our situation, have chosen the path of nonviolence of our own volition. Along this path we have organized many heroic campaigns.

The bitterness of the struggle mounts as liberty comes step by step closer to the freedom fighters' grasp. All too often, the protests and demonstrations of our people have been beaten back by force, but they have never been silenced.

Through all this cruel treatment in the name of law and order, our people, with few exceptions, have remained non-violent.

Nothing which we have suffered at the hands of the Government has turned us from our chosen path of disciplined resistance. It is for this, I believe, that this award is given.

The true patriots of South Africa, for whom I speak, will be satisfied with nothing less than the fullest democratic rights.

In government we will not be satisfied with anything less than direct individual adult suffrage and the right to stand for and be elected to all organs of government.

In economic matters we will be satisfied with nothing less than equality of opportunity in every sphere, and the enjoyment by all of those heritages which form the resources of the country which up to now have been appropriated on a racial "whites only" basis.

In culture we will be satisfied with nothing less than the opening of all doors of learning in non-segregatory institutions on the sole criterion of ability.

In the social sphere we will be satisfied with nothing less than the abolition of all racial bars.

We do not demand these things for people of African descent alone. We demand them for all South Africans, white and black.

Let me invite Africa to cast her eyes beyond the past and, to some extent, the present with their woes and tribulations, trials and failures, and some successes, and see herself an emerging continent, bursting to freedom through the shell of centuries of serfdom.

This is Africa's age—the dawn of her fulfillment, yes, the moment when she must grapple with destiny to reach the summits of sublimity saying, ours was a fight for noble values and worthy ends, and not for lands and the enslavement of man.

Still licking the scars of past wrongs perpetrated on her, could she not be magnanimous and practice no revenge? Her hand of friendship scornfully rejected, her pleas for justice and fair play spurned, should she not nonetheless seek to turn enmity into amity?

Though robbed of her lands, her independence and opportunities to become—this, oddly enough, often in the name of civilization and even Christianity—should she not see her destiny as being that of making a distinctive contribution to human progress and human relationships with a peculiar new African flavor enriched by the diversity of cultures she enjoys, thus building on the summits of present human achievement an edifice that would be one of the finest tributes to the genius of man?

In a strife-torn world, tottering on the brink of complete destruction by man-made nuclear weapons, a free and independent Africa is in the making, in answer to the injunction and challenge of history:

"Arise and shine, for thy light is come."

Acting in concert with other nations, she is man's last hope for a mediator between the East and West, and is qualified to demand of the great powers to "turn the swords into ploughshares" because two-thirds of mankind is hungry and illiterate.

Africa's qualification for this noble task is incontestable, for her own fight has never been and is not now a fight for conquest of land, for accumulation of wealth or domination of peoples, but for the recognition and preservation of the rights of man and the establishment of a truly free world.

RENATO CONSTANTINO

In this satiric essay, in the vein of Jonathan Swift's A Modest
Proposal, *Constantino reviews the history of Filipino-
American relations. With bitter humor he castigates his fellow
Filipinos for having wholeheartedly bought into an
Americanized system of values, characterized by Hollywood
movies, cosmetics, flashy cars, and conspicuous consumption.*

*More intense, however, is his criticism of the cruelty, vicious-
ness, and greed of the Americans from the very beginning of
their involvement in his country. Constantino reminds us that
when Admiral Dewey arrived in the Philippines to "liberate"
them from the Spanish, the Filipinos themselves had already
routed the Spaniards from most of the territory. The Filipinos
were, in fact, so unenthusiastic about their new American "allies" that it took six years of heavy fighting, and the murder of
many Filipinos, before the "hot-headed nationalists" allowed
themselves to be liberated.*

*Since "liberation" the United States has carefully cultivated
its interests in the Philippines, exploiting a highly favorable
trade balance and maintaining military bases strategic to the
U.S. defense posture in the Far East. Constantino alludes to
these bases in the first section of the essay, entitled "Territory."
He further refers to the common U.S. military practice of insist-
ing on maintaining jurisdictional rights over U.S. military
personnel, even in relation to offenses committed off-base. It
has been customary that crimes such as rape or murder of
Filipino citizens by American soldiers have been "punished" by
admonition or shipping the guilty party to the States or another
overseas base.*

*Since the time that Constantino's essay was written (1959),
President Marcos has declared martial law in the Philippines.
While some efforts seem to be being made to reduce American
influence, it is apparent that power has been seized by the weal-
thy, U.S.-oriented oligarchs, many of whom maintain homes in
Spain and the United States and bank accounts in Switzerland.
Thus it seems unlikely that the possibility Constantino*

*envisioned—that the nationalists may succeed in their struggle
to bring about a democratic government—will come about in the
near future.*

*The author is a historian, a political scientist, and a professorial lecturer at the University of the Philippines. Although he
has written a number of satires on Philippine society, he is
better known for his more serious historical and political works.*

The Filipinos in the Philippines

The Filipinos constitute the largest minority group in the
Philippines. The present native inhabitants are the survivors
of that race which suffered the brutalization of the Spaniards,
the "extermination campaign" of the American troops during
the Filipino-American War, and the mass executions of the
Japanese.

Ethnically, these people belong to the Malay group, though
strains of Chinese, Indian, and Spanish blood may be found.
Recently, however, a great deal of American blood has been
pouring into the country. The introduction of this strain into
the Filipino bloodstream has greatly improved the height of
Filipino basketball players and the shape of Philippine movie
stars.

Another school of thought would classify the Filipinos as an
almost sub-human species. U.S. Senator MacLaurin, during
the debate on the Paris Peace Treaty of 1898, expressed his
fears of the possible annexation of the Philippines because it
would mean the "incorporation of a mongrel and semi-
barbarous population into our body politic," which was "in-
ferior to, but akin to the Negro in moral and intellectual qualities and in capacity for self-government."

Territory

The Filipinos live in areas outside the military bases and
American recreation camps. The territory occupied by these
people is rapidly shrinking as Filipinos yield the choicest resi-
dential, commercial, and industrial sites to other minority

groups who have found in this land a haven from economic difficulties in their own countries of origin. The continuation of this trend can lead to only one result—namely, reservations for Filipinos, similar to those enjoyed by the Ainus of Japan and the American Indians in the United States. These reservations will constitute a guarantee from grateful foreign friends that the Filipinos will always have a place in the Philippines in recognition of their having been the first inhabitants of this country.

Physical Features

The Filipino race is the greatest answer to anthropologists who arbitrarily and unfairly classify peoples as white, black, brown, red, or yellow. The Filipinos may truly be called a super-race for, as a people, they show such varied physical characteristics that they defy categorization.

Brown and White

The men belong to the brown race; the women are definitely Caucasoid of the Hollywood type, for, by means of modern cosmetology, their skins are bleached, their hair is brunette, red, or even blonde. The female physical dimensions are 35-24-35, true or false. They have fairly straight limbs and pointed toes.

Blacks, Reds, and Yellows

The Negritos, along with certain Filipinos sporting P1.50 permanents, may be classified under the black race because of their characteristic kinky hair. There is a sprinkling of reds among the Filipinos, notably those lately of Central Luzon, who, according to outstanding "racial experts," may be easily recognized by their incorrigible tendency to infiltrate all manner of organizations and from those vantage points criticize American domination in this country. The yellow race is represented by those Filipinos who are descended from Chinese ancestors and other yellow individuals like those who cower before diplomatic and military representatives of foreign powers.

Character Traits

Hospitable and Generous

The Filipinos are a hospitable and generous people. With the exception of a certain Lapu-Lapu and some misguided "insurrectos" during the turn of the century, the Filipinos have been happy to open their shores to aliens in search of wealth. The majority have considered it a privilege to be able to offer their foreign friends all the opportunities for advancement. Their one obsession has been to make of this country what prominent foreign writers have called—"an island paradise." True to the wishes of their ancestors, the modern Filipinos have indeed transformed their country into a paradise—for non-Filipinos.

Of course, no paradise is without its serpent, and in the Philippine Eden the foreigners have discovered a species of venomous serpents whom they call "Ultra-nationalists."

Land of the Brave

Philippine history is replete with instances showing that the ancestors of modern Filipinos were proud, brave men. The modern Filipino is braver still, for he has fought and died for other nations and is willing to die again and again for America. Undaunted by the threat of nuclear obliteration, armed only with obsolete surplus American weapons, the Filipinos are willing to act as magnets to draw the enemy fire from continental America in a supreme gesture of gallantry which will surely amaze the world.

As a matter of fact, the Filipino is braver than the American. Time and again he has shown in the halls of the United Nations that he is not afraid to engage both the Soviet Union and Red China single-handed in mortal combat, whereas the Americans will not fight unless supported by loyal allies. The peak of Philippine bravery was reached during the time of Magsaysay. Unfortunately, because of the influence of cowardly nationalists who insist on fighting only for national interests, Filipino bravery has diminished.

A Cultured Race

The Filipino is a creature of immense talent for cultural acquisition. He has shown his discriminating taste by being receptive only to American culture, selecting for avid consumption such outstanding American contributions as cowboy movies, horror pictures, comics, rock and roll, soapbox derbies, beauty contests, teen-age idiosyncracies, advertising jingles, cocktail parties, and soft drinks. This talent of the Filipinos for assimilating only American culture, and moreover, only the best of that culture, was foreseen by T. H. Pardo de Tavera who in 1901 said:

> After peace is established, all our efforts will be directed to Americanizing ourselves; to cause a knowledge of the English language to be extended and generalized in the Philippines, in order that through its agency the American spirit may take possession of us, and that we may adopt its principles, its political customs, and its peculiar civilization, that our redemption may be complete and radical.

Heights of Ambition

The typical Filipino is ambitious. The male aspires to be a junior executive in a large American firm and later to head a subsidiary of some big American corporation. A few become politicians and seek office through any of the established parties. Failure to land in any major political slate could easily be remedied by establishing a grand alliance and calling the other office seekers "professional politicians." The female, both married and unmarried, aspires to be a fashion model or a cover girl.

The typical middle-class family dreams of an RFC or GSIS-financed bungalow with a terrace, a tiled bathroom, and a bubble lamp in the living room which simply must have a semi Hi-Fi radio and, if possible, a corner "bar" proudly displaying beer and coca cola bottles. Such a family raises children so that they may have the pleasure of giving them American nicknames and hearing themselves called Mommy and Daddy in contrast to less fortunate Nanays and Tatays. Their boys must go to colleges well known for their basketball teams, and their girls must receive an exclusive convent education. Of course, the family must have a second-hand car of the latest possible model or a least a re-conditioned jeep with tail fins.

In Manila, the aforementioned vehicle will most probably convey the family on its monthly outing to the exclusive Enlisted Men's Mess Hall of the JUSMAG compound, there to relish hamburger sandwiches and ice cream sundaes at PX prices.

Gratitude Springs Eternal

In the eyes of their foreign friends, one of the endearing traits of the Filipinos is their child-like gratitude for little gifts or imagined favors. The Filipinos have never stopped being grateful to the American administrators for their progress in agriculture, commerce, industry, public works, sanitation, etc. Like naive children, they received all these as if they were gifts from their benevolent conquerors. The truth is, as A.V.H. Hartendorp, an American oldtimer, said in his latest book:

A truly remarkable fact is that all this was accomplished without financial aid from the United States. The civil administration of the Philippines was self-supporting from the beginning of the American occupation in 1898. The only expense the Philippines constituted for the United States was the expense of maintaining the United States armed forces here.

More recently, the Filipinos have found new cause for gratitude in the establishment of packaging and assembly plants which are grandiosely called industries when in truth these plants are disguised forms of importation which consume plenty of dollars for raw material purchases and for capital and profit remittances.

The basic origin for this naive propensity to feel gratitude, out of all proportion to supposed favors bestowed, is the belief shared by almost all Filipinos that they should be grateful to the U.S. for having saved them from Spanish misrule. The entire thinking of the Filipinos at present is based on the assumption that the U. S. crossed the ocean to give succor to a people who were up in arms against a cruel tyrant and would have been crushed by said tyrant had not the noble-hearted American crusaders come to their rescue.

At this point, a discussion of early Philippine-American relations would be proper in order to establish the basis of that gratitude.

Pre-History and History

There is no need to touch on the history of the Filipinos during the pre-Spanish and Spanish periods. In the first place, there are many conflicting versions of Philippine history during this period. There is a history for Catholic schools and a history for Chinese schools although, strangely enough, there is as yet no proper history for Filipinos. In the second place, historians of the American period assert that prior to the arrival of the Americans, the Filipinos, in the words of President Theodore Roosevelt, were merely "a jumble of savage tribes."

Filipino life before the coming of the Americans would therefore more properly belong to pre-history, and we should not concern ourselves with it. After all, no less than Secretary of War Elihu Root, in a speech before the Marquette Club in 1899, denied the existence of a Filipino nation when he said:

Well, whom are we fighting? Are we fighting the Philippine nation? No! There is none. There are hundreds of islands inhabited by more than sixty tribes, speaking more than sixty languages, and all but one ready to accept American sovereignty.

This statement of the American Secretary of War was the basis of popular thinking in America during that period and thereafter.

The Original Professional Politicians

According to unimpeachable American sources, all the people of the Philippines were ready to welcome American occupation with the exception of the Tagalog tribe led by a group, who, in the words of General Otis quoting Manuel Manahan, were "professional politicians." We have the word of no less than President Taft that this group of revolutionaries kept up "a conspiracy of murder, a Mafia on a very large scale."

This group of Aguinaldo and Mabini was the only stumbling block to the realization of America's "manifest destiny" in these islands because, according to American intelligence, they were cruelly coercing the people to fight for the independence of their country.

Welcome Invaders

Indeed, the Americans were so welcome that it took them only six years to suppress resistance movements, and for this purpose they used only 120,000 American troops. Evidently, the hated revolutionists had been successful in forcing the Filipinos to fight for their independence against the Spaniards, and later the Americans, even though all the time the majority of them were just itching to be under American rule.

What techniques of mass hypnosis, what refinements of torture were used to turn a naturally pro-American people into fierce fighters for freedom, are secrets that the revolutionaries carried to their graves. The fact is that prior to the coming of that admirable Admiral George Dewey, the Filipinos had in effect deposed their cruel Castilian rulers. The revolutionary forces under Emilio Aguinaldo were in control of Luzon and the principal Visayan islands. The American liberators held only Cavite and Manila.

General Anderson stated, "We held Manila and Cavite, the rest of the Island (Luzon) was held not by Spaniards but by the Filipinos. On the other islands the Spaniards were confined to two or three fortified towns."

These were later captured by the Filipinos according to General Otis who, in his report of August 21, 1899, admitted:

Thus, in December, 1899, we find that in northern and southeastern Luzon, in (the islands of) Mindoro, Samar, Leyte, Panay and even on the coast of Mindanao and in some of the smaller islands, the aggressive Tagalog is present in person and, whether civilian or soldier, supreme in authority.

This was the lone tribe which was coercing the others to fight for independence, and a diabolically clever tribe it was too, to judge from the success of its nefarious schemes.

Fraternal Allies

The victory of Admiral Dewey in Manila Bay confronted the United States with the problem of what to do with a people who had dislodged their masters and who had declared their independence. Fortunately, the U.S. at that time was under the able leadership of William McKinley who had a tremendous compassion for the plight of backward peoples and knew exactly what was good for them. During the course of the war, he showed brilliant statesmanship when he said, "While we are conducting war and until its conclusion we must keep all we get; when the war is over we must keep what we want."

Under such inspired leadership, it is not surprising that the Americans executed a series of master strokes which finally released the Filipinos from the hypnotic control which the gang of revolutionaries had exercised over them. They regained their senses and gratefully relinquished control of their country to infinitely more capable hands.

One such master stroke was the maintenance of a semblance of friendship with the revolutionaries while joint action was necessary against Spanish troops. With the fall of Manila and the capture of the main bulk of the Spanish forces which was made possible only because Filipino troops then encircled the city, this silly friendship with misguided elements could be dropped. While the gullible Filipinos were jubilantly celebrating the fall of their old enemy and expecting to share with their American allies in the honors of victory, American policy makers, who were certainly more farsighted, decided it was time to put these revolutionaries in their proper place and cut them down to size before they began having an exaggerated idea of their own importance.

Judge James H. Blount in his book, *The American Occupation of the Philippines,* describes the fraternal relations between the two allies during the final act of the Spanish-American War:

As Aguinaldo's troops surged forward in the wake of the American advance they were stopped by orders from the American commander, and prevented from following the retreating Spaniards into Manila. They were not even allowed what is known to the modern small boy as a "look-in." They were not permitted to come into the city to see the surrender.

President McKinley's message to Congress of December, 1898, explains this treatment of Aguinaldo and his forces thus: "Divided victory was not permissible. It was fitting that whatever was to be done . . . should be accomplished by the strong arm of the U.S. alone."

American Altruism

A great deal of misunderstanding has been created by the verbal understanding between Dewey and Aguinaldo before the latter returned to the islands from his exile. On the question of Philippine independence, some biographers of the admiral and some Filipino historians claim that Dewey gave Aguinaldo to understand that the U.S. was fighting Spain in order to help the Filipinos gain their freedom. Aguinaldo states categorically, "Certainly Admiral Dewey did not bring me from Hong Kong to Manila to fight the Spaniards for the benefit of American trade expansion." Admiral Dewey has emphatically denied this and it is easy to believe him because as a soldier he was trained to follow orders. In May, 1898, Secretary of the Navy Long cabled Dewey "not to have political alliance with the insurgents . . . that would incur liability to maintain their cause in the future." Moreover, Dewey's attitude toward Philippine independence was expressed by him in these admirable succinct words: "That was my idea, not taking it seriously."

That he succeeded in making Aguinaldo believe otherwise is a measure of his diplomatic skill. The good admiral would have made an eminently successful Ambassador to the Philippines were he alive today. Who knows, if he had been allowed to use his extraordinary talents for a longer period in this country, the grateful Filipinos would probably have changed the name of Manila to Dewey City instead of honoring him with only one measly boulevard.

Thus did Dewey contribute to the salvation of the majority of the Filipinos who were eagerly awaiting the implantation of American sovereignty and the exercise of American altruism in their country. How then was American altruism to be practised in these forlorn islands of the Pacific? President McKinley's instructions to the peace commissioners in Paris answer this question. He said " . . . incidental to our tenure in the Philippines is the commercial opportunity. . . . The U.S. cannot accept less than the cession in full right and sovereignty of the island of Luzon."

Sen. Henry Cabot Lodge, the eminent ancestor of the present U.S. representative to the U.N., as permanent chairman of the Philadelphia convention which renominated McKinley for the presidency in 1900 said, "We make no hypocritical pretense of being interested in the Philippines solely on account of others. . . . We believe in trade expansion."

A more altruistic American, Secretary of the Treasury Lyman J. Gage, summed up his entire attitude in a brief "Philanthropy and five per cent go hand in hand."

But the most honest statement of American altruistic intention was made by the Hon. Charles Denby, a member of the Schurman Commission in 1899 who, in an article which appeared in the *Forum* of February, 1899, declared, "The cold practical question remains: will the possession of these islands benefit us as a nation? If they will not, set them free tomorrow and let their peoples, if they please, cut each other's throats."

Civilizing the Lowly Filipino

America was at the threshold of a new era. As Assistant Secretary of the Treasury Frank A. Vanderlip said, "We thus see with sudden clearness that some of the most revered of our political maxims have outlived their force, a new mainspring . . . has become the directing force . . . the mainspring of commercialism." So that the Filipinos might be better qualified to support this new directing force of commercialism, the Americans took upon themselves the task of civilizing the lowly Filipino.

Even before the effectivity of the Paris Peace Treaty, when America still had no legal right of title over the Philippines, McKinley issued on December 21, 1898, a proclamation of "benevolent assimilation" which in effect informed the Filipinos that they were already a possession of the United States who would rule them with benevolence if they accepted its sovereignty. Otherwise, the armed forces of the United States would compel them to submit. Apparently, the independent Filipino government did not know what was good for them and their country. They resisted the benevolent invasion.

With Solicitude and Care

Because of the recalcitrance of the Philippine government, the Americans had to civilize these barbaric peoples with the

Krag rifle. The U.S. army troops were made conscious of their mission to treat the natives with solicitude and care. The army song of the troops under Gen. Arthur MacArthur showed the high regard of the American soldier for the Filipino:

> Damn, damn, damn the Filipino
> Pock-marked Khakiac ladrone;
> Underneath the starry flag
> Civilize him with a Krag,
> And return us to our own beloved home.
>
> *(Sung to the tune of "Tramp, tramp, tramp,*
> *the boys are marching")*

The task of civilizing these people proved extremely difficult, for the Filipinos perversely insisted on living in their old savage ways. The Americans, therefore, had to resort to various civilized means of collective punishment, torture, and mass extermination in their sincere effort to bring the Filipinos to their senses in order that they would accept the superior civilization of America. For every attack made by Filipinos on American troops, whole villages were burned. Some quarters in the U.S. questioned the method of dealing with these people. The justification may be seen in the following testimony of Gen. R.P. Hughes during a U.S. Senate investigation—

Senator Rawlins. If these shacks were of no consequence what was the utility of their destruction?

Gen. Hughes. The destruction was as a punishment. They permitted these people to come in there and conceal themselves and they gave them no sign. It is always—

Sen. Rawlins. The punishment in that case would fall, not upon the men, who could go elsewhere, but mainly upon the women and little children.

Gen. Hughes. The women and children are part of the family, and where you wish to inflict a punishment you can punish the man probably worse in that way than in any other.

Sen. Rawlins. But is that within the ordinary rules of civilized warfare? Of course you could exterminate the family, which would be still worse punishment.

Gen. Hughes. These people are not civilized.

The techniques of benevolent assimilation were varied and ingenious. The most famous was the water cure. This particular technique is described in an article in *City and State* of January 2, 1909, quoting a letter to the *Omaha World* by Private A. F. Miller of the 32nd U.S. Volunteers:

Now this is the way we give them the water cure: lay them on their backs, a man standing on each hand and each foot, then put a round stick in the mouth and pour a pail of water in the mouth and nose, and if they don't give up pour in another pail. They swell up like toads. I'll tell you it's a terrible torture.

Mr. George Kennan, the special investigator of the *Outlook*, in an article of March 9, 1901, states:

The Spaniards used the torture of water, throughout the islands, as a means of obtaining information; but they used it sparingly, and only when it appeared evident that the victim was culpable. Americans seldom do things by halves. We come here and announce our intention of freeing the people from three or four hundred years of oppression, and say 'we are strong, and powerful, and grand.' Then to resort to inquisitorial methods, and use them without discrimination, is unworthy of us, and will recoil on us as a nation.

It is painful and humiliating to have to confess that in some of our dealings with the Filipinos we seem to be following more or less closely the example of Spain. We have established a penal colony; we burn native villages near which there has been an ambush or an attack by insurgent guerillas; we kill the wounded; we resort to torture as a means of obtaining information. . . .

Another technique is the so-called rope cure which is described in the *Chicago Record Herald:*

A light but strong rope is passed across the throat of the man to be examined. It is crossed behind his back and carried under the armpits, the ends are again brought around the neck and over to the back, turned under the armpits and shoulders, and then the free ends are carried as a girdle around the waist just at the end of the ribs, and tied fast and securely. A stick is put through the ropes where they cross between the shoulders, and then turned to suit. "Will it make a man talk?" Mr. Loughran was asked. "A wooden Indian would make a speech if you give him the rope cure," he replied. Mr. Loughran says that this was far more effective than the water cure, which is slow. The rope cure often persuaded a native to reveal the hiding place of his gun; and it did it quickly, because he knew that as soon as he consented to talk the stick would be loosened and would fly back, relieving the agony instantaneously. Of course, if the victim should have a weak heart, he might die of shock; but the native Filipino does not seem to be troubled with the malady.

"A Howling Wilderness"

Two famous generals produced by this period were General "Jake" Smith in Samar and General J.F. Bell in Batangas. In a letter to President McKinley on July 12, 1902, Secretary Root stated that Smith had given the following oral instructions:

"I want no prisoners. I wish you to kill and burn: the more you kill and burn the better you will please me," and further, that he wanted all persons killed who were capable of bearing arms and in actual hostilities against the United States, and did in reply to a question by Major Waller asking for an age limit, designate the limit as ten years of age.

According to Moorfield Story and Marcial P. Lichauco, in their book, *The Conquest of the Philippines by the United States:* "The accused bore his trial like a man. He admitted giving the orders. He did not seek to excuse them on the ground that his words were reckless talk—on the contrary, he sought to justify them. On the solitary question, therefore, of whether or not he had given the order the reviewing officers of high rank found him guilty and sentenced him to be admonished."

This, of course, was enough punishment for a man who after all was only doing his duty, albeit a bit overzealously, to make the God-forsaken island of Samar safe for democracy, and its near-savage people better qualified to profit from American tutelage.

Incidentally, all the current Filipino protestations against the brutalities of American military authorities in military bases do not take into consideration that the guilty personnel who have been shipped home to escape Philippine justice may have also been meted the supreme penalty of admonition and reprimand.

General Bell, not to be outdone by his colleague, General Smith, established his own claim to the gratitude of the Filipino people with his efficiently humane policies. In a report dated December 26, 1901, this gallant soldier proudly sets forth the tremendous job he has assigned himself:

I take so large a command for the purpose of thoroughly searching each ravine, valley and mountain peak for insurgents and for food, expecting to destroy everything I find outside of towns. All able-bodied men will be killed or captured.

As a result of General Bell's devoted labors, thousands were thrown into prison and, curiously enough, many died there. If we are to believe the records, they died in prison of various types of illnesses.

The population of Batangas in 1899 before Gen. Bell's fortuitous arrival was 312,192. In 1903 there were only 257,715 Batangueños left. This commendable attempt of Gen. Bell and his minions to solve the problem of population explosion in Batangas coincidentally resulted in weeding out those undesirable elements who senselessly refused to accept benevolent American rule. It is sad to note, however, that Gen. Bell's zealous efforts were not completely successful, for Batangas still harbors to this day enough of these undesirables to be characterized as a hotbed of nationalists, led by the most ungrateful ultra-nationalist of all—the notorious Claro M. Recto.

New Vistas Through the English Language

In the long run the Americans were able to suppress the resistance of the Filipinos who persisted in their unreasonable desire for independence. A half century of American rule followed, and it was during this period that the Americans demonstrated by words and by deeds their true benevolence, for everything they did for and to this country, they said they did for love of their little brown wards. To mention only a few of these charitable deeds:

The Americans established a system of education using English as a medium of instruction. This induced the Filipinos to forget their barbaric past, including the unwholesome lessons of the revolutionary firebrands of 1896. Moreover, English opened new vistas of Western culture to their dazed eyes and enabled them to write poetry about autumn and winter and snow on the fir trees, to know more of Paul Revere and less of Apolinario Mabini, to sing nostalgically about "My Old Kentucky Home" and "White Christmas."

But more important because of greater practical value primarily to the Filipinos and only incidentally to United States businessmen, their rudimentary command of English enabled Filipino citizens to import Hollywood movies, to purchase large quantities of American publications, and to consume a phenomenal amount of American-made goods. From Hollywood movies, the Filipinos imbibed many valuable lessons on life, love, Apaches, gangsters, and sex. Because they now possessed the advantage of reading in English, the eyes of Filipinos were opened to the wonderful world of Batman and Superman, the exciting underworld of Mickey Spillane, and the out of this world reporting of *Time* magazine. Their possession of English enabled the Filipinos to understand the masterpieces of advertising prose and thus elevated their hitherto brutish tastes so that now they ride in flamboyant cars and proudly chew gum, smoke Virginia cigarettes, and drink sparkling soft drinks. A concrete evidence of the educative effects of American advertising on Filipino throats may be found in the data on soft drinks and beverages. The yearly consumption of soft drinks and other beverages of 23,000,000 Filipinos is nearly 2,000,000,000 bottles or roughly 100 bottles per person including babies and centenarians.

Reciprocal Relations

In trying to spare the Filipino from the rigors of industrialization and to preserve the idyllic pastoral economy so suitable to their generally childlike nature, the Americans introduced a trade pattern for the islands which assured these people an unlimited supply of ready-made American goods and in return gave them magnanimously limited quotas for their raw material exports to the American markets. They were so solicitous about the welfare of their wards that even when formal independence was finally recognized, they spared their Filipino protégés the risks of over-development through industrialization by continuing the benevolent colonial pattern under the Bell Trade Act.

White Man's Justice

But this concern was not limited to the economic field, for desirous of protecting the Filipinos from Communist aggression, the Americans established and retained military bases and equipped the Philippine army with obsolete weapons. Of course, in the military bases, the superior American soldier had to be assured of real white man's justice by removing him from the pale of unreliable Oriental law. This, however, really constitutes one more instance of paternal solicitude, for in removing American criminal offenders from the jurisdiction of Philippine courts, the U.S. army is in effect relieving the congestion of Filipino court dockets. Anyway, most of the criminal offenses committed by American servicemen are minor matters such as running over slow-moving pedestrians or maltreating and raping unaccommodating Filipina hostesses.

The Filipinos are indeed a lucky people for they are allowed to share in the economic life of the country. There are a few Filipino manufacturers, businessmen, and importers. There are many Filipino market vendors, beauty salon proprietors, dressmakers and tailors, and gasoline station operators. Filipinos practically monopolize labor, sidewalk vending, and jeepney driving. Enterprising Filipinos have even taken over from the Chinese the lucrative and distinguished occupation of buying and selling old newspapers and empty bottles.

According to the Chairman of the National Economic Council, non-Filipinos control seventy per cent of Philippine foreign trade and eighty per cent of domestic trade. According to the census of 1948, the total non-Filipino assets in the Philippines for seven major industry groups; namely, forestry, transportation, mining, electricity, fisheries, manufacturing and commerce, constituted 48.1 per cent of the total assets. In other words, 23,000,000 Filipinos owned only a little more of the assets in these industries than less than half a million foreigners. It must be borne in mind that the share in the national wealth classified as belonging to Filipinos includes that owned by naturalized Filipinos. The native-born Filipinos, therefore, own considerably less than the figures mentioned above.

Insofar as the dollar quotas are concerned, the chairman of the NEC states:

During the periods 1956, 1957 and 1958, out of the total regular quotas allocated by the Central Bank, Filipinos (including the naturalized ones) were granted 48.12 per cent, 47.80 per cent, and 43.44 per cent, respectively. During the same period, foreigners were allocated 51.88 per cent, 52.20 per cent, and 56.56 per cent, respectively, which showed increasing trends in contrast to the decreasing Filipino participation or share.

These are government figures based on formal registration of ownership and consequently do not take into consideration the widespread institution of the dummy. If they did, Filipino participation would be found to be considerably lower.

Clouds on the Horizon

In spite of their participation in the economic life of the country, the Filipinos today are becoming increasingly dissatisfied with their position. Unfortunately, they are losing their traditional virtues of humility and hospitality and imbibing the harmful spirit of modern materialism. This makes them greedy and quite unreasonable. They believe that just

because they were here first and are numerically pre-
ponderant, this is primarily their own country, and they
should have a greater share of its resources. These are fal-
lacies, of course, and are disturbing the special relations between the Philippines and the United States. Any deteri-
oration of these relations, for whatever cause, weakens the
solidarity of the free world at a time when all nations must
forget their petty grievances and rally behind the leadership
of the United States.

The disturbances in the traditionally happy Philippine-
American relations may be laid squarely at the door of today's
nationalists and the Garcia administration which instituted
the Filipino First policy. The machinations of these nationalists have been so successful that they have already infected
the majority of the Filipinos with the incurable madness of
nationalism. Before the few Filipinos who happily still remain
untouched by this insanity succumb to the malady, it is the
considered opinion of the writer that they be transported immediately to the United States under the leadership of the
Grand Alliance and those of the Liberal Party who have
proven their loyalty to America. There they will find a haven
which they richly deserve.

As for the nationalists, these misguided elements who have
sorely tried American patience and forbearance should be
given their just desserts. They should be made to remain in
this country and forced to solve its numerous problems without American technical advisers, develop its resources without American aid, and shoulder the burdens of independent
existence.

If, after instituting their ill-conceived nationalist policies,
the country becomes industrialized and prosperous and in-
herits the problems common to wealthy nations, the nationalists will have no one to blame but themselves.

FIDEL CASTRO

*A Cuban revolutionary and political leader, Castro is premier
of Cuba. As a young lawyer, he openly criticized the dictator-*

ship of Batista in 1952, and on July 26, 1953, led an unsuccessful attack on an army post in Santiago de Cuba and was imprisoned. Released in 1955 in a general amnesty, he went to Mexico where he organized the 26th of July Movement. Despite severe setbacks and hardships, they built up a following and led the increasingly effective guerrilla campaign that toppled the Batista regime in 1959. Castro soon proved to be a brilliant propagandist and a powerful orator. By aligning himself and the Cuban revolution with the underprivileged peoples of Latin America, Asia, and Africa, he established his image as a folk hero. His writings include Ten Years of Revolution *(1964) and* History Will Absolve Me *(1968).*

Extracts from Words to the Intellectuals

There can be, of course, artists, and good artists, who do not have a revolutionary attitude towards life, and it is for precisely that group of artists and intellectuals that the Revolution constitutes a problem.

For a mercenary artist or intellectual, for a dishonest artist or intellectual, it would never be a problem: he knows what he has to do, he knows what is in his interest, he knows where he is going.

The real problem exists for the artist or intellectual who does not have a revolutionary attitude towards life but who is, however, an honest person. It is clear that he who has that attitude towards life, whether he is revolutionary or not, whether he is an artist or not, has his goals, has his objectives, and we should all ask ourselves about those goals and objectives. For the revolutionary, those goals and objectives are directed towards the change of reality; those goals and objectives are directed towards the redemption of man. It is man himself, his fellow man, the redemption of his fellow man that constitutes the objective of the revolutionary. If they ask us revolutionaries what matters most to us, we will say the people, and we will always say the people. The people in their true sense, that is, the majority of the people, those who have had to live in exploitation and in the cruelest neglect. Our basic concern will always be the great majority of the people, that is, the oppressed and exploited classes. The point of view through which we view everything is this: whatever is good for them will be good for us; whatever is noble, useful, and beautiful for them, will be noble, useful and beautiful for us. If one does not think of the people and for the people, that is, if one does not think and does not act for the great exploited masses of the people, for the great masses which we want to redeem, then one simply does not have a revolutionary attitude.

It is from this point of view that we analyze the good, the useful, and the beautiful of every action.

We understand that it must be a tragedy when someone understands this and none the less has to confess that he is incapable of fighting for it.

We are, or believe ourselves to be, revolutionaries. Whoever is more of an artist than a revolutionary cannot think exactly the same as we do. We struggle for the people without inner conflict, we know that we can achieve what we have set out to do. The principal goal is *the people*. We have to think about the people before we think about ourselves, and that is the only attitude that can be defined as a truly revolutionary attitude. . . .

The case was well made that there were many writers and artists who were not revolutionaries, but were, however, honest writers and artists; that they wanted to help the Revolution, and that the Revolution is interested in their help; that they wanted to work for the Revolution and that, at the same time, the Revolution was interested in their contributing their knowledge and efforts on its behalf.

It is easier to appreciate this when specific cases are analyzed: and among those specific cases are many that are not easy to analyze. A Catholic writer spoke here. He raised the problems that worried him and he spoke with great clarity. He asked if he could make an interpretation of a determined problem from his idealistic point of view or if he could write a work defending that point of view. He asked quite frankly if, within a revolutionary régime, he could express himself in accordance with those sentiments. He posed the problem in a form that might be considered symbolic.

He was concerned about knowing if he could write in accordance with those sentiments or in accordance with that ideology, which was not exactly the ideology of the Revolution. He was in agreement with the Revolution on economic and social questions, but his philosophic position was distinct from that of the Revolution. And this case is worthy of being kept well in mind, because it is a case representative of the group of writers and artists who demonstrate a favourable attitude towards the Revolution and wish to know what degree of freedom they have within the revolutionary conditions to express themselves in accordance with their feelings. That is the group that constitutes a problem for the Revolution, just as the Revolution constitutes a problem for them, and it is the duty of the Revolution to be concerned with these cases; it is the duty of the Revolution to be concerned with the situation of those artists and writers, because the Revolution ought to bend its efforts towards having more than the revolutionaries, more than the revolutionary artists and intellectuals, move along with it. It is possible that the men and women who have a truly revolutionary attitude towards reality do not constitute the greatest sector of the population: the revolutionaries are the vanguard of the people, but the revolutionaries should bend their efforts towards having all the people move along with them. The Revolution cannot renounce the goal of having all honest men and women, whether writers and artists or not, moving along with it; the Revolution should bend its efforts towards converting everyone who has doubts into a revolutionary. The Revolution should try to win over the greatest part of the people to its ideas; the Revolution should never give up counting on the majority of the people, counting not only on the revolutionaries, but on all honest citizens who, although they may not have a revolutionary attitude towards life, are with the Revolution.

The Revolution should give up only those who are incorrigible reactionaries, who are incorrigible counter-revolutionaries. Towards all others the Revolution must have a policy; the Revolution has to have an attitude towards those intellectuals and writers. The Revolution has to understand the real situation and should therefore act in such a manner that the whole group of artists and intellectuals who are not genuinely revolutionaries can find within the Revolution a place to work and create, a place where their creative spirit, even though they are not revolutionary writers and artists, has the opportunity and freedom to be expressed.

The Revolution cannot be trying to stifle art or culture when one of the goals and one of the fundamental purposes of the Revolution is to develop art and culture, so that our artistic and cultural treasures can truly belong to the people. And just as we want a better life for the people in the material sense, so do we want a better life for the people in a spiritual and cultural sense. And just as the Revolution is concerned with the development of the conditions and forces that will permit the people to satisfy all their material needs, so do we also want to create the conditions that will permit the people to satisfy all their cultural needs.

Is the cultural level of our people low? Until this year a high percentage of the people did not know how to read and write. A high percentage of the people have known hunger, or at least live or used to live under wretched conditions, under conditions of misery. Part of the people lack a great many of the material goods they need, and we are trying to bring about conditions that will permit all these material goods to reach the people.

In the same way we should bring about the necessary conditions for all cultural manifestations to reach the people. This is not to say that the artist has to sacrifice the artistic worth of his creations. It is to say that we have to struggle in all ways so that the artist creates for the people and so that the people in turn raise their cultural level and draw nearer to the artist. We cannot set up a general rule: all artistic manifestations are not of exactly the same nature, and at times we have spoken here as if that were the case. There are expressions of the creative spirit that by their very nature are much more accessible to the people than other manifestations of the creative spirit. Therefore it is not possible to set up a general rule, because we have to ask the questions: What principles of expression should the artist follow in his effort to reach the people? What should the people demand from the artist? Can we make a general statement about this? No. It would be oversimplified. It is necessary to strive to reach the people in all creative manifestations, but in turn it is necessary to do all we can to enable the people to understand more, to understand better. I believe that this principle is not in contradiction to the aspiration of any artist—and much less so if it is kept in mind that men should create for their contemporaries.

We say that there are no artists who create only for posterity because, without considering our judgement infallible, I believe that whoever is proceeding on this assumption is a victim of self-hypnosis.

And that is not to say that the artist who works for his contemporaries has to renounce the possibility of his work becoming known to posterity, because it is precisely by being created for the artist's contemporaries, regardless of whether his contemporaries have understood him or not, that many works have acquired historical and universal value. We are not making a Revolution for the generations to come, we are making a Revolution with this generation and for this generation, independently of its benefits for future generations and its becoming a historic event. We are not making a Revolution for posterity; this Revolution will be important to posterity because it is a Revolution for today and for the men and women of today.

Who would follow us if we were making a Revolution for future generations?

We are working and creating for our contemporaries, without depriving any artistic creation of aspirations to eternal fame.

—Translated by J.M. Cohen

NOVELLA

ALEX LA GUMA

Alex La Guma is a powerful writer whose work depicts in unflinching detail the misery and degradation characteristic of the plight of non-whites in South Africa, his homeland. La Guma was born in Cape Town in 1925, and, following his graduation from Cape Technical School, worked as a clerk, factory hand, bookkeeper, and journalist. Interested in South African politics since an early age and always concerned for the situation of his people, he was first arrested for treason in 1956. For the next ten years he was continually harassed, arrested, or detained under various restrictions. Finally he left South Africa in 1966 as a refugee and made his home in London with his family. He has written many short stories, which have appeared in Africa, Europe, and the U.S.A.

In A Walk in the Night, *La Guma paints a detailed picture of life in District Six, Cape Town's toughest quarter. The main story is about Michael Adonis, a colored young man, who, having lost his job and unwittingly murdered an old, decrepit man, falls into a pattern which can only lead to total moral dissolution and brutality. His walk in the night is counterpoised with the terrified flight of Willieboy, unjustly accused of the murder Michael Adonis committed. Parallel to these movements through the dark and filthy streets of the District is the prowling motion of the police van, carrying the vicious and violent Constable Raalt and his frightened rookie companion. The paths of the four men cross and recross, until Raalt's bullet puts an end to the futile and wasted life of Willieboy.*

Standing apart from the central action, yet concerned with it, is the ragged urchin Joe, whom Michael Adonis has befriended and has thereby earned his unflinching loyalty. Joe has had no more advantages than the other residents of District Six; abandoned by his family, homeless, uneducated, he is totally destitute. Yet somehow he seems to have a clear, direct moral sense and a feeling of compassion not expressed elsewhere in the story. Pleading with Michael Adonis not to get involved with a group of petty crooks, Joe says, "Please, Mike . . . I'm your pal. A man's got a right to look after another man. Jesus, isn't we all people?"

In the character of Constable Raalt, La Guma demonstrates how feelings of personal inadequacy and frustration may be given expression in unbridled acts of cruelty in a society which not only condones but promotes the doctrines of white supremacy. The younger officer, who shares the same beliefs, has not yet arrived at the level of corruption and flagrant abuse of authority which are the mark of Constable Raalt. In Raalt, La Guma shows clearly that the doctrine of apartheid is ultimately destructive of whites as well as blacks. "Where one is slave, none is free. . . . "

A Walk in the Night

> I am thy father's spirit;
> Doom'd for a certain term to walk the night,
> And for the day confined to fast in fires,
> Till the foul crimes done in my days of nature
> Are burnt and purged away.
>> *William Shakespeare: Hamlet, Act I, Scene V*

ONE

The young man dropped from the trackless tram just before it stopped at Castle Bridge. He dropped off, ignoring the stream of late-afternoon traffic rolling in from the suburbs, bobbed and ducked the cars and buses, the big, rumbling delivery trucks, deaf to the shouts and curses of the drivers, and reached the pavement.

Standing there, near the green railings around the public convenience, he lighted a cigarette, jostled by the lines of workers going home, the first trickle of a stream that would soon be flowing towards Hanover Street. He looked right through them, refusing to see them, nursing a little growth of anger the way one caresses the beginnings of a toothache with the tip of the tongue.

Around him the buzz and hum of voices and the growl of traffic blended into one solid mutter of sound which he only half-heard, his thoughts concentrated upon the pustule of rage and humiliation that was continuing to ripen deep down within him.

The young man wore jeans that had been washed several times and which were now left with a pale-blue colour flecked with old grease stains and the newer, darker ones of that day's work in the sheet-metal factory, and going white along the hard seams. The jeans had brass buttons, and the legs were too long, so that they had to be turned up six inches at the bottom. He also wore an old khaki shirt and over it a rubbed and scuffed and worn leather coat with slanting pockets and woollen wrists. His shoes were of the moccasin type, with leather thongs stitching the saddle to the rest of the uppers. They had been a bright tan once, but now they were worn a dark brown, beginning to crack in the grooves across the insteps. The thongs had broken in two places on one shoe and in one place on the other.

He was a well-built young man of medium height, and he had dark curly hair, slightly brittle but not quite kinky, and a complexion the colour of worn leather. If you looked closely you could see the dark shadow caused by premature shaving along his cheeks and around the chin and upper lip. His eyes were very dark brown, the whites not quite clear, and he had a slightly protuberant upper lip. His hands were muscular, with ridges of vein, the nails broad and thick like little shells, and rimmed with black from handling machine oil and grease. The backs of his hands, like his face, were brown, but the palms were pink with tiny ridges of yellow-white callouses. Now his dark brown eyes had hardened a little with sullenness.

He half-finished the cigarette, and threw the butt into the garden behind the fence around the public convenience. The garden of the convenience was laid out in small terraces and rockeries, carefully cultivated by the City Council, with many different kinds of rock plants, flowers, cacti, and ornamental trees. This the young man did not see, either, as he stepped off the pavement, dodging the traffic again and crossing the intersection to the Portuguese restaurant opposite.

In front of the restaurant the usual loungers hung around under the overhanging verandah, idling, talking, smoking, waiting. The window was full of painted and printed posters advertising dances, concerts, boxing-matches, meetings, and some of the loungers stood looking at them, commenting on the ability of the fighters or the popularity of the dance bands. The young man, his name was Michael Adonis, pushed past them and went into the café.

It was warm inside, with the smell of frying oil and fat and tobacco smoke. People sat in the booths or along a wooden table down the centre of the place, eating or engaged in conversation. Ancient strips of flypaper hung from the ceiling dotted with their victims and the floor was stained with spilled coffee, grease, and crushed cigarette butts; the walls marked with the countless rubbing of soiled shoulders and grimy hands. There was a general atmosphere of shabbiness about the café, but not unmixed with a sort of homeliness for the unending flow of derelicts, bums, domestic workers off duty, in-town-from-the-country folk who had no place to eat except there, and working people who stopped by on their way home. There were taxi-drivers too, and the rest of the mould that accumulated on the fringes of the underworld beyond Castle Bridge: loiterers, prostitutes, *fah-fee* numbers runners, petty gangsters, drab and frayed-looking thugs.

Michael Adonis looked around the café and saw Willieboy sitting at the long table that ran down the middle of the room. Willieboy was young and dark and wore his kinky hair brushed into a point above his forehead. He wore a sportscoat over a yellow T-shirt and a crucifix around his neck, more as a flamboyant decoration than as an act of religious devotion. He had yellowish eyeballs and big white teeth and an air of nonchalance, like the outward visible sign of his distorted pride in the terms he had served in a reformatory and in prison for assault.

He grinned, showing his big teeth as Michael Adonis strolled up, and said, 'Hoit, pally,' in greeting. He had finished a meal of steak and chips and was lighting a cigarette.

'Howzit,' Michael Adonis said surlily, sitting down opposite him. They were not very close friends, but had been thrown together in the whirlpool world of poverty, petty crime and violence of which that café was an outpost.

'Nice, boy, nice. You know me, mos. Always take it easy. How goes it with you?'

'Strolling again. Got pushed out of my job at the facktry.'

'How come then?'

'Answered back to a effing white rooker. Foreman.'

'Those whites. What happened?'

'That white bastard was lucky I didn't pull him up good. He had been asking for it a long time. Every time a man goes to the pisshouse he starts moaning. Jesus Christ, the way he went on you'd think a man had to wet his pants rather than take a minute off. Well, he picked on me for going for a leak and I told him to go to hell.'

'Ja,' Willieboy said. 'Working for whites. Happens all the time, man. Me, I never work for no white john. Not even brown one. To hell with work. Work, work, work, where does it get you? Not me, pally.'

The Swahili waiter came over, dark and shiny with perspiration, his white apron grimy and spotted with egg-yolk. Michael Adonis said: 'Steak and chips, and bring the tomato sauce, too.' To Willieboy he said, 'Well, a juba's got to live. Called me a cheeky black bastard. Me, I'm not black. Anyway I said he was a no-good pore-white and he calls the manager and they gave me my pay and tell me to muck out of it. White sonofabitch. I'll get him.'

'No, man, me I don't work. Never worked a bogger yet. Whether you work or don't, you live anyway, somehow. I haven't starved to death, have I? Work. Eff work.'

'I'll get him,' Michael Adonis said. His food came, handed to him on a chipped plate with big slices of bread on the side. He began to eat, chewing sullenly. Willieboy got up and strolled over to the juke-box, slipped a sixpenny piece into the slot. Michael Adonis ate silently, his anger mixing with a resentment for a fellow who was able to take life so easy.

Music boomed out of the speaker, drowning the buzz of voices in the café, and Willieboy stood by the machine, watching the disc spinning behind the lighted glass.

> When mah baby lef' me,
> She gimme a mule to rahd . . .
> When mah baby lef' me,
> She gimme a mule to rahd . . .

Michael Adonis went on eating, thinking over and over again, That sonavabitch, that bloody white sonavabitch, I'll get him. Anger seemed to make him ravenous and he bolted his food. While he was drinking his coffee from the thick, cracked cup three men came into the café, looked around the place, and then came over to him.

One of the men wore a striped, navy-blue suit and a high-crowned brown hat. He had a brown, bony face with knobby cheekbones, hollow cheeks and a bony, ridged jawline, all giving him a scrofulous look. The other two with him were youths and they wore new, lightweight tropical suits with pegged trousers and gaudy neckties. They had young, yellowish, depraved faces and thick hair shiny with brilliantine. One of them had a ring with a skull-and-crossbones on one finger. The eyes in the skull were cheap red stones, and he toyed with the ring all the time as if he wished to draw attention to it.

They pulled out chairs and sat down, and the man in the striped suit said: 'Het, Mikey.'

'Hullo.'

'They fired me.'

'Hell, just near the big days, too.' The man spoke as if there was something wrong with his throat; in a high, cracked voice, like the twang of a flat guitar string.

The boy with the ring said, 'We're looking for Sockies. You seen him?'

The man in the striped suit, who was called Foxy, said, 'We got a job on tonight. We want him for look-out man.'

'You don't have to tell him,' the boy with the ring said, looking at Foxy. He had a thin, olive-skinned face with down on his upper lip, and the whites of his eyes were unnaturally yellow.

'He's okay,' Foxy told him. 'Mikey's a pal of ours. Don't I say, Mikey?'

'I don't give over what you boys do,' Michael Adonis replied. He took a packet of cigarettes from the pocket of his leather coat and offered it around. They each took one.

When the cigarettes were lighted the one who had not spoken yet, said: 'Why don't we ask him to come in? We can do without Sockies if you say he's okay.' He had an old knife scar across his right cheekbone and looked very young and brutal.

Michael Adonis said nothing.

'Mikey's a good boy,' Foxy said, grinning with the cigarette in his mouth. 'He ain't like you blerry gangsters.'

'Well,' said the scarfaced boy. 'If you see Sockies, tell him we looking for him.'

'Where'll he get you?' Michael Adonis asked.

'He knows where to find us,' Foxy said.

'Come on then, man,' the boy with the scarface said. 'Let's stroll.'

'Okay, Mikey,' Foxy said as they got up.

'Okay.'

'Okay, pally,' the scarfaced boy said.

They went out of the café and Michael Adonis watched them go. He told himself they were a hardcase lot. The anger over having got the sack from his job had left him then, and he was feeling a little better. He picked up the bill from the table and went over to the counter to pay it.

Outside the first workers were streaming past towards Hanover, on their way to their homes in the quarter known as District Six. The trackless trams were full, rocking their way up the rise at Castle Bridge, the overflow hanging onto the grips of the platform. Michael Adonis watched the crowds streaming by, smoking idly, his mind wandering towards the stockinged legs of the girls, the chatter and hum of traffic brushing casually across his hearing. Up ahead a neon sign had already come on, pale against the late sunlight, flicking on and off, on and off, on and off.

He left the entrance of the café and fell into the stream, walking up towards the District, past the shopfronts with the adverts of shoes, underwear, Coca-Cola, cigarettes.

Inside the café the juke-box had stopped playing and Willieboy turned away from it, looking for Michael Adonis, and found that he had left.

TWO

Up ahead the music shops were still going full blast, the blare of records all mixed up so you could not tell one tune from another. Shopkeepers, Jewish, Indian, and Greek, stood in the doorways along the arcade of stores on each side of the street, waiting to welcome last-minute customers; and the vegetable and fruit barrows were still out too, the hawkers in white coats yelling their wares and flapping their brownpaper packets, bringing prices down now that the day was ending. Around the bus-stop a crowd pushed and jostled to clamber onto the track-less trams, struggling against the passengers fighting to alight. Along the pavements little knots of youths lounged in twos and threes or more, watching the crowds streaming by, jeering, smoking, joking against the noise, under the balconies, in doorways, around the plate-glass windows. A half-mile of sound and movement and signs, signs, signs: Coca-Cola, Sale Now On, Jewellers, The Modern Outfitters, If You Don't Eat Here We'll Both Starve, Grand Picnic to Paradise Valley Luxury Buses, Teas, Coffee, Smoke, Have You Tried Our Milk Shakes, Billiard Club, The Rockingham Arms, Your Recommendation Is Our Advert, Dress Salon.

Michael Adonis moved idly along the pavement through the stream of people unwinding like a spool up the street. A music shop was playing shrill and noisy,'Some of these days, you gonna miss me honey'; music from across the Atlantic, shipped in flat shellac discs to pound its jazz through the loudspeaker over the doorway.

He stopped outside the big plate window, looking in at the rows of guitars, banjoes, mandolins, the displayed gramophone parts, guitar picks, strings, electric irons, plugs, jews-harps, adaptors, celluloid dolls all the way from Japan, and the pictures of angels and Christ with a crown of thorns and drops of blood like lipstick marks on his pink forehead.

A fat man came out of the shop, his cheeks smooth and shiny with health, and said, 'You like to buy something, sir?'

'No man,' Michael Adonis said and spun his cigarette-end into the street where a couple of snot-nosed boys in ragged shirts and horny feet scrambled for it, pushing each other as they struggled to claim a few puffs.

Somebody said, 'Hoit, Mikey,' and he turned and saw the wreck of a youth who had fallen in beside him.

'Hullo, Joe.'

Joe was short and his face had an ageless quality about it under the grime, like something valuable forgotten in a junk shop. He had the soft brown eyes of a dog, and he smelled of a mixture of sweat, slept-in clothes and seaweed. His trousers had gone at the cuffs and knees, the rents held together with pins and pieces of string, and so stained and spotted that the original colour could not have been guessed at. Over the trousers he wore an ancient raincoat that reached almost to his ankles, the sleeves torn loose at the shoulders, the body hanging in ribbons, the front pinned together over his filthy vest. His shoes were worn beyond recognition.

Nobody knew where Joe came from, or anything about him. He just seemed to have happened, appearing in the District like a cockroach emerging through a floorboard. Most of the time he wandered around the harbour gathering fish discarded by fishermen and anglers, or along the beaches of the coast, picking limpets and mussels. He had a strange passion for things that came from the sea.

'How you, Joe?' Michael Adonis asked.

'Okay, Mikey.'

'What you been doing today?'

'Just strolling around the docks. *York Castle* came in this afternoon.'

'Ja?'

'You like mussels, Mikey? I'll bring you some.'

'That's fine, Joe.'

'I got a big starfish out on the beach yesterday. One big, big one. It was dead and stank.'

'Well, it's a good job you didn't bring it into town. City Council would be on your neck.'

'I hear they're going to make the beaches so only white people can go there,' Joe said.

'Ja. Read it in the papers. Damn sonsabitches.'

'It's going to get so's nobody can go nowhere.'

'I reckon so,' Michael Adonis said.

They were some way up the street now and outside the Queen Victoria. Michael Adonis said, 'You like a drink, Joe?' although he knew that the boy did not drink.

'No thanks, Mikey.'

'Well, so long.'

'So long, man.'

'You eat already?'

'Well . . . no . . . not yet,' Joe said, smiling humbly and shyly, moving his broken shoes gently on the rough cracked paving.

'Okay, here's a bob. Get yourself something. Parcel of fish and some chips.'

'Thanks, Mikey.'

'Okay. So long, Joe.'

'See you again.'

'Don't forget the mussels,' Michael Adonis said after him, knowing that Joe would forget anyway.

'I'll bring them,' Joe said, smiling back and raising his hand in a salute. He seemed to sense the other young man's doubt of his memory, and added a little fiercely, 'I won't forget. You'll see. I won't forget.'

Then he went up the street, trailing his tattered raincoat behind him like a sword-slashed, bullet-ripped banner just rescued from a battle.

Michael Adonis turned towards the pub and saw the two policemen coming towards him. They came down the pavement in their flat caps, khaki shirts and pants, their gun harness shiny with polish, and the holstered pistols heavy at their waists. They had hard, frozen faces as if carved out of pink ice, and hard, dispassionate eyes, hard and bright as pieces of blue glass. They strolled slowly and determinedly side by side, without moving off their course, cutting a path through the stream on the pavement like destroyers at sea.

They came on and Michael Adonis turned aside to avoid them, but they had him penned in with a casual, easy, skilful flanking manoeuvre before he could escape.

'Waar loop jy rond, jong? Where are you walking around, man?' The voice was hard and flat as the snap of a steel spring, and the one who spoke had hard, thin, chapped lips and a faint blonde down above them. He had flat cheekbones, pink-white, and thick, red-gold eyebrows and pale lashes. His chin was long and cleft and there was a small pimple beginning to form on one side of it, making a reddish dot against the pale skin.

'Going home,' Michael Adonis said, looking at the buckle of this policeman's belt. You learned from experience to gaze at some spot on their uniforms, the button of a pocket, or the bright smoothness of their Sam Browne belts, but never into their eyes, for that would be taken as an affront by them. It was only the very brave, or the very stupid, who dared look straight into the law's eyes, to challenge them or to question their authority.

The second policeman stuck his thumbs in his gun-belt and smiled distantly and faintly. It was more a slight movement of his lips, rather than a smile. The backs of his hands where they dropped over the leather of the belt were broad and white, and the outlines of the veins were pale blue under the skin, the skin covered with a field of tiny, slanting ginger-coloured hair. His fingers were thick and the knuckles big and creased and pink, the nails shiny and healthy and carefully kept.

This policeman asked in a heavy, brutal voice, 'Where's your dagga?'

'I don't smoke it.'

'Jong, turn out your pockets,' the first one ordered. 'Hurry up.'

Michael Adonis began to empty his pockets slowly, without looking up at them and thinking, with each movement, You mucking boers, you mucking boers. Some people stopped and looked and hurried on as the policemen turned the cold blue light of their eyes upon them. Michael Adonis showed them his crumpled and partly used packet of cigarettes, the money he had left over from his pay, a soiled handkerchief and an old piece of chewing gum covered with the grey fuzz from his pocket.

'Where did you steal the money?' The question was without humour, deadly serious, the voice topped with hardness like the surface of a file.

'Didn't steal it, baas *(you mucking boer)*.'

'Well, muck off from the street. Don't let us find you standing around, you hear?'

'Yes *(you mucking boer)*.'

'Yes, what? Who are you talking to, man?'

'Yes, baas *(you mucking bastard boer with your mucking gun and your mucking bloody red head)*.'

They pushed past him, one of them brushing him aside with an elbow and strolled on. He put the stuff back into his pockets. And deep down inside him the feeling of rage, frustration, and violence swelled like a boil, knotted with pain.

THREE

Pushing open the swing doors with the advertisements for beer on each wing, Michael Adonis entered the pub, and inside the smell of wine and sawdust and cigarette smoke enveloped him. The place was just filling with the after-work crowd and the bar was lined with men, talking and drinking, and most of the table space was taken. Through a doorway to a back room he could see a darts game in progress. Somebody was saying,

'... So I reckon to him, no, man, I don't fall for that joke
... 'Michael Adonis moved over to the bar and found a place
between a stout man in a shabby brown suit, and a man with a
haggard, wine-soaked, ravaged face. Around him the blurred
mutter of conversation went on, then swelling when an argument over a big fight or a football game provoked a little heat.

The pub, like pubs all over the world, was a place for debate
and discussion, for the exchange of views and opinions, for
argument, and for the working out of problems. It was a forum,
a parliament, a fountain of wisdom and a cesspool of nonsense,
it was a centre for the lost and the despairing, where cowards
absorbed dutch courage out of small glasses and leaned
against the shiny, scratched and polished mahogany counter
for support against the crushing burdens of insignificant lives.
Where the disillusioned gained temporary hope, where acts of
kindness were considered and murders planned.

There were two Coloured youths in alpaca jackets and a
balding Jew called Mister Ike serving behind the bar. He
greeted every customer with a phlegmatic geniality which
inspired a sort of servile familiarity.

One of the youths behind the bar came down from serving
somebody and said, 'Hullo, Mike.'

'Hullo, Smiling.'

The haggard man looked sideways at him and said, 'Hallo,
Mike. . . . ' But Michael Adonis did not return the greeting.

'Half white,' he said to the young bartender. While he was
waiting for the tumbler of wine he lighted a cigarette, leaning
on top of the bar, one foot on the rail over the trough on the
floor. His mind switched back to the incident with the police,
and then further back to the works' foreman with whom he had
had the argument resulting in him losing his job, and he
thought with rage, Effing sonofabitches.

The man in the brown suit looked his way and asked, 'What
came today? You know?'

'*Weet'ie.* Don't know.'

'Number eighteen,' the haggard man said.

'Jesus. Had two bob on nineteen. Hell, and I even dreamed
about eighteen last night. But thought I'd better play nineteen.' He began to recite the details of his dream, but nobody
seemed to be listening.

Michael Adonis took a sip at his glass and felt the sweet wine
warm his inside all the way down. Then he drank the rest in

one swallow and took in the pleasant, spreading, slightly sour warmth that spread out over the walls of his stomach and then drifted gradually to his head. He ordered another half-pint and let it stand for a while, feeling the rage subside, looking at himself in the mirror behind the bar and saying in his mind to the young, tan-coloured, dark-eyed face with the new stubble and the cigarette dangling from the lips, Okay, trouble-shooter. You're a mighty tough hombre. Fastest man in Tuscon, until he saw the swing doors behind him open and Foxy and the two youths in the tropical suits come in to wipe the fantasy away.

They looked around and, seeing him, came over.

'You seen Sockies, already?' the scarfaced boy asked.

'Nay, man.'

'*Hy is nie hier nie.* He isn't here,' Foxy said, looking around. 'Come, we blow.'

'Tell him we're looking for him, will you?' the scarfaced boy said. He had been smoking dagga and his eyeballs were yellow, the pupils dilated.

'Okay.'

They went out again, leaving the doors swinging and the man in the brown suit said, 'Those are hardcase lighties.'

'Seen them hanging around the Steps,' the haggard man, whose name was Mister Greene, said. 'That boy with the mark on his face, he was in reformatory last year. I know his people. Hendricks. Used to live up there in Chapel Street.'

'Bet they're out onto something.'

'They're just looking for one of their pals,' Michael Adonis told them.

'Fellow by the name of Socks.'

'No, jong. I don't like those boys.'

Michael Adonis picked up his drink and finished it, feeling the wine explode inside him and bring on a sudden giddiness. He stood against the bar, waiting for the nausea to pass, and then lighted another cigarette. The haggard man had been drinking gin and limejuice all the time and he was beginning to talk thickly. He belched loudly and swallowed.

'Hey, take it easy,' Michael Adonis said angrily to him. 'You'll mess up the whole blerry place.'

Greene hiccoughed and mumbled, 'Sorry,' wiping his mouth on a dirty handkerchief.

The pub was filling up and the tobacco smoke hung in a grey

undulating haze, so that at the far end of the room the men took on the vague forms of wraiths in a morning mist; and the voices merged into a solid blur of sound. The doors kept swinging back and forth as men moved in and out. Outside the sun had gone and the lights had come on inside the bar and in shop-windows and box signs along the street. Glasses clinked-clinked against the background of noise.

A man in a wind-breaker and an oilskin peaked cap, with a taxi-driver's licence badge pinned to the side of it, came in and pressed himself into the place between Michael Adonis and Greene. Under the cap he had a wily, grinning face and eyes as brown and alert as cockroaches. He grinned at Michael Adonis, showing tobacco-stained teeth and said:

'Howsit, Mikey?'

'Okay, how's business?'

'Not so bad. American ship came in this morning. Been driving those Yankees almost all day. Mostly to whore houses. Those johns are full of money. Just blowing it away on goosies.'

'Ya. Wish I could get a job on a boat,' Michael Adonis said. 'Go to the States, maybe.'

'Must be smart over there. You can go into any nightclub and dance with white geese. There's mos no colour bar.'

The haggard man, Greene, hiccoughed and chipped in, saying, 'I read how they hanged up a negro in the street in America. Whites done it.'

'Huh?' Michael Adonis said.

'Read it in the paper the other day. Some whites took a negro out in the street and hanged him up. They said he did look properly at some woman.'

'Well, the negroes isn't like us.' Michael Adonis said. He thought about the foreman, Scofield, and the police, and the little knot of rage reformed inside him again like the quickening of the embryo in the womb, and he added with a sudden viciousness: 'Anyway those whites are better than ours, I bet you.'

'They all the same all over,' the taxi-driver said, swallowing his drink and lighting a cigarette.

'I don't give a damn for a bastard white arse,' Michael Adonis said and stared morosely into his glass.

'That's politics,' Greene said. 'Cut out politics.' He was a little drunk.

'It's the capitalis' system,' the taxi-driver said. 'Heard it at a meeting on the Parade. Whites act like that because of the capitalis' system.'

'What the hell do you mean—capitalis' system?' Michael Adonis asked. 'What's this capitalis' system you talking about?'

'I can't explain it right, you know, hey,' the taxi-driver answered, frowning. 'But I heard some johns on the Parade talking about it. Said colour bar was because of the system.'

'Shit.'

'Cut out politics,' Greene said again. 'Those bastards all come from Russia.' He hiccoughed again, spraying saliva from his slack mouth.

'What's wrong with Russia?' the taxi-driver asked. 'What you know about Russia?'

'Have a drink and cut out politics,' Greene said.

The taxi-driver said crossly: 'Look, old dad. If you don't know what you talking about, then hold your jaw.'

'Okay mate, okay,' Greene replied, grinning sheepishly. 'But it's true what I said about that negro in the States.'

'Man, that's muck all,' the taxi-driver said. 'I seen somebody killed in the street, too. I remember the time,' he started narrating, 'I saw Flippy Isaacs get cut up. You remember Flippy? He was in for housebreak and theff. Got two years. Well,' he went on, 'while Flippy is up at the oubaas he gets word that his goose is jolling with Cully Richards. You remember Cully? He mos used to work down here in Hanover Street at that butcher-shop. Amin's butcher-shop, man. Well, while he's in the big-house Flippy gets to hearing about Cully messing around with his goose. Well, ou Flippy didn't like that. Man, that john was a bastard of a hardcase. Further, he gets blerry wild when he hears about Cully and his goose. Further, when he comes out he just collects his gear and walks straight down to Hanover and calls Cully out of the butcher-shop. Cully comes mos out and Flippy says to him: "I hear you been messing with my goose, hey? You been have a good time with my goose, hey?" Cully doesn't say nothing but just stands there looking at him. Cully was a pretty tough juba himself. He just stands there looking at Flippy, dead pan. That makes Flip even wilder and he pulls out a knife. Don't know where he got it, but it was only a pen-knife.

'Well, when he pulls that knife Cully sees red and he runs back into the butcher-shop and gets a butcher-knife. A helluva long knife. Just so long.' The taxi-driver indicated the size of the knife, holding the palms of his hands apart in front of himself. 'Well,' he went on, 'Cully comes running out of the shop, his face all screwed up with rage, and goes for Flippy. Just one cut with that knife, man. It must have been about a foot long and sharp like a razor. You know those butcher-knives, man. Just one cut, jong. Across the belly. Right through his shirt. Hell, ou Flippy just sat down on the pavement and held his stomach, with his guts all trying to come out between his fingers, and the blood running down into the gutter. His whole face was blue. He just sat there, trying to keep his guts in.'

The taxi-driver took a sip at his drink to wet his throat, and continued. 'I think ou Cully must've got a shock. I don't think he mean to do it. But Flip pulling that knife made him mad. Even if it was just a small knife. Anyway, he looked blerry sick himself. He took one look at Flippy sitting there trying to hold his guts in and it coming out all the time. And Cully sits down next to him and tries to help him push his guts back. Sitting there and shaking and trying to push Flippy's guts back like somebody trying to put back a lot of washing that had fallen out of a bundle. You should've seen the people. Anyway, somebody called the ambulance, and the law came along, too. Flippy was about dead when the ambulance took him away. Ou Cully didn't say a word. Just stood there while the law handcuff him and put him in the van. He got five years, I think.'

'That isn't like whites hanging a negroo up,' Greene said, when the taxi-driver had finished his story. 'What's that got to do with whites hanging a negroo up?'

'Awight, wise guy,' the taxi-driver told him. 'You know a lot.'

'No, I don't know a lot. But what's that got to do with hanging a negroo up in the street?' Greene had been drinking while the taxi-driver had been talking and he had grown steadily drunk. 'What's that got to do with hanging a negroo up in the street?'

'Ah, shut up,' the taxi-driver said and turned away.

'Well,' Michael Adonis said, 'if anybody messed around with my goose I'd give him the same.'

'Me go to jail for a toit?' the taxi-driver scowled. 'Never.'

'A man's a man,' Michael Adonis told him. He was a little drunk too, and full of the courage of four glasses of wine. 'What good's a john if he let some other bastard steal his goose?'

'You'se be-effed,' the taxi-driver said. 'Anyway, I've got to blow!' He took his cap off and looked inside it and put in on again, adjusting it carefully, examining himself in the mirror behind the bar. 'Well, okay, pally.'

'Okay,' Michael Adonis said. His head was muzzy and there was a slight feeling of nausea in his stomach. He watched the taxi-driver go out, the swing doors flapped and then swung gently. A car went up the street, its engine revving and the tires hissing on the asphalt. Michael Adonis turned and leaned on the bar and jerked his head at Smiling, the young barman. He ordered another pint of white wine and drank it down in two swallows, choking a little on the second, recovering and feeling the nausea replaced by a pleasant heady warmth. He put the glass down on the bar and lit another cigarette, then pulled himself out of the line. He picked his way through the press in the bar-room, through the smoke and liquor-smell laden atmosphere, and pushed through the swing doors.

FOUR

The air outside caught him suddenly in its cool grasp, making his skin prickle; and the glare of street-lights and windows made his head reel, so that he had to stand still for a moment to let the spinning of his brain subside. The spell of dizziness settled slowly, his head swinging gently back to normal like a merry-go-round slowing down and finally stopping. On each side of him the lights and neon signs stretched away with the blaze and glitter of a string of cheap, gaudy jewellery. A man brushed past him and went into the pub, the doors flap-flapping and the murmur of voices from inside had the sound of surf breaking on a beach. A slight breeze had sprung up over the city, moving the hanging signs, and scuttling bits of paper were grey ghosts in the yellow electric light along the street. There were people up and down, walking, looking into the shop-windows or waiting aimlessly.

Michael Adonis pulled up the zipper of his leather coat and dug his hands into the slanted pockets and crossed the street. The courage of liquor made his thoughts brave. He thought, To hell with them. I'm not scared of them. Ou Scofield and the law and the whole effing lot of them. Bastards. To hell with them. He was also feeling a little morose and the bravery gave way to self-pity, like an advert on the screen being replaced by another slide.

He turned down another street, away from the artificial glare of Hanover, between stretches of damp, battered houses with their broken ribs of front-railings; cracked walls and high tenements that rose like the left-overs of a bombed area in the twilight; vacant lots and weed-grown patches where houses had once stood; and deep doorways resembling the entrances to deserted castles. There were children playing in the street, darting among the overflowing dustbins and shooting at each other with wooden guns. In some of the doorways people sat or stood, murmuring idly in the fast-fading light like wasted ghosts in a plague-ridden city.

Foxy and the two youths in tropical suits stood in the lamp-light on a corner down the street. They were smoking and one of them spun the end of his cigarette into the street. They watched Michael Adonis cross the street, but did not move from where they stood or say anything.

Michael Adonis turned into the entrance of a tall narrow tenement where he lived. Once, long ago, it had had a certain kind of dignity, almost beauty, but now the decorative Victorian plaster around the wide doorway was chipped and broken and blackened with generations of grime. The floor of the entrance was flagged with white and black slabs in the pattern of a draught-board, but the tramp of untold feet and the accumulation of dust and grease and ash had blurred the squares so that now it had taken on the appearance of a kind of loathsome skin disease. A row of dustbins lined one side of the entrance and exhaled the smell of rotten fruit, stale food, stagnant water and general decay. A cat, the colour of dish-water, was trying to paw the remains of a fishhead from one of the bins.

Michael Adonis paused in the entrance on the way to the stairs and watched the cat. It tugged and wrestled with the head which was weighed down by a pile of rubbish, a broken bottle and an old boot. He watched it and then reaching out with a foot upset the pile of rubbish onto the floor, freeing the fish head. The cat pulled it from the bin and it came away with a tangle of entrails. The cat began to drag it towards the doorway leaving a damp brown trail across the floor.

'Playing with cats?'

Michael Adonis looked around and up at the girl who had come down the stairs and was standing at the bend in the staircase.

'I'd rather play with you,' he said, grinning at her. 'Hullo, Hazel.'

'You reckon.'

She came down and stood on the first step, smiling at him and showing the gap in the top row of her teeth. She had a heavy mouth, smeared blood-red with greasy lipstick, so that it looked stark as a wound in her dark face. Her coarse wiry hair was tied at the back with a scrap of soiled ribbon in the parody of a pony-tail, and under the blouse and skirt her body was insignificant except for her small, jutting breasts. She was wearing new, yellow leather, flat-heeled pumps that gave the impression of something expensive abandoned on a junk heap.

Michael Adonis thought, Knockers like apples, and said, 'Where you off to, bokkie?'

'Bioscope. And who's your bokkie?' She peered at him, her eyes sceptical.

'Okay. Don't be like that. What's showing?'

'What's it now again? *Love Me Tonight*. At the Metro.'

'That's a nonsense piece. I went to the Lawn last night. *The Gunfighter*.'

'No what. That isn't nice. They tell me the boy dies at the end.'

'Ah, you girls just like them kissing plays.'

He reached into the pocket of the leather coat and got out the cigarettes, shook two loose and offered the packet to the girl. His hand shook a little and she looked at him, smiling, and saying, 'You've got a nice dop in, hey?'

'I got troubles,' he replied, scowling at her.

'You drowning your sorrows?'

'Maybe,' The mention of sorrows brought back the sense of persecution again and he surrendered himself to it enjoying the deep self-pity for a while, thinking, I'll get even with them, the sonsabitches. They'll see.

The girl had taken a cigarette and he put the other between his lips, feeling for matches. He struck a light and held it to her cigarette, the flame wobbling between his fingers, and then lit his own.

The girl said, 'Well, I'm going to blow now.'

'Hell, wait a little longer. It's still early.'

'No, jong. I haven't booked.'

She edged past him, smiling, holding the cigarette between her lips with one hand in an exaggerated pose. He made a grab at her arm, but she skipped out of his reach, laughing, and darted out through the wide doorway, leaving him staring at it with a feeling of abandonment.

He said, aloud, 'Ah, hell,' and cursed, climbing the stairs and nursing the foetus of hatred inside his belly.

The staircase was worn and blackened, the old oak banister loose and scarred. Naked bulbs wherever the light sockets were in working order cast a pallid glare over parts of the interior, lighting up the big patches of damp and mildew, and the maps of denuded sections on the walls. Somewhere upstairs a radio was playing Latin-American music, bongos and maracas throbbing softly through the smells of ancient cooking, urine, damp-rot, and stale tobacco. A baby wailed with the tortured sound of gripe and malnutrition and a man's voice rose in hysterical laughter. Footsteps thudded and water rushed down a pipe in a muted roar.

From each landing a dim corridor lined with doors tunnelled towards a latrine that stood like a sentry box at its end, the floor in front of it soggy with spilled water. Michael Adonis climbed to the top floor and cigarettes and liquor made him pant a little. The radio was playing below him now, a crooner singing of lavender and shady avenues, and the child cried again and again.

The latrine at the end of the corridor opened and a man clawed his way out of it and began making his way towards one of the doors, holding onto the wall all the way and breathing hard with the sound of a saw cutting into wood. He was old and unsteady on his legs and hampered by his sagging trousers. His shirt was out dangling around him like a night-gown. He made his way slowly along the wall, like a great crab, breathing stertorously.

Michael Adonis stood at the head of the stairs and watched him for awhile, and then strolled forward. The old man heard his footsteps and looked up.

'Why, hallo, there, Michael, my boy,' the old man said in English, his voice high and cracked and breathless with age. In the light of the bulb in the ceiling his face looked yellowish-blue. The purple-veined, greyish skin had loosened all over it and sagged in blotched, puffy folds. With his sagging lower eyelids, revealing bloodshot rims, and the big, bulbous, red-veined nose that had once been aquiline, his face had the expression of a decrepit bloodhound. His head was almost bald, and wisps of dirty grey hair clung to the bony, pinkish skull like scrub clinging to eroded rock.

'How are you, Michael boy?'

'Okay,' Michael Adonis said, staring sullenly at the old man.

This old man, who was an Irishman and who was dying of alcoholism, diabetes, and old age, had once been an actor. He had performed in the theatres of Great Britain, South Africa, and Australia, and had served in two wars. Now he was a deserted, abandoned ruin, destroyed by alcohol and something neither he nor Michael Adonis understood, waiting for death, trapped at the top of an old tenement, after the sweep of human affairs had passed over him and left him broken and helpless as wreckage disintegrating on a hostile beach.

'Give us a hand, Michael boy,' the old man panted. 'Give us a hand.'

'What's the matter?' Michael Adonis asked. 'You got to the can, you ought to be able to get back.'

'That's not polite, Michael. You're in a bad mood. Tell you what, we'll sit down in my room and have a drink. You'd like a drink, wouldn't you? I've got a bottle left. Old age pension yesterday.'

'I don't want to drink your wine,' Michael Adonis said. 'I got money to buy my own booze with.'

'Who's talking about money?' the old man wheezed. 'Money's all the trouble in the world. Come on, Michael boy. Come on. Give your uncle a hand.'

'Youse not my uncle either,' Michael Adonis said, but took the stick-thin arm and eased the old man urgently over to a doorway. 'I haven't got no white uncles.'

'Thanks. What's the difference? My wife, God bless her soul, was a Coloured lady. A fine one, too,' the old man said, reaching for the knob and opening the door. He was partly drunk and smelled of cheap wine, sweat, vomit, and bad breath.

The room was as hot and airless as a newly-opened tomb, and there was an old iron bed against one wall, covered with unwashed bedding, and next to it a backless chair that served as a table on which stood a chipped ashtray full of cigarette butts and burnt matches, and a thick tumbler, sticky with the dregs of heavy red wine. A battered cupboard stood in a corner with a cracked, flyspotted mirror over it, and a small stack of dog-eared books gathering dust. In another corner an accumulation of empty wine bottles stood like packed skittles.

The old man struggled over to the bed and sank down on it, clawing at his sunken chest with bony, purple-nailed, fingers, and waited for his breath to come back.

Michael Adonis slouched over to the window and stared out through a gap in the dusty colourless curtain and the grimy panes. Beyond, the roofs of the city were sprawled in a jumble of dark, untidy patterns dotted with the scattered smudged blobs of yellow. Hanover Street made a crooked strip of misty light across the patch of District Six, and far off the cranes along the sea front stood starkly against the sky.

He turned away from the window, anger mixing with headiness of the liquor he had consumed and curdling into a sour knot of smouldering violence inside him. The old man was pouring wine into the sticky glass, the neck of the bottle rattling against the rim so that the red sloshed about and wet his knuckled fingers.

'There you are, Michael me boy,' he cackled, breathing hoarsely. 'Nothing like a bit of port to warm the cockles of your heart.'

He held the glass up, his hand shaking, slopping the liquor, and Michael Adonis took it from him with a sudden burst of viciousness and tossed the wine down, then flinging the glass back into the old man's lap. The thick, sweet wine nauseated him and he choked and fought to control his stomach, glaring at the wreck on the bed, until the wine settled and there was a new heat throbbing in his head.

'A bad mood,' the old man quavered, and poured himself a glassful. He drank it, the wine trickling down his stubbly chin, and gasped. He cocked his head at Michael Adonis and said: 'You shouldn't get cross over nothing. What's the matter with you?'

'Aw, go to buggery.'

'Now, now, that's no way to talk. We've all got our troubles.'

'Ya. Bloody troubles *you* got.'

'God bless my soul, I've got my troubles, too,' the old man said, with a sudden whine in his voice. 'Here I am and nobody to look after an old man.' Tears of remorse gathered in his pale, red-rimmed eyes, and he knuckled them with a tangled skein of dirty cord that was his hand. 'Look at me. I used to be something in my days. God bless my soul, I used to be something.'

Michael Adonis lit a cigarette and stood there looking at the old man through the spiral of smoke. He said: 'What the hell you crying about. You old white bastard, you got nothing to worry about.'

'Worry? Worry?' the old man whined. 'We all got something to worry about.' He mustered himself for a moment and shook a dried twig of a finger at Michael Adonis. 'We all got our cross to bear. What's my white got to do with it? Here I am, in shit street, and does my white help? I used to be an actor. God bless my soul, I toured England and Australia with Dame Clara Bright. A great lady. A great actress she was.' He began to weep, the tears spilling over the sagging rims of his eyes and he reached for the bottle again. 'We're like Hamlet's father's ghost. I played the ghost of Hamlet's father once. London it was.'

'You look like a blerry ghost, you spook,' Michael Adonis said bitterly. He jerked the bottle from the old man's hand and tipped it to his mouth and took a long swallow, gagging and then belching as he took the neck from his lips. His head spun and he wanted to retch.

The old man said: 'Don't finish the lot, boy. Leave some for old Uncle Doughty.' He reached frantically for the bottle, but Michael Adonis held it out of his reach, grinning and feeling pleasantly malicious.

'Want a dop, Uncle Doughty?'

'Oh, come on, man. Don't torment your old dad.'

'You old spook.'

'Give us a drink, give us a drink, sonny boy.'

'What was that you were saying about ghosts? I like ghost stories.' Michael Adonis grinned at him, feeling drunk. He waggled the bottle in front of the decayed ancient face with its purple veins, yellow teeth, and slack mouth, and watched the tears gather again in the liquid eyes.

'I'll tell you what,' the old man whined hopefully. 'I'll recite for you. You should hear me. I used to be something in my

days.' He cleared his throat of a knot of phlegm, choked, and swallowed. He started: 'I . . . I am thy father's spirit; doomed for a certain term to walk the night . . . ' He lost track, then mustered himself, waving his skeleton arms in dramatic gestures, and started again. 'I am thy father's spirit, doomed for a certain time to walk the night . . . and . . . and for the day confined to fast in fires, till the foul crimes done in my days of nature's . . . nature are burnt and purged away . . . But . . . '
He broke off and grinned at Michael Adonis, and then eyed the bottle. 'That's us, us, Michael, my boy. Just ghosts, doomed to walk the night. Shakespeare.'

'Bull,' Michael Adonis said, and took another swallow at the bottle. 'Who's a blerry ghost?' He scowled at the old man through a haze of red that swam in front of his eyes like thick oozing paint, distorting the ancient face staring up at him.

'Michael, my boy. Spare a drop for your old uncle.'

'You old bastard,' Michael Adonis said angrily. 'Can't a boy have a bloody piss without getting kicked in the backside by a lot of effing law?'

'Now, now, Michael. I don't know what you're talking about, God bless my soul. You take care of that old port, my boy.'

The old man tried to get up and Michael Adonis said, 'Take your effing port,' and struck out at the bony, blotched, sprouting skull, holding the bottle by the neck so that the wine splashed over his hand. The old man made a small, honking, animal noise and dropped back on the bed.

FIVE

Somewhere below a chain was pulled with a distant clanging sound and water welled and gushed through pipes, the sound dying with a hiss. The faraway mutter of a radio played rhumba music.

Michael Adonis stared at the bluish, waxy face of the old man and it stared back at him, with the blank artificial eyes of a doll. He said, 'Jesus,' and turned quickly and vomited down the wall behind him, holding himself upright with the palms of his hands and feeling the sourness of liquor and partly-digested food in his mouth. He stood like that, shaking, until his stomach was empty. His wine-stained hand made a big reddish mark on the wall.

The bottle had dropped to his feet, cracked at the base.

He straightened, staggering with the sudden reeling of his head and then sobered with the shock. He stared back at the wreck on the bed and said, aloud, 'God, I didn't mean it. I didn't mean to kill the blerry old man.' He wiped his mouth on the back of his hand and tasted the wine on it, then rubbed it dry on the seat of his jeans. A flood of thoughts bubbled through his mind. There's going to be trouble. Didn't mean it. Better get out. The law don't like white people being finished off. Well, I didn't *mos* mean it. Better get out before somebody comes. I never been in here. He looked at the sprawled figure that looked like a blowndown scarecrow. Well, he didn't have no right living here with us Coloureds.

He shivered a little as if he was cold, and lurched over to the door, holding onto the wall with one hand. He turned the knob and opened, looking out. His own room was a little way down the corridor. From the well of the stairs sounds drifted up: the radio was playing a smooth string number now, somebody laughed and feet thudded, a woman started scolding and a man's voice yelled back at her until she quietened, far away the sound of traffic interjected.

Comes from helping people, Michael Adonis thought, as he stepped out into the deserted corridor. He shut the door behind him and then walked quickly towards his room, hurrying as if the old man's ghost was at his heels. He reached his door and slid into the room, shutting the door quickly behind him. His head hurt and there was a sour taste in his mouth.

SIX

Police Constable Raalt lounged in the corner of the driving cabin of the patrol van and half listened to the radio under the dashboard. A voice, distorted by the mechanism, was claking away, reading out instructions in a monotone. The other half of Raalt's mind was thinking, I'm getting fed-up with all that nonsense, if she doesn't stop I'll do something serious.

The van was parked up a dark street and at the intersection at the end of it the flow of Hanover Street was like the opening of a cave. Raalt searched in the pocket of his tunic until he found a crumpled packet and drew out a cigarette. It was the last one and he crushed the packet into a ball in his thick hand

and flicked it out through the window. He lighted the cigarette and drew on it and thought: Well, her mother warned me she was a no-good bitch, but I was silly enough to think nothing of it. She won't get away with it, though. The bitch. He was thinking about his wife and it angered him that she was the cause of such thoughts. He eased his gun harness and scratched himself through the front of his tunic. There was a button missing on the shirt underneath. He had wanted to sew on the button before coming on duty but had been late and had not had the time to do it. He sewed and mended his own clothes and often he had to do the housework, too, and that angered him further. His wife had been good-looking before they had been married but now she had gone to seed, and that irritated him too. He sat in the corner of the van and nursed his anger.

The driver of the patrol wagon sat behind the wheel and listened intently to the radio. He had no other thoughts for what was being broadcast, and seemed oblivious of Raalt who lounged beside him. The policeman was young and slightly nervous and very careful to do everything according to regulations. That was something that irritated Raalt, too, but he did not reveal it except for little demonstrations of scorn, like smoking on duty.

After a while the voice on the radio ceased and the driver straightened and said: 'I think we ought to resume our patrol. Don't you think we've been parked long enough?'

Raalt removed the cigarette from his mouth, yawned and said: 'Okay, man. If you're not bloody fed-up with riding around looking at these effing hotnot bastards, let's go.' He tried to speak casually, hiding his anger from the driver, but it was there, like hard steel under camouflage paint.

The driver trod on the starter and worked the gears and they pulled away from the curb, heading towards the lighted end of the street.

SEVEN

The youth who was called Willieboy thought: I should've asked him for a couple of bob. Here I am right out of chink and he with the pay he just drew. Mikey's not cheap, he'll give some start. I need a stop badly.

He began to walk in the direction where he knew Michael Adonis lived.

Foxy and the two youths stood in the light of a shopwindow and saw Willieboy approaching. A trackless tram went past, hissing like escaping gas on the asphalt. The summer night was clear and warm, except for the thin breeze that carried a warning of a Southeaster. The boy with the skull-and-crossbones ring on his finger said, 'Man, we can't look for that bogger all bloody night.'

'He'll turn up,' Foxy said. 'We'll ask Willieboy here to look out for him.' They waited for Willieboy to come up and the boy with the skull-and-crossbones ring said, 'Hoit. You seen Sockies yet?'

'Nay, man,' Willieboy said.

'If you see him tell him we're looking for him. Say to him we will get him at the Club. He must wait for us there.'

'Okay.'

The scarfaced boy said, speaking to Foxy and the other, 'Well, let's go up to the Club. We might as well stick around there.'

'Ja, let's stroll,' the boy with the skull-and-crossbones ring agreed. They waved hands at Willieboy and went on down the street.

Willieboy thought, going in the other direction, I should've bummed a stop off them. I feel like a stop. He thrust his hands into the pockets of his trousers and wandered, shoulders drooping, along the pavement.

He passed the lighted windows, the pyramids of fruit, the price tags, the dismembered dummies draped in dusty dresses. Window-shoppers peered in through the plate glass, pointing and marking the surface with smudges, leaving galleries of fingerprints. In the darkened doorway of a tenement between a fruit shop and a shoe store a couple made love, their faces glued together, straining at each other in an embrace among the piled dirt-tins and abandoned banana crates.

In the entrance of the building where Michael Adonis lived a heavy, bloated man in a filthy singlet was trying to find his matches, searching through the pockets of his decrepit trousers. He gave up the search and looked at Willieboy mounting the two cracked steps.

'Give metchie, please.'

Willieboy paused and held out a box of matches. The man nodded thanks, struck one and held it in his cupped hands to the bedraggled stump of a cigarette between his chapped lips. He had a greyish, puffed skin under the charred stubble and he carried the smell of stale wine with him.

Somewhere up in the damp intestines of the tenement a radio was playing and Willieboy climbed up the worn, sticky staircase into a crescendo of boogie-woogie, past the stark corridors with their dead-ends of latrines staring back like hopeless futures.

The electric light on the last floor flickered but did not go out, clinging determinedly to life as if it refused to be overwhelmed by the decay spreading around it. Willieboy walked down the corridor in the struggling glow and reached the door of Michael Adonis's room. He tried the handle. It was locked and he rattled it calling out softly. Willieboy rattled the doorknob again and then scowled and turned away from the door. He walked a little way back towards the stairs. He thought, maybe this old poor white will part with some start. And he turned to the room of the old Irishman.

Tapping on the door he said, 'Hey, Mister Doughty,' speaking with his ear close to the panel of the door. When he received no reply he rapped a little louder, calling again. Then he turned the knob and looking in, looked into the dead blue-grey face of the old man, and it glared back at him, wide-eyed, the stained, carious teeth bared in a fixed grin, with the suddenness of a shot from a horror film.

EIGHT

On the floors of the tenements the grime collected quickly. A muddied sole of a shoe scuffed across the worn, splintery boards and left tiny embankments of dirt along the sides of the minute raised ridges of wood; or water was spilled or somebody urinated and left wet patches onto which the dust from the ceilings or the seams of clothes drifted and collected to leave dark patches as the moisture dried. A crumb fell or a drop of fat, and was ground underfoot, spread out to become a trap for the drifting dust that floated in invisible particles; the curve of a warped plank or the projections of a badly-made joint; the rosettes and bas-reliefs of Victorian plaster-work; the mortar that became damp and spongy when the rains came and then contracting and cracking with heat; all formed little traps for the dust. And in the dampness deadly life formed in decay and bacteria and mould, and in the heat and airlessness the rot appeared, too, so that things which once were whole or new withered or putrefied and the smells of their decay and putrefaction pervaded the tenements of the poor.

In the dark corners and the unseen crannies, in the fetid heat and slippery dampness the insects and vermin, maggots and slugs, 'roaches in shiny brown armour, spiders like tiny grey monsters carrying death under their minute feet or in the suckers, or rats with dusty black eyes with disease under the claws or in the fur, moved mysteriously.

In a room down the corridor Franky Lorenzo lay on his back on the iron bedstead and stared at the ceiling. The ceiling had been painted white once, a very long time ago, but now it was grey and the paint was cracked and peeling and fly-spotted over the grey. The boards had warped and contracted so that there were dark gaps between them through which dust filtered down into the room whenever anything moved on the roof of the building. There were small cobwebs in the corners of the room, too, against the cornice. But he did not see these things now, because he was tired and irritable and happy and worried, all at the same time.

He wore a singlet and a pair of old corduroys and the singlet was dark with sweat and dust, and the corduroys shiny with wear, and there was coal dust in the grooves where the furry cotton had not been worn away. He had an air of harassment about him, of too hard work and unpaid bills and sour babies. An old scar above his left eye made a white mark in his bristly brown face. He had received the scar in a fight many years ago, when a man had hit him with a bottle. Under the singlet he had a massive chest, covered with thick, wiry hair, and his arms were thick and corded with veins and muscles, and he had a thick, heavy neck. The lines in his face, around the mobile mouth, and under the dark, deep-socketed eyes were full of old coal dust which he had never succeeded in washing away, and the eyes themselves, under the overhang of frontal bone and eyebrows, were soft and bright and young, like those of a little boy. His hands, clasped behind his head now, were hard and horny and calloused from wielding a shovel, and there was a faint odour of stale sweat and tobacco about him.

His wife had, a few minutes earlier, announced that she was once more pregnant and he was trying to decide whether it was good news or bad.

Four of their children lay sleeping in the narrow single bed against the wall on the other side of the room. They slept under the one thread-bare, worn, sweaty blanket, fitted together like parts of a puzzle into the narrow sagging space, two at each end of the bed with their legs carefully arranged. In time they would turn and twist in their sleep and the legs would become entangled, or they would kick one another and wake up, complaining and whimpering. Now they slept, the two boys together, their mouths open, and the two girls, their stringy hair plaited into tight ropes, all the heads pressed into the coverless, partly disembowelled, greasy striped pillows.

The fifth child was on her mother's hip, sucking noisily from a ginger-beer bottle fitted with an ancient teat, drinking sugared water. Grace, Franky Lorenzo's wife, held the child straddled on her hip and hoped that it would not cry and disturb her husband. She had a young-old face to which the beauty of her youth still clung, although her body had become worn and thickened with regular childbirth. Her face had the boniness and grandeur of an ascetic saint, and her eyes were dark wells of sadness mixed with joy.

Franky Lorenzo thought, They say, mos, it's us poor people's riches. You got no food in your guts, and you got no food for your children, but you're rich with them. The rich people got money but they got one, two kids. They got enough to feed ten, twenty children and they only make one or two. We haven't got even enough for one kid and we make eight, nine—one a year. Jesus.

He said aloud, 'Again. For what you want to get that way?'

'Well, it isn't my fault,' she told him.

'No. It isn't your fault.'

'You talk like it's my fault. Whose fault is it then?'

He sat up and shouted angrily, 'Christ, you could mos do something. Drink something for it. Pills.'

'Maybe you ought to stop thinking of your pleasure every blerry night,' she flared back.

'Well, I got a right. Don't I say?'

'Ja. That's all you think about. Your rights.'

She started to cry softly, hugging the child at her hip. The children on the bed woke up, stared out over the ragged edges of their blanket.

Franky sank back on the bed and stared at the ceiling again. He felt a little ashamed now, hearing her quiet sobbing, and he began to wish he could do something good and beautiful for her. He looked at her with his deep, soft eyes and wanted to say something kind, but he could not find the words, and rubbed the back of one hand across the back of his mouth instead. He had hurt her, he felt, and love suddenly welled up inside him and choked his throat. He was tired, he thought. That made him angry. He was a stevedore and worked like hell in the docks and he felt angry with himself, too, now.

His wife sat down on a chair and looked at him and saw him only in a blur of tears and her own love beat like a pulse inside her.

She said huskily, 'Franky . . . '

From the bed Franky Lorenzo's voice held a gentle quality: 'Awright. It's awright. I'm sorry I shouted.' He did not look at her, out of embarrassment.

'Really, Franky?'

'Ja. Really.' He coughed, as if something was obstructing his throat, and said again, 'It's awright, woman. It's okay. Yes. Everything's okay.' Then with forced brusqueness: 'How about some tea, huh?'

'You . . . you hold the baby?'

'Of course. Why not?'

There was a table between the beds covered with newspapers, the edges cut into a frieze, on which were the kitchen things, and a primus stove. She picked up a saucepan and went out of the room to fill it at the tap in the latrine, while Franky Lorenzo held the child beside him on the bed.

NINE

Willieboy slammed the room door shut. A shout of fright rattled in his throat and he stood stock still for a moment, his face twitching with shock.

In that same moment a woman came out of the room opposite that of Michael Adonis. She was holding a saucepan in one hand and she had a young-old face and the body that bore the signs of regular childbirth. She stared at Willieboy sharply and said: 'Here, what you doing there?'

Willieboy turned quickly in panic, bolting for the head of the stairs and was gone down them, taking the steps three at at time, blundering into the banisters at the angle of each landing, while the woman reached the old man's door.

She rapped on the panels, calling out, 'Uncle Doughty. Uncle Doughty,' and receiving no reply turned the handle and looked in. She dropped the saucepan and her scream of terror reached Willieboy as he cleared the last steps of the staircase.

In the lobby he crashed into the bloated man to whom he had given a match, sending him staggering and cursing, and then was out past the piled-up-dust-bins, running up the street in the lamp-lit darkness.

It's enough to make a man commit murder, Constable Raalt told himself, sitting in the driving cabin of the patrol van. I'd wring her bloody neck but it's a sin to kill your wife. It's a sin the way she carries on, too. If I ever find out something definite she'll know all about it.

He glanced sideways at the driver beside him. The driver had a young face with plump, girlish jowls and light brown eyes. He was nervous of Raalt and perhaps a little afraid, although he tried now and then to break down the barrier it formed between them by attempting to be as co-operative as possible. Now he said, trying to make conversation: 'Things are quiet tonight, ne?'

'Quiet,' Raalt answered with a small sneer. 'I wish something would happen. I'd like to lay my hands on one of those bushman bastards and wring his bloody neck.' He found little relief in transferring his rage to some other unknown victim, but he took pleasure in the vindictiveness and his manner increased the discomfort of the driver who did not know what it was all about, but only sensed the rage that was consuming his companion.

He said: 'Well, the quieter the better. I don't like any trouble. Anyway, let these hottentots kill each other off for all I care. I want to get through this patrol and go home.'

They cruised down a dark street past leprous rows of houses, an all-night delicatessen making a pallid splash of light against the gloom, bumped over cobblestones, and swung into the garish strip of Hanover Street. The driver was turning over in his mind the idea of requesting a transfer to another station, anywhere else, as long as he would be away from Raalt. He did not like Raalt. He was becoming convinced of that. There was something about Raalt that increased his nervousness all the time they were together, so that it mounted at times almost to the point of fear. The driver was young and perhaps over-conscientious of his status both in the police force and in society, and he thought, He is one of those who will disgrace us whites. In his scorn for the hottentots and kaffirs he is exposing the whole race to shame. He will do something violent to one of those black bastards and as a result our superiority will suffer. They ought to post him somewhere, in a white area where he will have little opportunity of doing anything dishonourable.

'Stop here,' Raalt said and the driver eased his foot from the accelerator so that the van slowed down and stopped by the curb side. The driver looked out and saw that they were outside a shuttered drapery.

Raalt climbed out without a word and slammed the door, and then, looking into the cabin, his eyes in the shadow with his back to the street-light, their irises hard and shiny as plate-glass, said: 'Hang on for me, *kerel.*'

The driver said: 'Okay, man,' and moving over looked out and back to watch Raalt go a little way down the pavement to where a sign over a door next to a darkened shop said: Jolly Boys Social Club. He thought, I wonder what rule he is going to break now.

Constable Raalt pushed open the street door and climbed a flight of chipped cement steps littered with cigarette butts, burned out matches and rubbish left by the nebulous community of loungers and hangers-on who frequented the club upstairs. At the top of the steps was a blistered brown door. Raalt tried the handle, found it locked and slapped the panels hard with the flat of his hand.

In the narrow dusty room beyond the door two men played snooker on the green table under the big shaded lamp and at another table a crowd threw dice, watching intently as the bone cubes sprang and bounced against the raised sides of the table, while at a third a quartet played cards with silent concentration. From the walls film stars stared down or away in various poses and a big blonde, wearing very few clothes, smiled toothily from under the cracked gloss surface of the picture. A painted sign pleaded vainly for the patrons to use the ashtrays since the floor was fed up; and smoke, laden with the tang of dagga, hung like a fog so that one could become pleasantly doped by merely drawing a few deep breaths.

When the banging of Raalt's hand on the door came to them the players in the room raised their heads, their eyes turned to where the sound came from, alert as foxes catching the scent of a hunter.

The two men at the snooker table stopped playing and rested on their cues, lighting cigarettes and blowing smoke casually in order to give the impression of nervelessness while a short, olive-skinned man in a once-white shirt and grey cardigan detached himself from the suspended dice game and made his way towards the door.

He had a round, flabby belly that protruded like a pregnancy over his belt, a round flat face and heavy grey lips with a fresh cigarette jutting at an angle from a corner of his mouth. The cigarette seemed to divide his face unequally on that side and on the other an old knife scar showed through the stubble on the cheek from the temple to the tip of his round chin, so that his whole face had the look of having been roughly split by a meat cleaver and then forgotten. His eyes were small and round and brown and flat and gritty as weathered sandstone under the blunt ridge of his forehead.

This man slid the bolt on the door and opened it a few inches, looking out, then stepped back, saying, 'Hullo, Boss Raalt,' as the constable pushed his way inside.

The silence hung now like armour-plate, hard and protective, and Raalt's smile was a crooked grimace, ugly as a razor slash. He shifted his grey-as-dust eyes onto the olive-skinned man who had shut the door now, and asked bitterly, 'How's business, Chips?'

'Slow, Boss Raalt, slow,' the olive-skinned man replied, the lids lowered like screens over the brown eyes, the cigarette jerking with each word.

'Take that cigarette out of your jaw when you talk to me,' Raalt said.

'Okay, Boss Raalt, okay,' Chips said and removed the cigarette, dropped it on the floor and put a wide foot on it.

Under the lowered lids the eyes were hard and flat and shiny as the ends of cartridge shells, but the heavy grey mouth remained curled in the fixed smile.

He said to nobody in particular: 'Die baas Raalt, always making jokes. Always making jokes.'

Raalt held the dusty grey eyes on him and lifting his right hand up near his left shoulder struck the olive-skinned man across the mouth with the back of it, saying, spitting out each word: 'You don't have to smile at me, jong. I'm not your playmate.'

The olive-skinned man, Chips, stood quite still, only his head having jerked under the impact of the blow, with a faint stain of blood forming between the heavy grey lips, while behind him the people watched tautly in the smoke haze.

He said: 'Ja, baas,' speaking without humiliation, but with a heavy irony in his tone, and Raalt struck him again, so that the blood formed in a pool in the corner of his mouth and slid out and down that side of his chin in a thin, crooked trickle.

'You think mos you're a big shot,' Raalt said bitterly.

The olive-skinned man lifted a thick hand and wiped his mouth with it, looked at the bloodstain on the palm of his hand and then wiped it away slowly and deliberately on the leg of his stained trousers. He dug the same hand casually into the hip-pocket of the trousers and drew out a fistful of greasy crumpled notes. He counted off five pounds, put the rest away, and smoothed them carefully, arranging them with all their faces up, folded the sheaf neatly down the middle and passed it to Raalt. Raalt took it without a word and slipped it into the top pocket of his tunic, buttoning the flap down over it again, and gazed around at the silent men standing in the grey-smoke-filled room, then said: 'Well, you bastards are lucky I'm on this beat.' And to the man, Chips, he said, 'Don't do anything you don't want me to know about.'

The man made no reply, and Raalt asked, 'Do you hear me?'

'Ja, my baas,' smiling now thinly under the veiled, dark-copper eyes with the traces of blood beginning to congeal at the corner of his mouth and in the bristly stubble on his chin.

He held the door open and Raalt went by him and down the cement steps to the street. The olive-skinned man shut the door again, sliding the bolt carefully into place and then walked back to where the two men were chalking their cues again, not looking at him, and to where the crowd was gathering around the gambling table again, another man rattling the dice and saying, 'Come baby, make nick. Make nick.'

TEN

Michael Adonis lay on the iron bed in his dark room and heard the doorknob rattle. The room faced the street and from below the street-light made a pale white glow against the high window-panes and filtered a very little way into the gloom so that the unwashed curtains seemed to hang like ghosts in midair. The stained, papered walls were vague in the dark and the ceiling invisible. The door rattled again and somebody called softly outside in the corridor.

His flesh suddenly crawling as if he had been doused with cold water, Michael Adonis thought, Who the hell is that? Why the hell don't they go away. I'm not moving out of this place. It's got nothing to do with me. I didn't mean to kill that old bastard, did I? It can't be the law. They'd kick up hell and maybe break the door down. Why the hell don't they go away? Why don't they leave me alone? I mos want to be alone. To hell with all of them and that old man, too. What for did he want to go on living for, anyway. To hell with him and the lot of them. Maybe I ought to go and tell them. *Bedornerd.* You know what the law will do to you. They don't have any shit from us brown people. They'll hang you, as true as God. Christ, we all got hanged long ago. What's the law for? To kick us poor brown bastards around. You think they're going to listen to your story; Jesus, and he was a white man, too. Well, what's he want to come and live here among us browns for? To hell with him. Well, I didn't mos mean to finish him. Awright, man, he's dead and you're alive. Stay alive. Ja, stay alive and get kicked under the arse until you're finished, too. Like they did with your job. To hell with them. The whole effing lot of them.

He shivered and fumbled around until he found a cigarette and lit it, the match flare lighting his face, revealing the curves of his cheekbones and throwing shadows into the hollows below them and around his eye-sockets. The rattling of the doorknob had stopped and he heard vaguely the sound of footsteps along the corridor. He puffed at the cigarette and blew smoke into the darkness.

You ought to get yourself a goose, he thought. You've been messing around too long. You ought to get married and have a family. Maybe you ought to try that goose you met downstairs. Her? *Bedonerd.* When I take a girl she's got to be nice. Pretty nice. With soft hair you can run your hands through and skin so you can feel how soft her cheeks are and you'd come home every night mos and she'd have your diet ready and Friday nights you'd hand over your pay packet and she'd give you your pocket money and you'd go down to the canteen and have a couple of drinks and if you got too fired up she'd take care of you. Funny how some rookers are always squealing about having to hand over their pay Friday nights. Jesus, if I had a wife I'd hand over my ching without any sighs. But she's got to be one of them nice geese, not too much nagging and willing to give a man his pleasure.

Then he sat bolt upright as a woman screamed in the corridor outside and the thought that jumped into his mind was, Oh, God, they found that old bastard. The woman screamed again and a door banged and a man began shouting and then some more doors were opening and banging, and feet pounded upstairs, along corridors, voices started speaking together. There was an uproar in the corridor outside and a man's voice said over and over, 'What the hell, what the hell, what the hell.'

Michael Adonis scrambled off the bed, the cigarette falling from his lips to the floor, sending off a shower of red sparks while he plunged towards the door. For a moment he was about to open it and dash out in his excitement, but he checked himself in time and clung to the handle, pressing himself against the woodwork, listening. He felt cold and shivery and then hot, and his mind raced.

There were several people in the corridor outside and above a hubbub of voices a woman was saying hysterically, ' . . . old man. I saw who done it. I saw who done it. That skolly . . . ' A man's voice told her to shut up and Michael Adonis thought, How could she? She never saw a thing. We were all alone. There was nobody around. How could she have seen me? The bloody lying bitch. The bloody lying bitch.

The man started talking again and the hubbub ceased. ' . . . better call the law . . . No . . . ambulance no use . . . dead, isn't he? . . . the law . . . don't want no trouble . . . ' Somebody else said something and the man shouted, 'Christ, we leave it alone and the blerry law will grab the whole building on suspicion. Jesus, don't I know the law; I been in court four times all.'

Voices interjected, the man spoke again, his voice bearing a note of pride in his knowledge of the workings of the judiciary. Experience gave authority to his opinions. Conversation recommenced and the blur of voices rose, but without coherence in the room where Michael Adonis crouched. After a while it subsided to the muttering sound of distant breakers whispering against rocks, and then there was the sound of footsteps going downstairs, until the silence hung like a shroud on the upper floor of the tenement.

Michael Adonis released the doorknob and found the palm of his hand slippery with sweat. The liquor had gone from his brain now, and his mind was jumpy as a newborn child. He crossed over to the window, his heart beating hard, and stood by one side of the window peering down past the edge of the curtain. The street was quiet in the haze of the electric lights, the catacombs of darkened doorways beyond the grey pavements, and where lights were on in windows, they were yellow glows behind cut-out squares in black cardboard. Far beyond the rooftops of lower buildings neon signs cast a haze like a misplaced dawn over the city.

Then Michael Adonis saw the tenement crowd spill onto the pavement and into the street, eddying for a moment and then drawn in a small whirlpool around the vortex of a man in shirtsleeves and baggy grey flannel trousers. The light made a scar of the bald patch on his head and he waved his bared-to-the-elbow arms while he talked. The crowd stood around him, listening, and sometimes somebody said something, so that his arms and hands gestured again, as if he was making a speech. They went on talking for some minutes and after a while another man broke from the crowd and hurried up the street and into the dark.

Michael Adonis thought, coldly sober now, if they call the law they'll come up here sure and maybe want to know who lives here in these rooms. If they find me here then I'll go. I don't want no blerry questions asked. To hell with them. What's the bloody law done for them? Why, they can't have a little drink in and be found on the street without the law smacking them around. Christ, what a people. That smart son of a bitch down there who's doing all the talking is trying to be a laan, a big shot. What's it got to do with him? What'd that old bogger ever do for him? To hell with the lot of them. Stabbing a man in the back.

He watched the crowd in the street below for a while and then dropped the curtain and went back to the door. He turned the key and opened the door carefully. There was nobody out in the corridor. The old man's door looked stark and bare as a tombstone. Michael Adonis went out and shut the door quietly behind him. He walked carefully along the corridor and to the head of the stairs and looked down into the well. Somewhere the radio was still on, playing soft, syrupy music, all violins and horns. He went down the staircase slowly, listening all the time, until he reached the first landing, and then turned quickly towards the back of the building. A filthy window gave onto a low roof behind the tenement and below that into a squalid alleyway. Michael Adonis eased himself onto the roof which sheltered a disused boiler-house, and dropped down into the alley thick with accumulated muck. He ploughed his way towards the exit, stumbling over debris generations old and slimy with stagnant water, past dustbins and piled offal and into a sidestreet. It was blocked at one end by a wall so that he had to walk towards the street where the crowd had gathered. They were a distance below the spot where he emerged and were talking together. He cut quickly out of the cul-de-sac and darted up the street away from the crowd.

A little way up the street Foxy and the two young men watched him go off into the darkness, and the scarfaced youth said: 'That looks like Mikey, don't I say?'

'Ja,' said Foxy noncommittally. And to the boy with the skull-and-crossbones ring he said: 'Hey, go and find out what those jubas are gabbing about.'

The boy with the skull-and-crossbones ring sauntered off in the direction of the crowd in front of the tenement.

The scarfaced boy said: 'I wonder where in Jesus Sockies is. Looks like we get to search for him all blerry night.'

'He'll turn up,' Foxy said, not looking at him but at the crowd. 'I wonder what that is all about?'

ELEVEN

In the dark a scrap of cloud struggled along the edge of Table Mountain, clawed at the rocks for a foothold, was torn away by the breeze that came in from the southeast, and disappeared.

In the hot tenements the people felt the breeze through the chinks and cracks of loose boarding and broken windows and stirred in their sweaty sleep. Those who could not sleep sat by the windows or in doorways and looked out towards the mountain beyond the rooftops and searched for the sign of wind. The breeze carried the stale smells from passageway to passageway, from room to room, along lanes and back alleys, through the realms of the poor, until massed smells of stagnant water, cooking, rotting vegetables, oil, fish, damp plaster and timber, unwashed curtains, bodies and stairways, cheap perfume and incense, spices and half-washed kitchenware, urine, animals, and dusty corners became one vast, anonymous odour, so widespread and all-embracing as to become unidentifiable, hardly noticeable by the initiated nostrils of the teeming, cramped world of poverty which it enveloped.

Willieboy strolled up the narrow back street in District Six, keeping instinctively to the shadows which were part of his own anonymity, and thought with sudden anger: Well, I had mos nothing to do with it. They can't say it's me. I found him mos like that. But years of treacherous experience and victimization through suspicion had rusted the armour of confidence, reduced him to the nondescript entity which made him easy prey to a life which specialized in finding scapegoats for anything that steered it from its dreary course. So that now he longed for the stimulants which would weld the seams of the broken armour and bring about the bravado that seemed necessary in the struggle to get back into the battle that was for hardened warriors only.

The look-out in front of the house halfway up an alleyway that was half stone steps and half cobbles was an old decrepit ghost of a man that sat in a ruined grass chair beside the doorway in the darkness of the high stoop facing the entrance of another street.

He saw Willieboy emerge from the lemon-coloured light of a street-lamp, recognized him, and relaxed, but maintaining an expression of officiousness with which he tried to hide his identity as another of the massed nonentities to which they both belonged. He nursed a sort of pride in his position as the look-out for a bawdy house, a position which raised him a dubious degree out of the morass into which the dependent poor had been trodden.

'Hoit,' Willieboy said, moving up the three steps onto the stoop.

An expressionless grunt, neither of welcome nor rejection, answered him. The old eyes were dull and damp as pieces of gravel in a gutter.

'Place open?'

'Ja,' the old man said reluctantly. 'Waiting for some sailors.'

He did not move as the boy turned to open the door. His business was to warn at the approach of enemies. He withdrew himself into the shelter of his own old untidy thoughts as Willieboy went inside.

The front of the house was in darkness but beyond the dangling lace curtain at the end of the passageway light glared in the sitting-room. The floor was covered with bright linoleum decorated with geometrical designs, and there was a low table with a large clay vase containing coloured paper flowers held up in a piece of netting-wire. A big new radiogram stood against one wall and a sideboard displayed a pair of vases and a glass-covered tea tray with pictures of the Royal family behind the glass. The wallpaper was old, but there was still colour in the pattern of cabbage-like flowers and ribbons. A brocaded divan stood against another wall and its armchairs across two corners.

When Willieboy came into the room a woman stepped out of the kitchen. She was tall and big-boned and had a hard face with small dark eyes like two discoloured patches in brown sandstone. Her hair was tied back untidily into a bun and she wore two big gold rings in her ears. The rings were too big and did not suit her so that you noticed them all the time. Her mouth was crudely painted with bright lipstick. She was a lean, powerful woman with long arms, knobby wrists, and big hands which displayed several rings.

The dark eyes looked suspiciously at Willieboy, and she asked sharply: 'Ja? And what do you want?'

Willieboy grinned at her, but under the harsh stare his bravado dwindled and he looked sheepish, saying: 'Hullo, Miss Gipsy. Miss Gipsy, I thought maybe you'd give us a little something on the book. You know, mos.' His hands came up, describing a bottle in the air.

'That'll be the day. You think I'm here to support all you bum-hangers?'

'Hell, come on, Miss Gipsy. I'll mos pay you soon as I get money.'

'Soon as you get money? You mean soon as you rob somebody again.'

'Come on, man, Miss Gipsy,' Willieboy said, whining a little. 'You know me, mos.'

'Well,' Gipsy said, 'Okay. But you don't pay up soon and you'll see.'

'Thanks, Miss Gipsy,' Willieboy smiled. 'You're real sporting.'

The woman went back to the kitchen and Willieboy sat down on a chair. When Gipsy came back she brought a bottle of cheap wine which she put on the sideboard with a glass. She said: 'And don't sit here all night. I'm expecting some customers.'

'Okay, Miss Gipsy.'

Willieboy broke the seal of the bottle and poured the glass full. He emptied it at a swallow and felt the hot, raw liquor strike his stomach and burn for a moment before it spread out. It went to his head immediately and he felt a little dizzy, but after the second drink he settled into the sensation.

The woman did not come out of the kitchen again, and he drank on his own, taking his time and allowing himself to slip gently into a state of intoxication.

He had finished three-quarters of the bottle when there was a sound of a car pulling up outside, voices laughed and talked, and then the front door opened and people clattered into the passageway. The curtain parted and three men and three young women came in.

Two of the men were white, and the third was swarthy, with very black hair in shiny waves and a thin black moustache. One of the other men had red hair flowing back in a beautiful, natural pompadour. They all wore smart suits with loose draped backs and polo shirts.

One of the girls went over to the radio immediately and started a record. The dark seaman waited for her, while the other girls sat down on the divan with his companions.

A girl on the divan looked at Willieboy and said: 'How's it, pal?'

'Nice, Nancy, nice,' he said, smiling back at her. He did not look at the men, and thought lugubriously that she had no right to be there.

She was tan-coloured, and the bright dress she wore added

something so that you had to look at her again, and then you saw that she was beautiful. There was beauty in the depths of her dark eyes and in the lines of tragedy around her mouth, in the lost youth of the used shape of her body.

'You look cross,' she said to Willieboy, and to the redheaded seaman, 'He's my old pally.'

The seaman said, 'Uh huh,' grinning.

Then the woman, Gipsy, sailed in from the kitchen and said loudly, smiling at them all: 'Hullo, gentlemen. See you brought my girls home.'

The seamen got up and shook her hand, and the dark one stopped dancing for a moment to do likewise. The girl with whom he was dancing said: 'Bring us a bottle of brandy, Gipsy.'

'Right away,' Gipsy said. She laughed and said to the men: 'Make yourselves at home, boys.'

The music stopped and the black-haired man released his partner, guiding her over to an armchair, saying something in Spanish that she did not understand, but which made her giggle. She sat down and crossed her legs and the seaman sat on the arm of the chair with one hand on her neck. Willieboy watched him sullenly.

Gipsy came back with brandy and glasses and poured a row of drinks. They all drank, clinking glasses, and the girls laughed breathlessly as the spirits went down. Willieboy thought, I bet she put tobacco in that stuff.

The redhead said to him: 'How about you, buster? Have a drink?'

Willieboy looked at him. The redhead seemed to waver and undulate before him, and he was feeling drunk. He said with dignity: 'I got my own, pal.' He reached for his bottle of cheap wine and poured a drink. His hands shook a little.

'You better go slow on that,' the girl, Nancy, said.

'I can take it,' Willieboy said thickly. 'What do you think I am? A squashie?'

'Man, you put that stuff down real solid,' the other man on the divan said patronizingly.

Willieboy looked at him sullenly and asked: 'Youse guys from the States?'

'Yeah, man,' the seaman said. 'This here's Red and mah name's George. Red here, he from Chicago, see. That's some burg, that is. You all heard abaht Chi, Ah guess.'

'Yes,' Willieboy said. 'Gangsters.'

'Yeah, man. That's raht, man. Nah me, Ahm from down Looziana way. That's dahn Sahth.'

'South America?'

'Naw, man. Ah mean the Sahthern part o' Northern 'Merica, see?'

Willieboy did not understand this and directed his attention at the Spanish-speaking one and asked: 'Who is he? Cesar Romero?'

The Spanish-speaking man looked up and across at him, frowning, and George laughed and said: 'Naw, he ain't Cesar Romero, that's Ray Ybarra. He's Puerto Rican, but comes from Noo York.'

'Ain't he American?' Willieboy asked, feeling confused and drunk.

'Of course he's American,' the girl with George said. 'Don't be so blerry stupid.'

They all laughed and Red hugged the girl, Nancy, to his body, and the Puerto Rican from New York began to fondle the girl in the armchair. They had some more drinks and then Gipsy came in again.

The men smiled at her and George said: 'Hallo, little girl.'

She grinned at him and said: 'You better treat my girls nice, hey?'

'Sure ma'am,' Red replied. He smiled at the girl, Nancy, and stroked her hair.

Willieboy was drunk and angry from being laughed at and now he said to the woman: 'Listen, Gipsy, what you let the girls mess with these boggers for? They foreigners.'

The woman, Gipsy, turned on him. 'You. What the hell you talking about?'

'These jubas. They just messing our girls.'

'That any of your business?'

'I don't like them messing our girls,' Willieboy said again, staring at the three men. 'To hell with them.'

'Leave him alone, Gipsy,' the girl, Nancy, said to the woman.

'You stick to your business,' Gipsy told her, and to Willieboy, 'And what right you got talking about my guests?'

'Guests—' Willieboy sneered, looking at the seamen and feeling angry. 'They got no right messing with our girls.'

The seamen were quiet now, looking at him. They could not

understand what he was saying, but they sensed his antagonism.

Gipsy said: 'You got a cheek coming to drink on the book and then insulting my real customers.'

'Awright, I'll pay you for it. They can keep their blerry brandy too. I don't want their blerry brandy.'

'You keep quiet if you want to stay here,' Gipsy snapped at him. 'You don't know how to act in front of respectable people.'

'Awright, Gipsy,' Willieboy said and looked at the seamen. 'Let them mess with the girls.'

'Keep quiet, man,' Nancy told him, speaking kindly. 'It's all right, man. You just keep quiet. You want another drink?'

'No,' Willieboy said. 'Why don't you leave them, Nancy?'

'He's just a little drunk,' Nancy told Red. 'He don't mean nothing.'

'Why don't you throw him out, the unmannerly bogger,' the girl with the Puerto Rican said.

'Gwan,' Willieboy said to her. 'Who's you?'

The Puerto Rican seaman looked at him and said: 'Listen, don't talk to a lady like that.' He got up and went on looking at Willieboy.

George stood up, too, and said: 'Now, Ray. This don't call for no fight, boy.' And Gipsy said: 'I don't want trouble here. This is a respectable place.'

'Then tell him to lay off,' the Puerto Rican said. He looked mean and dangerous.

'Come on, get out,' Gipsy said to Willieboy. 'You drunk and you make trouble.'

Willieboy ignored her, but was looking at the seaman. He was still a little drunk and spoiling for a fight.

'Go, man, Willieboy,' Nancy said. 'Come around in the morning.'

'That juba got no right talking to me that way, mos,' Willieboy said, still looking at the seaman.

'You better go, kid,' the Puerto Rican told him.

Willieboy lunged at him suddenly and he stepped back startled, but Gipsy had her arms around Willieboy before he could do anything else. She was strong and she held onto him while Willieboy struggled. The girls began to scream and the two other seamen stepped forward. Willieboy suddenly went berserk and threw Gipsy from him with a savage twist, so that she staggered into the table upsetting it and scattering the glasses and the near-empty brandy bottle.

'God, I'll chop you,' Willieboy shouted and reached for his jacket pocket.

'Watch out for his knife,' Gipsy shouted, and they saw the sharpened kitchen knife gripped in his hand.

'Willieboy. No, man,' the girl, Nancy, cried out.

The seaman whose name was George reached out, picked up the fallen brandy-bottle and flung it. He was drunk, too, and his aim was bad, so that it missed Willieboy by a yard and splintered against the wall somewhere, leaving a stain on the wallpaper. Willieboy swung at him with the knife, but his feet became entangled with the legs of the overturned table and he lurched, and at that moment Gipsy hit him expertly behind an ear. He fell on his face over the table, dropping the knife, and groaned.

The Puerto Rican seaman stepped forward and prepared to kick him in the head, but Gipsy said sharply: 'Don't do that. Leave him.' The Puerto Rican drew back, cursing in Spanish.

Meanwhile the front door had opened and the look-out came in, running down the passageway and saying: 'No man. No, man.' His mouth was open and his old eyes looked startled.

Gipsy looked at him and said derisively: 'A hell of a time for you to come.'

The old man looked at Willieboy who stirred in the wreckage of the table and broken glasses, and asked: 'What'd he do, Gipsy?'

'Ran amuck and tried to chop these visitors. You better put him out in the street.'

'Don't hurt him,' Nancy said.

'Garn,' Gipsy said to her. 'You talk like he was your man.'

'I know him a long time,' Nancy said. 'He is always so luff.'

Red put an arm around her and said: 'Now you all don't get excited, kid.'

The look-out got his hands under Willieboy's armpits and hauled him over, then started to drag him down the corridor to the front door. His heels made a squealing sound on the oil-cloth. Gipsy stooped and picked up the fallen knife and placed it on the sideboard.

'He'll get into trouble over that knife, one day,' she said.

'Now you girls better clear up. These blerry skollies always making trouble for respectable people.'

'Put on the gram,' one of the girls said.

George laughed and said: 'That little scrap just give me a thirst. You reckon you can rassle up another bottle, ma'am?'

'Yes,' Gipsy said. 'That's another twenty-five bob.'

Outside the old man dumped Willieboy on the stoop. He was wheezing from dragging the limp youth, and he grumbled irritably: 'Always got to do the dirty work. Always doing the blerry dirty work.' Inside the radio began to play again.

Willieboy came to slowly and sat up, holding his head where Gipsy had hit him. He blinked at the look-out and asked angrily: 'You hit me, you effing bastard?'

'It must have been the woman,' the look-out said. 'She got a blow like the kick of a horse. I already seen her knock the front teeth out of a sailor once. You better go, pal.'

Willieboy looked at him for a moment, and then rolled over suddenly to the edge of the stoop and was sick onto the pavement. He lay there, panting for a while, after retching was over. Then he stood up and lurched down the steps and went down the street, walking unsteadily in the dark.

TWELVE

The driver saw the crowd first and said, bringing Constable Raalt out of his thoughts, 'What goes on here?'

He eased his foot on the accelerator bringing the patrol van slowly up to the crowd. Raalt had been thinking morosely about his wife again and the sight of the crowd pleased him a little with its relief from his gnawing thoughts. He was out on the running-board before the van came to a stop and his hard grey eyes swung over the crowd from face to face like the expressionless lenses of a camera.

The crowd was scattered from the entrance of the tenement, across the pavement in front of it and onto the street. Now, as the van pulled up, those in the street withdrew partially towards the edge of the pavement, faces passive and eyes downcast in the presence of the law. A few slid quietly away into the shadows beyond the lamp-light, for there was no desire in them to cooperate with these men who wore their guns like appendages of their bodies and whose faces had the hard metallic look, and whose hearts and guts were merely valves and wires which operated robots.

'Nou ja, what goes on?' Raalt's voice cracked out.

The crowd eddied and rippled for a few moments and then parted as a heavy, wine-bloated man pushed his way forward. 'What you scared of?' he muttered to all in general. 'Can't you blerry well talk?' He looked at Constable Raalt and grinned ingratiatingly. He said: 'There's a dead man upstairs. Look like murder, baas.'

Constable Raalt stared back at him and said: 'How the hell you know what's murder and what isn't, jong?'

The bloated man grinned again and moved his feet. He said: 'Well, Konstabel, I reckon I saw who did it.'

'Oh, you did? And what is your name, kerel?'

'John Abrahams, baas.'

Somebody in the crowd cried: 'Hey, jou fif' column,' and Raalt's flat grey eyes glanced around from face to face. The crowd muttered and shuffled again, and now their eyes were on Abrahams. He could feel hostility in the stares and he grinned sheepishly, but turned his head and said: 'Well, we must mos cooperate with the law, don't I say?'

'Ja,' another man said, looking at him and ignoring the police. 'Yes, cooperate like they did with Noortjie.'

'What of Noortjie?' Abrahams scowled.

'You know mos. Because he was little drunk one night they took him to the cells and boggered hell out of him all night. Lost his teeth, and when he came in front of the court they said he'd resisted arrest and he got extra for that, too. Okay, cooperate with them, man.'

'Well, who told him to get drunk?' the puffy man asked. He turned back to Constable Raalt and said: 'Don't listen to them, baas. I believe in law and or'er.'

'Oh,' Constable Raalt said, smiling at him with a small sneer. 'You believe in law and order. That's very good, jong.' He looked at the driver and said: 'He believes in law and order.' To the man he said again: 'Good. Give us some of your law and order.'

Abrahams looked at his shoes and shuffled and smiled. 'Well, baas, I was standing there in the doorway and this rooker came along and I ask him for a match and he give me one to light my endtjie, my cigarette-end, then he go in upstairs and I stand but here all the time and the next thing I hear a woman screaming and this rooker come running down and almost run me over and I see him running up the street fast.' He paused for breath and continued, 'Further, I go upstairs, and the people here who live inside also go upstairs and there we see this old man dead.' He stopped and then looked about him with a sort of shabby pride. The people surrounding him stared back and he shook off their antagonism with a shrug and said again to Constable Raalt: 'You see how it is, baas? These people.'

Constable Raalt did not offer comment, but without turning his head, said to the driver: 'We'd better go in and look.' To the bloated man he said: 'You better come with us. The rest of you can eff off.'

He scattered the crowd as he walked through it to the entrance of the tenement, the driver following and Abrahams bringing up the rear. The throng closed again and some ventured in behind them, voices muttering that they lived here, anyhow.

Climbing the smelly staircase into the heights of the building, the driver thought, with disgust, that he did not mind if the whole population of this place killed themselves off as long as it was not done while he was on duty. This was a bloody nuisance, and he relegated them all to hell, including Constable Raalt. At the same time he was glad Raalt was with him, for he was new to the force and this district where the people had little regard for the authority of the land, and he was not sure that he would have been able to handle this thing, which seemed to be murder, too.

They reached the top floor and the driver felt trapped there by the smell of decay and disintegration. He heard Raalt snapping at the group that crowded behind them and somebody shuffled over to gesture at a door. The dim, half-burned-out bulb in the socket in the ceiling glowed weakly so that the shadows of the people were blurred and blotched.

He went behind Raalt into the room and the crowd behind tried to push in with them and he turned and shouted irritably: 'Listen here, muck off. Keep outside.'

The stench of vomit hit him with a sour blow and he stared at the bluish dead face of the old man on the bed. He said: 'Jesus Christ.'

Raalt went over and looked closely at the dead face, examining it without touching it. It was the first time he had looked at a corpse this way, but he tried to give the driver an impression of experience. He felt a little disgusted. He straightened up and said to the driver:

'Looks like he was hit on the head.'

'It's a job for the detectives,' the driver said, looking around with a grimace of nausea. 'I'll get the station on the wireless.'

'What's your hurry, man?' Constable Raalt asked. 'This is our patrol, isn't it?'

'Naturally. But it is a case for the criminal investigation volk,' the driver replied, without looking at him.

Raalt said: 'Nobody kills anybody on my beat and gets away with it. No bloody bastard.'

Looking again at the corpse, the driver said: 'A white man, too. What would a white man be doing living in a place like this?' He looked away from the corpse and around the room, wrinkling his nose at the smell of vomit, wine, decay.

Raalt said nothing, but unbuttoned the flap of his pocket and took out his notebook. He glanced at his wristwatch and then began to write in the book. The driver said, a little impatiently: 'I had better get onto the wireless.'

Constable Raalt looked up at him from his writing with his hard grey eyes and then said, grinning: 'Very well. Get the station on your beautiful wireless and tell them to send the detectives. Also give them my greeting and best wishes. Also a blessed Christmas.'

The driver glanced at his eyes, shook his head and went out. Constable Raalt wrote again in his notebook and through the writing thought, I wonder what she's doing now, the verdomte bitch, I'll break her neck if I catch her at something. He finished writing and then went to the door of the room. He had become oblivious of the sour smell in the room and it was now merely a smell, like stale tobacco or the smell of disinfectant in the police station.

The people gathered in the corridor, near the upper landing, gazed back at the constable, some of them nervously, some with surreptitious boldness, all with the worn, brutalized, wasted, slum-scratched faces of the poor. They saw the flat grey eyes under the gingerish eyebrows, hard and expressionless as the end of pieces of lead pipe, pointed at them.

'Now,' he said coldly. 'Now, where is the woman who is supposed to have screamed?'

The people on the landing and in the corridor said nothing, looking away, and Constable Raalt thought, These bastards don't like us; they never did like us and we are only tolerated here; I bet there are some here who would like to stick a knife into me right now.

He said, sneering: 'What's the matter? She didn't do it, did she?'

The man, John Abrahams, laughed a little and said: 'They won't say a thing, baas. You know how it is.'

'No, I don't know how it is,' Raalt told him. 'You tell me how it is.'

'Well, baas . . . '

'All right, forget it, man. What's your name, anyway?'

'John Abrahams, Konstabel. I told baas.'

Raalt wrote it down in his notebook, together with the address. 'What is the name of the man inside?' Gesturing with his head towards the door of the room where the body lay.

'Mister Doughty,' the man Abrahams said.

'Doughty? What sort of a name is that? How do you spell it?'

'I don't know, baas. We just called him Mister Doughty.'

'Doughty,' Constable Raalt repeated. 'What a peculiar name. These people have bloody peculiar names.' Then he remembered that the body was that of a white man and he asked: 'What was he doing here? How did he get here?'

'He lived here a long time.' Abrahams replied. 'He got a pension and he was in the big war. I heard him talk about it once.' He added with a grin, 'Drank like hell, too.' He looked down at his feet when Raalt stared at him.

'Now,' Raalt said, when he had written down the old man's name in his notebook without bothering to try to spell it correctly: 'Tell me, how did this man look whom you saw running away.'

Before Abrahams could answer Franky Lorenzo said to him from the crowd in the corridor: 'You've said enough already, Johnny.'

Constable Raalt raised his head and looked at Franky Lorenzo, his grey eyes bleak. He said: 'Listen, jong, you seem to have a lot to say. You had a lot to say downstairs, too. Do you want to be arrested for intimidating a witness and defeating the ends of justice?'

Franky Lorenzo did not understand these high-sounding phrases but he sensed the threat. Still he met the constable's eyes holding them with his own, until he felt his wife tugging at his arm, pleading: 'Franky, don't get into trouble, please. Remember . . . remember. . . .'

'All right,' Franky Lorenzo said sullenly. 'All right.' He looked across at Abrahams for a moment and then looked away again.

Constable Raalt said: 'Pasop,' to him and then to Abrahams: 'Now, then. Come on.'

'Well, baas,' Abrahams hesitated, feeling a little nervous and embarrassed now. 'Well, baas, you see I didn't execkly see . . .'

'Oh,' Constable Raalt said, his voice hard. 'You didn't exactly see. What exactly did you see?'

'Well, baas, he was just a boy. One of these young rookers that hang out on the corners. I can't say execkly . . .'

John Abrahams was now begining to feel the effect of the abrasive stares of those around him and his bravado commenced to collapse, falling from him like dislodged coloured paper decorations. He shuffled and stared at his feet and fingered his nether lip, trying to salvage some of the disintegrating sense of importance.

'Listen, man,' Raalt told him. 'If you don't want to talk now you can still be forced to appear in court and say what you know before the magistrate. So make up your mind.'

John Abrahams collapsed completely and said quickly: 'He was just a young rooker, baas. He had on a yellow shirt and a sports coat and had kinky hair. That's all I seen, baas, true as God. That's all.' He looked around helplessly and cried out: 'Well, I got to tell what I saw, mustn't I?'

The crowd was silent and Constable Raalt, writing in his notebook again thought, They hate us, but I don't give a bloody hell about them, anyway; and no hotnot bastard gets away with murder on my patrol; yellow shirt and kinky hair; a real hotnot and I'll get him even if I have to gather in every black bastard wearing a yellow shirt.

He said, his grey eyes narrowed with rage: 'All right, the rest of you can bogger off. Abrahams, you stay here and wait for the detectives.'

'Can't I go, baas?' Abrahams asked, whining now.

'No, God, jong. I said wait for the detectives.'

He added to his thought, Detectives; I can look after my own troubles; that boy and his detectives.

He stared at the crowd in the corridor, his eyes like pieces of grey metal, and they started to disperse, slowly trickling away. Franky Lorenzo looked again at Abrahams and spat on the floor, then walked down the corridor with his wife. Constable Raalt returned his notebook to the pocket of his tunic and buttoned the flap. He waited for the detectives to arrive, and began to think again of his own wife.

THIRTEEN

Michael Adonis turned into the little Indian café and saw the boy, Joe, sitting at one of the baize-covered tables, eating. Michael Adonis had seen the café as he came into the short, grey, yellow-lamp-lighted street with its scarred walls and cracked pavements, and had headed towards it because he had been walking about for an hour and wanted to sit down. He saw the pale glow of the café light behind the greasy window piled with curry-balls and Indian sweetmeats and headed for it like a lost ship sighting a point of land for the first time after a long and hopeless voyage.

He parted the sparse wooden-bead curtains and saw Joe at the table. Behind a glass case full of stale rolls an old, bearded Indian dozed, his betel-stained mouth half-open and his beard stirring as he breathed. There was nobody else in the café.

Joe looked up as Michael Adonis came over, and smiled. He was eating curried peas and rice with one hand, arranging the food skilfully into a little mound and then shovelling it into his mouth with his grouped fingers. Some of the food had spilled onto his disreputable old raincoat, adding fresh stains to many others.

He said: 'Hey, Mikey. You out late.'

Michael Adonis sat down opposite him and said, scowling: 'Same with you. Where in hell do you live?'

Joe smiled, shrugging, and waved his free hand. The nails were rimmed with black, and the smell of fish still clung to him. 'Anywhere,' he said.

Then he added, still smiling, but a little shyly: 'Bought the curry with the shilling what you gave me. The old Moor sells shilling's worth.'

'I had supper,' Michael Adonis told him and lighted a cigarette. He smoked silently, brooding.

'What you walking about for, Mikey? You look sick, too.'

'I'm not sick. I got troubles.'

Just then the old Indian woke up and saw him, and came over, wiping his hands on his stained and greasy apron. 'You want eat?' he asked.

'No,' Michael Adonis said. 'Bring me some coffee.'

'No coffee. Tea.'

'Awright.'

The old Indian went over to the hatchway in the back wall and called through into the kitchen.

Michael Adonis got out his cigarettes and lit one, watching Joe eating the curry. Joe scooped some of the food into his mouth, chewed, the yellow gravy staining the outer corners of his lips. He said, philosophically: 'We have all got troubles. Don't I say?'

'You. Troubles,' Michael Adonis said, looking at him with some derision. 'What troubles you got?'

He was suddenly pleased and proud of his own predicament. He felt as if he was the only man who had ever killed another and thought himself a curiosity at which people should wonder. He longed to be questioned about it, about the way he had felt when he had done it, about the impulse that had caused him to take the life of another. But the difficulty was that to reveal his secret was dangerous, so he had to carry it with him for all time or accept the consequences. The rights and wrongs of the matter did not occur to him then. It was just something that, to himself, placed him above others, like a poor beggar who suddenly found himself the heir to vast riches. And the fact that he dared not declare his newly acquired status irritated him, too, so that now he felt a prick of jealousy for this nondescript boy who was in a position to disclose his own problems with ease if he wished to.

He said, surlily: 'Where the hell you get troubles from?'

But at that moment the bead curtains over the doorway of the café parted and Foxy and the two youths in their smart tropical suits came in. They saw Michael Adonis and Joe at the table and came over.

They looked with some disgust at the ragged boy and then immediately ignored him, and Foxy turned to Michael Adonis, saying: 'We still looking for that bastard Sockies. Did you see him yet?'

'No, man.'

The boy with the scarface spat on the floor and said: 'We walking around all night looking for that hound. We ought to find another look-out.'

'You feel like doing something with us?' Foxy asked Michael Adonis.

'What?'

'Leave him alone,' the boy with the skull-and-crossbones ring growled.

'We need a man to hold candle at a job,' Foxy replied, ignoring the youth. 'We'll give you a cut.'

'Who the hell is he?' the boy asked, looking at Michael Adonis scornfully.

I wonder how many people you killed, Michael Adonis thought with his distorted pride, staring back at the boy with the ring, a thin smile on his lips, and said: 'What do you know about me?'

The one with the scarface then said: 'Maybe he's okay.'

Foxy asked: 'You want to come in, Mikey?'

Michael Adonis looked again at the boy with the ring. 'What about him?'

'He's okay,' Foxy told him, grinning. 'He's just a little hard-case, that's all. But he's awright.'

'Well,' Michael Adonis considered, rubbing the faint stubble on his chin. 'Well, maybe. I don't know yet.' He felt a stir of pleasure at being approached, but he was still hesitant.

Foxy shrugged and said: 'We going down to the Club now. We not going to bogger around looking for Sockies no more. We'll be down at the Club, so get us there when you make up your mind.'

He added: 'You could make some chink now you haven't got a job no more. Maybe you can come with us always.' To the other he said: 'I know Mikey a long time. He's awright, man.'

The old Indian came back with the cup of tea Michael Adonis had ordered and put it down on the table. Some of the tea had slopped over into the saucer. He looked at the three who had come in, chewing his betel nut. The boy with the scarface looked around at him and said: 'Okay, baas, we going. We want nothing.'

He looked at Michael Adonis again, while the old Indian went away. Then he said: 'We saw some law going into your place. Heard a rooker got chopped or something.'

'And we seen you come out the side lane, too,' the boy with the skull-and-crossbones ring said, with smiling malice.

Michael Adonis stared at them and felt suddenly trapped. On the one hand he would have liked to have proclaimed it to them like a victory over their own petty accomplishments, but on the other hand the mixed feelings of fear and caution gagged him. He did not like the boy with the ring and wanted to tell him that he, Michael Adonis, was a bigger shot now than he was, but he smiled back into the depraved eyes of the boy and said: 'And then? What the hell it got to do with me?'

Foxy reached out and patted the shoulder of his scuffed leather coat and said: 'Mikey's a good boy. He's not like you jubas. He got class. Don't I say Mikey?' Then directly to the two with him: 'Now let's muck off.'

They went over towards the doorway, but before he went out Foxy stopped and turned, smiling again at Michael Adonis.

'You don't have to worry niks, Mikey. We okay. We don't give a eff for the law. You come in with us. We okay.' He waved a hand and then went out through the bead curtains.

Joe had finished his meal now and he looked at Michael Adonis and asked: 'What they talking about, Mikey? That stuff about the law down at your place.'

'I don't know. *Ek weet nie,*' Michael Adonis answered, feeling angry. 'How the hell should I know? I told them, didn't I?'

'Listen, Michael,' Joe said, speaking seriously now, and feeling awkward about it at the same time. 'Listen, maybe you got big troubles. Bigger than I got.' He felt somewhat ashamed of the comparison, but he went on. 'Like I said, we all got troubles. But johns like them don't help you out of them. They in trouble themselves. You'd only add to the whole heap of troubles. I don't know how to tell it, but you run away with them and you got another trouble. Like those rookers. They started a small trouble, maybe, and then run away from it and it was another trouble , so they run away all the time, adding up the troubles. Hell, I don't know.' He felt desperate and a little sad, and did not know quite what to say.

Michael Adonis scowled at him and asked: 'What the blerry hell you know? What troubles you got?'

Joe looked down at the plate which he had wiped clean so that the tiniest morsel of food had not escaped his belly. He said, embarrassed: 'I don't know. I got nothing. No house, no people, no place. Maybe that's troubles. Don't I say?'

'Where's your people, then?' Michael Adonis asked. He tasted his tea, which had gone cold during all the talking.

'Somewhere. I don't know. Hear, we used to live in Prince Lane, mos, a long, long time. Me, my old woman and my father and my sister, Mary, and my small brothers, Isaac and Matty. Then one day my father goes out and he never comes back again. He just went out one morning and we never saw him again.'

'What the hell he do that for?' Michael Adonis asked. 'What for he want to do a thing like that?'

'Don't know. He never mos told us nothing. He just went out that morning and that was the last we saw of him.'

Joe said, shaking his head and frowning, looking at his plate: 'I don't know. Maybe he had troubles, too. He didn't have no job. He was out of a job for a long time and we didn't get things to eat often. Me and my brother Matty used to go out mornings and ask from door to door for pieces of stale bread. Sometimes we got some last-night's cooked food with it from the people. But it was never enough for all of us. My old woman never used to touch the stuff, but shared it out among us lighties. Also the rent of the house wasn't paid and after a while my old woman gets a letter we got to get out. The landlady sends a lot of letters, saying every time we got to clear out, and afterwards some bastards come with a paper and walks right in and stacks all the furniture on the pavement outside and then locks the door and says if we go back we will all be thrown in jail.'

Joe wasn't happy any more. He looked old and very serious. He said:

'My old woman just sat there by the pile of furniture with Mary and Isaac and Matty and me, and cries. She just sit there and cry. Then after some time she says, Well, we got to go back to the country to stay with my ouma, my grandmother. So she sells the furniture to a secondhand man, and they go away.'

'They?' Michael Adonis said. 'What about you?'

'Me, I ran away when I heard they was going. I just ran away like my old man.' Joe looked at Michael Adonis and said: 'I wasn't going to the outside. To the country. Man, that would be the same like running away, too. Some bastards come with a piece of paper and tell you to get the hell out because you haven't got money for the rent, and a shopkeeper tell you you got to have money else you don't get nothing to eat, and you got to go away somewhere else where it's going to start all over again. No, man,' he shook his head again, 'What's the use. I rather stay around here and starve on one spot or maybe pick up something here and there to get something in my belly. My old man, he ran away. I didn't want to run, too.'

Michael Adonis stared at him for a moment. He felt a little embarrassed now in the presence of this boy. He had never heard Joe say anything as lengthy and as serious as this and he wondered whether the boy had spoken the truth or was a little queer. Then he picked up his neglected cup and drank. The tea was quite cold now and a scum of milk had started to form on the surface.

He said, uncomfortably: 'You like some tea?'

'No thanks, man. It's okay.'

Michael Adonis put his cup down and took out his cigarettes. He shoved the packet over to Joe and said gruffly: 'Well, have a smoke, then.'

Joe shook his head and smiled gently and somewhat shyly. He said: 'No thanks. I don't mos smoke.' Then he added, serious again: 'You mustn't go with those gangsters, Mikey. You leave those gangsters alone.'

'What's it to you?' Michael Adonis asked, feeling both angry and embarrassed. 'What's it to you?'

'Nothing. Nothing, I reckon. But they mean boys.'

'Ah, hell,' Michael Adonis said and got up. He went over to the counter where the old Indian dozed and got some money out. He paid for his tea, feeling the ragged boy's eyes on him, and did not look back when he went out.

FOURTEEN

Night crouched over the city. The glow of street lamps and electric signs formed a yellow haze, giving it a pale underbelly that did not reach far enough upwards to absorb the stars that spotted its purple hide. Under it the city was a patchwork of greys, whites, and reds threaded with thick ropes of black

where the darkness held the scattered pattern together. Along
the sea front the tall shadows of masts and spars and cranes
towered like tangled bones of prehistoric monsters.

Willieboy came up a street that was flanked on one side by
the great blank wall of a warehouse, and on the other by a row
of single-storied houses fronted by wooden fences. Lights
burned in some of the windows and in one of the houses a radio
was playing. He went up the street, his hands deep in the
pockets of his trousers, pushing the sides of the trousers out-
wards so that they looked like riding breeches. He was feeling
muzzy and his head ached. And he felt angry and humiliated
by the manhandling he had received at Gipsy's shebeen. He
clenched his fists in his pockets and thought, They can't treat a
man like that, where can they treat a juba like that? Hell, I'm a
shot, too. I'll show those sonsabitches.

He was also aware of his inferiority. All his youthful life he
had cherished dreams of becoming a big shot. He had seen
others rise to some sort of power in the confined underworld of
this district and found himself left behind. He had looked with
envy at the flashy desperadoes who quivered across the screen
in front of the eightpenny gallery and had dreamed of being
transported wherever he wished in great black motorcars and
issuing orders for the execution of enemies. And when the
picture faded and he emerged from the vast smoke-laden
cinema mingling with the noisy crowd he was always aware of
his inadequacy, moving unnoticed in the mob. He had affected
a slouch, wore gaudy shirts and peg-bottomed trousers,
brushed his hair into a flamboyant peak. He had been thinking
of piercing one ear and decorating it with a gold ring. But even
with these things he continued to remain something less than
nondescript, part of the blurred face of the crowd, incon-
spicuous as a smudge on a grimy wall.

He turned from the street into another equally as gloomy
and quiet and up ahead he saw the dark form of somebody
approaching along the pavement. It was a man and he was
walking with a lurch that sent him from side to side as he came
on.

It was with a sense of shock that he came face to face with
Willieboy. He pulled up with a hiccough, his mouth dropping
open, drooling, and his bloodshot eyes widening with fright. He
tried to turn away and run, but his drunken legs would not

allow him to, and he lurched awkwardly. Then Willieboy had hold of him by the front of his coat and he wailed in terror.

'Hullo, old man,' Willieboy said. 'Give us five bob, man.'

'No, man, I haven't got, man.' Mister Greene gasped, his voice quavering with fear. He was scared that the boy would pull a knife.

'Come on, pally. Let's have five bob.'

'Please, man. Please.'

Greene tried to pull away, but the boy held onto him, and then suddenly his legs were kicked expertly from under him and he was flat on the pavement with the boy standing over him.

He shouted: 'Please. No, man, No, man.'

Willieboy kicked him viciously in the ribs and he squealed more from fear than pain. Then hands were running through his pockets while he crouched trembling.

'Ah, effit,' Willieboy sneered. 'You bare-arsed bastard. You got nothing.'

'If I had I'd give you, man,' Greene cried. 'Leave me alone, man.'

'I got a good mind to chop you,' Willieboy told him savagely. 'I got a good mind to chop you.'

'Please.'

'Gwan. Muckoff to your wife and kids.'

He kicked Greene again and again, then stood back while the groaning man climbed to his feet. Shock and fear had sobered the haggard man, and he stumbled away, tripping in his haste to get away. Willieboy took a step towards him and he screamed with terror and started to run, gasping painfully. Willieboy watched him running into the darkness and when he had disappeared, turned away down the street.

Willieboy reached the end of the street and turning the corner he saw the police van. It was coming along the rows of shuttered shops and dim tenements, cruising slowly, and the glare of its headlights caught him as he hesitated on the pavement.

FIFTEEN

Michael Adonis was almost at the end of the street when he heard Joe coming after him. One of Joe's shoelaces was loose and it flick-flicked on the asphalt as he ran. He came beside the young man and said, a little breathless: 'Mike. Mikey, listen here . . . '

Walking along the dark street Michael Adonis did not look at him, but thought, Well, what you want now. You reckon you going to be around me for the rest of my blerry life? You spook.

Somewhere up ahead people were singing.

'Mike,' Joe was saying, 'Mike, maybe it isn't my business, you see? Maybe it got nothing to do with me, but you like my brother. I got to mos think about you. Jesus, man, why, you even gave me money for food. There's not a lot of people give me money for food. Awright, maybe now and then. But most of the time I do what I can out on the rocks.'

He was getting out of breath again because Michael Adonis was quickening his pace and the boy, Joe, had to step out to keep up with him. He spoke quickly as if he had very little time in which he had to say what he wanted to say.

'Listen, Mikey,' he said. 'You don't know those boys. They have done bad things. I heard. To girls, also. I heard about Mrs. Kannemeyer's daughter. And they use knives, too. They'se a bunch of gangsters, Mike, and they'se going to land up somewhere bad. They was in reformatory, one of them at least. I forget what one. But they'll get you in trouble, Mikey. They break into places and steal, and I heard they stabbed a couple of other johns. Christ, I don't want to see you end up like that, Mike. Hell, a man'd rather starve. They'll murder somebody and get hanged, Mikey. You want to get hanged?'

Michael Adonis suddenly stopped in his stride and looked at Joe. 'What the hell you following me around like a blerry tail for?' he asked angrily. 'What's it got to do with you what I'm going to do?'

'Please, Mike,' Joe said. He looked as if he was going to cry. 'I'm your pal. A man's got a right to look after another man. Jesus, isn't we all people?'

'Ah, go to hell,' Michael Adonis shouted at him. 'Go to hell. Leave me alone.'

He turned his back and went on down the street, leaving Joe staring after him, his face puckering with the beginning of weeping.

Blerry young squashy, Michael Adonis thought as he turned up another street. For what's he got to act like a blerry god-father?

A few blocks further up a street that led back into Hanover

was the Club. It was on the ground floor in what had once been a shop. Behind the painted plate-glass windows billiard cues clacked against balls, and a strip of light escaped from under the door. Overhead was an old balcony that fronted a row of shabby rooms.

Michael Adonis tried the door and found it locked. He rattled the knob and waited. It was unlocked and opened a few inches to reveal a part of Foxy's scrofulous face.

'Hoit, Mike,' Foxy said, and opened the door for him to enter. 'Glad you thought it over, pally.'

Inside the two youths were shooting balls across the billiard table. One of them had his coat off, showing the bright metal links of his new armbands. They looked up as Michael Adonis came in. The boy with the skull-and-crossbones ring was leaning on his cue. At the back of the room another man slept on an old disembowelled sofa, breathing harshly through his mouth. The room smelled badly of tobacco smoke and marijuana, which is called dagga here, mingled with the stench of stagnant water from a puddle under a filthy sink in a corner.

Michael Adonis stood under the harsh light of the room, his hands in the pockets of his leather coat, looking at the two youths. Foxy finished locking the door and came over saying: 'Well, Mikey here's come along, so to hell with Sockies. Don't I say, Mike?'

'I reckon so,' Michael Adonis answered.

'We got a job we going to do later on. Sockies was supposed to hold candle for us while me and these two jubas did the work. He did not turn up, so he can forget it. You coming with us, Mike?'

'Of course, ja, man.'

'Mike's a good juba,' Foxy smiled at the other two, slapping Michael Adonis on the back. 'You'll see. He going to be with us a long time.'

The boy with the ring put his cue aside and felt in the pockets of his trousers, while the other boy went on playing. He got out a packet of cigarette papers and extracted two leaves, returning the rest to the pocket. He arranged the leaves carefully, wetting the end of one and pasting it over an end of the other, thus joining the two into one long strip. He worked with the care of a surgeon performing a delicate operation. Then he formed the strip into a trench, holding it gently between the thumb and third finger of one hand, with the tip of the index finger in the hollow of the trench, keeping it in shape. With his other hand he got out a small cylinder of brown paper and bit off one end, and from it poured some of the dagga evenly along the length of the trench and then put the brown paper packet away. Next he got out a cigarette and split it with a thumbnail and scattered the tobacco from it onto the dagga, and then mixed the two carefully without spilling any. When he was satisfied he rolled the cigarette paper deftly into a tube, licked one edge with the tip of his tongue and pasted it down, pinched an end shut and stroked the tube caressingly into shape. Then he twisted the other end shut and put it in his mouth and lit it.

He took two long puffs at the dope and let the smoke out through his nostrils in long twin jets. Then he looked at Michael Adonis and said: 'Pull a skuif, pal?'

The other boy had stopped working at the billiard balls, poised over the table about to make a shot, but not finishing it, standing quite still as if a motion picture of him had suddenly been stopped, looking at Michael Adonis.

'Take a pull, pally,' the boy with the skull-and-crossbones ring said again.

'Why not, man?' Michael Adonis said, meeting his look, and reached out. He took a deep puff at the dagga and felt the floor move under him and the walls tilt, then settle back, and there was a light feeling in his head. He took another puff and handed it back to the boy.

'Come on,' Foxy said suddenly. 'That pill's going in a line. I'm next.'

When he had had his share and it had been passed on to the scarfaced boy he said: 'We better talk about this job. We got a car, too, and Toyer is going to drive.' He walked around the billiard table to the back of the room and seized the sleeping man by a shoulder, shaking. 'Come on, you bastard, wake up. Shake it up.'

The man grunted in his sleep, tried to turn over and then opened his eyes when Foxy slapped his face. He said: 'Whatter? Whatter? What goes on, man?'

'Come on. Come on. We got to talk business.'

The man sat up and rubbed his eyes. He asked: 'Sockies turn up?'

'Nay, man. We got another pally. Mikey, here.'

Toyer got to his feet and came towards the front of the room, looking at Michael Adonis. He said: 'Hoit, pally.'

'How's it?' Michael Adonis asked and giggled suddenly. He was feeling happy after the dagga.

The scarfaced boy at the billiard table said quickly: 'What's that?'

They all turned and looked at him. He was staring in front of him, holding the cue underarm, like a rifle, and listening.

'What the hell's the matter with you?' Foxy growled.

'Sounded like somebody shooting,' the scarfaced boy said.

'Shooting, shit,' Foxy said. 'Who's shooting?'

'Well, it sounded like somebody fired a gun,' the boy told him.

Foxy went to the door, unlocked it and went out. He stood on the pavement and looked up the street for a while. Then he came in again and relocked the door.

He said: 'What you think this is? The bio? Cowboys and crooks?'

'Well, I only said what I heard,' the scarfaced boy replied.

Then they all heard the sound. It sounded like a cannon craker going off far away, many blocks away in another part of the District. Later it came again, the flat sharp sound of a pistol shot.

SIXTEEN

The driver was glad that they were out of that smelly tenement again and back on patrol. At the same time he was somewhat irritated by the sullen presence of Constable Raalt who nursed gloomy thoughts about his wife. Driving the patrol van, he thought it has to be this one. I have to be put up all night with this one. He's got trouble with his wife, and what have I got to do with his troubles? What has his troubles got to do with this patrol? Let him leave his domestic troubles at home. He is dangerous, too, when he's like this and I don't want to get involved in anything. The way he behaved back there in that place, sneering and putting on in front of those hotnots. That's the way they lose respect. You've got to set an example with these people. Train them like dogs to have respect for you. If you whip them they'll turn on you. You've got to know how to handle these people. Pa knew how to handle these people. I wonder how he's getting on out there on the farm. He's got a lot of these hotnots working out in the orchards and the vineyards and he's never had any trouble with them. Give them some wine and drive them into town Saturday nights and they're all right.

He remembered the long bumpy drive through the wide rich farmlands at dusk in the lorry, swaying and rolling along the dirt roads with the dust boiling up behind in a long dark screen and the farm hands singing and shouting in the back, and the sky growing dark and purple with the first stars beginning to show and the crickets beginning to make their sounds. Only you couldn't hear the crickets then because of the noise of the lorry. Once one of the hands had fallen off the tailgate and they'd had to stop. He'd grazed his head and shoulder on the gravel and was half silly from shock, and the driver's father had cursed him for a *donder se bliksem* of a hotnot, and the others had looked on from the back of the lorry, laughing in the growing darkness. They had all called the driver *jong baas*, the young boss, and now and then he had joked with some of them, about their wives and daughters and sweethearts, and they always laughed and had never showed any resentment. For a while he had thought about sleeping with one of the meide, the girls, but he had never got around to it, and anyway, he thought that it would bring great dishonour upon himself, his family, and the volk if ever such a thing was done and discovered. There was a girl in the town who he liked very much, and to whom he now wrote occasional letters. He had not decided whether he was in love with her, for he considered himself a very serious young man and did not wish to fling himself headlong into marriage unless he was absolutely sure. She was beautiful, tall, and suntanned, with short curly blonde hair and merry eyes and long lovely legs, and he remembered her with some excitement. Still, he did not wish to get himself into the kind of mess Raalt was in, although, the driver thought, this girl was not a woman that would cause a man any misery. He wondered whether he ought to write to her and try to make things permanent, but this thought was interrupted suddenly by Raalt's harsh voice.

'Pull up, man.'

'What?' the driver asked with a start, jamming on the brakes.

'Isn't that not that donder se hotnot, the one with the yellow shirt?'

Constable Raalt was already opening the door and beginning to climb out when the driver looked ahead through the windshield and saw the Coloured boy caught in the glare of the headlights. He saw the brown anonymous face, the short kinky hair and the front of the yellow T-shirt and a jumble of thoughts sprawled through his mind, Yellow shirt; farmhands; hotnots; the lorry; I've got to write to her; that yellow shirt; yellow shirt; a young rooker with a yellow shirt, baas; and Constable Raalt was out of the van shouting:

'Hey, you bogger, stand still there.'

The driver climbed quickly out of the van, slamming the door, and he saw Raalt stepping towards the boy. The Coloured boy stood on the edge of the pavement, his feet widespread and his arms slightly spread, still frozen by the shock of the sudden appearance of the police van. Then the driver saw him duck suddenly as Raalt drew near and his body snapped into action like a released spring and he was going up the street fast.

'Stand still, jong,' Raalt shouted, and started off in pursuit.

The driver dashed after them, running hard. The boy was up ahead, weaving and sprinting, panic speeding him on, and the driver saw with a shock that Constable Raalt was unbuttoning his holster.

He drew up close to Raalt and shouted hoarsely: 'Moenie skiet nie, man. Don't shoot.'

But the pistol came up, its lanyard whipping, and then came the hard flat crack and the tongue of orange-yellow flame.

The boy darted suddenly sideways and was gone down a narrow lane, and when the two policemen reached it they were in time to see him bounding and leaping over piles of refuse and overturned dust-bins. Constable Raalt paused to fire again, but the driver was panting: 'Don't shoot. We'll get him. Keep after him, I'll take the van and circle the block.'

Raalt saw the boy reach the end of the lane and turn up the street beyond and he looked at the driver. What the driver saw in his eyes were what he thought were the fires of hell.

Constable Raalt said, spitting out the words: 'All right man, get the effing van and see if you can catch him.'

The driver dashed back along the street towards the patrol van, saying to himself, Don't let him shoot. I don't want any shooting. He's mad now and there's no knowing what he'll do. But don't let him shoot. Lord, don't let him shoot.

At the end of the lane Constable Raalt paused again, looking up the street. He saw no sign of the boy and started to run again. His wind was good and he was a trained sprinter, and he knew that usually these people did not last very long running. He told himself that the bliksem had probably tired after the first hard effort and had ducked in somewhere to hide. He dropped to a trot, his eyes scanning the rows of buildings on each side of the street.

People, attracted by the sound of the shot, were beginning to come into the street, but Raalt took no notice of them. Voices chattered and laughed, cursed, jeered, but Raalt passed up the street, his eyes restless, watching. He was a hunter now, stalking.

He found another alleyway half-way up the street and he stopped by it. Behind him the procession of onlookers came to a halt. He still had his revolver out and he turned to the crowd for the first time, waving it at them.

'Get back, you donders. You'll get hurt.'

After that he ignored them again and looked up the alleyway. It was a dead-end, running into a blank, plastered wall that was the back of another building. Against it was piled a collection of junk, rotting boxes and packing cases, ruined furniture and decaying mattresses and the usual dust-bins. Constable Raalt drew his flashlight with his left hand and sent the beam around the alley. Walls enclosed it on either side and he stepped forward between them.

He told himself that the boy in the yellow shirt couldn't have got very far down the street in the few moments he had been out of sight, and that he was probably hiding somewhere around. He could have come down an alley such as this one, and this was the first one off the street. Then he heard the sound of movement on the roofs above him, and he flicked off the light, his teeth showing slightly in a tight grin.

Constable Raalt started to mount the pile of rubbish that reached almost to the parapets of the buildings on each side of the alleyway. Behind him the crowd around the entrance of the alley began to scream warnings upwards and he cursed under his breath, looking backwards at them for a moment and climbing quickly. He kicked aside boxes and warped and rotten planking as he ascended, upsetting some of the stacked rubbish. He wondered vaguely where the driver had got to, but he was not concerned with him very much, preferring to hunt alone and undisturbed. He reached the top of the pile and heaved himself upwards to look over a parapet. He saw nothing but the uneven jumble of roofs, chimney-pots, and drain-pipes partly illuminated by the moonlight and street lamps.

Willieboy lay flat on his face, thrusting his body into the hard, unyielding surface of the roof. He felt the rough corru-gated iron against his chest through the shirt and coat, and the touch of something cold and metallic against his chin. There was a sour taste in his mouth and his head ached badly. Also, he was out of breath and his chest heaved and jerked from the wild dash down the street and the scramble onto this roof. There was a smell of cat droppings and urine around him. But he noticed none of these things for the cold clutch of fear deep down inside him.

He had dodged the police many times before, but never like this; neither had he been shot at, and he was afraid. He shiv-ered suddenly and his face puckered in the dark, the tears forming in his eyes. He thought, What they want to chase me for? What did I do? I did nothing. I did nothing. What they want to chase me for?

Lying there in the dark he felt the chill of his fear that was colder than the touch of metal or the breeze that had come up over the city.

He thought again, What did I do? I never did nothing. His mind jumped and he saw his mother standing over him, shout-ing: 'You been naughty again,' He was seven years old and had been selling the evening paper. The sub-agent for whom he hawked the papers had paid him a few pence commission he had earned and he had bought a big parcel of fish and chips instead of taking the money home. He had not eaten since early that morning, and then only a bowl of porridge without milk or sugar and a slice of stale bread, and by evening he was very hungry. He had gone home to the ramshackle room in a tenement with the smell of fish about him and when he could not produce his commission his mother slapped his face and shouted: 'You naughty little bastard.' She slapped him again and again so that his head jerked loosely on his shoulders and his face stung from the blows. He wept through the pain.

His mother beat him at the slightest provocation and he knew that she was wreaking vengeance upon him for the beat-

ings she received from his father. His father came home drunk
most nights and beat his mother and him with a heavy leather
belt. His mother crouched in a corner of the room and shrieked
and whimpered for mercy. When his father was through with
her he turned on Willieboy, but sometimes he managed to
escape from the room and did not return until late in the night
when the father was snoring drunkenly and his mother had
cried herself to sleep. His mother, unable to defend herself
against her husband, took revenge for her whippings on Willieboy.

Now he lay on the rooftop and heard her again, saying: 'You
naughty little bogger.'

He raised a hand and wiped the tears from his eyes. I've got
to get away, he told himself, I've got to get away. I don't want
to be shot. Please don't let me get shot.

He lay quite still and listened for sounds on the roof. Somewhere below people were shouting and talking, a jumble of
words. But he was not concerned about them. He peered ahead
around the end of a projection that crossed the roof in front of
his face, searching for any sign of the policeman. Once he
heard the crunch of a boot on the corrugated iron and fear
leapt in him and he tried to force himself into the hard metal
under his body. That law's somewhere out there waiting, he
thought. What they want to chase me for? I did nothing. You
should not have run, he told himself. Soon as you run they
come for you. Well I did nothing, I can give myself up. They
kicked the lights out of you. You think they going to chase you
all this way and on top of a roof and then just let you go? Us
poor bastards always get kicked around. If it's not the law it's
something else. Always there's somebody to kick you around.
What kind of blerry business is that? he asked himself with
remorse.

Then he heard the policeman's footsteps blundering around
on the iron of the roof as he came forward and Willieboy sprang
to his feet in fright and dashed for the far end of the row of
rooftops.

Constable Raalt had been crouching against an old and disused water tank, waiting for some sign of the boy. He knew for
sure that the boy was somewhere on that row of roofs and he
waited for him to show himself. Constable Raalt was determined to take his time about this. He had his quarry trapped

and he was quite sure that he would conclude the hunt successfully. He crouched there in the dark and smiled with satisfaction.

The water tank was on his left and a few feet to his right was a pigeon loft. He could hear the soft rustling sounds that came from inside it and smell the odour of bird-lime. Below in the street the crowd was moving about growling. For a moment he wondered what had happened to the driver, but he thrust the thought quickly from his mind along with every other thought and concentrated coldly on what he had to do there on the rooftops.

After a while he decided that he would move forward a little. He did not want to turn on the flashlight because he was enjoying this stalk in the dark. He took a long step forward and his face struck a clothes-line, the taut, stretched wire causing him to step back stumbling on the corrugated surface of the roof.

He cursed and ducked under the wire and it was then that he saw the dark form of the Coloured youth spring up from behind a projection ahead of him and start off, bounding across the roofs.

Raalt flung himself forward, firing as he did so. The flash of the pistol made a bright flare of light for a second and the bullet struck a drainpipe and sang off. Then Raalt was running across the roofs, his boots drumming the surface.

A roar went up from the crowd in the street below and a woman screamed shrilly. Raalt pounded on, leaping projections, holding his head low to evade the clothes-lines. He saw the boy poise himself for an instant on the edge of the far wall and drop out of sight.

Willieboy struck the asphalt below and the shock of the awkward drop jarred through his body. A hot stab of pain seared through an ankle and he screamed with pain, then he was stumbling and hobbling crookedly into the middle of the street with the crowd breaking back ahead of him. Then he saw another section of the mob split and the patrol van sweeping down on him.

He turned with fear and despair disfiguring his face, hearing the van screeching to a halt and seeing Constable Raalt drop expertly from the roof he had left. He stared bewilderedly about him. Then with the policemen moving on him from the

front and back he crouched like a fear-crazed animal at bay
and shouted hysterically at the one with the gun:

'You ... boer. You ... boer.'

He cursed Constable Raalt, unloading the obscenities like
one dumping manure and then reached frantically for the
pocket where he carried the sharpened kitchen-knife.

Before his hand reached the pocket and before he could discover that the knife was not there Constable Raalt fired again.

The bullet slapped into the boy, jerking him upright, and he
spun, his arms flung wide, turning on his toes like a ballet
dancer.

SEVENTEEN

The crowd roared again, the sound breaking against the
surrounding houses. They wavered for a while and then
surged forward, then rolled back, muttering before the cold
dark muzzle of the pistol. The muttering remained, the
threatening sound of a storm-tossed ocean breaking against a
rocky shoreline.

'Shot him in cold blood, the bastards.'

'They just know to shoot.'

'Is he dead?'

'How the hell do I know.'

'Move over, I want to see.'

'Shot him down in cold blood.'

'Awright, they'll get it, one day. You'll see.'

'Who is it, anyway?'

'Don't know. Some rooker they was chasing.'

'Must have been one of those skollies. Always interfering
with people. They all end up like that. Did he have a knife?'

'Shot the poor bastard in cold blood.'

'That's all they know. Shooting us people.'

'Move over, man, I also want to see mos.'

'Stop shoving. The bastards.'

The mutter of dark water eroding the granite cliffs, sucking
at the sand-filled cracks and dissolving the banks of clay.

The driver had a shocked look on his face and he said, his
voice cracking: 'What did you want to shoot for? We had him. I
could have got him from behind.'

Constable Raalt told him. 'What's the matter with you, Andries? Aren't you a policeman?' His eyes were hard and grey, like two rough pebbles in the dark, and his mouth was bitter.

The driver looked down at the boy. He lay groaning, holding himself where he had been shot, and a pool of blood was forming under him, spreading on the asphalt.

'Jesus, man,' the driver said. 'We'd better call an ambulance.'

'Ambulance,' Constable Raalt scoffed. 'Hell, we'll take the bliksem down to the station. They'll patch him up. He's not hurt so terribly.'

'I think we'd better call an ambulance,' the driver insisted nervously. He looked as if he was about to cry.

Then Willieboy suddenly screamed aloud. 'Oh mamma, oh, mamma,' he screamed. 'It hurts. Oh, my mamma, my mamma.'

The crowd surged forward again, growling, and then fell back under the hard, threatening muzzle of Constable Raalt's pistol. Somebody threw a tin can and it curved over the milling heads and struck the fender of the police van.

'You bastards,' Raalt shouted, waving the revolver. 'You bastards, you want to get shot, too?'

The driver was worried, and he said: 'Come on, man, let's go. Let's go.'

He looked down at the boy who had been shot. The front of the yellow shirt was dark with blood and there was some blood on the edge and lapels of his coat. He had fainted and in the light of the headlamps his face bore a stark, terrible look, the skin coarse and drawn tight so that the bone structure of the adolescent, undeveloped face showed gauntly, covered with a film of sweat.

The driver said: 'Christ, man, we'd better hurry up. Get him out of here. We ought to call an ambulance, I say.'

'Muck the ambulance,' Constable Raalt snapped. 'Load him in the back of the van and take him down to the station. They'll fix him up there, the bloody hotnot.'

'We'd better go,' the driver repeated impatiently. 'I don't like this crowd.'

'This crowd. A lot of bloody baboons. All right, man, let's get this bogger into the back. You take him by the feet.'

The driver stooped quickly and took the boy by his ankles. He was in a hurry to get away from there, and felt nervous and anxious. Raalt bent over the boy's head and gripped the collar of his coat, hauling him roughly into a sitting position. His other hand still held the pistol, and his eyes watched the murmuring crowd. The driver raised the boy and they carried him, his limp body sagging in the middle like a half-empty sack, to the back of the van. Around them the crowd rolled forward again and the driver prayed that there wouldn't be any more shooting. He told himself that Raalt was crazy to have shot the youth and that there would probably be a hell of a lot of trouble over this.

They got the double doors of the van open and bundled the unconscious boy into the back. In his hurry to get away the driver pushed and thrust him quickly, so that he rolled and flopped on the bed of the van, groaning. They slammed the doors and came around to the driving cabin, Raalt still holding the gun, watching the sullen crowd.

The driver was in the cabin first, fumbling with the ignition in his hurry and grinding the gears. Beside him Constable Raalt holstered his pistol and the van moved forward into the crowd. The driver was still scared and nervous and he caused the van to bounce and jerk, scattering the people around it and raising an uproar. Fists thumped on the metal bodywork and a shower of brickbats rained suddenly down on it, but the driver got the vehicle under control and ploughed slowly through the mob.

EIGHTEEN

'You was naughty again,' his mother shouted and slapped his face so that pain leapt through him. He stood against the door jamb of the ugly room, rubbing one stubby-toed bare foot against the instep of the other and wept, wiping his running nose on the ragged, filthy sleeve of his Khaki shirt.

The inside of the van was dark and there was no sound but the purr of the motor. There was something cold and metallic against his cheek, which conjured up a vague recollection of rooftops, but he did not know what it was, nor did he attempt to find out. He did not move his head and did not try to wipe his running nose. The effort was too much for him, and when he moved his head he vomited and his head spun so that he would go into a coma. So he rode with the pain that lapped at him. It was a dull formless pain that caressed him, trembling through his body with the throbbing of the van's engine. There was another pain in his ankle but it had the feeling of being apart from the rest of his body.

He wanted to get up and go home, but he decided there was no point in going home because his father would only beat him again. He'd go down to the Daffodil Club and play some billiards, or get a drink. He could do with a drink. His head ached and he had a very bad hangover, and there was this pain rolling backwards and forwards, up and down inside him, like a loose, heavy iron bearing in a cylinder.

Through the dull pain the coldness against his cheek was irritating and he decided to turn his head in order to discover what caused it. It was caused by one of the metal strips that were fixed on the floor of the van, but before he could realize that, he choked and bile filled his mouth, welling up and bursting from the corner of his lips. He tried to sit up, but could not, and the bile receded into his throat so that he retched and the pain lanced him as his body twitched and he screamed and fainted.

The patrol van was in Hanover Street again, passing between the rows of locked shops with their lighted glass box-signs and price-cards and the peeling placards, and above them the rows of shabby rooms behind painted-over glass doors and splintering and reinforced balconies; past the dark public houses and black caverns of tenement hallways, the cafés with dim lights behind the beaded curtains and soda-fountain parlours with late customers sipping bottled drinks, leaning against the marble-topped counters and the display stands; past the street corners where the knots of youths lounged, smoking and laughing, the laughter breaking off to be replaced by silent stares in the dark as the police cruised by; past the neon sign that said Coca-Cola, Coca-Cola, Coca-Cola over and over throughout the night.

Constable Raalt felt in his tunic pocket for his cigarettes and found that he had none. He said: 'Pull up at the Portuguese, will you? I want to get some smokes.'

'Jesus, man,' the driver said. 'We haven't got time to get cigarettes. We've got to get this jong to the station.'

'Ach, there's lots of time, man. That bastard isn't going to die yet. These hotnots are tough. Stop at the damn café, man.'

The driver shook his head. He was worried and nervous and a little frightened, but he knew that it was no use arguing with Raalt. He said: 'Well, it's your responsibility then,' thereby purging himself of all blame for whatever had happened or might happen afterwards. Constable Raalt looked sideways at him, and smiled, curling his lips from his teeth.

The driver shook his head again and did not look at Raalt, but he slowed down and brought the van to a stop.

'Don't be long, man,' he said keeping his eyes away from Constable Raalt's face. He heard Raalt climbing out, slamming the door of the cabin and cross the pavement into the restaurant.

In the back of the van Willieboy had come to with the small jolt the stopping had made. He awoke with the faint smell of petrol and carbon-monoxide in his nostrils. It made him retch again and he shook until the retching turned to weeping and he cried, the sobs wrenching at him, jerking the pain through his abdomen. He reached down to where the pain was worst and felt the wet stickiness of his clothes and then the bleeding mouth of the wound where the bullet had torn through him, smashing into his insides. Then he seemed to realize for the first time what had happened to him.

'Help! Oh, God, help me! Oh, mamma, oh, mamma. Oh, Lord Jesus, save me. Save me. I'm dying! I'm dying! Save me. Save me. Oh, Christ, help me. Help me. Help me. Please. Help me. God. Jesus, Mother. Help me! help me!'

His screams crashed against the sides of the van, confined within the metal walls. His father's leather belt whistled and snapped through the air, its sharp edge ripping at his legs and buttocks, the pain jumping through him.

Constable Raalt had entered the café. The place was quiet and there were only a few people scattered in the booths and at the long table down the middle of the room. Heads and eyes glanced at him before returning to the chipped cups, the bottles of icy soft drinks and the stale doughnuts. A taxi-driver read the evening paper and did not look up from it when Raalt came in. The fat proprietor behind the counter wiped its marble top and nodded at the constable.

'Hullo,' Raalt said, grinning and pushing his cap back on his head. 'Give us a packet of twenties, please.'

The fat man dropped the package of cigarettes on the counter and asked: 'How's things, meneer?'

'So so,' Constable Raalt told him. 'Always blerry trouble with the skollies up here.'

He broke open the packet and worked a cigarette out of it,

stuck it in his mouth and searched for his matches. The Portuguese pushed a box over towards him and he lit the cigarette, puffing.

'Always got trouble with those skollies,' the proprietor said. 'Me, I've got me a nice fish-club under this counter. They don't mess with me. Just the other night a bogger came in here. . . . ' He began to relate the incident which had taken place.

While they were talking the door opened again and the driver came in. He was looking frightened and his young face had a shocked expression on it.

He said to Raalt: 'We must go, man. That jong . . . '

'What's the hurry?' the café proprietor asked, leaning his thick arms on the counter.

Constable Raalt said: 'We've got one of those blerry skollies in the wagon.' To the driver he said: 'What are you looking so troubled about, man?'

'Look, Raalt,' the driver said. 'That jong . . . we'd better get him to the station quickly, man.'

'Hell,' Raalt said maliciously.

The proprietor asked amiably: 'Would you gents like a Coke?'

Willieboy allowed himself to ride with the pain. It was not so bad any more and had taken a dull, numbing character. He felt cold, however, and wished that his mother would spare another blanket to warm him. The rain beat against the window of the tenement room and he shivered under the thin scrap of blanket on the floor. On the bed his father and mother slept together in a bulky jumble. Once his mother woke up and turning her head shouted at him to stop complaining. He said: 'I'm cold, ma,' but received no further reply.

Delirium was an anaesthetic and he no longer felt pain. But his fingers and hands seemed to have thickened and begun to lose all sense of feeling, so that even when he knew that he moved them over his body they did not seem to touch anything. They were like thick, swollen, lifeless things. Also he had difficulty in seeing the darkness inside the van, and there was a high-pitched ringing sound running through his brain.

'They's always kicking a poor bastard around,' he said, and was surprised at the loudness and clarity of his voice. He tried to look through the darkness but the power of sight had gone from his eyes. They remained open although he could no longer see. Then his mouth was suddenly full of bile and blood and he tasted the sourness and the salt for an infinitesimal instant before he was dead.

NINETEEN

Now, after midnight, it was cooler. A breeze had sprung up out of the south-east and stirred the hot air, but the stars remained bright, flickering and shimmering so that the sky was alive with them. In the gutters of the District ragged ends of paper stirred and whispered in the breeze and in the windows of the sweaty tenements, greasy curtains undulated. On the sagging bedsteads and the cramped staircases the sleeping moved and turned in their slumber, sensing the coolness in the air. If the breeze held on and strengthened it would develop into the old summer South-easter by the morning.

At the Club the painted glass doors rattled gently and Foxy commented idly: 'I reckon she's going to blow tomorrow.'

'We'd better blow ourselves,' the youth with the skull-and-crossbones ring said. 'We going to stand here all blerry night?'

'Awright. Awright,' Foxy said. 'Let's go then.' He looked at Toyer and asked: 'You sure the car's okay?'

'It's okay, man,' Toyer replied. He was feeling sleepy and yawned loudly. 'Parked around the block.'

'Well, we better blow.' Foxy smiled at Michael Adonis and winked.

'You ready, pally?'

'Naturally. Why not? What about these scared boggers?'

'Who's scared?' the boy with the scarred face asked. Then added sullenly: 'Your mother, man.'

'And yours too, pally,' Michael Adonis said, smiling, and led the way to the door.

They all went out and Foxy turned off the lights and locked the door. He stood on the pavement with the rest of them and looked up at the sky. 'Ja,' he announced. 'It's going to blow.'

From a crack under the skirting-board in a dark room a cockroach emerged cautiously, feeling through the gloom with its antennae, the fine hairlike wands waving this way and that, searching for an obstruction. Finding none, the cockroach moved forward on its jointed, angled legs, crossing the floor, stepping over the tiny hedges caused by the splintered sides of the floorboards. It encountered some stickiness and it tasted the mixture of spilled liquor and vomit on the floor of the room of the slain old man. The old man's body had been removed earlier and the room locked by the police, and now the cockroach was alone in it, with the smell of decay and death. The cockroach paused over the stickiness and a creaking of boards somewhere startled it, sending it scuttling off with tiny scraping sounds across the floor. After a while the room was silent again and it returned and commenced to gorge itself.

In a downstairs room John Abrahams lay with his face towards the wall. He could not sleep and he stared at the dim blankness near his eyes. He had not undressed and he could smell the sweatiness of his clothes and the staleness of the ruin that was his body. He thought dully, What's it help you, turning on your own people? What's it help you? He kept on thinking the same thought over and over again, so that after a while he did not have to put any more effort into thinking because the thought just went on and on its own, What's it help you? What's it help you? What's it help you?

Somewhere the young man Joe made his way towards the sea, walking alone through the starlit darkness. In the morning he would be close to the smell of the ocean and wade through the chill, comforting water, bending close to the purling green surface and see the dark undulating fronds of seaweed, writhing and swaying in the shallows, like beckoning hands. And in the rock pools he would examine the mysterious life of the sea things, the transparent beauty of starfish and anemone, and hear the relentless, consistent pounding of the creaming waves against the granite citadels of rock.

Franky Lorenzo slept on his back and snored peacefully. Beside him the woman, Grace, lay awake in the dark, restlessly waiting for the dawn and feeling the knot of life within her.

JOURNALS

NESTOR PAZ

Néstor Paz was born in 1945 in Sucre, Bolivia. Though he came from a comfortable upper-middle-class family—his father was first a general in the Bolivian Armed Forces and then governor of Sucre—Néstor was deeply affected by the plight of the poor and oppressed in his country. As a young student he was strongly influenced by the examples of Camilo Torres and Che Guevara and dedicated his life to the struggle to end oppression and bring about revolutionary change. He was deeply religious and strove throughout his brief life to synthesize his Christian beliefs with Marxist thought.

Néstor Paz joined the National Liberation Army (ELN) in July of 1970 and died of starvation on October 8, 1970. His campaign journal, from which we reprint selections here, is written mainly in the form of letters to his young wife, Cecy.

The editors of the journal, Ed Garcia and John Eagleson, speak of its significance: "The Campaign Journal is ... more than just an extraordinary document of a revolutionary engaged in armed struggle. For anyone who reads the moving account with openness and. honesty, the Campaign Journal poses an unsettling challenge—a challenge which questions the direction of one's life and the worth of one's cause. Because Néstor Paz speaks with his life, and because his message is written in blood, his message cannot be ignored."

On the last page of Francisco's campaign journal, Omar, the Marxist leader of the small surviving group and Francisco's cousin, briefly noted:

Néstor Paz Zamora, "Francisco,"
died on October 8th at 12 noon.
Cousin: You have given me the greatest lesson
of love for mankind.
Thank you.
Omar.

Selections from My Life for my Friends: The Guerrilla Journal of Néstor Paz, Christian

Message of Néstor Paz on Leaving to Join the Guerrillas in Teoponte, July 17, 1970

"Every sincere revolutionary must realize that armed struggle is the only path that remains" (Camilo Torres, January 7, 1966).[1]

Following the glorious path taken by our own heroes, the guerrillas of the Peruvian highlands, and by the continental heroes, Bolívar and Sucre, and the heroic commitment of Ernesto Guevara, the Peredo brothers, Darío,[2] and many others who lead the march of the people's liberation, we take our place in the long guerrilla file, rifle in hand, to combat the symbol and instrument of oppression—the "gorilla" army.[3]

As long as blood flows in our veins we will make heard the cutting cry of the exploited. Our lives do not matter if we can make our Latin America, *la patria grande*, a free territory of free people who are masters of their own destiny.

I realize that my decision and that of my companions will bring upon us a deluge of accusations, from the paternalistic "poor misguided fellow," to the open charge of "demagogic criminal." But Yahweh our God, the Christ of the Gospels, has announced the "good news of the liberation of man," for which he himself acted. We cannot sit and spend long hours reading the Gospel with cardinals, bishops, and pastors, all of whom are doing fine right where they are, while the flock wanders about in hunger and solitude. Doing this is called "nonviolence," "peace," "Gospel." These persons, sadly, are today's Pharisees.

People no longer listen to the "Good News." Man is always betrayed by his "brother."

"Peace" is not something one finds by chance; it is the result of equality among people, as Isaiah says in his chapter 58. Peace is the result of love among people, the result of an end to exploitation.

"Peace" is not attained by dressing up in silk and living in a medieval palace, or by robbing the people in order to have a millionaire's salary, or by playing on the people's religious superstition in order to live at their expense.

"Greater love than this no man has than to lay down his life for his friends." This is the commandment which sums up the "Law."

For this reason we have taken up arms: to defend the unlettered and undernourished majority from the exploitation of a minority and to win back dignity for a dehumanized people.

We know that violence is painful because we feel in our own flesh the violent repression of the established disorder. But we are determined to liberate man because we consider *him a brother*. We are the people in arms. This is the only path that remains. Man comes before the "Sabbath," not vice versa.

They say violence is not evangelical; let them remember Yahweh slaying the first-born of the Egyptians to free his people from exploitation.

They say that they believe in "non-violence." Then let them stand clearly with the people. If they do, the rich and the "gorillas" will both demand their lives, just as they demanded Christ's. Let them take courage and try it; let us see if they are consistent enough to face a Good Friday. But all that is demagoguery, isn't it, you canons, generals, *cursillistas*,[4] priests of the established disorder, you priests of the peace enforced by violence, of the massacre of San Juan,[5] of the complicity of silence, of the 200-peso salaries, of the widespread tuberculosis, and of pie in the sky when you die. The Gospel is not mechanical moralism. It is a shell hiding a "life" which must be discovered if we are not to fall into pharisaism. The Gospel is "Jesus among us."

We have chosen this path because it is the only path left open to us, painful though it may be.

Fortunately, there are some, and their numbers are growing, who recognize the authenticity of our position and who either help us or have joined our ranks. We need only consider what the right-wing "gorilla" government of Brazil does to a committed Church: Father Pereira Neto was assassinated in a most cruel and inhuman manner.[6] Or recall Father Ildefonso, a Tupamaro, assassinated in Uruguay. Or Father Camilo Torres, silenced by the government and the servile church. But Camilo Torres ratified with his blood what he had said about Christianity:

In Catholicism the main thing is love for one's fellow men: " . . . He who loves his fellow man has fulfilled the Law." For this love to be genuine, it must seek to be effective. If works of beneficence, almsgiving, the few tuition-free schools, the few housing projects—everything which is known as "charity"—do not succeed in feeding the majority of the hungry, in clothing the majority of the naked, or in teaching the majority of the ignorant, then we must seek effective means to achieve the well-being of this majority. . . . This is why the revolution is not only permissible but obligatory for those Christians who see it as the only effective and far-reaching way to make love for all people a reality.[7]

I believe that taking up arms is the only effective way of protecting the poor against their present exploitation, the only effective way of generating a free man.

I believe that the struggle for liberation is rooted in the prophetic line of Salvation History.

Enough of the languid faces of the over-pious! The whip of justice, so often betrayed by elegant gentlemen, will fall on the exploiter, that false Christian who forgets that the force of his Lord ought to drive him to liberate his neighbor from sin, that is to say, from every lack of love.

We believe in a "New Man," made free by the blood and resurrection of Jesus. We believe in a New Earth, where love will be the fundamental law. This will come about, however, only by breaking the old patterns based on selfishness. We don't want patches. New cloth can't be used to mend old garments, nor can new wine be put into old wineskins. Conversion implies first an inner violence which is then followed by violence against the exploiter. May both men and the Lord together judge the rightness of our decision. At least no one can imply that we look for profit or comfort. These are not what we find in the struggle; they are what we leave behind.

The Lord said, "He who loves father or mother more than me is not worthy of me, and he who loves son or daughter more than me is not worthy of me" (Matthew), and "He who does not hate even his own life cannot be my disciple" (Luke). We believe that the Lord is referring to the person tied to his "own little world" and his "own little problems." The "other person" is out there beyond our "own comfort."

There are those who defend themselves with lyrical discourses about the "revolution"; yet at the moment of truth, because of their cowardice, they take the side of the oppressor.

The sin of "omission" is the fault of our Church, just as it was of the "lukewarm" members (Rev. 3:14–22), just as it is of those who do not want "to get their hands dirty." We don't want to bequeath to our children a vision of life based upon competition as a means of possession, or on possessions as a measure of man's value.

We believe in a man who has value for who he is, and not for what he has. We believe in a completely liberated man who will live and build brotherly structures through which love may be expressed.

I am certain that we can achieve this goal, for the Lord "is ready to give us far more than all we can ask or think" (Ephesians 3:20).

"The duty of every Christian is to be a revolutionary. The duty of every revolutionary is to bring about the revolution."[8]

Victory or Death.

Francisco

Sunday, July 26

My dear princess,[9]

I'm sitting at the foot of a very steep sandstone hill waiting for the minutes to pass by before suppertime.

Yesterday marked our first week in this new life. First of all, I want to tell you I've missed you as part of my being, my very substance. Things are going well in spite of the fact that we have in the same band seventy different individuals.[10]

I'm going to play cards. I'll be back soon.

There was no card game, but I spent the time talking to Choco. He's completely discouraged and can't take it anymore. I tried to encourage him. I think I helped a little. Our biggest problem is to feel that we are protected by our comrades and closely related to them.

When we left Teoponte I was terribly sad. I began needing you. In this place I didn't find the one I love, the one who has never let me down—and this made me panicky, afraid.

We are getting ourselves together as a group, and this is the most difficult stage. Yesterday we went down to a poor town to buy a few things. We are behind the town of Guanay. We talked with some peasants who were friendly enough and willing to lend us a hand. Our feast of pork was good, with some bananas and yucca. Today, I think, we'll eat roasted corn. We miss food a lot, and the most wretched morsel seems like a great delicacy.

I am well, and things are beginning to take shape. Yesterday two of our men got lost. I prayed for them. Today they found their way back.

I hope my ability to love continues to grow at the same rate as my ability as a guerrilla fighther. It is the only way of qualitatively improving the revolutionary spirit.

I think of you a lot and I love you.

July 30, 10:30 A.M.

I'm taking advantage of this rest period to write you. We're doing fine. I think of nothing but you. I'm beginning to pray with a basis and a foundation, and this unites me with everything that is ours, besides providing me with the dimension of the Lord Jesus.

Yesterday eight men left us, the first ones to crack. One of them was Choco. I gave him some things for you in case he gets the chance to give them to you. I especially asked him to encourage you to keep on going, because this is the most practical way of expressing our love for each other. I asked him to tell you that I am strong and loving you more every day.

The column is being purified to a great extent, although I think that more will be leaving. We have not clashed with the army, but we are about to. We've learned about Ovando's son.[11]

The words in that *zamba* song are true: "Everything I look at, we've already seen together." Everything here reminds me of you—everything you've prepared for me with so much affection. All my equipment is complete, thanks to you. I have everything I need.

I have great confidence in the coming victory and in the ability of the men to achieve it, although I doubt that many of us will see it.

I miss you and I love you totally. I never thought we could be so together as we are now. To become as one.

Anyhow, we've done all we could, don't you think? Even if I die, I know that I'm one with you. The Resurrection now has a real meaning in my life, and it is no longer just a "truth." I want to grow in depth and penetrate more profoundly into "life" and "man." I want to reach the point of total humanization. This is the vocation of my life and definitely our fulfillment.

My closest companions are those of the first squad of the vanguard. They are excellent men, and almost all of us have learned to get along well together.

Yesterday we had a delicious meal and ate like mad. It's funny how every bite has an "inexhaustible" worth. We're on to "something" here. We've stopped the march.

August 1

Today is "the day,"[12] right, princess? One more anniversary. I remember you with a special affection. I love you.

I had two difficult days before yesterday. We had two favorable encounters with the army, but I had to revise my whole way of thinking. It probably had to do with the violence, the commitment, the meaning of the struggle, the value of a sacrifice, the effectiveness of our troops, etc., and at the root of all this, your absence. I thought about it, and it made me bitter. But I grew. It was really hard to leave behind the model of the "old man" and exchange it for the model of a "new man." All growth means pain, and this is what I felt. Growth also means not being sure if these are the paths of the Lord. But today I am more at peace, more calm, and I've made a resolution that I'm determined to keep:

First, I am in this struggle until victory or death.

Second, this is the path on which history advances; there is no other.

Third, if this is so, then this is Christian, especially if we keep in mind the prophetic role of Camilo Torres.

Fourth, being here I am more fully with you because we are fulfilling the ideal of our lives.

I remember you once again and the parties at Muda García's place, the motorcycle, the Sunday mornings, our first kiss, every happy moment we spent together—and the tragic ones too. I better not keep thinking about all these things because it makes me want to be by your side, and that is not bad.

Things are going well. We've already gone through our baptism of fire. The prospects are excellent, and only our own shortcomings and weakness can make them change. These first three months are decisive. Afterward I think everything will go better. I have begun praying with more fulness and confidence.

Well, I'll leave you for now. I love you. Oh, by the way, I lost my cap with the cross on it and the handkerchief with the words "Everything and always." You'll make me a new one, won't you?

Sunday, August 2

We've started the march, and it's already 10:30 A.M. The men are very tired, and I think it's because we don't have any good food. Our main dish every day is one or two spoonfuls of boiled rice with salt. Sometimes we have dried meat, sometimes we don't. This is making us very weak. I'm already feeling some pain and fatigue in my legs. Other than this, my body has served me well.

It seems that the eight men who left us the other day were killed. They were not armed and were killed in cold blood. Before he left, Choco left me the photo which we had taken together in San Pedro.

That's how things are going. We are looking for sources of supplies and ways to strike at the army.

Yesterday all of us who had not done it before swore an oath before a picture of Che Guevara. It will be a day of double memories for me—a double pledge of love for you and love for the revolution. Deep down they are the same thing.

We've been apart for two weeks, and today I was looking again at your picture and your little note. What you tell me is so incredibly beautiful that I get a lump in my throat every time I read it. I love you. I hope the time flies by so that I can see you or at least get to some place where I can hear some news from you. For now, I trust that you are well. I can imagine how worried you all must be, the folks and Mario and Jaime,[13] etc. What bothers me most is that I can't be in touch with all of you. But I better not keep on thinking of these things because it just makes matters worse. We have come to a beautiful sandstone mountain and a quiet woods, dry and filled with small fruits. It was our Sunday walk. I thought of you and how nice it would be to take a walk here with you.

Wednesday, August 12

My adorable love, we're taking a short rest now during our long march. It's 10:40 and we're about to enter into a new stage of the guerrilla campaign. We've more or less finished our training, and now we'll see who's taken advantage of it and how. We'll be going into the Valley of Mapiri where there is a concentration of the military and peasants.

It's 11:50 and we have seen fields with a few houses. I make note of this for two reasons: First, because it means a bad beginning to the struggle. We'll have to face the peasants' inconsistency, the mountains, and the army—and all at once. Second, because there is FOOD there. It's funny how you can risk your own skin for a little corn, a pig or some other animal, yucca, bananas, a corn cake or any other little thing. The truth is that not only do we have empty stomachs, but we're weak, and that makes it really tough when we walk all day as we've usually been doing all this time. . . . It seems we have to cross the river. The army might be on the other side, or at least that seems most logical.

The men's faces are saying, "Let's stop." Since we saw the fields it's clear to everybody that a little meat with toasted corn, some fried bananas and yucca, would be a dish worthy of the Hotel Crillón.

The day after tomorrow is another anniversary, right?[14] I'll make a note of it so I won't forget. I don't even want to imagine your reaction to an oversight of such magnitude.

The education of the will is really essential if you haven't been concerned with it before. This week we've had the loss of cans of preserves—condensed milk, sardines, corned beef—and the men reported them as if they had been lost or stolen. But now some have confessed their weakness to the leader. It makes me really mad to know that some bastard either by himself or with somebody else can down a can of condensed

milk and deprive four or five comrades of such vital suste-
nance. But at least they recognized their own weakness. The
punishments have been given, and we hope that these things
don't happen again. Che ordered a combatant shot in the
Sierra for stealing food. I'm not saying that we should take
such a drastic measure, since I don't think it would be the best
thing for us to do here, but I don't think the idea should be
rejected if the offense is serious.

I feel well and in good spirits. My whole being, my body and
soul, my mind and all that I am, have come together. I'm a
leaven, but one that works steadily. At least that's the feeling I
have. A great peace and a great calm fill me completely. In a
vital way I'm even moving from the idea of "death" as a
diminishment to the reality of "death" as fulness, and I am
moving into a new dimension. I'm not seeking death, not in any
way, but if it comes I'll meet it with the peace and calm that
such a moment deserves, and I'll even ask them to report that
I've gone to the Father, that "Come, Lord Jesus" has become
real in me. If there's any shadow in all of this, it's you, your
absence. I won't even say that it's physical, for I feel you
within me, and this makes me a little anxious. How I'd like to
share all this with you, but that time will come. I haven't lost
hope.

Saturday, August 15

Feast of the Virgin. I'm in an ambush. I think we're going to
meet the army face to face. I'll write you later. I love you. I miss
you terribly. We've already been hiding here for three hours.
There's nothing abnormal, except that I'm sitting on an ant-
hill, and they really bite.

Sunday, August 16

How are things, my dear princess?

We're on the move again, knapsacks on our backs and eyes
ready to spot the enemy. We've had four or five unusual days.
Fantastic! We went into a small town and rested, ate, and
relaxed our spirits. For the first time in my life my stomach

seems like it's dancing, jumping around like a madman. Yesterday morning we left the town, and in the afternoon the planes came. It seems that they've gotten some information.

They bombed and machine-gunned quite close to where we were camped. Our group is disorganized. Morale is down, and this really worries me. It's not that anything serious has happened, but in different ways and circumstances the men are reacting aggressively, neurotically. I think that there is still a great crisis of faith among us, a crisis in the complete confidence needed in the command group and in their ability to bring this war to a successful end. I sincerely think they are capable, although there's no denying their lack of experience, especially in ordinary, everyday organizational details. But otherwise they've acted with clear vision and awareness of what they were doing and the decisions they were making.

I think that we're going to be fighting, most importantly in circumstances advantageous to us. This will either reduce certain problems or make them more serious, especially the problems of a personal nature which we have been dragging along with us. There's no doubt we still need a strong catalyst, as we would have had in Inti, Ricardo, or Pombo, or even. . . . [15] But I don't think that this has any direct relation to the degree of commitment to the revolutionary ideal that the troops demand of themselves.

I'm well and I think the others can see this, since in general they have nothing against me and I even think they respect me. If I can develop certain aspects of my life as a guerrilla, and prove I've developed by my deeds, that is, by my daily consistency, I think I'll be able to help the troops even more. I'm telling you all this because I want to continue with the kind of sincerity we've always had. To be an open book for each other. It's not that I have a great desire for promotions, but if I have something to contribute I want to do it completely. "My eternal vocation of service" is fashioned again here, a kind of priesthood—not ritual or externally sacramental—but very rich in concrete possibilities for love.

Omar told me that they were proposing my name as "political officer" in the column. This is a post which is based completely on the moral strength of the comrade who holds it. We'll see. If I get the post, I'd like to earn it either in combat or right here, after a while spent in this everyday life itself.

Guerrilla life is really a convergence point of many different dimensions and concerns. It is here that the most intimate part of each person comes into play, his metaphysical being, his personal complexity, his shortcomings and strengths, in a word, his everything.

It's exciting, but it also makes me very afraid. Because if it's not well-directed and channeled the whole thing can turn into a nuthouse.

But in and beyond all this—I LOVE YOU. Today we would be sleeping and getting ready to listen to "Agitando Pañuelos" on Radio Altiplano. Princess, it's incredible how I love you. Every time I repeat these words I find them more and more meaningful and real.

In general the people in the towns have received us well, at least they helped us in every way we asked them (always in exchange for money, of course). I wish I was in charge of this so that our conscientization efforts would have been presented as simply as possible, so that we would have a chance of coming back again, resting, leaving behind one of our sick or wounded.[16]

Men are still leaving. Yesterday another disappeared. I think we'll still have a big shake-up. I hope it finds us well prepared.

The national situation seems to be in our favor: It's a shame we don't have a good communications network. Okay, I'll leave you for now. I'm sleepy.

Monday, August 17

We're ready to begin the march. Yesterday we made a trail, a long one so we'll be able to move ahead fast, even with the mule and the small bull we have with us. We don't know what to expect since the army must be trying to surround us. I just hope we meet them so we can better define our real capabilities and test our morale. And I hope we meet them under good conditions for us so that our evaluations can be clear and genuine.

I'm happy, my love. We're moving ahead with confidence on a qualitative level. Yesterday I read a little of the Apostles, their first steps, their hesitations, their discoveries, their cowardice, their confidence in the "triumph." It gave me new courage and strengthened my desire to be in the vanguard, to be a prophet of a people on the march. I especially liked the summary made by Stephen, the first Christian martyr of salvation history. It tells of the deeds of liberation, God's presence in history, and Stephen's unbreakable faith and desire to discover the Lord beyond the shadows.

We're in a dry thicket. I think we're climbing again. We'd gone down to an altitude of 400 meters and in our previous excursions we've gone up to 1500. We've already spent a month which has been really productive in experiences and contact with real situations. Maybe tomorrow or a little later on I can give you a summary and an analysis.

Tuesday, August 18

It's been a full month, dear princess. Yesterday we missed our chance to score our first victory. We planned an ambush, but because of our carelessness and negligence the soldiers detected the trap and didn't enter the area. Today I don't know what the command group will decide, whether to move away from the enemy or wait to strike them even though they are already alerted.

This month's experience has helped us a lot. As I told you before, we've come to know each other quite well, our weaknesses, our strengths, and our real possibilities. I think it's been a positive experience, because it's turned out well for us, both in the operations we planned and unforeseen situations. We've noted who is strong and who is weak and who hasn't progressed. There are some who can be salvaged, but there are others who almost surely are lost. Some will leave us at any moment or will give us some kind of surprise, which I hope won't be unpleasant.

Personally I'm doing fine. I'm clear in what I'm doing, and, I think, convinced of everything that all this means. My life has a goal that is well marked out, and I feel sure that I'm heading toward it with great and complete confidence in what I'm doing, both personally and communally. As for our prospects, I think they're good. But they could be better because we are not yet fully capable of catalyzing the people. This is directly related to our internal and external effectiveness, things which have been affecting us recently.

My life with the Lord has deepened, and I think we're overcoming that "old man," who is like a snare keeping me from moving ahead and tangling up my path every time I am careless. Later I'll tell you more, but now I'm going to read Che.[17]

Saturday, September 5

My love: We have come to a stop in our march. We heard some shots to our left, but we don't know exactly where they came from.

I've been with you constantly. These days have been very intense, charged with meaning. They might be our last—or the first of our victory. I think more of the second possibility because, analyzing things coldly, I think we still have good chances. In the midst of our group we have an excellent "family" life. In Black Omar especially I've found a brother more than a comrade. This reassures me and gives me tremendous confidence. The political situation is very good, but we're a little tied up by our own situation.

Allende won in Chile, and this opens up great possibilities. If in Latin America an entire people is capable of choosing socialism, it means that the conditions are established—no doubt about it.

I LOVE YOU. I'll write again soon.

Tuesday, September 8

My love: We find ourselves in an interesting situation. There are twenty-three of us left. At last we're ready for ANYTHING. We have a tight-knit column. Yesterday we had our first political session, with a talk, an analysis of the situation, and some readings. I directed it, my debut as political officer. It was very profitable, and we came to some clear-cut conclusions on our goals. There were contributions from comrades like Kolla, peasants who gave their points of view on rural conditions and the reactions of the people who work in the fields.

Others contributed in the same way, and Chato summarized the discussion. It was a good start.

Things are going well in the midst of the drama of the moment. On the one hand, we know what we have created as catalysts within the national situation. On the other hand, we also know how tough a blow our physical annihilation would be to the cause and how much of the effort would collapse with our defeat.

My own life is going well. I was happy to find a New Testament which one of the men was carrying with him. It's like gold. As a group we have reached a certain level of intimacy. Besides having a good friend in Black Omar, there are two others from Tarija, Jesús and the Chapaco Adrián. There's also the old group of priceless friends like Quiridito, Rogelio, Omar, and the others.

Something good will come out of this, something truly good that will change the future history of this country.

I miss you terribly. How I wish we could live through this more closely together so we could grow in it, even though what you are doing is the same thing.

Saturday, September 12

My dear Lord: It's been a long time since I've written. Today I really feel the need of you and your presence. Maybe it's because of the nearness of death or the relative failure of our struggle. You know I've always tried to be faithful to you in every way, consistent with the fulness of my being. That's why I'm here. I understand love as an urgent demand to solve the problem of the other—where you are.

I left what I had and I came. Maybe today is my Holy Thursday and tonight will be my Good Friday. Into your hands I surrender completely all that I am with a trust having no limits, because I love you. What hurts me most is perhaps leaving behind those I love the most—Cecy and my family —and also not being able to experience the triumph of the people, their liberation.

We are a group filled with authentic humanity, "Christian" humanity. This, I think, is enough to move history ahead. This encourages me. I love you, and I give to you all that I am and all that we are, without measure—because you are my Father.

Nobody's death is useless if his life has been filled with meaning, and I believe ours has been.

Ciao, Lord, perhaps until we meet in your heaven, that new land that we yearn for so much.

My dear love: Just a few lines for you. I don't have the energy for any more. I have been tremendously happy with you. It hurts me deeply to leave you alone, but if I must, I will. I'm here till the end, which is Victory or Death.

I love you. I give you all that I am, all that I can, with all the strength I have. I'll see you soon—either here or there. I'm giving you a big kiss and protecting you in my arms.

[Francisco's last entry]

October 2

My dear princess: I haven't written for many days because I just haven't had the strength. Yesterday I was thinking a lot about everything that is OURS.

We are undergoing extremely difficult and discouraging moments.

My body is broken, but my spirit is whole. I want to give myself to you, first of all, and then to others. I love you with all my strength and with all that I am able, for you are the incarnation of my life, my struggle, and my dreams.

It will be difficult for us to be together on the 9th. Maybe the 29th or at Christmas.[18] But I'm confident that we will be together.

We're a small group. It's good to be with comrades who are also friends or relatives. It gives me a lot of peace. At times like these it's hard not to despair. It's trust in the Lord Jesus that gives me the courage to go on till the end.

We have lost the battle, at least this one, and there's nothing that can be done. We'll have to recoup our resources and decide clearly and realistically what we can do in the future. We'll see.

I only hope that we'll see each other on this side of death, even though after death our reunion would be complete and full of happiness. I believe in this and it comforts me.

I hope to be with you soon, to have long talks, to look at each other, to bring a little Paz into this world who will fill our days with joy, and to move ahead. I'm afraid something's happened to you, but I hope you're okay.

I'll leave you now. As always paper isn't enough for what I want to say. I'm no good at writing. I can hardly express myself. I'm thinking of the folks, my brothers and sisters. I'll be hugging them soon. More than anything else I want to eat and eat and eat the first few days. We haven't had anything for a month except for a little bite of whatever we could find here or there. I love you and I want you to understand this perfectly. I love you more than anything and I love you completely....

—*Translated by Ed Garcia and John Eagleson*

NOTES

1. Camilo Torres, a Colombian priest and sociologist, university chaplain and editor of *Frente Unido*, joined the Colombian National Liberation Army and explained the reasons for this decision in "A Message to Colombians from the Mountains" on January 7, 1966. A month later he was killed in an encounter with a national army patrol. The example and writings of Camilo Torres had a deep impact on Néstor Paz. See *Revolutionary Priest: The Complete Writings and Messages of Camilo Torres*, ed. John Gerassi (New York: Vintage, 1971).

2. Inti and Coco Peredo as well as "Darío" (Arturo Alvarado Durán) were combatants in Che Guevara's Bolivian campaign.

3. "Gorilla" refers to reactionary military forces.

4. The *cursillo* is a renewal movement of Spanish origin geared toward deepening the commitment of lay Catholics. In Bolivia its composition is largely from the middle and affluent classes and it has come to be identified with a conservative or reactionary orientation.

5. Massacre of miners and their families in the mining centers of Siglo XX and Catavi perpetrated by Bolivian soldiers on St. John the Baptist's Day, June 24, 1967. The massacre was ordered by then President René Barrientos, who feared the solidarity of the miners with the forces of Che Guevara. The date is widely commemorated among opposition forces in Bolivia today.

6. Henrique Pereira Neto, a university chaplain in Recife, Brazil, was an assistant to Archbishop Dom Helder Camara, world renowned champion of the poor and oppressed. Father Pereira Neto was kidnapped, tortured, and killed by para-military right-wing forces in Brazil in May 1969.

7. Camilo Torres, "Message to Christians," published in *Frente Unido*, August 26, 1965.

8. Ibid.

9. Néstor addresses most of the entries in his campaign journal to his wife Cecilia, whom he calls "Cecy," Reina adorada, Querida reinita, Amorcito, and other affectionate names.

10. The ELN's official list of combatants put the number at sixty-seven (see *Presencia*, January 16, 1971). Father Jaime Zalles, a member of the Peace Commission which mediated between the government and the last surviving members of the ELN in Teoponte, confirmed this figure, while in *Teoponte: Experiencia guerrillera boliviana,* Hugo Assmann puts the number at 75.

11. Marcelo Ovando, twenty-one-year-old son of General Alfredo Ovando, then head of the Bolivian military regime. On the return from a reconnaissance flight over the Teoponte guerrilla zone, the military plane in which he was flying accidentally crashed near Lake Titicaca on July 29, 1970.

12. August 1 commemorates Néstor and Cecy's first meeting at the Universidad de San Andrés in La Paz, where he was studying medicine and she was studying biochemistry.

13. Mario is the eldest of the Paz family. Jaime, like Néstor, studied in the seminary; later he went to Louvain, Belgium, to study sociology and is now a militant member of the Bolivian resistance. Néstor was the third child. The two youngest are Rosario and Edicita.

14. Néstor and Cecy were married on April 14, 1968, and they commemorated this date every month.

15. When the young combatants of the ELN entered the guerrilla zone, they elected "Chato" Peredo as temporary leader of the Teoponte Campaign. Although committed to the cause, "Chato" did not possess the strong leadership qualities of a Che Guevara or his lieutenants in the Ñancahuazú campaign, among whom were Inti Peredo, eldest of the three Peredo brothers and acknowledged leader of the ELN after Che's death; Ricardo, a Chilean militant who was in charge of operations in the Cochabamba area; and Pombo, a veteran of the Cuban Sierra Maestra and survivor of Ñancahuazú who was one of Che's closest associates.

16. Successful efforts at conscientization, that is, increasing political awareness, would have led to greater understanding of and support for the guerrilla forces on the part of the people in the area.

17. Ernesto Che Guevara's *Revolutionary Works.*

18. October 9 is Néstor's birthday; October 29 is Cecy's birthday.

CARLOS ALBERTO LIBANIO CHRISTO

In November 1969, a twenty-five year old Dominican seminarian was arrested on charges of subversion against the military government of Brazil. After twenty-two months in prison before trial, he was sentenced in September 1971 to four more years in prison without his guilt having been proven.

Tragically, there is nothing novel or newsworthy in what happened to Carlos ("Betto") Libanio Christo. Thousands have been arrested and imprisoned on false charges in Brazil, Chile, and much of Latin America.

Betto's parents collected his letters and distributed them in mimeographed form. They have since been published in Italian, French, and Spanish editions, and are taking a place alongside Dietrich Bonhoeffer's Letters and Papers from Prison *as a challenge to those of us who carry the invisible shackles of complacency and conformity.*

Selections from
Against Principalities and Powers:
Letters from a Brazilian Jail

To his sister Teresa

DOPS,[1] Porto Alegre
November 25, 1969

Dear Teresa, this is my first letter to you from prison. I have been here for two weeks now, and I probably will be here for a long time to come. I have committed no crimes. My crime was to try to be a Christian in the true sense of the word. My crime was not to accept injustice, not to stoop to compromise with privilege. My crime was to help those who are in trouble risking their lives.

I'm not afraid. I have no regrets. I spend my days reading, thinking, and dedicating myself more to prayer. I live in complete inner freedom, content to believe that I am sharing in the mystery of Jesus Christ who was persecuted, imprisoned, and condemned for the sake of our freedom.

Time will make everything clear. I hope you all are well.

To his parents

São Paulo
November 27, 1969

Dearest Mom and Dad, look beyond the factual details of what has happened. Disregard the reports and conjecture in the press. Disregard the accusations against me. Only one thing is important right now: I am in jail, and it is a source of joy to me. As the Bible tells us, what is wisdom in the eyes of human beings is folly in the eyes of God, and what is wisdom in the eyes of God is folly in the eyes of human beings. My arrest should cause you no shame but pride, as it does me. I am content. My conscience is at peace because what I said and did was in the interest of a more just world and a freer earth. With so much injustice around us it's not surprising that I find myself here.

I have not felt one moment of discouragement in prison. In fact I find it a truly enriching experience. Here you learn many things and become more of a realist. In particular you discover that a person is not judged by what he does in the sight of others but by what he is within himself. I am convinced that freedom of movement is not the whole meaning of human freedom. There are cloistered monks who are completely free, and no one is free who has not yet encountered himself. Prison makes possible this encounter with oneself and with others. It leads us to explore the infinite riches of the mind and spirit.

In Porto Alegre they decreed preventive detention for me, but I learned that the trial will take place in São Paulo. Everything indicates that the whole matter will be concluded rather quickly, the president of the Republic being among those who want it that way. Our lawyer here is Mario Simas, whom I met briefly at DOPS headquarters.

I believe that my visiting hours are from one to four o'clock on Wednesday afternoons. Anyone outside my immediate family who wishes to visit me must get a permit from Judge Nelson of the Second Military Court. I'm told that no formalities are required to obtain the permit.

As for letters, please write as often as you wish and can. Thanks for the hippy shorts. Shorts are our usual dress here.

Here in prison I met Doctor Madeira, who treated me when I had hepatitis. He's been in prison for ten months and is now the prison doctor, in fact if not by official decree. He's a marvelous person.

I embrace the two of you and all our friends. Let us remain united in prayer that God's will, not ours, be done.

A big hug to everyone, with much trust and affection.

To his parents

Tiradentes Prison
São Paulo
December 7, 1969

(. . .) The only news here is my new prison life. Since I only arrived here a week ago, everything is still new to me. It's likely that I will be in Tiradentes Prison for some time.[2] There are about two hundred of us political prisoners here, young people of both sexes. Our cell is big, roomy, and airy. We have two bathrooms with showers, a washtub, and a kitchen with stoves. There are thirty-two people in our cell, almost all of them young. The few older men have adapted perfectly to their new style of life. We have two injured people. One was beaten up by the police when they seized him; the other threw himself out of a fourth-floor apartment window. Both are convalescing now. The group is divided into teams, which take daily turns at housekeeping. Yesterday it was my team's turn. We got up early, swept the cell, and made coffee (with milk and bread and butter). Some members of our team helped bathe the injured, while others did the cooking. I was a cook and by some miracle did not do too badly.

Occupations: French lessons, gymnastics, yoga, theology, conversations. When you have a strong spirit, prison life is tolerable. No one here seems to be unnerved or beaten down. Everyone is taking it in stride. The interrogations are finished, thank God. Now we must make the best possible use of our time here. I do not consider this time in prison a hiatus in my life. It is the normal continuation of it, and I feel keenly that I am going through a great experience.

To a religious community

February 22, 1970

(. . .) It is a rainy and gloomy Sunday here. Now there are fifty of us in this cell, and we are trying to make the best of it. Many are sleeping on mattresses on the ground because there is no room for more beds. The silence reflects the darkness of this gray day. It is not the silence of tranquility or inner peace; it is a kind of suffocation. So many people together and so little talk. It's as if we wanted to scream but the sound dies in our throat, and we simply keep silent and wait. For what? I don't know. No one does. Waiting is a permanent part of life in prison. It's like waiting on a railroad platform, but here there is no train and no track. Our silence is heavy-hearted like the weather. We are like people who, being provoked, bide their time and store up energy to react and counterattack later. We can feel our own impotence. No one can help us, and we ourselves can do nothing. It isn't a dead end because we have not yet given in to discouragement. Nor is it hate because we have not yet given in to despair. Perhaps it's rage—patient, silent rage at the labyrinth of absurdity before us.

What did the Jews think about in the concentration camps, knowing they would soon die in the gas chambers? Perhaps they thought about nothing, just as many of us are doing right now. Perhaps they simply waited in silence, but not for anything in particular—not for death and certainly not for some miraculous release. Perhaps they were incapable of thinking about the unthinkable or fearing the inevitable. Once people realize that nothing depends on them any longer, that their fear is no longer a symptom of resistance, then they have nothing to do but wait in silence.

To his parents

March 23, 1970

(. . .) Your courage in facing up to reality and your confidence in the future gives me much courage. At times, to tell you the truth, I become annoyed with myself for causing you so much anxiety. Then I realize that something else is involved here, that it has to do with the natural desire we all have to regain our freedom. But what is freedom? It is a question I frequently ask myself. There is the freedom that is based on money and the labor of others, and then there is the freedom of the human being who finds himself by giving himself, by service to others. Were the great men of history, such as Julius Caesar and Napoleon Bonaparte, free only because they did not owe obedience to anyone? Jesus Christ and Francis of Assisi chose the path of self-sacrifice, of service to others, of absolute obedience. Were they free?

In a study of freedom in the present-day world, Marcuse states that one can hardly find a free person in the United States. Yet that country is regarded as the model of freedom in the Western world. There is a high degree of social organization, resulting from the breakneck speed of a technological advance in which people are conditioned by the machine. Because of this the industrial and governmental systems strictly control the individual. The choices available to average Americans are extremely limited. They can pick a make of a car, a particular plane flight, a brand of film, or a six-pack of beer. But they have little chance to choose some alternative to the "American way of life." And despite deep-rooted religious sentiments and patterns of conduct, Americans lack spiritual depth and philosophical objectivity. They do not question or ponder their existence, much less consider changing the status quo; quite the contrary, they seek to propagate it. The results of American freedom are plainly to be seen in the newspapers: a persistent and spreading plague in Southeast Asia and the Middle East, the world's record consumption of toxic drugs, unbridled eroticism, artistic productions devoid of any constructive content (like the Hollywood productions that teach you nothing but to drink Coca-Cola), racial segregation, and so on. Such technological freedom was well analyzed and criticized by Aldous Huxley in *Brave New World.*

Even less can you talk about freedom under regimes ruled by the likes of Hilter and Stalin, where all power comes from the state and is exercised exclusively in its name, where the people are all but excluded from the political process and dissidents are imprisoned, outlawed, or killed.

The fundamental point of these examples is the fact that the state can restrict or take away freedom but can never confer it. *For freedom is something that must be won.* People must continually fight for it, even at the cost of their lives.

I believe that freedom, as a societal achievement, has not yet come into existence. So far there have been occasional moments of freedom, areas of freedom, free individuals. But freedom as a condition of life has not yet come into being. Slavery as a legal status was abolished only a century ago. But people go on creating new myths to compensate for their frustrations—new forms of subjugation, like colonialism and imperialism. The very social structure in which we live is funda-

392   *Carlos Alberto Libanio Christo (Brazil)*

mentally coercive. From the moment we come into the world we are taught what we "must not" do, we are subjected to repressive laws, and we can see a policeman on every corner. The existing social structure so exacerbates this condition that many human beings do not know what to make of freedom even when they have a chance to be free.

A century ago humankind began to discover itself through psychology, sociology, and biology. But we are still too much "outside" ourselves. We have made little use of the psychic and spiritual riches within us. I believe we will attain true freedom only when we arrive at the stage of evolution that Teilhard de Chardin calls the "noosphere," the realm of the spirit. Surely the spirit will be the last great discovery of humankind. Then we will be free because freedom will exist, first and foremost, within us.

The witness of free human beings helps us to believe in freedom and desire it. Real freedom develops inside us and radiates outward. No prison can destroy it. I have received this kind of witness from my cellmates, from children, from poets and saints, and from the poor. They are people who cannot be imprisoned by bars. They speak with their eyes, with their silences, and with their serenity. They are prophets of the spirit, who know how to lay hold of the reins of history. It is they who are really dangerous, who should be feared above all others by those who don't wish to hear the word "freedom" or admit its existence.

It's to be expected that since I'm a prisoner, I should speak of freedom. I do so because every day I discover it within myself and my cellmates and realize its value and its price.

To his parents

March 31, 1970

Dearest Mom and Dad, I would be very happy if you could look at everything that is happening to me from my own point of view, which is the point of view of faith, of abandonment to God's plans, of service to our people, to history. We were born and raised in a middle-class environment, where you always have to preserve appearances. By now I could have had my B.A. and been earning a good salary on some newspaper, secure in the esteem and admiration that certain people had for me before they learned what choices I've made. But none of that has anything to do with my vocation as a Christian. History is not built on appearances but on choices. You have to choose, and you can't please two opposing sides. Either you align yourself with the poor and the oppressed, or your acquire the badge of the oppressor. You have to live either by human logic and common sense or by the impulses of the Spirit.

I know how hard it is to live for the future. Those who live in the past and wish at all cost to preserve the present (as if they could) do all they can to destroy us. They heap lies, abuse, and threats on us, and they take away our freedom. But they can't make us stumble into contradictions. We must be courageous and consistent. We must commit ourselves to the future because God's promises are there. The book of Genesis tells us that Abraham, out of faith in God's promise, forsook his native land and his wealth to journey to the promised land, a land flowing with milk and honey. That journey symbolizes the attitude of the Christian. Jesus came to proclaim the kingdom of justice and peace to us. Each of us in our own way, according to the abilities we have been given, contributes to the making of this kingdom and the quest for it. The kingdom can not be established outside history, so our journey toward it must take place within history.

To Marco, a student friend

April 7, 1970

Dear Marco, those who know that they have to stay here a long time are more relaxed. They follow a schedule, a program of study, and so they continue to live their lives. They don't waste time recalling the past or dreaming of some imminent, utopian future. They integrate their activities into the rhythm of life that you can establish in prison. As far as our personal life is concerned, the rhythm of prison life can be as intense and productive as our pattern of living outside. Idleness is the most dangerous temptation facing a prisoner. It is what turns prison into a school for crime for ordinary prisoners. Lacking any formal education and unable to devote himself to reading, the average inmate spends the whole day sleeping, rehashing

the past, and talking nonsense. Abandoned to his own useless-
ness, he wears himself out day by day. (There is no chance for
rehabilitation because our prison system is punitive rather
than corrective.) His only prospect is to learn new techniques
of theft and crime from his cellmates.

We can hear the conversations in the other cell block. They
shout to each other from cell to cell, always in underworld
slang and never using their real names. They use nicknames
so that there is no danger of being informed on. (. . .) If one of
them doesn't have a nickname, he is labelled by the place he
comes from. They usually sleep all day and sing all evening,
banging out the rhythm of their songs. (. . .) The most curious
thing of theirs is the *teresa*. It's a looped string that they use to
pass objects from one cell to another. If a person can handle
the *teresa* well, he can do wondrous feats. For example, a
prisoner may throw a cigarette down the corridor, so that it
stops right in front of the intended recipient. But then a prisoner in another cell shoots out his *teresa* and lassoes it for
himself. Another easily learned technique is sign language. If
you want to talk to someone at night, you use sign language so
you don't wake up other prisoners.

To his brothers and sisters

May 10, 1970

Greetings to you all! The most beautiful gift I've gotten recently was Mom's visit, bringing Dad's written statement
about my imprisonment. It is remarkable in both form and
content. I have no changes to make, no criticism to offer.
Among other things, it's well written. Mom and Dad have
managed to express beautifully everything that has been
happening to me in this dynamic period of church renewal.
There is a direct relationship between that renewal and my
imprisonment.

For centuries the church has justified the social order in
which it has lived. The values of that social order (the family,
private property, tradition, individual liberty, democratic
government, etc.), were considered Christian. Social order and
Christianity became so closely identified that we came to

speak of "Western Christian civilization." In reality this was an ideological interpretation of Christianity propounded by those in power. And the social order, which created its own peculiar abuses, found the justification for its existence in this interpretation.

So Eisenhower (who was Protestant) sends troops into Vietnam "to defend the Catholic minority."

Cambodia is invaded and its population decimated "in defense of the free world."

In South Africa Christians appeal to the Bible to prove the divine origin of apartheid.

And here at home Archbishop Siguad can say, without risking the accusation of heresy, that the class divisions into rich and poor derive from the will of God, who did not desire equality among people.

Now, in this postconciliar period, our problem is to return to the sources and to see clearly that Christianity is not identical with any social order; that it challenges and questions all social orders; that the state does not represent any divine right, that laws are made by people and these people are wholly concerned with protecting their own privileges.

So we will inevitably see a clash between Christianity and the social order, between the church and the state, between Christians animated by love and those who are attached to their laws.

To Pedro[3]

May 16, 1970

Dear Pedro, the only news from prison comes from our own experiences and thoughts. Today I've been thinking a great deal about these six months that I've been in prison to date. You on the outside, who have never experienced it (I would not wish it on you for the world!), cannot imagine what it is really like, however much I might write to you about it. Although I have been here for six months, I think it's too soon to make a definitive judgment. That will have to wait until I have been free again for two or three years. Only then will I be able to say something about the meaning of prison life and its impact on us.

Based on my brief experience so far, I must say that prison is an absurd institution. It is as ridiculous as burying a man alive. It does not punish, and it does not correct. Its sole objective is to remove from society those who have threatened the security of its "masters." Countless human beings have spent long years in prison and, on leaving, returned to the same life they had led before. Their imprisonment did not increase or diminish the security of those outside one bit. Nor did it serve as an example. The example was provided by the ideals for which these prisoners fought and for which others would take the same risks.

It is abominable that society feels obliged to confine the best of its youth, those capable of transcending self-interest and egotism, behind bars. A waiting room is a good image of what prison is like. You wait there, among total strangers, for your turn to come. You wait for hours, and after reading all the magazines and chewing over all your thoughts you suddenly realize that the waiting time is indeterminate and that it is impossible to leave the room. So your only recourse is to start up a conversation with the other people there. At the same time every detail in the waiting room takes on importance. After several days, you know the pattern in the tablecloth and the upholstery, and you could describe every detail of the room with your eyes closed. The people and things in the room become as intimately familiar as the parts of your own body. To make the interminable wait less awful, you make up a game: Everyone changes seats—you rearrange the furniture—but you have no chance at all to make any decision that will change the basic situation. The door can only be opened from the outside; no one inside has a key.

In the past six months I have passed through three different prisons and experienced eight different cells. I came to know each one of them as well as I now know cell seven. Although there are fifty of us in here, I have no trouble at all in finding something I need. I know exactly where everything can be found, just as I know for a fact that my fellow prisoners are capable of loving. Prison can humanize a person or turn him into a brute. It teaches us to love, to smile at suffering, to get over moments of depression, to nurture patiently the strength of our will and our ideals. On the other hand, prison can drive a person crazy (it has happened to two people here), crush his moral strength, or fill him with hatred and destructive impulses.

Living together is a great help. It lightens the burden for all. There are also moments of tension, when the atmosphere becomes charged and everyone is suddenly transformed with fearful expectation.

As for myself, I feel that something has grown inside me, something firmly rooted. It is as if I have emerged from fog and can now see things clearly. I can see what I want and why I want it. I can see my capabilities and what I am up to facing. I feel I have reached some point of no return, from which it would be suicide or treason to go back. I must go on without a backward glance. I no longer have anything to lose because everything I now possess is within me. All that is left to me is the road ahead. Even if it does not take me very far, every step will make a difference.

To his cousin Maria

December 31, 1970

(. . .) There are three Dominicans left in prison with me: Fernando, Ivo, and Tito. Tito is included in the list of prisoners demanded in exchange for the Swiss ambassador, but the negotiations have bogged down. Roberto was freed on October 28 after he had attempted to commit suicide by slitting both wrists. It was the psychological effect of prison life that led him to it. It was not an act of weakness but the protest of a man who had been in prison for almost a year without any charge whatever having been lodged against him. Maurizio, who has left the order (he decided to leave even before his arrest), was freed in November. Our Christmas gift was the release of Giorgio, an Italian, on December 24. There had been no charge against him either. So the four of us are left, waiting for a trial whose date has not yet been set. We are accused of a "crime," namely, that we hid people wanted as subversives by the police and helped them to flee the country. This is an offense according to Brazilian law, but not according to church tradition. Church precedent for aiding fugitives dates from the time when Mary, Joseph, and the child Jesus fled into Egypt to escape Herod's persecution—as I told the Joint Military Council.

There are more than three hundred political prisoners here, both men and women. For seven months there were forty of us in a cell that had room for twenty. For four months I slept on the floor. In September the inmates organized protest demonstrations against the terrible prison conditions and the excessive slowness of the judicial proceedings. Because Giorgio went on a hunger strike, retaliatory measures were directed against us priests. We were taken from prison and sent separately to different barracks. I spent twenty days in solitary confinement in a cell belonging to the cavalry barracks. It measured one meter by three, with hardly room for a bunk. It had no water or sanitary facilities, and I was only allowed to use the washroom once a day—at 8:00 A.M. I faced total solitude there, surrounded by soldiers but unable to exchange a single word with anyone. My only reading material was my New Testament. I was later transferred to headquarters where conditions were slightly better. There at least I could wash up, because there was a water faucet in the cell.

At the end of October we were brought back to Tiradentes prison. We were kept completely separate from the other prisoners, confined in cell 17. It measures two and one-half by six meters. The walls are damp and gray, and there are a lot of holes in the ceiling. So there is a constant dripping of water when it rains. At the back of the cell is a water pipe with a faucet. There we wash up and get water to drink and to cook with. We cook our own food that is sent to us from the monastery because the prison food is unbearable. We get out of the cell for an hour and a half in the sun only twice a week, and we have visiting hours once every two weeks.

We spend our time in prison reading, doing calisthenics, and studying theology. We are not idle. Every evening we get together for prayer. We recite the Psalms, chant hymns, and receive the body of our Lord. We have not received permission to celebrate Mass, but the chaplain of the military police comes with consecrated hosts every so often.

For me all this represents a revival of the life lived by the church during the first three centuries of its existence. It would be incredible if the church were not present somehow in prisons under a regime that oppresses human beings. Here we are in fellowship with "the wretched of the earth." We are in communion with those who have been invited to the Lord's banquet. All this is grace, as is any suffering endured in a Christian spirit.

I can assure you that prison has effected a radical transformation—a profound conversion—in us. Behind these bars many things lose the value they once had, and new discoveries turn us into new people. It is good for the church to go through prison. There it rediscovers the way that Christ had pointed out, the way of poverty and persecution.

To his parents

January 2, 1971

Dearest Mom and Dad, my first letter of the year is to you. I was hoping to send it by T., but I don't think it will be ready in time. She came to see me. Her decision to come to São Paulo seems sound to me. There comes a time when it's important to take off on your own.

We had our New Year's Eve party here in prison. It was pretty much the Christmas party all over again. We sang everything we knew, in a concert that lasted from eleven at night to three in the morning. Very lively and very off-key. I listened more than I sang. I don't have the gift of song, which belongs to the birds and which God has kindly granted to some people. But my three companions sang till they were hoarse. They are the most singular trio that I have ever encountered. Tito knows the lyrics of all the songs, even the old *boleros* that were popular at the same time as the maxi-skirt. Ivo knows the tunes, and Fernando shouts them out. From every cell a small chorus sang together, making the whole prison resonate. And hands thrusting through the bars beat time on the heavy iron doors.

One year has ended, another begun. For some of us it means one year less in prison, for others one year more of waiting. We, for instance, don't know now much longer we will have to stay here. Now rumor has it that we'll be out soon, and we hope the rumor turns out to be true. But rumor does neither us nor you any good. It's better to assume that we'll get out when the discharge papers arrive. These flights of fancy may nurture hope, but the prison bars remain impassable as ever, with us on the inside. I prefer not to cherish any illusions because nothing is more dangerous for a prisoner than impatience. Imprisonment is not like illness, in which the doctor's contagious optimism is a real psychological aid to the patient's recovering. This is different, as I noticed with Giorgio. In the last six months of his internment somebody came by at least once a week to assure him that he would be released the following week. Result: As the weeks passed and his irritability mounted, he gradually lost all power of concentration. So it is better to wait for freedom to come to you than to try to grab it. I suspect that the family's impatience is greater than mine.

(. . .) And I see people here who will not go free for ten or twenty years. There was a kid here, just recently transferred to a penitentiary, twenty-nine years old and sentenced to sixty-seven years in prison. He has already served ten. I have thought about it for a long time, and I ask myself how in the name of justice it can take sixty-seven years in prison to rehabilitate a nineteen-year-old! Compared to people like him, I have no right to feel sorry for myself, particularly since I always knew what I was getting into and why. Some people are convicted for actions for which they are not wholly responsible. In a sudden burst of anger they commit an act that has irreparable consequences. There are prisoners who will have to pay for such a lapse with many years of their lives. For example, I think I would not be able [censored]. A longing bearhug to you all.

To Marlene, a friend

June 20, 1971

Marlene, your letter, which I've read twice from beginning to end, is very human and as beautiful as the sunflowers you have planted on your farm. It is like you. To be in touch with the earth is a good thing. Here I miss it very much. It's been quite a while since I've seen fields, or anything green—my landscape is all cement and iron. It's an oppressive panorama. I miss the open air and the vistas in which you can lose yourself. . . . I was born in the mountains and spent my first years on the seacoast. My earliest memory of myself is that of a small boy playing with a little pail on the Copacabana beach. That was when I was three or four, and it's my only memory of that time—the rest is gone. This has stayed with me because I love the sea above anything else in nature. It frightens me and consoles me at the same time because it hides a mysterious richness.

There is another spectacle I never tire of contemplating: human beings. What could be more beautiful or more terrible? People can cultivate roses, write poetry, compose music—and they can also make weapons of war, oppress each other, and condemn each other to death. We have a long way to go to recapture the unity described in the first chapter of Genesis. Right now we are a mass of contradictions, undoubtedly because we are self-deceived.

One of the most important moments of my life came when I realized that my existence had a social dimension. Only then did I begin to grasp its personal dimension. Until that moment I had believed in the law of the jungle, in which competition, not cooperation, was the key. I left off competing in order to cooperate. I ceased wanting so that I would be able to choose. It suddenly came to me that every choice entails a renunciation. You cannot flutter through life from one possibility to the next without ever committing yourself to any. Choosing one path at a crossroads necessarily excludes the others. At times you are overtaken by the temptation to turn back or take dubious shortcuts that at first glance seem easier but always turn out more tortuous. You must keep going, patiently and determinedly, trusting your own legs and nurturing your hope in the destination that awaits you.

The things we have been taught don't emphasize the social dimension of human existence. . . . I learned to read and write from the Uncle Paperone books. I piously believed that one day I would be as rich as he. I spent my childhood with Captain Marvel and Zorro. My heroes were strong men, and they won with force. I could sleep in peace because they would protect me. . . . The enemies of my heroes—the outlaws, thugs, and trouble-makers—looked a little bit like Mexicans. All these books taught me that crime doesn't pay, but also that it was no crime to make money. They also taught me that the ideal man, the prototype of virility, was super-fed, super-equipped, and super-envied. I learned that I must become one of them at all costs, and I dreamed of my future as I chewed gum and drank Coke. I had a passionate admiration for Uncle Sam.

My sensibilities were further developed by the movies. They continued the education that my comic books began, reinforcing the same values vividly and crudely. They taught me that love is a pretty face and a nice figure, and that I would have to plunge headfirst into incredible adventures in order to be a real man. From the movie screen I learned a whole host of things that no one would have the courage to teach anyone in real life. The fulfilled man was rich, clean-shaven, stylishly dressed, successful with women, and surrounded by flunkies who jumped to satisfy his every whim. When I left the movie house, I was convinced that my own life would duplicate in every respect what I saw on the screen, provided that I could make money. This was the primer of Uncle Sam, who was to me the incarnation of progress, civilization, and freedom.

My adolescent idols were the technicolor images of movie stars. David Niven in his Rolls Royce, driven by a black chauffeur from Harlem. Elizabeth Taylor as the queen of Egypt, worshipped by thousands of Oriental slaves. Gary Cooper leveling his unerring rifle at the head of some Mexican bandit. John Wayne carrying victory over death around the world. They were the invincible whites, superhuman and superb, every man capable of winning a blonde goddess for his love.

In every feature of body and mind I sought to resemble Marlon Brando, James Dean, Frank Sinatra, and Glenn Ford. I wished to be nothing like the bandits whom they killed, the enemies they conquered, the servants who catered to them on the screen. I tried to identify with my heroes and their glory, their wealth, and their power over women. But most of my illusions died with the death of Marilyn Monroe, and a good thing too.

In the city I learned the law of the jungle and the use of intelligence to accumulate riches. I too could learn to be insensitive to other people's sufferings.

Women were brought up to believe in even worse illusions than ours. You were trained to be man's living tools. You were taught to be beautiful. You were taught to walk, smile, sit, bat your eyes, speak, eat, diet, and dress so as to arouse men's desire. You were taught that men are the ones who study, make decisions, build things, make mistakes, give orders, and fulfill themselves. Man is the warrior, woman the warrior's rest. You were to satisfy his whims; to be beautiful, docile, and patient. You must belong to him alone, even if he amused himself with other women. All you had to be was beautiful. It didn't matter if your head had nothing to recommend it but hair. You were the body; he was the mind. He thought; you did. His body was not supposed to matter to you, only his money, his social prestige, his intelligence. That is what you were to look for in him, even though he saw neither your mind nor your spirit, only your body.

The worst poison in our society is not sold at the drug store. It is sex. It is an effect, not a cause. It is the fruit of our inability to love, a symptom of contemporary man's asexuality. We are preoccupied with sex because we are impotent. All the super-men of our childhood were asexual beings. All the movie stars of our adolescence were romantic fakes: They could kiss beautifully, but love was only supposed to happen *after* "The End" flashed on the screen.

In this school we were taught the artifices and the vicissitudes of love, but we never learned to love. A line was drawn between mind and body. As mind, the male has lost his virility, his ability to perceive his body; his sexual aggressiveness stems from the repugnance he feels for his own body. As body, the female has lost her personality, her inner self; her sexual passivity is that of a mere receptacle.

The Don Juans of our day are not supermen, as James Bond might suggest. They are impotent, never-satisfied creatures who must always be trying someone new. And the superseduc-tress in reality is super-frigid. The body cannot satisfy the mind, and the mind is unaware that it must satisfy the body's spirit.

If you walk in the rain, you are bound to get wet. If we have deceived ourselves about love, then our lives will be ones of amorous deceit and deceptive loves. Only when we discover the social dimension will we free ourselves from this modern Babylon!

(. . .) Only then will we recover the unity of body and mind, of flesh and spirit. Competition will be succeeded by cooperation. Personal success will come to mean success in and for society. Heroism will be the prerogative of the whole people, achieved in the fulfillment of common aspirations. Power will mean service, love, self-giving.

(. . .) Why all these years of psychotherapy? Why all these

incurable guilt complexes? They are the price of the illusions in which we have grown up, of the daydreams to which we were addicted. We are maladjusted to life.

At this point it seems to me that the only cure for the evil is to uproot it. But first we must find the roots.

Next time tell me about your daughter. Much friendship to you and your family.

To a brother in Rome

July 28, 1972

(. . .) Our situation today is not what it was when I wrote my last letter to you. We were then in the infirmary, in the course of a total fast that lasted thirty-three days. (. . .) When we finally ended the fast, we went through days of tense waiting. Would we be kept here? Would we be returned to São Paulo? (. . .) Finally we learned our fate: We will be kept here like common prisoners. (. . .) On the twenty-fifth we were processed into the population of this prison. This means that we are now known by numbers: Betto 25044, Fernando 25045, Ivo 25046, Vanderley Caixa 25047, Maurice Politi 25048, Manoel Porfirio de Souza 25049. We wear the prison uniform, we are not allowed food parcels from home, and we must follow prison regulations. Since they were made for a population of four hundred inmates, they are hardly flexible enough to allow for individual needs.

We are also subject to the same punishments as the other prisoners. These range from a simple warning through loss of visiting rights to solitary confinement. We live in individual cells, two meters by three, one next to the other. In each cell is a toilet, cement blocks that serve as chair and table, and a faucet for washing our dishes and ourselves. In the afternoon we can be together in one room; there we study theology.

(. . .) The other prisoners' attitudes toward us are excellent. They all come to talk and listen to us. They show us great sympathy and seem immensely curious on the subject of faith. We feel useful. (. . .) We protest the regimen to which we have been subjected, but we find ourselves adapting to it bit by bit. It is the radicalism of the gospel that bids us to do so. Now we must share our lives wholly with our brothers, the ordinary offenders, and carry on our struggle for the justice to which we are entitled. As always, we are counting on your prayers.

To his cousin Agnese

January 2, 1973

This is in reply to the letter you wrote me exactly a month ago on the First Sunday of Advent. So far I haven't been able to find out whether you got my other letters. I have answered all of yours, but I have no idea whether you got mine because you make no reference to them. Besides I don't have your new address, so I can't write to you directly.

You say that in Italy a lot of people are asking: "What do you believe in now?" You also talk about the need for finding new sources of spirituality. It is precisely this need, I think, that makes it possible to answer such a question.

The problem is a consequence of theology's growing maturity expressed in its ability to criticize its own premises. Nowadays there is nothing that cannot be questioned. Just as in the latter half of the nineteenth century post-Hegelian philosophy criticized the methodology and objectives of everything that had come before, so today theology is impelled to a similarly radical self-revision. Among Catholics this process began with Vatican II and constitutes a real Copernican revolution. Just consider the problems raised by Bultmann, for example. . . .

Scientific progress is the root of all philosophical progress. One cannot write a history of philosophy without taking into account the data arising from man's perception of nature. Plato was the genius beneficiary of Greek mathematics, as Descartes was of Galileo's physics, Kant of Newton's discoveries, and Marx of the English economists.

Theology is not an isolated science. It cannot help but reflect innovations in science and philosophy. But theology has had a falling-out with the secular sciences. Science has definitely become the mainspring of all human progress. Philosophy has ceased to contemplate the world and has decided to change it. But what about theology? Will it manage to be more than a polite way of saying something about revealed truths?

"What do you believe in now?" People find the question hard

to answer and the reason for the difficulty, I think, is the centuries-long divorce between theology and spirituality in the Western church. You say, quite rightly, that we must discover new sources of spirituality. I think we can only accomplish this through a new mode of theologizing in which theology and spirituality will be inextricably linked. The foundation of theology nowadays is threefold: divine revelation, tradition, and signs of the times. Theological interpretation of the signs of the times is not something new; the Old Testament prophets did it long ago. It is new only for us who have reinstituted it after long disuse, albeit we still lack the tools to practice it. We must clean our glasses well to see what's happening in the world. Otherwise we will be in danger of mistaking the burning bush, the breeze on Mount Horeb, and the star over Bethlehem for purely natural phenomena.

Every historical period has its own structures. To understand the period we must know how these structures were formed, for the word of God is supposed to reverberate through them. Hence a contemporary theologian simply must know how to judge the impact of economics as a determining element in the lives of peoples and in international relations. It is not enough to say *what* we must do to be faithful to the Lord. One must also spell out *how* we are to do it, what our praxis should be, how we must act within the context of our fidelity to him. Chapter 21 of Luke's gospel presents a masterful lesson by Jesus on reading and interpreting the signs of the times. He tells us the sign: Jerusalem besieged by an invading army. He tells us the outcome: Its destruction is at hand. Then he tells people how to act according to their circumstances: Those in Judea are to flee to the mountains; those in Jerusalem are to get away. Those in the countryside are not to enter the city. Then he reveals the meaning of the event: These are days of chastisement in which all that had been written will be fulfilled.

The church finds it hard to interpret present-day events prophetically. It seems perplexed by events like the wars in Vietnam, the struggle in the Middle East, the various wars of liberation, the emancipation of women, student and worker movements, dictatorships.... In general the hierarchy limits itself to voicing vague desires for peace without giving any concrete indications of how committed Christians should act in these real situations. Hence it's hard for the church to show the profound significance of Christian praxis for the course of salvation.

I believe that two ideological factors influence the positions that the hierarchy takes. First of all, prophecy has given away to diplomatic expediency. Pronouncements are phrased so as to offend no one, therefore they touch no one. They provoke no questioning, no changes of heart. The second factor is the false notion that the world can evolve without birth pangs. This fallacy is reflected in the pessimistic attitude toward all social conflicts, as if they represented a backward step. But Jesus tells us exactly the opposite: "When you hear of wars and insurrections, do not fall into a panic. These things are bound to happen first; but the end does not follow immediately. . . . When all this begins to happen, *stand upright and hold your heads high, because your liberation is near*" (Luke 21:9–28).

I can see the possibility of a synthesis between theology and spirituality only in an evangelical praxis. We ask each other, What do you believe in now? because the object of our faith is a body of doctrines subjected to rigorous criticism. That sort of faith should not exist among us. The true object of a Christian's faith is a person, Jesus Christ; and the relationship established by faith is one of love. Whoever experiences a crisis of faith because the assumptions of theology are being revised confesses thereby that he lacks spirituality. By spirituality I mean a way of possessing Christ in one's own life, not merely as someone believed in but above all as someone loved. Theology must be rooted in love.

When we observe Jesus' relations with his apostles, we are amazed to find that he was never concerned to transmit to them a body of doctrine. He did not copy the Greek Academy or even the Hebrew synagogue. He did not train his disciples in the manner of Plato and Aristotle. We do not find in the gospel an academic Jesus, concerned to demonstrate to his disciples the principles in which they are to believe. In Christianity the object of faith is a person, which implies a relationship of love.

Jesus is one who loves and who is loved. He lives with his friends and teaches them what the simplest happenings of life mean in the light of the "good news." He is not in a hurry, and their vacillation does not upset him. Peter vacillates. So does

Thomas. And Matthew tells us that some were unsure even after they had seen him risen from the dead (Matt. 28:17). But they all loved him.

So the question should be phrased differently: "What do you love?" A person may believe everything that the church tells him to believe, and still love worldly wisdom, the trappings of luxury, money, and power. When a person tells you what he loves, he reveals who he really is: "For where your treasure is, there will your heart be also" (Matt. 6:21). Belief without love is possible only when theology and spirituality are completely separated. We have much to learn from the Eastern church about how to overcome this defect. The Eastern church has no such dualism. Its theology is not *rational science* but *wisdom*, and it grows out of and is nurtured by a profoundly spiritual life.

Latin rationalism has so subdivided the duties of Christians that we have ended by losing the unity and dynamism of the gospel. Some are to contemplate; others to act. Some are to be concerned for the poor, others not. Some are to follow the beatitudes, others may even observe the evangelical counsels.

This is a serious distortion. I don't think that Jesus established different categories of Christians. The so-called evangelical counsels are for all: priests and laypeople, married people and celibates. So are prayer and contemplation.

The only allowable differences are in charisms and functions. All the other differences derive from our imperfections and our infidelity.

Well, I'll sign off. At home everything is fine. Mom and Dad have celebrated their thirty-first wedding anniversary, and Leonardo has gone to the United States. Please let me know whether you've gotten this letter. Keep writing to me. Fernando, Ivo, and I send you and your friends all our best wishes for a happy 1973.

—Translated by John Drury

Epilogue

Betto was released from prison in October 1973, and today lives in a shanty in a desperately poor section of Vitória, capital of the state of Espírito Santo. Together with other young people, he is participating in the life of the poor to concretize his commitment to the oppressed. According to him it is not a matter of trying to serve them but above all to be one of them. Betto believes only in a church that is born of the people.

One year after his release from prison he said: "We have finished the first year in freedom and we have not found freedom; it still does not exist. I try always to be prepared, knowing the next time will be the last." (Betto is referring to a new imprisonment.)

With regard to his status in the Dominican order, Betto has written to his general superior asking that he be officially considered a lay brother: "I do not want to be ordained a priest because it would be the first step in rising to power within the church. I am more convinced every day that any type of power tends to corrupt. Furthermore, the priority is no longer sacramental but rather evangelical and I can continue to evangelize without being ordained a priest."

NOTES

1. Department for Political and Social Order. There is a branch in each state of the Brazilian Federation.

2. Tiradentes is an old prison in downtown São Paulo, built in the colonial era. Abandoned for decades because of its unhygienic conditions, it has recently been returned to use, primarily for political prisoners.

3. Pedro is a member of a religious order and a biblical exegete.

ACKNOWLEDGEMENTS

*Grateful acknowledgement is made
to authors, translators, and publishers
for permission to reprint
previously published selections.*

Peter Abrahams: "Nkrumah, Kenyatta, and the Old Order" from Peter Abrahams' *The Blacks*, published in *Holiday* magazine, April 1959. Copyright 1959 Curtis Publishing Company. Reprinted by permission of Curtis Brown, Ltd., New York, N.Y.

S.Y. Agnon: "Tehilah" from *Israeli Stories*, edited by Joel Blocker, translated by Walter Lever. Copyright 1962 Schocken Books, Inc. The story first appeared in the publication, *Israel Argosy*, The Jewish Agency, Jerusalem, Israel. Reprinted by permission of Schocken Books Inc.

Yosano Akiko: "A Mouse" from *The Mentor Book of Modern Asian Literature*. New American Library (1969), edited by Dorothy Blair Shimer, translated by Shio Sakanishi. Copyright Shio Sakanishi. Reprinted by permission of the translator.

Domingo Alfonso: "Arte Poética," translated by J.M. Cohen, from *Writers in the New Cuba*, edited by J.M Cohen. Copyright 1967 J.M. Cohen. Reprinted by permission of Penguin Books, Ltd.

Chairil Anwar: "At the Mosque" and "My Love Far in the Islands" from *Anthology of Modern Indonesian Poetry*, edited by Burton Raffel. Copyright 1964 Asia Society, Inc. Reprinted by permission of the University of California Press.

411

Jawa Apronti: "Funeral" from *Modern Poetry from Africa* (1963, 1967), edited by Gerald Moore and Ulli Beier (1963). The poem first appeared in the publication *Transition.* Copyright 1964 Jawa Apronti. Reprinted by permission of the author and Penguin Books, Ltd.

Onelio Jorge Cardoso: *The Cat's Second Death,* translated by Dr. J.G. Brotherston. Copyright J.G. Brotherston. Reprinted by permission of the translator.

Fidel Castro: Extracts from "Words to the Intellectuals," translated J.M. Cohen, from *Writers in the New Cuba* edited by J.M. Cohen. Copyright 1967 J.M. Cohen. Reprinted by permission of Penguin Books, Ltd.

Aimé Césaire: Extract from "Return to My Native Land," translated by John Berger and Anne Bostock from *African Writings Today* (Penguin Books, Ltd., 1967), edited by Ezekiel Mphahlele. These extracts are taken from the definitive edition of Aimé Césaire's *Cahier d'un retour au pays natal* published by *Présence Africaine,* Paris (1956). Reprinted by permission of the publishers.

Fen Chih: "I Sing of Anshan Steel" from *Twentieth Century Chinese Poetry* by Kai-yu Hsu. Copyright 1963 Kai-yu Hsu. Reprinted by permission of Doubleday & Company, Inc.

Jong Chol: "Out of Favor" from *The Ever White Mountain,* translated and edited by Inez Kong Pai. Copyright 1965 John Weatherhill, Inc. Reprinted by permission of the publishers, John Weatherhill, Inc.

Yu-Wol Chong-Nyon and Daniel Milton: "The Non-revolutionaries," copyright 1969 and 1970 by Yu-Wol Chong-Nyon and D.L. Milton, in New American Library, Plume Books, *A Treasury of Modern Asian Stories,* edited by D.L. Milton and W. Clifford. Translated from the Korean by the author and Daniel L. Milton. Reprinted by permission of the author and Daniel L. Milton.

J.P. Clark: "Ibadan" from *Poems,* published by Mbari Publications, Ibadan, Nigeria. Copyright J.P. Clark, 1962. Reprinted by permission of the author.

Renato Constantino: "The Filipinos in the Philippines" from *The Filipinos in the Philippines and Other Essays* published in 1959. Copyright Renato Constantino. Reprinted by permission of the author.

José Craveirinha: "Poem of the Future Citizen" and "Song of the Negro on the Ferry" by Kalungano, translated by Philippa Rumsey, from *African Writings Today* (Penguin Books, Ltd., 1967), edited by Ezekiel Mphahlele. Copyright Ezekiel Mphahlele 1967, poem copyright Kalungano 1967, translation copyright Philippa Rumsey 1967. Reprinted by permission of Philippa Rumsey.

José de Broucker: Prayer poems from *Dom Helder Camara: The Violence of a Peacemaker.* Originally published in 1969 as *Dom Helder Camara: la violence d'un pacifique.* Copyright 1969, Librairie Arthéme Fayard, Paris. English translation copyright 1970, Orbis Books.

David Diop: "Africa," translated by Anne Atik, from *African Writings Today* (Penguin Books, Ltd., 1967), edited by Ezekiel Mphahlele. The poem "Afrique" appears in David Diop's *Coups de pilon,* first published by *Présence Africaine,* Paris (1956). Reprinted by permission of the publishers.

Aguinaldo Fonseca: "Tavern by the Sea," translated by Alan Ryder, from *Modern Poetry from Africa,* edited by Gerald Moore and Ulli Beier. Copyright 1963 Gerald Moore and Ulli Beier. The original was first published in *Anthologie La poésie Africaine d' expression portugaise,* edited by Mario de Andrade, by Editions Pierre Jean Oswald, Paris. Reprinted by permission of Editions Pierre Jean Oswald, and Penguin Books, Ltd.

He Guyan: "Maple Leaves," translated by W.J.F. Jenner, from *Modern Chinese Stories* edited by W.J.F. Jenner. Copyright Oxford University Press. Reprinted with permission of Oxford University Press.

Sinai C. Hamada: "Tanabata's Wife" from *Philippine Pen Anthology of Short Stories 1962,* edited by Francisco Arcellana. Copyright Sinai C. Hamada. Published by the Philippine Center of International PEN. The story first appeared in the Philippines in the following publications: Philippine Free Press, Sunday Times Magazine, Manila Chronicle, Graphic and Literary Apprentice. Reprinted by permission of the author.

Bak In-Ro: "A Rope of Iron" and "Three Brothers" from *The Ever White Mountain*, translated and edited by Inez Kong Pai. Copyright 1965 John Weatherhill, Inc. Reprinted by permission of the publishers, John Weatherhill, Inc.

Muhammad Iqbal: "Ghazal No. 9" from *Poems From Iqbal* translated by E.G. Kiernan. Copyright John Murray, Ltd. Reprinted by permission of John Murray (Publishers), Ltd.

Kobayashi Issa: "3 Haiku" from *An Introduction to Haiku* by Harold G. Henderson. Copyright 1958 Harold G. Henderson. Reprinted by permission of Doubleday & Company, Inc.

Antonio Jacinto: "Monangamba," translated by Alan Ryder, from *Modern Poetry from Africa*, edited by Gerald Moore and Ulli Beier. Copyright 1963 Gerald Moore and Ulli Beier. The original was first published in *Anthologie La Poésie Africaine d' expression portugaise*, edited by Mario de Andrade, by Editions Pierre Jean Oswald, Paris. Reprinted by permission of Editions Pierre Jean Oswald, and Penguin Books, Ltd.

J.E. Kariuki: "New Life" from *African Writings Today* (Penguin Books, Ltd., 1967), edited by Ezekiel Mphahlele. Copyright J.E. Kariuki. Reprinted by permission of the author.

Alex La Guma: "A Walk in the Night" from *A Walk in the Night and Other Stories* by Alex La Guma. "A Walk in the Night" was first published by Mbari Publications, Ibadan, Nigeria. Copyright 1962 Mbari Publications. Published in the United States by Northwestern University Press (1967) by special arrangement with Heinemann Educational Books, Ltd. Reprinted by permission of Northwestern University Press.

Aquah Laluah: "The Souls of Black and White" from *The Poetry of the Negro, 1746–1970*, Doubleday (1970, 1973), edited by Langston Hughes and Arna Bontemps. Copyright The Atlantic Monthly. Reprinted by permission of The Atlantic Monthly.

Carlos Alberto Libanio Christo: Selections from *Against Principalities and Powers: Letters from a Brazilian Jail* by Carlos Alberto Libanio Christo, translated by John Drury. Originally published in 1971 as *Dai Sotterranei della storia*.

Copyright 1971 Arnoldo Mondadori Editore, Milan, Italy. English translation copyright 1977 Orbis Books.

Albert Luthuli: "The Dignity of Man" (1961 Nobel Peace Prize Acceptance Speech), from a series entitled *Nobel Lectures*. Copyright Elsevier Publishing Company. Reprinted by permission of the Elsevier Scientific Publishing Company, Amsterdam, The Netherlands.

Una Marson: "Nightfall" from *Towards the Stars*, by Una Marson. Copyright Hodder & Stoughton. Reprinted by permission of the publishers, Hodder & Stoughton Educational.

Kasu Maruyama: "A Rhinoceros and a Lion" from *The Many Worlds of Poetry* (1968), edited by Jacob Drachler and Virginia Terris (New Directions). "A Rhinoceros and a Lion" first appeared in *Poetry*. Copyright 1956 The Modern Poetry Association. Reprinted by permission of the Editor of *Poetry* and the translators, Satoru Sato and Constance Urdang.

John S. Mbiti: Prayers from *The Prayers of African Religion* by John S. Mbiti. Copyright 1975 John S. Mbiti, and first published by SPCK, London (1975). Reprinted by permission of the U.S. publisher, Orbis Books and SPCK, London, for the author.

Ho Chi Minh: "On the Road," "Morning Sunshine," "Cold Night" from *The Prison Diary of Ho Chi Minh*, Bantam Books, Inc. "Declaration of Independence of the Democratic Republic of Vietnam" from *Ho Chi Minh on Revolution: Selected Writings 1920–1966*, edited by Bernard B. Fall. Copyright Phaidon Press, Ltd. Reprinted by permission of the publishers, Phaidon Press, Ltd.

Bloke Modisane: "Lonely" from *Modern Poetry From Africa* (Penguin Books, Ltd., 1963, 1967), edited by Gerald Moore and Ulli Beier. Copyright Bloke Modisane. Reprinted by permission of the author.

Pablo Neruda: "Ode to Laziness" and "The United Fruit Company" from *Selected Poems of Pablo Neruda*, by Pablo Neruda. Copyright 1961 Grove Press, Inc.; English texts copyright 1961 Ben Belitt. Reprinted by permission of Grove Press, Inc.

Abioseh Nicol: "The Meaning of Africa." Copyright Oxford University Press. Reprinted by permission of Oxford University Press and David Higham Associates, Ltd. *The Truly Married Woman*, copyright Katz and Milton, Ltd. Reprinted by permission of the publishers, Katz and Milton and David Higham Associates, Ltd.

Nicanor Parra: "Epitaph" from *The Many Worlds of Poetry* (1968), edited by Jacob Drachler and Virginia Terris, translated by Jorge Elliott. Copyright New Directions Publishing Corporation. Reprinted by permission of New Directions Publishing Corporation for the author.

Néstor Paz: Selections from *My Life for My Friends: The Guerrilla Journal of Néstor Paz, Christian*, translated and edited by Ed Garcia and John Eagleson. Copyright 1975 Orbis Books. Reprinted by permission of Orbis Books.

Octavio Paz: "In Her Splendor Islanded" from *Selected Poems of Octavio Paz*, a bilingual edition with translations by Muriel Rukeyser. Copyright 1963 Octavio Paz and Muriel Rukeyser. Reprinted by permission of Indiana University Press.

Lenrie Peters: "After They Put Down Their Overalls" from *African Writings Today* (Penguin Books, Ltd., 1967), edited by Ezekiel Mphahlele. Copyright Lenrie Peters. Reprinted by permission of the author.

Virgilio Piñera: "The Dragée," translated by J.M. Cohen, from *Writers in the New Cuba, 1967*, edited by J.M. Cohen. Copyright 1967 J.M. Cohen. Reprinted by permission of Penguin Books, Ltd.

"Plácido": "Mother, Farewell!" from the Spanish of Plácido, translated by James Weldon Johnson, from *Saint Peter Relates an Incident* by James Weldon Johnson. Copyright 1935 James Weldon Johnson. Copyright renewed 1963 Grace Nail Johnson. All rights reserved. Reprinted by permission of The Viking Press, Inc.

Taufiq Rafat: *Poem 4*. Copyright *Beloit Poetry Journal*. Reprinted by permission of *Beloit Poetry Journal*, Beloit, Wisconsin.

W.S. Rendra: "Little Sister Narti," translated by Burton Raffel, from *Anthology of Indonesian Poetry*, edited by Burton

Raffel. Copyright 1968 by the State University of New York. Reprinted by permission of the State University of New York Press.

Roberto Fernández Retamar: "Of Reality," translated by J.M. Cohen, from *Writers in the New Cuba*, edited by J.M. Cohen. Copyright 1967 J.M. Cohen. Reprinted by permission of Penguin Books, Ltd.

Emil Roumer: "The Peasant Declares His Love," translated by John Peale Bishop, from *An Anthology of Contemporary Latin American Poetry*, edited by Dudley Fitts. Copyright 1942, 1947, New Directions Publishing Corporation. Reprinted by permission of New Directions Publishing Corporation.

Léopold Sédar Senghor: "Prayer to Masks," translated by Gerald Moore and Ulli Beier, from *Modern Poetry from Africa*, edited by Gerald Moore and Ulli Beier. Copyright 1963 Gerald Moore and Ulli Beier. Reprinted by permission of Penguin Books Ltd.

Sembène Ousmane: "Black Girl" from Charles R. Larson's *African Short Stories*. Reprinted with permission of the translator, Ellen Conroy Kennedy. English copyright 1970 Ellen Conroy Kennedy from the French of Ousmane's collection *Voltaique*, originally published by *Présence Africaine*, Paris in 1962, and Macmillan in 1970.

Fang Shumin: "Moon on a Frosty Morning," translated by W.J.F. Jenner, from *Modern Chinese Stories*, edited by W.J.F. Jenner. Copyright Oxford University Press. Reprinted with permission of Oxford University Press.

Khushwant Singh: "Riot" from the collection *The Mark of Vishnu* by Khushwant Singh. Published by Sakira Press, London. Copyright Khushwant Singh. Reprinted by permission of the author.

Mohan Singh: *Evening*. Copyright *Beloit Poetry Journal*. Reprinted by permission of *Beloit Poetry Journal*, Beloit, Wisconsin.

Sitor Situmorang: "Swimming Pool" from *Anthology of Modern Indonesian Poetry*, edited by Burton Raffel. Copyright 1964 Asia Society, Inc. Reprinted by permission of the University of California Press.

Wole Soyinka: "Telephone Conversation" from *Modern Poetry from Africa, 1963*, edited by Gerald Moore and Ulli Beier. Copyright Wole Soyinka. Reprinted by permission of the author.

José Juan Tablada: "The Monkey," reprinted from *The Seer and the Honeycomb: A Book of Tiny Poems*, edited by Robert Bly, Beacon Press, 1971. Copyright 1968 Robert Bly, reprinted with his permission.

J.E. Tatengkeng: "Traveler First Class," copyright *Beloit Poetry Journal*. Reprinted by permission of *Beloit Poetry Journal*, Beloit, Wisconsin. "On the Shore, Twilight" from *Anthology of Modern Indonesian Poetry*, edited by Burton Raffel. Copyright 1964 Asia Society Inc. Reprinted by permission of the University of California Press.

Rabindranath Tagore: "Songs from Gitanjali," from *Collected Poems and Plays* by Sir Rabindranath Tagore. Copyright Macmillan Publishing Co. Published in the United States by Macmillan Publishing Co., Inc., reprinted with permission of Macmillan.

Mao Tse-tung: "The Long March," "After Swimming Across the Yangtze River," from *Twentieth Century Chinese Poetry*, by Kai-yu Hsu. Copyright 1963 Kai-yu Hsu. Reprinted by permission of Doubleday & Company, Inc.

Cesar Vallejo: "Common Sense" from *Poemas Humanos: Human Poems*, translated by Clayton Eshelman. Copyright 1968 Grove Press, Inc. Reprinted by permission of Grove Press, Inc.

Baku Yamanoguchi: "Marriage" from *The Many Worlds of Poetry* (1968), edited by Jacob Drachler and Virginia Terris (New Directions). "Marriage" first appeared in *Poetry*. Copyright 1956 The Modern Poetry Association. Reprinted by permission of the editor of *Poetry* and the translators, Satoru Sato and Constance Urdang.

Wen Yi-tuo: "Dead Water" from *Twentieth Century Chinese Poetry* by Kai-yu Hsu. Copyright 1963 Kai-yu Hsu. Reprinted by permission of Doubleday & Company, Inc.

Kim Sang-yong: "Perfumed Incense" and "Your Love is a Lie" from *The Ever White Mountain*, translated and edited by

Inez Kong Pai. Copyright 1965 John Weatherhill, Inc. Reprinted by permission of the publishers, John Weatherhill, Inc.

"Zawgyi" (U Thein Han): *His Spouse.* Copyright U Thein Han. Reprinted by permission of the author.

The editors regret that although they have made every effort to trace the original copyright proprietors for the works listed below, they have met with no success and hope they have not unknowingly infringed on any existing rights.

"Dada" from *Philippine Pen Anthology of Short Stories*, edited by Francisco Arcellana.

"Boarding House" from *New World Writings No. 14* by Manuel Bandeira.

Jamaica Market and *Lizard* by Agnes-Maxwell Hall.

"The Dragée" by Virgilio Piñera.

"Of Reality" by Roberto Fernández Retamar.

"Arte Poética" by Domingo Alfonso.

"Cold Winter Storm" and "The Winter Sea Gulls" by Kato Shuson.

BIBLIOGRAPHY

Abrahams, Peter. *The Blacks*. New York: Curtis Publishing Company, 1959.

Arcellana, Francisco, ed. *Philippine Pen Anthology of Short Stories*. Manila: Philippine Pen, 1972.

Banderia, Manuel. *New World Writings #14*. Rio de Janeiro, Brazil.

Blocker, Joel, ed. *Israeli Stories*. New York: Schocken Books, Inc., 1962.

Bly, Robert, ed. *The Seer and the Honeycomb, A Book of Tiny Poems*. Boston: Beacon Press, 1971.

Clark, J.P., ed. *Poems*. Ibadan, Nigeria: Mbari Publications, 1962.

Cohen, J.M., ed. *Writers in the New Cuba*. London/Baltimore: Penguin Books, 1967.

Constantino, Renato. *The Filipinos in the Philippines and Other Essays*. Quezon City, Manila, 1959.

De Broucker, José. *Dom Helder Camara, The Violence of a Peacemaker*. New York: Orbis Books, 1970.

Drachler, Jacob and Virginia Terris, eds. *The Many Worlds of Poetry*. New York: New Directions, 1968.

Fall, Bernard B. *Ho Chi Minh on Revolution: Selected Writings 1920–1966*. London: Phaidon Publishers.

Fitts, Dudley, ed. *An Anthology of Contemporary Latin American Poetry*. New York: New Directions, 1942, 1974.

Garcia, Ed, and John Eagleson, eds. *My Life for My Friends: The Guerrilla Journal of Néstor Paz, Christian*. New York: Orbis Books, 1975.

Henderson, Harold G., ed. *An Introduction to Haiku*. New York: Doubleday, 1958.

Hsu, Kai-yu, ed. *Twentieth Century Chinese Poetry*. New York: Doubleday, 1963.

Hughes, Langston and Arna Bontemps, eds. *The Poetry of the Negro, 1746–1970*. New York: Doubleday, 1970, 1973.

Jenner, W.J.F., ed. *Modern Chinese Stories*. London: Oxford University Press, 1974.

Johnson, James Weldon, ed. *Saint Peter Relates an Incident*. New York: Viking Press, 1935.

Kiernan, E.G. *Poems From Iqbal*. London: John Murray Ltd.

La Guma, Alex. *A Walk in the Night and Other Stories*. Evanston: Northwestern University Press, 1967.

Larson, Charles R., ed. *African Short Stories*. New York: Macmillan, 1970.

Libanio Christo, Carlos Alberto. *Against Principalities and Powers: Letters from a Brazilian Jail*. Maryknoll, New York: Orbis Books, 1977.

Marson, Una. *Toward the Stars*. London: Hodder & Stoughton Educational.

Mbiti, John S. *The Prayers of African Religion*. Maryknoll, New York: Orbis Books, 1976.

Milton, D.L. and W.C. Clifford. *A Treasury of Modern Asian Stories*. New York: New American Library, 1961, 1970.

Minh, Ho Chi. *The Prison Diary of Ho Chi Minh*. New York: Bantam Books, Inc.

Moore, Gerald, and Ulli Beier, eds. *Modern Poetry From Africa*. London/Baltimore: Penguin Books, 1963, 1967.

Mphahlele, Ezekiel, ed. *African Writing Today*. London/ Baltimore: Penguin Books, 1967.

Neruda, Pablo. *Selected Poems of Pablo Neruda*. New York: Grove Press, 1961.

Nicol, Abioseh. *The Truly Married Woman*. London: Katz and Milton.

———. *The Meaning of Africa*. London: Oxford University Press.

Pai, Inez Kong, ed. *The Ever White Mountain*. New York: John Weatherhill, Inc., 1965.

Paz, Octavio, ed. *Selected Poems of Octavio Paz*. Bloomington: Indiana University Press, 1963.

Rafat, Taufiq. *Poem 4*. Beloit, Wisconsin: *Beloit Poetry Journal*.

Raffel, Burton, ed. *Anthology of Modern Indonesian Poetry*. New York: State University of New York Press, 1964.

Shimer, Blair Dorothy, ed. *The Mentor Book of Modern Asian Literature.* New York: New American Library, 1969.

Singh, Khuswant, ed. *The Mark of Vishnu.* London: Sakira Press.

Singh, Mohan. *Evening.* Beloit, Wisconsin: *Beloit Poetry Journal.*

Tatengkeng, J.E. *Traveler First Class.* Beloit, Wisconsin: *Beloit Poetry Journal.*

Tagore, Rabindranath. *Collected Poems and Plays.* New York: Macmillan.

Vallejo, Cesar. *Poemas Humanos (Human Poems).* New York: Grove Press, 1968.

SUGGESTIONS FOR RELATED READING

FICTION

Achebe, Chinua. *Arrow of God.* New York: Doubleday, 1969.
———. *A Man of the People.* New York: Doubleday, 1966.
———. *No Longer at Ease.* Greenwich, Conn.: Fawcett, 1961.
———. *Things Fall Apart.* Greenwich, Conn.: Fawcett, 1976.
Alegria, Ciro. *Broad and Alien Is the World.* New York: Farrar, Straus & Giroux, 1941.
Asturias, Miguel A. *El Señor Presidente.* New York: Atheneum, 1964.
Azuela, Mariano. *Two Novels of Mexico: The Flies and the Bosses.* Berkeley: University of California, 1956.
———. *The Underdogs.* New York: New American Library.
Carpentier, Alejo. *The Lost Steps.* New York: Knopf, 1967.
Conton, William. *The African.* Atlantic Highlands, New Jersey: Humanities, 1960.
Cortazar, Julio. *The Winners.* New York: Pantheon, 1960.
Donoso, José. *Coronation.* New York: Knopf, 1965.
Fuentes, Carlos. *The Good Conscience.* New York: Farrar, Straus & Giroux, 1961.
Gonzalez, N.V.M. *Bamboo Dancers.* Chicago: Swallow, 1960.
———. *Season of Grace.* Manila: Benipayo, 1956.
Icaza, Jorge. *The Villagers.* Carbondale: Southern Illinois University Press, 1974.
Kim, Richard. *The Martyred.* New York: Braziller, 1964.
La Guma, Alex. *A Walk in the Night and Other Stories.* Evanston: Northwestern University Press, 1967.
Mphahlele, Ezekiel. *The Living and the Dead and Other Stories.* Washington, D.C.: Black Orpheus, 1961.

423

Related Reading

Ouologuem, Yambo. *Bound to Violence.* Atlantic Highlands, New Jersey: Humanities, 1976.

Paton, Alan. *Cry the Beloved Country.* New York: Scribner, 1948.

―――. *Too Late the Phalarope.* New York: Scribner, 1953.

Roa Batos, Augusto. *Son of Man.* London: Gollancz, 1965.

Rojas, Manuel. *Born Guilty.* New York: Literary, 1955.

Tutuola, Amos. *My Life in the Bush of Ghosts.* New York: Grove, 1962.

―――. *The Palm-Wine Drinkard.* New York: Grove, 1954.

Vargas Llosa, Mario. *Time of the Heroes.* New York: Grove, 1966.

―――. *The Green House.* New York: Harper, 1969.

Yanez, Augustin. *The Edge of the Storm.* Austin: University of Texas Press, 1963.

COLLECTIONS AND ANTHOLOGIES

Benson, Rachel. *Nine Latin American Poets.* New York: Las Americas, 1968.

Bhalo, Ahmad, Nassirbin Juma Bhalo and Lyndon Harries. *Poems From Kenya.* Madison: University of Wisconsin Press, 1966.

Cardenal, Ernesto. *Psalms of Struggle and Liberation.* New York: Seabury, 1971.

Cohen, J.M. *Latin American Writings Today.* Gloucester, Massachusetts: Peter Smith.

Drachler, Jacob. *African Heritage.* London/Toronto/New York: Collier-Macmillan, 1964.

Kgositsile, Keorapetse. *The World is Here: Poetry From Modern Africa.* New York: Doubleday, 1973.

Larson, Charles R. *Modern African Stories.* London: Fontana, 1971.

Manzalaoui, Mahmoud. *Arabic Writing Today: The Short Story.* Cairo, Egypt: American Research Center, 1968.

Mersmann, James F. *Out of the Vietnam Vortex: A Study of Poets and Poetry Against the War.* Lawrence/ Manhattan/Wichita: The University Press of Kansas, 1974.

Mistral, Gabriela. *Selected Poems of Gabriela Mistral.* Bloomington: Indiana University Press, 1957.

Nicol, Abioseh. *The Truly Married Woman and Other Stories.* London: Oxford University Press, 1965.

Nwoga, Donatus. *West African Verse.* Atlantic Highlands, New Jersey: Humanities, 1967.

Paz, Octavio. *Anthology of Mexican Poetry.* Bloomington: Indiana University Press, 1958.

———. *Configurations.* New York: New Directions, 1971.

Pieterse, Cosmo. *Seven South African Poets: Poems of Exile.* Atlantic Highlands, New Jersey: Humanities, 1971.

Ramchand, Kenneth. *West Indian Narrative: An Introductory Anthology.* Atlantic Highlands, New Jersey: Humanities, 1966.

Rutherford, Peggy. *African Voices.* New York: Vanguard, 1959.

Salkey, Andrew. *Breaklight: The Poetry of the Caribbean.* New York: Doubleday, 1971.

———. *Stories from the Caribbean.* Philadelphia: Dufour, 1965.

Swanzy, Henry. *Voices of Ghana.* Accra: Ministry of Information and Broadcasting, 1958 (Out of Print).

Tarn, Nathaniel. *Con Cuba: An Anthology of Cuban Poetry.* New York: Grossman, 1969.

Troupe, Quincy, and Rainer Schulte. *Giant Talk.* New York: Vintage, 1975.

Williams, Miller. *Chile: An Anthology of New Writing.* Kent, Ohio: Kent State University Press, 1968.

Yip, Wai-Lim. *Modern Chinese Poetry: Twenty Poets From the Republic of China 1955–1965.* Iowa City: University of Iowa Press, 1970.